GENDER AND THE GREAT WAR

Gender and the Great War

Edited by

Susan R. Grayzel and Tammy M. Proctor

OXFORD
UNIVERSITY PRESS

OXFORD
UNIVERSITY PRESS

Oxford University Press is a department of the University of Oxford. It furthers
the University's objective of excellence in research, scholarship, and education
by publishing worldwide. Oxford is a registered trade mark of Oxford University
Press in the UK and certain other countries.

Published in the United States of America by Oxford University Press
198 Madison Avenue, New York, NY 10016, United States of America.

Library of Congress Cataloging-in-Publication Data
Grayzel, Susan R., editor of compilation. | Proctor, Tammy M., 1968– editor of compilation.
Title: Gender and the Great War / edited by Susan R. Grayzel and Tammy M. Proctor.
Description: New York : Oxford University Press, [2017] |
    Includes bibliographical references and index.
Identifiers: LCCN 2017002554 (print) | LCCN 2017017799 (ebook) |
    ISBN 9780190271091 (Updf) | ISBN 9780190271107 (Epub) | ISBN 9780190271077 (hardcover : alk. paper) |
    ISBN 9780190271084 (pbk. : alk. paper)
Subjects: LCSH: World War, 1914–1918—Women. | World War, 1914–1918—Participation, Female. |
    World War, 1914–1918—Social aspects. | Sex role—History—20th century.
Classification: LCC D639.W7 (ebook) | LCC D639.W7 G395 2017 (print) | DDC 940.3082—dc23
LC record available at https://lccn.loc.gov/2017002554

9 8 7 6 5 4 3 2 1

Paperback printed by Webcom, Inc., Canada
Hardback printed by Bridgeport National Bindery, Inc., United States of America

In memory of Gail Braybon, pioneering scholar of gender and the Great War

Contents

Acknowledgments   ix

Contributors   xi

Introduction   1
Susan R. Grayzel and Tammy M. Proctor

1. Gender and Citizenship   10
Kimberly Jensen

2. Gender and Resistance   27
Erika Kuhlman

3. Gender and Work   46
Deborah Thom

4. Gender and Race   67
Richard S. Fogarty

5. Gender and Sexuality   91
Ana Carden-Coyne and Laura Doan

6. Gender and Age   115
Tammy M. Proctor

7. Gender and Occupation   133
Jovana Knežević

8. Gender and Everyday Life   149
   Karen Hunt

9. Gender and Warfare   169
   Susan R. Grayzel

10. Gender and Violence   187
    Michelle Moyd

11. Gender and Mourning   211
    Joy Damousi

12. Gender and Memory   230
    Karen Petrone

13. The Scholarship of the First World War   248
    Susan R. Grayzel and Tammy M. Proctor

SELECTED BIBLIOGRAPHY   259
INDEX   283

Acknowledgments

THE EDITORS WOULD like to thank the organizers of the 2014 Sixteenth Berkshire Conference on the History of Women, Gender and Sexualities for allowing us to present the earliest versions of these essays at two linked roundtables. Special thanks to audiences at that conference who tolerated very crowded rooms in order to participate in the ensuing conversation. We are extremely grateful to the contributors— our friends and colleagues—for participating in the roundtables and for the pleasure of working with them as we prepared this volume.

As co-editors, we also appreciate enormously the opportunity to have worked together from vision to roundtable to volume and look forward to future collaborations.

Special thanks go to Nancy Toff, whose enthusiasm for and attention to our work have been extraordinarily generous. Thanks to her, Elda Granata, and the other staff at Oxford University Press for helping us bring this book to life. We would like to express our gratitude to Abigail Fritz and Jessica Nelson, students at Utah State University, who assisted with the bibliographic and indexing work.

Each of us has benefited from the rich intellectual life of our institutional homes, the University of Mississippi, Wittenberg University, and Utah State University. We are grateful for the years of student questions, which have enriched our perspectives on questions of gender and war. The assistance and encouragement of students, faculty, and staff at our universities have been invaluable.

Finally, as always, we thank Joe and Todd for all of their support.

Contributors

Ana Carden-Coyne, Senior Lecturer in war and conflict and co-Director of the Centre for the Cultural History of War, University of Manchester. Author of *Reconstructing the Body: Classicism, Modernism and the First World War* (2009).

Joy Damousi, Professor of history, University of Melbourne. Author of *The Labour of Loss: Mourning, Memory, and Wartime Bereavement in Australia* (1999).

Laura Doan, Professor of cultural history and Sexuality Studies and co-Director, Centre for the Study of Sexuality and Culture, University of Manchester. Author of *Disturbing Practices: History, Sexuality, and Women's Experience of Modern War* (2013).

Richard S. Fogarty, Associate Professor of History and Associate Dean, University at Albany, State University of New York. Author of *Race and War in France: Colonial Subjects in the French Army, 1914–1918* (2008).

Susan R. Grayzel, Professor of History at the University of Mississippi. Author of *At Home and Under Fire: Air Raids and Culture in Britain from the Great War to the Blitz* (Cambridge, 2012) and *Women's Identities at War: Gender, Motherhood, and Politics in Britain and France during the First World War* (1999).

Karen Hunt, Professor of modern British history, Keele University. Author of *Equivocal Feminists* (2002) and "The Politics of Food and Women's Neighborhood Activism in First World War Britain" *International Labor and Working-Class History* 77, no. 1 (2010): 8–26.

Kimberly Jensen, Professor of history and gender studies, Western Oregon State University. Author of *Mobilizing Minerva: American Women in the First World War* (2008).

Jovana Knežević, Associate Director, Center for Russian, East European and Eurasian Studies, Stanford University. Author of "Prostitutes as a Threat to National Honor in Habsburg-Occupied Serbia during the Great War," *Journal of the History of Sexuality* 20, no. 1 (2011): 312–335.

Erika Kuhlman, Professor of history and Director of the Women's Studies Program, Idaho State University. Author of *Of Little Comfort: War Widows, Fallen Soldiers, and the Remaking of the Nation after the Great War* (2012) and *Reconstructing Patriarchy after the Great War: Women, Gender, and Postwar Reconciliation between Nations* (2008).

Michelle Moyd, Associate Professor of history, Indiana University. Author of *Violent Intermediaries: African Soldiers, Conquest, and Everyday Colonialism in German East Africa* (2014).

Karen Petrone, Professor and Chair of the Department of History, University of Kentucky. Author of *The Great War in Russian Memory* (2011).

Tammy M. Proctor, Professor and Department Head in the Department of History, Utah State University. Author of *Civilians in a World at War, 1914–1918* (2010) and *Female Intelligence: Women and Espionage in the First World War* (2003).

Deborah Thom, Fellow and Director of studies in history, Robinson College, Cambridge University. Author of *Nice Girls and Rude Girls: Women Workers and the First World War* (1998).

Introduction

Susan R. Grayzel and Tammy M. Proctor

WHAT DO WE think we know about the First World War? To talk about the First World War means addressing a story that developed out of the troubled decades following the conflict, a tale that has had incredible staying power over the past century. The dominant account of the first modern total war is one of blunders and of a lost world of innocence; it contains a beautifully simple buildup to 1914 and reveals the lie of the "war to end all wars." The players in this version of the war are young male soldiers sent to their doom by old men, beautiful yet tragic female nurses tending the wounded, and fiery revolutionaries fomenting the violence that permeated the postwar world. This version holds some truth, but it obscures a central reality of the experience of the conflict: that this modern, total, global war was a messy and unpredictable affair. Its central players included men and women of all ages and classes, both combatants and noncombatants. Across the globe, societies rose and fell as a result of these four years.

We are the inheritors of the postwar world of failed imperial ambitions and political violence, as well as the revised international order that solidly placed the United States on top. We need to understand this war, and this book aims to help. The essays that follow consider the ugly, uncomfortable parts of the war in order to tell a more complex story of the 1914–1918 conflict through the lens of gender. World War I touched the lives of millions of men and women around the world, from the deserts of southern Africa to the Siberian tundra, but in quite varied ways. A man living in occupied Poland experienced the conflict in a much different way than a man of the same age serving as a soldier in Mesopotamia. Female refugees in northern France saw a different side of war than did women who nursed soldiers in war-ravaged Galicia. A child in Vienna received a meager food ration while a child in the United States could still enjoy abundance. The scope of the war and the complexity of its impact on world history make the Great War a challenging but essential conflict to study.

1914: A WORLD LOST?

When some teachers of history talk about Europe during the summer months of 1914, they tend to paint a picture of a halcyon surface with the dark tensions of nationalism, imperialism, and militarism swirling underneath. Looking back at the years from the end of the nineteenth century to the start of the twentieth century, writers coined the phrase the "belle époque" (beautiful era). Nostalgia led them to see a prosperous, ordered society set adrift by an assassin in Sarajevo, who in killing Archduke Franz Ferdinand, the heir to the Austro-Hungarian Empire, set in motion the devastation of the Great War. The "Guns of August" appear in this story as an inevitable end to the peaceful world of prewar Europe, and the month between Gavrilo Princip's bullets in Sarajevo and the first artillery bombardment of Belgrade to start the war fits nicely into the tale.

Yet there was nothing inevitable about the beginning of war, and Europe was far from a peaceful place. Revolutionary movements in most European countries sparked riots, political reform, and even all-out revolution in the years leading up to 1914, and European empires fought bloody conflicts in their extended colonies throughout much of the late nineteenth and early twentieth centuries. The major powers—Austria-Hungary, Britain, France, Germany, and Russia—had also witnessed war on the European continent since the end of the Napoleonic Wars in 1815. But much had changed by 1914.

Politically, new ideas that emphasized national belonging and new currents that allowed for greater, if uneven, democratization had transformed European societies. More men voted and held political office than ever before; robust labor movements gave voice to industrial workers seeking better lives. The emergence of new voices and opportunities inspired others living on the margins of political and economic power. Ethnic and religious minorities organized associations to challenge their perceived and real oppression. Educational opportunities created more educated citizenries that could read, write, and speak their dissent, leading to a widespread feeling at the turn of the century that the world was transforming the certainties of the past. Even women increasingly demanded equal political and legal rights in this new world.

Nationalists and imperialists provided one response to the instability that democracy brought by taking aim at the threat to political control by elites. They offered national glory and the promise of imperial might to counter transnational class-based ideas like socialism or Marxism. Cecil Rhodes, creator of the Rhodes Scholarships and consummate empire builder in southern Africa, captured this idea in his oft-quoted statement: "If you want to avoid civil war, you must become imperialists."[1] The fear of social revolution and civil war was real, and it was fueled even more by a wave of assassinations and violent actions by anarchists in the early decades of the twentieth century. Assassins killed American presidents, British diplomats, and Russian tsars, demonstrating the vulnerability of those in power.

In the meantime, smaller-scale wars, internal conflicts, revolutions, and the brutal violence of imperial conquest had helped encourage new tactics and test new weaponry. Yet they had not shown the bulk of Europeans what modern war could bring. By 1914, a series of wars in imperial territories and in the Balkan Peninsula in particular exposed the insecurity of existing power structures. Neither Russia nor the Ottoman Empire nor Austria-Hungary was prepared to concede its influence in this area. Mounting international tensions had also created an alliance system that could turn local struggles into international ones. The emergence of the powerful new nation of Germany in 1871 prompted that government to seek to contain its enemies, and the Triple Alliance of Germany, Austria-Hungary, and Italy offered a bulwark against threats from the French and Russians, and then from the expanded Triple Entente that added the British to this side. Germany's industrial might, second only to that of the United States by 1914, and its newly built Imperial Navy only increased international anxieties.

As a result, the assassination of Archduke Franz Ferdinand and his wife, Sophie by Bosnian Serb nationalist Gavrilo Princip on June 28, 1914, soured the already tense relationship between Serbia and Austria-Hungary. Many historians have sought to make sense of the "July Crisis," the series of steps and missteps that led Germany to condone the actions of Austria-Hungary and Russia to stand behind Serbia, with France lending support. Piece by piece, the groundwork of national competition and the buildup of arms turned what could have been a Third Balkan War instead into a conflict that consumed much of the world. From July 28 to August 5, participating states mobilized the largest armies that had ever been seen. Some voices predicted a long, bloody conflict, others promised victory by Christmas, and an anguished minority cried out in opposition. States and colonies around the world declared their allegiances or their neutrality, taking a stance in this increasingly dangerous conflict. Japan and Britain fired on the German colony in China; German and African forces clashed with British and African forces in East Africa; troop ships left the harbors of Senegal, Australia, Canada, and South Africa.

Quickly, in the fall of 1914, a war of movement turned into a quagmire in the West (Belgium and France); on the Eastern Front, armies invaded and occupied large parts of Eastern Europe. In a war between continental empires, colonies under European control became spaces of conflict and places to supply resources and labor (military and otherwise), voluntarily and under coercion. As the war continued into 1915, new combatants entered the conflict such as the Ottoman Empire on the side of the Central Powers and Italy on the side of the Entente. Neutral states such as the United States and Sweden found themselves acting as diplomatic arbiters between the warring states. New weapons—lethal poison gas, Zeppelins and airplanes, submarines, large-scale artillery—entered the war with devastating consequences. These advances further extended the zones affected by conflict as well as expanded the range of people who could now lay down their lives for a nation at war. A stalemate sank into the Western Front, and the trench became a lasting symbol of the war.

By 1916, the seemingly intractable nature of the war led to calculated risks, and the bloodbaths of Verdun and the Somme on the Western Front and the Brusilov offensive in the East. In the meantime, the Allied naval blockade cut short the food supply in continental Europe, helping to make hunger a weapon of this modern, industrialized war. The year 1917 witnessed mutinies, strikes, and ultimately a revolution in Russia that brought down the reign of the tsars. In the aftermath of the fall of the Romanovs, the world's first communist regime took power and Russia plunged into the carnage of civil war. Having tacitly lent aid to Britain, the United States abandoned its neutrality in the middle of 1917 and helped sway the balance in the remaining eighteen months of the conflict. When the fighting stopped in Europe on November 11, 1918, nearly 75 million military and civilian lives had been lost or damaged, and millions of other lives had been reshaped by the global war. Four imperial dynasties disappeared: the Ottomans (Turkey), the Habsburgs (Austria-Hungary), the Hohenzollerns (Germany), and the Romanovs (Russia). In the wake of these historic political upheavals, new nations arose to vie for legitimacy. Physical destruction near the battle zones was catastrophic, and material deprivation threatened whole populations in the immediate postwar period.

This is the standard narrative of this war, cut to its bare bones. It conjures images of landscapes destroyed by the modern methods of fighting and the devastation that reigned in its wake. Yet this account very much obscures the diversity of the wartime experiences of those caught up in the First World War. By using gender as a framework for looking at men's and women's lives in the war, this book presents a different picture, one that not only alters our understanding of the years 1914–1918 but also helps us to see why the problems of the postwar world were so thorny.

MEN, MASCULINITY, AND THE WAR

"Gender" is a term that often becomes code for "women," but it is a powerful tool for understanding men's lives as well, especially in wartime. Prior to World War I, most European nations passed legislation mandating military service for all men, and this practice marked a new milestone in preparing nations for modern war. Each nation's legislation differed in terms of length of service, options for deferral, and exceptions, but these laws meant that a whole generation of young men now learned the basics of soldiering at an early age (typically eighteen). Even in Britain, which had no mandatory draft, schools, universities, and organizations encouraged voluntary training in order to create a defense force in reserve. The result of these mandatory military exercises was a new expectation for all men; war service became proof of manliness. Boys' magazines and books emphasized the qualities of honor and heroism for teen boys to prepare them for the service they would someday need to perform. Heroes of far-off imperial wars made especially good role models for boys, emphasizing both the manly qualities of the soldier and the racial superiority of Europeans.

What this meant for young men in 1914 is that they had been prepped—by training experiences, the media, and public enthusiasm for uniforms—to see their war service not only as a duty but even more as an exciting adventure. This is not to say that there were not men who opposed the war and who attempted to stay out of uniform—chiefly religious pacifists and leftists—but there was a gendered expectation that men fight, which provided a strong incentive for men to embrace their roles as soldiers. Not all men could fight because of age, health, or jobs, so those who stayed home sought to justify their masculinity and their civic duty through other forms of war service and nationalism. Those unwilling to support the war suffered ostracism and prison. For men in occupation zones, the war meant inactivity, which threatened their sense of themselves as breadwinners, as heads of families, and ultimately as males. Even though some resisted enemy occupation, many men living in occupied regions felt inadequate. A similar feeling of helplessness and inadequacy appears in accounts left by prisoners of war, whose imprisonment might be tainted by a hint of cowardice or weakness. Like those men who could not fight for a multitude of other reasons, prisoners tried to justify their patriotism in alternative ways.

In short, men in every nation had to prove themselves in this war, whether or not they were actively involved in battle. Opting out was not possible. Masculinity played an important role in virtually all aspects of the war, and this collection helps us reconsider how and why men served in an increasingly brutal conflict. Men living in colonial empires sought to prove themselves not just as males but often in racial terms. War service conferred citizenship and respect, or at least that is what many "marginal" groups of men thought would happen if they performed their civic duty. Jews in the massive European empires of the day saw the war as a chance to demonstrate their loyalty to state and nation, to gain legitimacy. Other members of historically marginalized populations within the nation such as African-Americans similarly sought to prove their worth as citizen-soldiers. Colonial subjects labored and fought in multiple theaters of war with the idea that their patriotic acts would prove their loyalty and their manliness to colonial governments. In all these cases, gendered visions of what a man could and should be shaped public perception of the war.

WOMEN AND THE WAR

Gender also crucially defined the role of women. The eve of the First World War saw dedicated activists across Europe and elsewhere vigorously campaigning to bring full citizenship rights to women. Denied full enfranchisement in all the combatant nations, an increasing number of women were arguing that their states needed to grant them a voice in deciding the fates of their countries. As the international crisis of June–July 1914 unfolded, women in the main states confronting the potential for international violence (such as Austria-Hungary, France, Germany, Great Britain, Italy, Russia, the Ottoman Empire, and Serbia) still had no officially sanctioned political voice. They thus faced the potential outbreak of war indirectly, unable to participate in political decision-making. The nations mobilizing for war tended to see women as the wives, lovers, mothers, sisters, and daughters of combatants, but not as the ones who could be called upon to wage war in its most traditional sense. Thus, from the outbreak of war in 1914, some factors clearly set women apart from their male counterparts.

No state compelled or requested women's service as combatants. Mobilization in 1914 meant calling up men. This is not to say that women had no public role. For instance, although some nations, like France, were fearful that certain political groups that espoused internationalist values (like socialists) might protest full-scale mobilization, few were as concerned that women as a whole would obstruct the mobilization for war. Some leaders of international feminist organizations asked members to pressure governments to halt the rapid call to arms. However, few women's voices publicly criticized their state officials or their nation's stance once war was actually declared, even if overt support for the war might have been less widespread among women. Even so, while women were not called immediately to active military service, all participant states demanded their loyalty and sacrifices. As the initial phase of the First World War extended into 1915 and then into long years of action and waiting, enduring and suffering, the full panoply of what it meant to wage a modern, total war engaged women more fully than prior wars.

Women took on an enormous range of active roles in and for their nations at war. In terms of waged and volunteer labor for their wartime states, women served in roles as diverse as agricultural laborers; ambulance, bus, tram, and trolley drivers; clerks; cooks; doctors; domestic servants; drivers; engineers; factory workers; forestry workers and foragers; machinists; nurses; police officers; railway workers; secretaries; spies; telegraph and telephone operators; typists; and, in few extraordinary circumstances, combatants. They filled in for absent men in communal labor, religious organizations, and local charities; they created new organizations to cater to the wartime needs of children, mothers, refugees, and, above all, soldiers. They gained new visibility and new opportunities, even if their work was often couched in terms of "doing their bit" and "for the duration." Yet, one thing was clear by war's end—their labor was vital to sustaining the war effort even if some aspects of their work made their societies anxious.

In addition to women's visible waged and unwaged work to sustain their nations' war effort—and just as important—women continued to perform their domestic tasks of homekeeping, child-rearing, and emotional (and sometimes financial and physical) support for their families. Wartime restrictions upon, and in some cases lack of access to, food and fuel made carrying on daily home life even more challenging for women in many places. Women carried the burden of queuing for food and managing meager rations. Yet, voices throughout the war continued to call upon women to "keep the home fires burning" and safeguard an image of the tranquil home life for which men made sacrifices of life, limb, and livelihood.

In addition, a few women were happy to claim the mantle of being separate from the war. A manifesto issued by the International Women's Suffrage Alliance (the umbrella organization for women's suffrage movements in individual nations) proclaimed:

> In this terrible hour, when the fate of Europe depends on decisions which women have no power to shape, we, realising our responsibilities as the mothers of the race, cannot stand passive by.... [W]e call upon the Governments and Powers of our several countries to avert the threatened unparalleled disaster.[2]

And the war did divide feminists, with only a minority who continued to adhere in public to the movement's internationalist ideals and to advocate for peace in the face of the virulent nationalism that emerged as the war got underway. This left a complex legacy for the organized women's movement and for women as individuals in the aftermath.

WHY THIS VOLUME?

The centenary of the First World War in 2014–2018 offers an opportunity to reflect upon the role of gender history in shaping our understanding of this pivotal international event. Ideas about gender, particularly about how men and women should act, became newly contentious in many areas of the world as a result of this conflict. From the moment of its outbreak, contemporary observers and postwar commentators viewed the gendered experiences of the war as being especially significant for defining how the war can and must be understood. Over the past twenty-five years, the scholarship on gender and this war has grown, yet there has never been a forum such as the one that we present here that has sought to place so many of the varying threads of this complex history into conversation with one another in a manner that is at once accessible and provocative.[3]

The chapters assembled in this volume emerge from a series of roundtables presented at the 2014 Berkshire Conference on the History of Women, Genders, and Sexualities that gathered scholars together to reflect on where the gender history of the war stood at its hundredth anniversary. The book is organized to showcase the various themes and to group together those that build upon earlier topics. While each author has written with a transnational framework in mind, the realities of uneven historical scholarship across these broad topics and the space limitations of this volume leave inevitable gaps. The centrality of Eastern and Central Europe to the conflict and its aftermath deserves much more attention than what we have given it here, for instance.[4] New work on Italy will also expand the field, as will historical studies of the Ottoman Empire and sub-Saharan Africa. In short, there are many exciting projects in the works, but we believe that even more scholarship is necessary. Thus we anticipate that this initial focus on gender and significant intersecting categories of historical inquiry can play a key role in illuminating the war on all its fronts. What we collectively hope this volume may do is spur interest in investigating the gaps and questions that remain, providing even richer scholarship on the absolutely crucial functions of gender in wartime.

NOTES

1. Rhodes's speech quoted in Patrick Brantlinger, *Rule of Darkness: British Literature and Imperialism, 1830–1914* (Ithaca, NY: Cornell University Press, 1990), 34.

2. International Women's Suffrage Alliance, *International Manifesto of Women* reprinted in *Votes for Women*, August 7, 1914, and also Margaret R. Higonnet, ed., *Lines of Fire: Women Writers of World War I* (New York, 1999).

3. Two similar volumes are based more loosely around research essays: Christa Hämmerle, Oswald Überegger, and Birgitta Bader Zaar, eds., *Gender and the First World War* (Houndmills: Palgrave Macmillan, 2014), and Nicole Dombrowski, ed., *Women and War in the Twentieth Century: Enlisted with or without Consent* (New York: Routledge, 1998).

4. One useful study in this area is Nancy M. Wingfield and Maria Bucur, eds., *Gender and War in Twentieth-Century Eastern Europe* (Bloomington: Indiana University Press, 2006).

1

Gender and Citizenship

Kimberly Jensen

THE FIRST WORLD WAR reinforced the links between masculinity, military service, and citizenship but also offered the possibility for marginalized men, including men of color and men in colonized states, and women of various communities, to claim enhanced civic roles through patriotic service on the home and war fronts. The world war was, for most combatant nations, a total war that required the transformation of national economies for war production and the support of citizens and residents. National leaders needed people to engage in the work of wartime production and soldiering, to practice food rationing or conservation, and to follow other government policies designed to result in victory. And the First World War paralleled the expansion of movements for woman suffrage and reform in many countries, movements that emphasized women's contributions to state economies and civic progress.

However, leaders of nation states reinforced traditional gender and racial practices in defining loyalty and citizenship. The growth in state bureaucracies and surveillance on citizens and noncitizens developed in some cases into a war on civil liberties during the conflict. Wartime violence and these attacks on civil liberties caused many people to challenge state policies and to include civil liberties in new conceptions of citizenship rights. The war also led many advocates to develop the concept of a transnational or world citizenship that would allow people to work together above and across nation states for reforms such as woman suffrage and international peace. This chapter explores these contested meanings and practices of citizenship as women and men from a variety of groups and nations challenged and redefined their civic roles.

CITIZENSHIP AND CIVIL LIBERTIES IN CONTEXT

What does it mean to be a citizen of a particular nation, and who is eligible for citizenship? What are the rights and obligations of individual citizens? The answers to these questions have shifted across time and national boundaries and have been framed by social and cultural ideas about gender and gender identity, sexuality, race, ethnicity, immigration status, and class. When the First World War began in 1914, citizenship for residents of many Western imperial nations was based on male military service to the state. Those men who were eligible and who fulfilled their obligation of military service would, in return, be invested with the rights of citizenship, including voting, office holding, and other elements of administering and deciding on political questions in one's community and nation. The practices of racism and imperialism limited citizenship rights for men and women of color and colonized status. Women as a group were not eligible for official military service, and so they were "outside the boundaries of reciprocity and entitlement" that conferred the rights of citizenship.[1] The links between citizenship and military service were also based on the idea of men as the protectors and women as the protected in society.[2]

In the early twentieth century, people in many nations were engaged in vigorous debates about the nature of, and qualifications for, citizenship. Across many countries, women worked for the right to vote, to hold political office, and to help shape policies that would reform their communities. Members of colonized states and members of communities of color and ethnicity worked to address policies that limited their political participation, engaging in campaigns against racism and imperialism. Yet there was also resistance to these calls for change, and some political leaders took steps to exclude immigrants, challenge reform policies, and limit the rights of citizenship and privilege. The First World War erupted in the midst of these currents of debate and reform. For those who opposed the war, for those who named particular wartime violence against women, and for those who identified the war's role in the building of colonial empires, expanding the rights of citizenship became an important goal in urgent calls for postwar change.

For some women and men excluded from state policies of citizenship or having only limited civic roles, the war offered opportunities to support their nation's program and to define such active patriotism as service worthy of citizenship. By undertaking the obligations of service to the state, they could claim the reciprocal rights of citizenship. Men would need to work or fight, and women would need to engage in industrial and agricultural work, to volunteer with Red Cross and Red Crescent societies or the hundreds of other voluntary agencies. They would need to let their husbands, sons, and fathers go to war. Through taxation, "fight or pay" contributions, war bonds, and Liberty Loans, governments called on citizens and residents to contribute to the war effort. Leaders used propaganda and coercion and legislated against civil liberties to produce results in authoritarian regimes and in more liberal nations. In the United States, for example, which remained officially neutral until April 1917, Congress passed the Espionage Act in 1917 and the Sedition Act in 1918 criminalizing opposition to the war and the military. The Habsburg Empire eliminated civil liberties and censored most communication through a wartime surveillance office. Leaders of the Ottoman Empire transferred some criminal proceedings from civil to military courts. Many nations suspended jury trials. The Russian military could detain or deport suspects without trial. Wartime officials in Great Britain expanded the Defense of the Realm Act to encompass a wide range of actions, from censorship of printed material thought harmful to the war effort to sexual behavior.[3]

GENDER, WARTIME SERVICE, AND CITIZENSHIP

Across many nations, the wartime work of women made news, and women's active patriotic service formed a key part of women's claims to a more complete female citizenship. For example, hundreds of thousands of women engaged in voluntary work on the home front, including providing bandages and comfort kits for soldiers in national and empire branches of the Red Cross and Red Crescent. British women joined the Voluntary Aid Detachment (VAD), and some women who were colonial subjects in India and Australia engaged in such home front service to bolster their claims for more representation and equality within the empire. Indigenous women established the Six Nations Women's Patriotic League in Ontario, Canada, to emphasize their contributions to the wartime state.[4] In the United States, women's wartime service included work under the umbrella organization the Woman's Committee of the Council of National Defense. More than 6,000 women volunteered for service abroad, including work with the Red Cross, the Young Women's Christian Association, the Jewish Welfare Board, and the American Library Association.[5] African American women across the nation engaged in war work to support black troops and their families and established local branches of the Emergency Circle of Negro War Relief. African American women also filed lawsuits to challenge racial segregation and engaged in active protest against the East St. Louis Riot of 1917 with a vigorous public awareness campaign, silent marches, and prayer meetings.[6] In Los Angeles, California, women who were members of racial and ethnic minorities in the city made their claims for patriotic citizenship in ethnically segregated auxiliaries of the Red Cross, including Japanese American and Jewish women. At Brownson House, a settlement house under Catholic auspices, Mexican American women organized for Red Cross service. African American women worked within the Harriet Tubman and Phyllis Wheatley auxiliaries.[7]

Other women served with national armies, and many of them thus made claims for full inclusion as female citizens in military institutions. Women doctors provide a strong example of this call for inclusion in the military as part of a more complete female citizenship. They campaigned as professional women who claimed a more equal place in military medicine and for more complete economic citizenship that would include equality with male medical colleagues. Women physicians from many nations who participated in national militaries and as volunteer war workers faced powerful cultural ideas and practices about gender, work, wartime service, and citizenship. They had broken barriers within the medical institutions of their nations, claiming the right to pursue an equal medical education and practice, but still faced considerable challenges to equality with men in their field. Many women doctors saw wartime service as a way to demonstrate their professional skills but also to expand their opportunities in the military workplace. Yet cultural representations of women healers at war often focused on women as auxiliaries to men, unequal partners in wartime medicine. This, too, stemmed from traditional associations among masculinity, military service, and citizenship. The uneven gains women doctors experienced during the war suggest that ideas about women as the "weaker sex" continued to define the results.

When the war began, medical women numbered some 3,000 across Great Britain. Many sought an official place within the British military, but when this was denied them, they formed all-female medical units to provide needed wartime medical care and to demonstrate their skills and equality with male doctors. The largest and most famous of the British all-female medical units was the Scottish Women's Hospitals (SWH), organized by suffragist physician Elsie Inglis, a graduate of Edinburgh Medical School. The Scottish Federation of Women's Suffrage Societies sponsored SWH units over the course of the conflict, with fourteen units serving in France, Belgium, Serbia, Macedonia, Romania, and Russia. The SWH included women on its staff from England, Wales, Ireland, Canada, and Australia.[8]

Women physicians in the United States, numbering some 6,000 during the war years, also linked wartime medical service with a fuller economic citizenship for women. The Medical Women's National Association (MWNA), established in 1915, sponsored a registration drive to demonstrate women's readiness for military medical service, organized petitions, and lobbied the American Medical Association for support. In the meantime, women physicians supported other avenues for wartime medical service. Several all-female medical units, modeled on the SWH, were staffed entirely by women. The National American Woman Suffrage Association (NAWSA) created the Women's Oversea Hospitals with two units in France, and the MWNA supported two French units and dispensaries under the title of the American Women's Hospitals during the conflict. Many other medical women served at home and with voluntary organizations overseas such as the Red Cross. At least seventy-six were serving with various organizations by November 1918. They included two African American women physicians living in France: Mary L. Brown, a Howard University Medical School graduate with the Red Cross, and Harriet Rice, who served in a French military hospital and was awarded the *Reconnaissance française*. Fifty-five women physicians served in the Army Medical Corps without rank or commissions as contract surgeons, eleven had military duty overseas, and forty-five worked in US states and territories, including Puerto Rico.[9]

More numerous than female physicians were women nurses, who served while reiterating claims for patriotic service but also professional and gender equality. Nursing as a female profession had grown in industrializing nations in the late nineteenth and early twentieth centuries, and many supporters hoped that exposure of their successful work on the global stage of war would increase their status in the medical profession. Yet female nurses faced powerful barriers for full and permanent inclusion in the institution of the military and as citizens. In France, the Service de santé militaire established a category of medical worker in 1916 known as the "temporary military nurse," which underscored women's needed but impermanent place in the military.[10] Across the course of the conflict, more than 28,000 German women served in hospital and aid stations and in the occupied territories in the Volunteer Nursing Corps. Yet the low salary (one-quarter to one-eighth of a daily wage of factory work for women) meant that military nurses were primarily elite women who did not necessarily want to engage in nursing as a profession.[11] The Ottoman Red Crescent Society opened a school of nursing in 1914; another school of nursing opened that same year at Istanbul University. During the war, the Center for Women in Istanbul trained nurses and challenged cultural practices that it believed were detrimental to women nurses by "maintaining that men and women could work together." Women "broke through their segregation, worked together with male physicians, and took care of male patients at hospitals and on battlefields."[12]

Some nurses served as ambassadors and diplomats for their nations. Elite Austro-Hungarian Red Cross nurses visited prisoners of war in Russia in 1915 and 1916, represented Austria-Hungary, and used their connections to visit camps and direct relief.[13] When Japan entered the war against the Central Powers, its leaders sent Japanese Red Cross relief groups to act as medical ambassadors to the Allied nations of Great Britain, France, and Russia. On their way to Great Britain in January 1915, twenty-two Japanese Red Cross nurses served 2,500 patients at the Netley Royal Victoria Military Hospital from February to December 1915, in Japanese Red Cross wards and British wards.[14]

In Great Britain, professional nurses were an official part of the military as members of Queen Alexandra's Imperial Military Nursing Service (QAIMNS). Reserve nurses served in the Territorial Forces Nursing Service (TFNS) and the QAIMNS Reserve. British women who wished to volunteer their services for wartime nursing joined the Voluntary Aid Detachment (VAD), an organization established in 1909. Nursing VAD membership consisted primarily of elite and upper-middle-class women.[15] Class and professional experience created conflict between rank-and-file trained nurses and elite volunteers such as VAD Vera Brittain. Professional, working nurses in the QAIMNS and the reserve corps hoped that the war would illustrate the powerful need for trained nurses during and after the war. They were generally women who saw the war as a way to demonstrate their economic citizenship and medical professionalism and who believed that the war would expand their career opportunities. These VADs, most of whom were elite women, most often understood their wartime service as an expression of their patriotism and service to the empire. They did not have the same experience of or commitment to professionalization as did military nurses.[16]

In the United States, more than 21,480 women served in the Army Nurse Corps during the First World War, 10,660 of them with the American Expeditionary Force abroad. African American nurses, led by Adah Thoms and joined by community organizations, lobbied across the war years for entrance into the Red Cross and Army Nurse Corps. In the fall of 1918, in the midst of the global influenza pandemic and crisis, eighteen African American nurses were accepted into the Army Nurse Corps for service in two training camps for African American soldiers, Camp Sherman in Ohio and Camp Grant in Illinois. During the conflict, no army nurse had any official rank in the military. Nurses and their allies, including many supporters of woman suffrage, mounted a campaign to change military regulations so that all army nurses would be commissioned as officers. They waged this campaign for rank until 1920, when army nurses received relative rank as officers but not on a male scale, without many of the benefits and without complete military command authority. For many male policymakers, the campaign for rank challenged the notion of female nurses as symbols of self-sacrifice serving soldiers and the nation. The compromise policy of relative rank suggests that most could not accept women nurses as full citizens with claims to equality through military service.[17]

FROM WARTIME SERVICE TO VOTES

When the First World War began in 1914, activists in many nations had already been engaged in campaigns to win the right to vote for women, a right that had tradition-ally been limited to elite men. These movements took place in a vibrant era of reform in which many people worked to redefine women's roles and participation in an industrializing and technologically expanding age. The work of women during the conflict certainly had an impact on various national struggles for woman suffrage, but the effects of the war on votes for women were mixed.

In the United States, the war years and their aftermath brought an over seven-decade struggle for women's voting rights to a successful conclusion with ratifica-tion of the Nineteenth Amendment in 1920. Women in eleven US states and one territory had achieved full voting rights by the time the nation entered the war in April 1917. This meant that women in these locations could cast a vote in all elections, from those in their cities and counties all the way to selecting members of Congress and the president of the United States. Activists in some other states had won partial voting rights such as the ability to vote in school elections or to vote only in the election for US president, referred to as "presidential suffrage." During the war years, women in four other states won complete voting rights, and women in eleven others secured the right to presidential suffrage. In 1919, the year following the war's end, both houses of Congress approved an amendment to the US Constitution that provided for women's full voting rights. The Nineteenth Amendment was ratified on August 26, 1920, when three-quarters of state legisla-tures voted to support it.[18]

The wartime momentum given to the woman suffrage question in the United States was mirrored in other national movements. By the close of the conflict, women in the new Soviet Union, Great Britain, Canada, the Netherlands, Germany, Poland, Hungary, Austria, Luxembourg, and Czechoslovakia had gained some vot-ing rights. French feminists such as Marguerite de Witt-Schlumberger argued for the vote for women as citizens in their own right and as a result of Frenchwomen's wartime service. Some policymakers such as Maurice Barrès argued that widows and mothers of fallen soldiers should receive fuller civic rights and votes because of their relationship to men who had sacrificed their lives for the nation, a way of continuing to relate women's citizenship to their family status rather than to them as individuals. Others worried that politicized women would be the downfall of the French nation. The debates on woman suffrage in the French legislature from 1919 to 1922 are significant because of the extent to which these arguments became part of the discourse of wartime and its aftermath, even if women did not achieve suffrage as a result. In both Britain and France, women's contributions to war were linked to debates emerging directly from the wartime experience of service, sacrifice, and loss.[19]

Within nations, women were often divided about whether the campaign for woman suffrage should be linked to a national war effort. Pacifist and socialist women opposed any links because they often viewed the vote as a tool to end militarism and exploitation.[20] Montreal suffragists were divided over Canada's Wartime Elections Act of 1917. The act gave voting privileges to women whose husbands and sons were already serving in the military. Opponents argued that if only these women were enfranchised, then the law linked the vote unquestionably with militarism and a proposed conscription law.[21] In the United States, members of the moderate NAWSA, including the organization's president, Carrie Chapman Catt, engaged in patriotic voluntary service, and national leaders used the service of suffrage women to convince male politicians to support the cause. The conflict provided a forum for the more radical National Woman's Party (NWP) to challenge the notion of America's war as one to make the world safe for democracy while denying women the citizen's right to vote at home. Two hundred women protesters from the NWP were arrested when they picketed the White house. Some 2,000 women protesters from the NWP picketed the White House from 1917 to 1919, and authorities arrested some 200 of them. Their hunger strikes and force-feeding by prison staff provided strong publicity for the cause.[22]

RACE, ETHNICITY, AND CIVIC STATUS

Some men and women of color and those in marginalized communities and colonized states also saw the war as offering them an opportunity to claim expanded rights of citizenship and equality. Ely Green, one of almost 400,000 African American men who were part of the US military in World War I, and among the 200,000 who saw service in France, believed that army service with the American Expeditionary Force would be his way to "win my rights as a citizen" and to fight racism at home.[23] Addie Waites Hunton, Kathryn Johnson, and Helen Curtis provided support services for African American troops through the Young Men's Christian Association and challenged government segregation, working as both "race women and cultural ambassadors."[24] Addie Hunton used the paradigm of patriotic motherhood but also went beyond it to voice "a political consciousness that was critical of the nation." As "trusted guardians of African American soldiers in France, Hunton, Johnson, and Curtis 'fought for the community as a whole,'" with black women and men working together for a common goal.[25]

Native American men who were not citizens of the United States were required to register for the draft but did not have to be drafted. However, Indian men who were citizens were subject to the draft. Some 17,000 Indians served during the war, most of whom were not citizens. Native American soldiers were integrated into regular army units, including service in France in the American Expeditionary Force. In June 1919, the US Congress passed a law providing for citizenship for Indian veterans of the World War as "real Americans . . . of right entitled to citizenship." Full citizenship for all Indian men and women came with the Indian Citizenship Act of 1924. Citizenship in this case was complicated by the continuing politics of the Bureau of Indian Affairs, poverty, and local laws effectively preventing Indians from exercising the vote. In these cases, race and ethnicity formed bases of political organizing that transcended gender identity.[26]

The wartime instituting of a military draft created a civic divide among men in the United States. During the conflict, some 70 percent of US soldiers were in the military through conscription. Policymakers wanted control over the formation of military forces and saw the draft as a way to accomplish that. Noncitizen men who had completed their "first papers" as the initial step in the naturalization process were eligible for the draft and had to register. This included men from neutral nations, whose diplomats protested this as a violation of treaty rights and the rights of the men in question. In April 1918, responding to these critiques, the Wilson administration made it possible for men from neutral nations residing in the United States to be discharged from the military upon diplomatic request, and men with "first papers" could withdraw them if they did not wish to be drafted. Many local draft boards continued to support drafting of these "alien" men, and Congress responded by penalizing those men who withdrew their declarations of intent, making them ineligible for citizenship after the conflict.[27] The draft also reinforced race and class hierarchies. In the American South, elite white men found exemptions more commonly than others, but African American laborers, needed by white farmers, also were exempted. White men without class or community connections were drafted more frequently. Questions of full citizenship in the period of the First World War, as these cases demonstrate, involved intersections of gender, race, region, and status.[28]

GENDER NORMS, CIVIL LIBERTIES, AND
CHALLENGES TO CITIZENSHIP

The powerful cultural views that linked the qualities of citizenship to patriotic motherhood, military service, or a prescribed public loyalty also created a mirror image of the dangerous anticitizen. Disloyalty, opposition to the war, militant feminism, or a homosexual, transgender, or queer identity all violated proper expressions of the positive qualities of citizenship. Because the war also engendered a rapid growth of state surveillance on citizens and noncitizens as a way to identify those men eligible for the draft and those who were enemy aliens or opposed to the war and wartime policies, all residents were potentially under state scrutiny as never before.[29]

In the United States, the army borrowed and adapted surveillance and mass examination techniques from the prewar work of the Bureau of Immigration to scrutinize gay men and used psychological testing to stigmatize recruits whose sexuality did not conform to a masculine/feminine binary and thus challenged their ability to be full citizens.[30] The Bureau of Immigration had also honed a practice of admitting women who were respectable wives and mothers into the United States and refusing those whom they believed did not conform to these standards of respectability.[31] The US Department of Justice and local branches of the American Protective League, a vigilante group, conducted raids against "slacker" men who sought to avoid military service or the draft. Purported slackers and men who sought conscientious objector status were often considered "effeminate" and labeled as "perverts" and demonized and subjected to violence and imprisonment.[32] Men from other combatant nations who avoided military service or who objected on religious or ethical grounds also faced powerful consequences. In Great Britain, "shirkers" faced everything from violent attacks to prison terms for war resistance.[33] A man who avoided wartime service in France was known as an *embusqué*. Popular culture images in France, such as those in cartoons, contrasted the easy life of an *embusqué* characterized by "weakness, fear, incompetence" with the steadfast French poilu soldier of the trenches.[34]

Many women who opposed the war were labeled as disloyal subjects who forfeited their citizenship rights because they did not conform to the imperative of patriotic motherhood. In the United States, Emma Goldman was deported after the conflict for her opposition to the draft and outspoken challenges to the war's effects on the people and democracy. Dr. Marie Equi of Portland, Oregon, was sent to San Quentin Prison, her prosecution and persecution heightened due to her overt radicalism and her lesbian identity. Kate Richards O'Hare insisted that mothers were being exploited by being asked to send their sons into the trenches, and she was convicted under the Sedition Act for so saying. By refusing to adopt the civic qualities of "patriotic motherhood," women who opposed the war became "scurrilous citizens" instead.[35]

Residents of various nations who held citizenship in an enemy nation brought a particular focus to the question of anticitizenship, violence, and civil liberties. The surveillance of resident enemy aliens took place in all of the combatant nations, and those individuals deemed most dangerous were interned in camps for the duration of the conflict. Hundreds of thousands of people were affected.[36] Those deemed "enemy aliens" were considered anticitizens, and they were targeted by government officials and community leaders not because of their actions but because of their identities. Colonial subjects were stigmatized even more: in the German internment camp in Ruhleben near Berlin, British subjects who were African or Jamaican were housed in a segregated barracks for blacks.[37]

In the United States, in the context of powerful anti-German speeches, the removal of German language instruction and music from schools, and heated local violence and conflict targeting German Americans, President Woodrow Wilson declared on November 6, 1917, that all men residing in the United States who were German citizens aged fourteen or older would have to register with the US government. On April 19, 1918, Wilson expanded the registration to include all women of the same age and status. Women throughout the country would have to bring photographs and fill our registration forms from June 17 to 26, 1918. Just as had the men before them, in cities with 5,000 or more residents, women had to go to police headquarters to register; outside of those cities, registration took place under the watchful eye of the postmaster or postmistress at the local post office.[38] German citizens came fully under government surveillance, now required to have their registration cards on their persons at all times or be subject to arrest. This program lasted until after the Armistice on December 25, 1918. If one wished to move, whether across the country or across the street, a permit was required. Those who worked in restricted military or industrial zones, such as the Port of Portland, had to have a special permit to travel within that security zone.[39]

Ten years before the United States had entered the war, in 1907, fears of increased numbers of immigrants and expanding nativism led Congress to pass the Expatriation Act of 1907. Women who were US citizens and then married a man who was not a citizen were required to take the nationality of their husband and were prohibited from following the naturalization process as individuals.[40] The US Supreme Court upheld the Expatriation Act in *Mackenzie v. Hare* (1915), when the First World War was in its early stages.[41] This meant that women who were US citizens, often born in the United States, who were married to German citizen men were defined not as citizens but as anticitizen enemy aliens. They had to register and be surveilled under the provisions of Wilson's proclamation. Similar policies relating to married women's nationality were in place in Great Britain and Germany.[42]

These US-born "enemy alien" women provide a powerful case study in the ways that wartime fears and gendered citizenship policies combined to remove civil liberties during the war and to further erode some women's civic credentials in the wartime expansion of the surveillance state. The case of the state of Oregon is illustrative. Across the state, 3,729 people, including 2,245 men and 1,484 women, registered as enemy alien Germans. A startling 394 women, more than a quarter of the total number of Oregon women who registered, were born in the United States but were labeled enemies because of their marriages to German citizen men. Women resisted in a number of ways, making claims to the citizenship of their birth on the registration documents, protesting directly at the time of registration, and even divorcing husbands in service in the German army.[43]

In Germany, international activist Elizabeth Rotten assisted German-born wives of British men who had also lost their citizenship as a result of marriage and were deemed "enemy aliens." Rotten worked with the Information and Assistance Bureau for Germans Abroad and for Foreigners in Germany, founded in 1914, to assist such women whose British husbands were interned at the Ruhleben camp. With their German citizenship forfeited because of marriage, wives of these "enemy aliens" lacked benefits and separation allowances, exacerbating their precarious wartime situation. Rotten was able to raise funds for assistance from major corporate donors and provide significant relief, building on a feminist critique of war and nationalism highlighted by the plight of enemy alien women in these circumstances.[44]

CITIZENSHIP AND TRANSNATIONAL ACTIVISM

The question of married women's nationality became a focus of postwar transnational activism. Because other national policies restricted a woman's nationality and citizenship to that of her husband, this became, in addition to calls for universal enfranchisement of women, a common element of a human rights platform for women. Support came from a range of organizations, including the International Suffrage Alliance and the Inter-American Commission on Women, culminating in the inclusion of the independent right of nationality in the United Nations Universal Declaration of Human Rights in 1948.[45]

For some women across nations, the First World War engendered similar programs for action that embraced concepts of a transnational citizenship, shared principles of what would later be known as human rights in the United Nations Declaration of Rights in 1948 and other documents. Women pacifists during the war were isolated by nationalists who saw internationalism and pacifism as unpatriotic, and also by members of women's organizations who defined citizenship as patriotic motherhood and advocated support of wartime national goals. Forming transnational relationships of shared ideals and goals was one way to redirect this isolation to productive work. The women from various nations, including former combatant nations, who formed the Women's International League for Peace and Freedom (WILPF) in 1919 developed a discourse of citizenship as a "shared humanity, often based on women's identity as mothers, which allowed them to reach across national divides and to maintain a sense of the humanity of the enemy," an "active and dynamic" vision of world peace. In their Hague resolutions of 1919, WILPF leaders affirmed the importance of the vote for women as an element of national citizenship but also called for a larger human rights program that affirmed "preventing future war at [the] international level and through transnational activism."[46]

Women doctors took similar transnational action to achieve both women's rights and human rights in the postwar period with a vision of a collective set of rights and responsibilities as global citizens. Many of the 10,000 women physicians of the world joined the Medical Women's International Association (MWIA), established in 1919, with this goal in mind. Many of the early leaders of the MWIA also had a shared wartime experience with medical work in hospitals in France or other nations such as Serbia, or were in neutral nations impacted by the conflict. During the war, they found medical women from other nations doing similar work, and this engendered an identity that they shared not just as physicians but as doctors whose perspectives had been changed because of their professional experiences overseas or with military hospitals in their own nations. Esther Lovejoy of the United States, the first president of the MWIA, urged her colleagues to embrace this transnational civic view by working to end war and thereby addressing the violence against women in its wake, to empower women in their local communities with the vote and the power to regulate health matters, and to build a strong organization of women doctors above and across nation states campaigning for women's rights on a global scale. The MWIA worked to include women physicians whose nations had been at war with the Allied powers during the conflict, including Safieh Ali of Turkey, Dora Teleky of Austria, and Vera Lebedeva of the new Soviet Union.[47]

The transnational and international civic hopes of many people in the postwar world did not always translate into success. The leaders of the League of Nations, with its promise of an internationalist civic body and membership, failed to include women in most positions of authority and action and did not resolve many citizenship claims relating to colonial peoples and states. International labor and suffrage groups made gains but faced continuing barriers to a broader world citizenship and empowerment.

CONTESTED CITIZENSHIPS

During the First World War, many people tested the enduring and forceful connections among masculinity, military service, and citizenship. By engaging in home and war front service to their nation states, many women and marginalized and colonized men made the claim that such service made them deserving recipients of a more complete citizenship status, including having the right to vote. The results of these claims were mixed, with some women and men achieving civic rights such as the vote, and others facing continuing oppression and discrimination and defeat in national debates about citizenship status and wartime service. Other activists did not want to connect social and civic reform with militarism. People in opposition to the wartime programs of their nation states, men and women labeled "enemy aliens," and individuals who challenged the prevailing "qualities" of a citizen such as homosexuals and radicals, found themselves labeled and persecuted as "anticitizens." Authoritarian and also more liberal states engaged in the suppression of civil liberties and increased surveillance on citizens and residents, engendering new calls for civic protections and freedoms as part of postwar citizenship gains. And some activists in quest of more complete civic powers began to identify a transnational or world citizenship and shared goals above and across national boundaries. The scholarship on citizenship and the First World War underscores that citizenship was not an unchanging status but that many people worked to create new definitions of civic identity in this period. The achievement of increased civic rights was not a steady line of progress; gender, race, ethnicity, sexuality, class, and colonial status all impacted the possibilities and results for individuals and groups.

Many fruitful avenues of research on citizenship and the First World War remain. Scholars who are investigating the impact of wartime actions and ideas on indigenous peoples may draw on the work of the many scholars reviewed here, with the opportunity to find new case studies and to understand how gender and citizenship were central to these stories. Local case studies will continue to enrich our analysis of the ways that transnational events influenced communities and gender relations. A transnational approach offers the chance for scholars to compare similar groups across national boundaries and to assess in even more detail the results of wartime claims for citizenship rights and the complicated relationship between wartime service and categories of identity and status based on gender. And, in turn, scholars of the First World War and its aftermath may also contribute to our understanding of the twentieth century and beyond as a "long war," with conflict broadly conceived as including, but not limited to, declared war, revolution, and civil war, and the civic conflicts relating to citizenship. More scholarship will help to uncover the important threads connecting campaigns for civil liberties during and after the First World War with the broad movement for human rights in the twentieth and twenty-first centuries. Such work will reinforce the importance of the First World War as a vital event and process in the modern and postmodern world.

NOTES

1. Linda K. Kerber, *No Constitutional Right to Be Ladies: Women and the Obligations of Citizenship* (New York: Hill and Wang, 1998), 223.

2. Judith Hicks Stiehm, "The Protected, the Protector, the Defender," *Women's Studies International Forum* 5 (1982): 367–376.

3. Kimberly Jensen, *Mobilizing Minerva: American Women in the First World War* (Urbana: University of Illinois Press, 2008); Christopher Capozzola, *Uncle Sam Wants You: World War I and the Making of the Modern American Citizen* (New York: Oxford University Press, 2008); Susan Grayzel, *Women's Identities at War: Gender, Motherhood, and Politics in Britain and France during the First World War* (Chapel Hill: University of North Carolina Press, 1999), 36; Tammy Proctor, *Civilians in a World at War: 1914–1918* (New York: New York University Press, 2010), 78–80; Belinda J. Davis, *Home Fires Burning: Food, Politics, and Everyday Life in World War I Berlin* (Chapel Hill: University of North Carolina Press, 2000); Desmond Morton, "Supporting Soldiers' Wives and Families in the Great War: What Was Transformed?," in *A Sisterhood of Suffering and Service: Women and Girls of Canada and Newfoundland during the First World War*, ed. Sarah Glassford and Amy Shaw (Vancouver: University of British Columbia Press, 2012), 195–218.

4. Proctor, *Civilians in a World at War*, 177–189; Allison Norman, "'In Defense of the Empire': The Six Nations of the Grand River and the Great War," in *A Sisterhood of Suffering and Service*, 29–50.

5. Penelope Brownell, "The Women's Committees of the First World War: Women in Government, 1917–1919" (PhD diss., Brown University, 2002); Capozzola, *Uncle Sam Wants You*, 83–103; and Susan Zeiger, *In Uncle Sam's Service: Women Workers with the American Expeditionary Force, 1917–1919* (Ithaca, NY: Cornell University Press, 1999).

6. Nikki Brown, *Private Politics and Public Voices: Black Women's Activism from World War I to the New Deal* (Bloomington: Indiana University Press, 2006), 1–29.

7. Lynn Dumenil, "Women's Reform Organizations and Wartime Mobilization in World War I–Era Los Angeles," *Journal of the Gilded Age and Progressive Era* 10, no. 2 (2011): 213-245.

8. Esther Pohl Lovejoy, *Women Doctors of the World* (New York: Macmillan, 1957), 282–291; Leah Leneman, "Medical Women at War, 1914–1918," *Medical History* 38, no. 2 (1994): 160–177; Kimberly Jensen, "Volunteers, Auxiliaries, and Women's Mobilization: The First World War and Beyond," in *The Brill Companion to Women's Military History*, ed. Barton C. Hacker and Margaret Vining (Leiden: Brill, 2012), 189–232.

9. Jensen, *Mobilizing Minerva*, 75–115.

10. Margaret H. Darrow, *French Women and the First World War: War Stories of the Home Front* (Oxford: Berg, 2000), 134–156.

11. Bianca Schönberger, "'Motherly Heroines and Adventurous Girls': Red Cross Nurses and Women Army Auxiliaries in the First World War," in *Home/Front: The Military, War and Gender in Twentieth-Century Germany*, ed. Karen Hagemann and Stefanie Schüler-Springorum (Oxford: Berg, 2002), 87–114.

12. Zuhal Özaydin, "Upper Social Strata Women in Nursing in Turkey," *Nursing History Review* 14 (2006): 161–174; quotations on 164–165.

13. Alon Rachamimov, "'Female Generals' and 'Siberian Angels': Aristocratic Nurses and the Austro-Hungarian POW Relief," in *Gender and War in Twentieth-Century Eastern Europe*, ed. Nancy M. Wingfield and Maria Bucur (Bloomington: Indiana University Press, 2006), 23–46.

14. Gordon Daniels, "Humanitarianism or Politics? Japanese Red Cross Nurses in Britain 1915–1916," in *Japanese Women: Emerging from Subservience, 1868–1945*, ed. Hiroko Tomida and Gordon Daniels (Kent, UK: Global Oriental, 2005), 222–231.

15. Janet S. K. Watson, "Wars in the Wards: The Social Construction of Medical Work in First World War Britain," *Journal of British Studies* 41, no. 4 (2002): 484–510.

16. Janet S. K. Watson, *Fighting Different Wars: Experience, Memory, and the First World War in Britain* (New York: Cambridge University Press, 2004).

17. Jensen, *Mobilizing Minerva*, 116–141.

18. In 1917, women could vote in the states of Wyoming, Colorado, Idaho, Utah, Washington, California, Oregon, Kansas, Arizona, Montana, and Nevada and in the territory of Alaska. Women in New York secured the right in 1917, and in Michigan, South Dakota, and Oklahoma in 1918. Presidential election–only suffrage came to women in North Dakota, Nebraska, and Rhode Island in 1917, and in Indiana, Maine, Missouri, Iowa, Minnesota, Ohio, Wisconsin, and Tennessee in 1919. National American Woman Suffrage Association, *Victory: How Women Won It: A Centennial Symposium 1840–1940* (New York: H. W. Wilson, 1940), 161–166, 172. For an overview, see Sarah Hunter Graham, *Woman Suffrage and the New Democracy* (New Haven, CT: Yale University Press, 1996).

19. Grayzel, *Women's Identities at War*, 190–225.

20. Frances H. Early, *A World without War: How U.S. Feminists and Pacifists Resisted World War I* (Syracuse, NY: Syracuse University Press, 2007).

21. Tarah Brookfield, "Divided by the Ballot Box: The Montreal Council of Women and the Election of 1917," *Canadian Historical Review* 89, no. 4 (2008): 473–501.

22. Graham, *Woman Suffrage and the New Democracy*, 99–127; Christine A. Lunardini, *From Equal Suffrage to Equal Rights: Alice Paul and the National Woman's Party, 1910–1928* (New York: New York University Press, 1986).

23. Adriane Danette Lentz-Smith, *Freedom Struggles: African Americans and World War I* (Cambridge, MA: Harvard University Press, 2009), 4, 81.

24. Brown, *Private Politics and Public Voices*, 84–107.

25. Melinda Plastas, *A Band of Noble Women: Racial Politics in the Peace Movement* (Syracuse, NY: Syracuse University Press, 2011), 44; Lentz-Smith, *Freedom Struggles*, 102.

26. Steven Sabol, "'It Was a Pretty Good War, but They Stopped It Too Soon': The American Empire, Native Americans and World War I," in *Empires in World War I: Shifting Frontiers and Imperial Dynamics in a Global Conflict*, ed. Andrew Tait Jarvoe and Richard S. Fogarty (New York: Palgrave Macmillan, 2014), 193–216; quotation on 209.

27. Candice Bredbenner, "A Duty to Defend? The Evolution of Aliens' Military Obligations to the United States, 1792–1946," *Journal of Policy History* 24, no. 2 (2012): 224–262.

28. Jeanette Keith, *Rich Man's War, Poor Man's Fight: Race, Class and Power in the Rural South during the First World War* (Chapel Hill: University of North Carolina Press, 2004).

29. Capozzola, *Uncle Sam Wants You*; Keith, *Rich Man's War, Poor Man's Fight*, 135–161.

30. Margot Cannady, *The Straight State: Sexuality and Citizenship in Twentieth-Century America* (Princeton, NJ: Princeton University Press, 2009), 23, 55–90.

31. Martha Gardner, *The Qualities of a Citizen: Women, Immigration, and Citizenship, 1870–1965* (Princeton, NJ: Princeton University Press, 2005).

32. Cannady, *Straight State*, 60; Capozzola, *Uncle Sam Wants You*, 41–53.

33. Proctor, *Civilians in a World at War*, 28–29.

34. James P. Daughton, "Sketches of the Poilu's World: Trench Cartoons from the Great War," in *World War I and the Cultures of Modernity*, ed. Douglas Peter Mackaman and Michael Mays (Jackson: University Press of Mississippi, 2000), 35–67.

35. Kathleen Kennedy, *Disloyal Mothers and Scurrilous Citizens: Women and Subversion during World War I* (Bloomington: Indiana University Press, 1999).

36. Proctor, *Civilians in a World at War*, 203–238; Capozzola, *Uncle Sam Wants You*, 173–205.

37. Proctor, *Civilians in a World at War*, 216.

38. "Registration of Women On Today," *Oregonian*, June 17, 1918, 5.

39. US Executive Office of the President, "By the President of the United States of America: A Proclamation, November 16, 1917," in *United States Statutes at Large*, vol. 40, pt. II, 1716–1718; US Executive Office of the President, "By the President of the United States of America, A Proclamation, April 19, 1918," in *United States Statutes at Large*, vol. 40, pt. II, 1772–1773; Jorg Nagler, "Enemy Aliens in the USA, 1914–1918," in *Minorities in Wartime: National and Racial Groupings in Europe, North America and Australia during the Two World Wars*, ed. Panikos Panayi (Oxford: Berg, 1993), 191–215; Capozzola, *Uncle Sam Wants You*, 187, 273n37.

40. Candace Lewis Bredbenner, *A Nationality of Her Own: Women, Marriage and the Law of Citizenship* (Berkeley: University of California Press, 1998), 4.

41. Bredbenner, *Nationality of Her Own*, 65–70.

42. M. Page Baldwin, "Subject to Empire: Married Women and the British Nationality and Status of Aliens Act," *Journal of British Studies* 40, no. 4 (2001): 522–556.

43. United States Department of Justice, World War I Alien Registration Forms, Oregon, MSS 1540, Oregon Historical Society Research Library, Portland, Oregon, Boxes 1–5. See also Kimberly Jensen, "From Citizens to Enemy Aliens: Oregon Women, Marriage, and the Surveillance State during the First World War," *Oregon Historical Quarterly* 114, no. 4 (2014): 427–442. The 1910 federal census reveals that men and women born in Germany were the largest group of foreign-born residents in Oregon, some 18,000 people out of a total state population of 672,765.

44. Matthew Stibbe, "Elisabeth Rotten and the 'Auskunfts und Hilfsstelle für Deutsche im Ausland und Ausländer in Deutschland' 1914–1919," in *The Women's Movement in Wartime: International Perspectives 1914–19*, ed. Alison Fell and Ingrid Sharp (London: Palgrave Macmillan, 2007), 194–210.

45. Bredbenner, *Nationality of Her Own*, 195–242.

46. Ingrid Sharp, "Feminist Peace Activism: 1915 and 2010: Are We Nearly There Yet?," *Peace and Change: A Journal of Peace Research* 38, no. 2 (2013): 155–180; quotations on 163, 165, 166.

47. Kimberly Jensen, *Oregon's Doctor to the World: Esther Pohl Lovejoy and a Life in Activism* (Seattle: University of Washington Press, 2012), 193–207; National Representatives, *Bulletin Association Internationale des Femmes-Médicins* 2 (June 1930): 2.

2

Gender and Resistance

Erika Kuhlman

BOTH WOMEN AND men used ideas about masculinity and femininity to resist participation in the First World War. Resisting war means acting against a nation's claims to the resources—human, economic, and cultural—that it uses to prosecute the war. Resistance takes many forms and includes individuals refusing to participate in the conflict either through direct action or inaction (for example, refusing to register for the draft or deserting one's military unit) or by the act of publicizing one's resistance, such as writing an antiwar editorial. Beyond individual initiatives, resistance also encompasses collective actions and pronouncements. Here we find such activities as holding mass protests against a war or publishing a manifesto outlining why a group or organization is resisting armed conflict. The goal of any act of resistance—either an explicit act or publicly explaining one's resistance—is to prevent the nation from making claims upon the resources that are necessary to prosecute the war and thereby either stopping the nation from going to war or ending a war that is already in progress.

Men and women who resist conflicts often act in response to a specific war or the buildup to a conflict, although some people always oppose war no matter what the dispute involves or how it is prosecuted. Others may find only a particular war to be immoral or unworthy of support. The Great War, often defined as the first war to be fought by multiple industrialized nations, was fought by whole societies rather than by armies of (typically) men isolated from the rest of society. Resisting the Great War, then, involved not only men refusing to fight but also civilians resisting the pressure put upon them by governments and others favoring the war to conform to and support the conflict. In order to obtain consent to war, nations utilized conventional gender norms to create hegemonic gender roles for women in support capacities and men in combat.[1] Resisting those roles is a key component to understanding the myriad reasons and ways men and women resisted war, including pacifism, pacifism influenced by feminism and socialism, and religious pacifism as practiced by Quakers and others. Methods of countering the Great War included writing essays, editorials, and books on pacifism; practicing one's pacifism by calling attention to wounds caused by war; draft resistance; and deserting the military. Understanding the history of resistance to war illuminates how and why nations are able to obtain citizens' consent to war and the conformity necessary to prosecute a "total" war involving nearly all aspects of democratized, industrialized societies. Using the lens of resistance to analyze a conflict reveals the ways in which going to war was a process of negotiation between governments and their citizens rather than a preordained event that simply "happened." The line separating conformity from resistance, however, was not always clear, just as the presumed boundary dividing femininity and masculinity shifted constantly over the course of the war. Some people may have complied with wartime gender expectations in some instances but may have resisted the war at other times.

People responded to war in complicated ways, shaping how they conceived of and made use of gender in their responses, and how their understandings of gender reflected and produced a transnational concept of resistance to the Great War. In the final analysis, the multiple ways in which what people did and what they thought about the war transcended national boundaries.

WOMEN'S AND MEN'S ROLES DURING WAR: EXPECTATION
AND RESISTANCE

Gender influenced the steps that women and men took when the Great War began in August 1914 (the United States entered the war in April 1917), at times signaling conformity to their nation's entrance into the war, and at other times, resistance. To support the war, women were recruited by their governments and joined military auxiliaries in England, Germany, France, and the United States, and in Russia they were trained as fighters.[2] Males volunteered to join the military and took up arms against the perceived enemy in a war that some have deemed to be an "invitation to manliness" for the young men who heeded such calls.[3] Many other men were drafted into the military by governments that had conscription laws. Outside the military itself, men and women participated in war bond drives to encourage citizens to lend their money to the war effort, and in relief organizations designed to aid those displaced or injured during the war. Male artists—often coming from the advertising industry—drew illustrations for the myriad patriotic posters hung in public places in all belligerent nations to encourage citizens to participate in the nation's war effort in whatever way they could.[4]

Women's primary and expected contribution to the war effort lay in nursing, an occupation requiring both a "mother" and a "fighting spirit," according to nursing instructor Isabel Maitland Stewart.[5] In this activity, women both conformed to gender expectations of nurturing and resisted those expectations. The tie between nursing and war began, at least in a professional sense, with the Crimean War. Florence Nightingale, a British nurse, received a call from the War Office to come to the aid of soldiers who lay untreated in what barely passed for army hospitals. There, she discovered that poor hygiene and overcrowding were causing the most harm. Nightingale's work revolutionized the field of army nursing.[6] Tens of thousands of women served as nurses during the First World War. Some worked through the auspices of humanitarian aid groups such as the Red Cross, while others were attached to military units. Some were professionals; others volunteered and were trained on the job.

By the First World War, nursing leaders in the United States were attempting to professionalize an occupation that required special training and skill but also, it was thought, white skin and middle-class origins to lift nursing to a level of professional respectability.[7] Regardless of where and how nurses worked, nursing was considered women's natural role in wartime, an extension of the nurturing roles—as mothers, teachers, and caregivers—that they performed in peacetime. By acting as nurses, women conformed to expected gender roles and to their nation's call to participate in the Great War. However, when professional nurses fought for greater recognition and pay, they moved aggressively beyond the expected behind-the-scenes helpmeet role and into the public sphere.[8]

In all the fighting nations, too, however, women and men acted individually to resist the war, and they formed pacifist organizations to try to keep their nations out of the war. "Pacifism" is here defined as persons or groups of people who oppose war and/or violence as a means to solve conflicts, usually between nations. Indeed, just prior to the Great War, pacifism had reached its peak, in terms of membership, as a reform movement in the United States.[9] Women joined mixed-gender organizations but also formed their own groups, where they would be guaranteed an opportunity to achieve leadership positions.[10]

Men's resistance to war included refusing the draft by failure to comply with registration notices, hiding from draft boards, and obtaining conscientious objector status. These men faced prosecution for the offense of resistance, since most at-war nations punished men who refused to comply with draft laws. They also faced public scorn and sometimes heavy punishment when they did not act according to the hegemonic manly ideal of brave soldier. However, not all males were subject to the draft, rendering the supposed ideal male model open to question, since by law some men's attempts to conform to the ideal were rejected. In the United States, the Selective Service Act of 1917 exempted legislators (who made up the very body that declared war and that crafted the law), clergy, police, firemen, and religious pacifists. Men deemed physically, mentally, or morally deficient were not inducted into military service. Draft boards were formed to hear men's requests for exemptions, and boards in southern states admitted to allowing exemptions for some whites but not for black men.[11] By refusing to admit certain kinds of men into the military, the nation indicated that the supposed "gender ideal" of manly warrior was flexible, and also that the requirement of conformity was not universal and was therefore open to negotiation.

In addition, thousands of rural, southern men resisted conscription in other ways. Some failed to register for the draft, others helped diversify conscientious objection from its roots in certain religious orders, and others banded together and left their units after being inducted. These deserters, who were not necessarily pacifists, armed themselves and hid out in the countryside; it took federal troops to round them up for punishment.[12] "Desertion" is defined as servicemen and servicewomen deciding to leave their units with the intention of not returning. German deserters were legion especially during the last half of 1918, when expectations for a swift and decisive end to the war had long since passed and many men believed they would face senseless slaughter, since victory by that point seemed impossible to achieve. These men did not necessarily oppose all wars, or war in general; instead, they were against participating in this particular conflict and refused to take part in it any longer by escaping.[13] The story of a unit of French soldiers taking heavy casualties in a 1914 battle, then mutinying and refusing to fight in a second engagement a year later, and finally returning to fight valiantly toward the end of the war demonstrates a pattern of conformity and resistance, underscoring the ways in which war is negotiated between and among those who conceive of it, those who direct it, and those who fight it.[14]

WAR, PEACE, AND WOMEN

For women in many parts of Europe and the United States, the Great War occurred just as female activists grew hopeful that women would be granted the right to vote (suffrage) by their governments. Gaining access to the ballot box meant that women were increasingly seen as being equally capable of self-government as their male counterparts. However, since in most European and American nations, women were not able to join the military, the concept of woman suffrage conflicted with the conventional notion that to be a citizen meant to be willing and able to defend the nation militarily. Therefore, gender seemed to limit women's ability to participate fully as citizens in their nations, and this was used against them in their fight for the right to vote. Some British suffrage advocates substituted other forms of social service for women's presumed inability to perform military service; others emphasized women's presumed moral superiority over men's protective function.[15] The Great War also coincided with the rise of peace movements throughout Europe and America. Women, often seen as the "gentler sex," took part equally with men in these organizations. This notion of the softer nature of femininity, of course, is precisely what kept women from joining the military and becoming full citizens. Feminist pacifists, then, faced difficult choices during the war. They could continue to lobby for the vote in at-war nations where special attention was being paid to military defense, and they could echo the need for citizens to provide armed (and other) support. Or, feminist pacifists could choose to stop campaigning for suffrage and start paying exclusive attention to how women could prove themselves capable of helping their nations defend themselves during war and thereby hope to have their activities rewarded through the passage of suffrage laws. Or, if pacifists, they could continue to lobby for the vote and, if successful, demonstrate women's ability to govern in such a manner (more "gently") that would reduce the likelihood of war in the future. It was this last method that sustained the international feminist pacifist movement that developed after the war.

There are examples of diverse women in different places making all of these choices simultaneously. In England, the National Union of Women's Suffrage Societies (NUWSS), founded in 1897, continued to lobby quietly and respectfully for women's right to vote during the war. In the United States, the National Woman's Party, headed by Alice Paul, who had worked in England with suffrage activists, challenged the US president publicly to grant women the liberty that American soldiers were presumably fighting for in the Great War.[16] The *Bund Deutscher Frauenvereine* (Association of German Women's Organizations) kept pushing for woman suffrage in overtly nationalistic terms that underscored the nation's need for a strong military defense.[17] In the United States, the Woman's Peace Party (WPP), which after the war helped form the Women's International League for Peace and Freedom (WILPF), continued to make pacifist arguments and female suffrage arguments throughout the conflict.

Jeannette Rankin, for example, had campaigned for suffrage in the states of Washington and Montana. In 1916, she was elected US representative from Montana (where women had already achieved the right to vote); she arrived in her nation's capital, Washington, DC, just in time to vote against the US declaration of war against Germany in April 1917. When Rankin voted "no," she proclaimed that she voted against war as a woman (though her brother Wellington Rankin had advised her to vote a man's vote, in favor of war).[18] Rankin also helped establish the WPP, which was the first US women's pacifist organization to form after the Great War began.

Rankin's proclamation demonstrated her belief that women and men approached the topic of war differently. Ideas about masculinity and femininity shaped the responses of those who conformed to gendered expectations of what women were supposed to do regarding the war. Women also resisted stereotypes by refusing to conform. The line separating conformity and resistance fluctuated within individuals and in differing social circumstances.

GENDER, CONFORMITY, AND RESISTANCE

One of the clearest illustrations of both gender conformity and resistance appeared in a publication written by the New York City WPP. The New York City branch distributed its newsletter, called *Four Lights*, throughout the nation (until the US Postal Service censored the publication under the 1917 Espionage Act). In one issue, editor Sarah N. Cleghorn used a drawing of a card and white feather that a Canadian man had been sent through the mail when he refused to enlist in the British military. The card read, "Wanted: Petticoats for all able-bodied men who prefer staying at home when their country needs them." Women who secured the enlistment of ten men received a brooch for their efforts, according to Cleghorn. The editor was decidedly unimpressed by the ritual of shaming men who did not do their perceived military duty and of praising women who goaded them to conform to the masculine military ideal. "It is of such conditions," she wrote sarcastically, "that the new courage is being born."[19]

This incident illustrates a number of conventional notions about gender. During the First World War, proper masculine behavior meant that men should volunteer for military service to their country. Men who refused to serve were shamed publicly for their nonconformity. The method of shaming involved "soft" symbols of femininity—petticoats and white feathers—being handed to the male resisters, implying that because they were not man enough to conform to masculine gender norms, they should wear feminine clothing instead.[20] At the same time, the womanly thing to do during war was to secure men's military service. This activity was rewarded with a piece of feminine jewelry. Overall, the ritual implied that men should behave as manly soldiers and defend their nation. Women were to behave as though they expected men to protect them, even if that meant men leaving women at home while they fought for the nation overseas, the assumption being that women could not take up arms themselves. This was an extension of conventional gender roles in peacetime, where men were considered the protectors and women were those whom men were to protect. Notice the *active* role for men versus the inactive role for women—females are the protected, not the protectors. Wartime, however, prompted women to actively seek men's protection by shaming those men who shirked that presumed duty. It is worth noting that until 1916 Britain—including Canada—fought the Great War without instituting a conscription law, relying solely on volunteers who, it was assumed, would answer the call to arms more enthusiastically if women were seen as requesting male protection.[21] In the act of writing her article, Sarah Cleghorn demonstrated women's awareness of the wartime pressure to conform to gender ideals, and she showed how women could resist that social pressure through publications such as *Four Lights*.

The masculine and feminine roles that women and men were to conform to during war were grounded in long-standing cultural norms. In general, European societies in the eighteenth and nineteenth centuries expected men to play three roles in society; first, to marry and be husbands and fathers; second, to bear arms; and third, to be active citizens. In Switzerland, for example, upon marriage those three roles were conflated within a single male. Bridegrooms were expected to wear a military uniform, and after marriage they were expected to participate in military drills conducted in the village square.[22]

In the context of the Great War in Germany, the masculine ideal was a cold-hearted, strong, dominating figure ready for battle physically and mentally. At the same time, however, there were a multitude of ways in which actual German soldiers negotiated that expectation, communicating in letters to their wives or girlfriends, for example, that they secretly longed for feminine emotional support (some also sought and received emotional and physical support, and sometimes sexual gratification, from their male comrades).[23] In this instance, evidence suggests that men both conformed to and resisted gender norms. They complied with gender expectations by not resisting the draft—by taking up arms and fighting in the ways suggested by the soldierly ideal. They resisted, however, by seeking out the emotional support of their wives. Interestingly, women, too, both conformed to and resisted gendered expectations during war. While some wives eagerly came to their soldier-husbands' aid and provided a compassionate shoulder, some in effect told their men to "buck up" and keep fighting.[24]

INTERNATIONAL WOMEN'S ORGANIZATIONS AND RESISTANCE

Although wars have traditionally been understood as a series of battles pitting one nation against another, historians have more recently argued that wars actually brought people from disparate nations together, for example, in efforts to provide relief to injured soldiers and in commemorating the war.[25] Women's international organizations included members from nearly all the at-war nations, and they combined their efforts to resist the war. International activists, however, were challenged in this endeavor by the heightened nationalism of wartime. Historians have deemed the late nineteenth century to be the "age of nationalism" in Europe.[26] This was a period when the nation had hit its stride as the primary way that humans organized themselves into political units with definable geographical boundaries and increasingly centralized power and authority over its citizens. At the same time, some nations proved to be more open to allowing their citizens greater say over and participation in national governments.

Leading up to the Great War, international activists began imagining international institutions that could aid in solving conflicts between nations diplomatically and legally rather than militarily. This was part of Progressive Era reform movements, when elite women and men began conceiving of human beings as capable of using their ability to reason to solve problems rather than resorting to violence. One such international institution was the Hague Convention of 1899 and 1907, where nations collectively wrote international treaties, some of which were designed to avert war between nations (for example, the convention for the pacific settlement of international disputes, which created a permanent court of arbitration). A third convention was planned for 1914, but the First World War made it impossible for nations to participate. Importantly, the development of the conventions signaled that men no longer viewed militarism as necessary to a nation's well-being, nor to men proving themselves to be manly men. However, this shift did not signal that male elites were open to women participating in international politics, nor did it mean that women themselves were prepared to be involved. In fact, some members of the International Council of Women, founded in the United States in 1888, welcomed the opportunity to be involved at the Hague Conventions, while others hesitated to comment on the proceedings, shunning a move that would involve them overtly in politics.[27]

When European nations declared war against each other in August 1914, progressive-minded individuals who had conceived of these conventions as likely to avert international conflicts were severely disappointed and disillusioned. Female pacifists then sought an outlet for their continued feminist pacifism in the International Woman Suffrage Alliance (IWSA). The history of this organization, which was founded in Berlin in 1904 and headquartered in London, reveals the shifting of women's concerns regarding both the right to vote and how women resisted the Great War.

Women suffragists around the world had established a strong network that helped activists help each other in other nations where they found themselves in the same boat: struggling to obtain the right to vote from governments that were run primarily by men. To be successful, they had to convince men that women were capable of self-government. The IWSA shared news, tactics, and strategies that helped women determine how to go about winning the right to vote. When the war began, suffrage organizations in the belligerent countries found their materials being censored by their own governments. States also restricted travel. Previously, the IWSA had held congresses in cities throughout Europe periodically since its founding a decade earlier.

In April 1915, a group of women pacifists declared their desire to meet in an international congress to try to stop the current war and prevent future conflicts from erupting. The organizers of the congress were founders of the IWSA, who perceived a connection between women being denied the vote in almost all the world's nations and the use of war as a method of solving international conflicts. The connection lay in women's awareness of and their discomfort with injustice, where the conference-goers perceived denying females the right to vote as an injustice, and they understood conflicts between nations as disagreements that arise when one nation behaves unjustly toward another. Therefore, they believed that because they were women subject to the first injustice (being denied the right to vote), they better understood the second injustice (one nation treating another nation unfairly). More than a thousand women participated in the conference, held in The Hague, Netherlands. For German delegate Lida Gustava Heymann, women's purpose at The Hague was international and transnational. Heymann urged women to "do their duty as wives and mothers, to protect life, to fight against national hatred, to guard civilization, to further justice—justice not only for their own country, but for all the countries of the world."[28] Participants made plans for the next congress, which occurred at the end of the war in 1919.

At that May 1919 meeting, held in Zurich, Switzerland, members changed the name of their organization to the Women's International League for Peace and Freedom and adopted a document that countered the Treaty of Versailles, the agreement that officially ended the Great War. In its document, WILPF, which was the first organization to actually read the treaty, condemned the harsh measures punishing Germany and its allies, which it viewed (correctly, as it turns out) as likely to start another war. The statement issued in May 1919 reflected WILPF's views of the importance of how women understood gender—both femininity and masculinity.

The Great War and its aftermath had heightened WILPF members' sense of gender differences. They acknowledged that their previous efforts to end the war (particularly the conference that they had held at The Hague in 1915) had failed, and they felt that they were unsuccessful because women had no power in the realm of international relations and war. This notion was confirmed by the fact that women were not given a seat at the negotiating table at Versailles as the peace terms were being worked out.[29] Members realized that they had no voice in the diplomatic or war-making world because of who *did* have that power. Men, claimed the women, who "have no respect for human life, or for the counsel and needs of women," controlled international relations. Therefore, pacifist women were unable to make a difference in the prosecution of, or the outcome of, the Great War.

The response by WILPF to the Treaty of Versailles was written at a time when woman suffrage laws were beginning to be considered seriously and even passed in many formerly belligerent countries. Germany, for example, passed its woman suffrage law in 1918. Women's ability to vote was clearly on the minds of WILPF members as they composed their response to the treaty. In order to create a "sane world order," the women declared, "we [women] must have freedom in every field of activity and the power that freedom brings. In the struggle for our emancipation, we have not destroyed a single human life." By "emancipation" WILPF meant the right to vote, although they probably meant much more than just that right. Next, WILPF outlined the succeeding steps it would take as an organization. The women's goal was to emancipate men from their bondage to the violence and brutality that millions of soldiers had experienced during the war. In doing so, the women would also liberate themselves, as "women can never know true liberty in a society dominated by force."[30]

The postwar statement by WILPF nicely summarizes why the international organization felt that women should resist both war and some conventional gender roles for men and women. War equaled violence, and in a violent world women and men could never realize true freedom. They had seen that women's roles in society did not include international policymaking, and in that regard they felt that women should resist the conventional sense that women should remain in the private, domestic realm, versus the public world of international politics. Some members of the women's peace movement, such as Jane Addams (WILPF's first president) argued that women's prerogative in the home was precisely the quality that was needed to make the public sphere more moral.[31]

The document also provides a sense of what the organization saw as essential gender differences between men and women. While calling for women to expand their roles and enter international politics, their statement nevertheless relies on the presumed sense of women as "gentler," and men as naturally forceful, domineering, and disrespectful of human life. Sometimes statements such as that released by WILPF regarding the Treaty of Versailles are as insightful for what they do *not* say as they are for what they *do* say. The document does not suggest that men may find themselves less anxious to make war, given their recent experiences in "the war to end all wars" (see the discussion of international veterans' peace organizations later in the chapter). In other words, WILPF seemed convinced that men were naturally aggressive and had to be taught—by women—to be less so. In addition, the statement does not indicate that in fact the Great War provided evidence that women could be every bit as aggressive as men, as indicated by the numbers of women who expressed their nationalist devotion militantly, such as Christabel Pankhurst in England, and those who actually took up arms in response to the Great War.[32]

By the end of the conflict, some women activists were ready to participate in international politics. In fact, having secured the right to vote in several of the formerly at-war nations, activists found that their job of helping each other gain woman suffrage in their respective nations was largely finished. Members of WILPF believed the organization's next major piece of activism, supporting and advocating for the League of Nations and working for disarmament, was work that would largely be done by female internationalists, or women whose activism, in concert with men's, focused on international relations.

UNDERSTANDING GENDER AND RESISTANCE TRANSNATIONALLY

More recently, transnational historians have illuminated women's and men's fluctuating connection to the nation-state in the context of war. During the Great War, nations declared war against one another and mobilized their militaries to fight the war in the hopes of achieving their specific national war aims. The state encouraged men to do their duty by serving in their country's military. Two men, one a German Lutheran (Friedrich Siegmund-Schultze) and the other an English Quaker (Henry Hodgkin), met each other and pledged to resist the war in their respective countries. Hodgkin held a meeting of multidenominational Christian men who resisted the war in London in December 1914, at which time the Fellowship of Reconciliation (FoR) was born. A year later, FoR boasted 1,500 members in fifty-five locations across the United Kingdom.[33]

When soldiers demobilized after the war, many of them faced the prospect of a new fight: receiving compensation from their governments for their war-induced injuries. A substantial number of casualties left millions of servicemen without limbs, blinded, with compromised eyesight, and suffering from mental and emotional trauma. Veterans' activism stirred complacent governments to do more for those who returned from the war.[34] Because soldiers had served their nations' militaries during the war, the act of demanding restitution from their nations' governments after the war reinforced the presumed ties between military men and the nations they served.

However, the post–Great War era also saw a rise in the number and stature of international veterans' organizations. These organizations were based on veterans' similar war experiences and memories, regardless of what nation they happened to be fighting for. War often highlights the ways in which individuals from disparate nations experienced armed conflict in very similar ways.[35] For example, all participant nations recruited soldiers using similar methods, all offered veterans benefits and pensions upon their return, and all nations sought to intensify the image of sacrifice for the nation during the war, often by "memorial day" military cemetery rituals and burial of "unknown soldiers."[36] These commonalities resulted in the rise of international cooperation among those presumed, ironically, to be the living symbols of nationalism: the World War I veteran. In addition to men separating themselves from the nation during the war, by declaring themselves conscientious objectors, refusing the draft, or joining organizations such as FoR, veterans who had already completed their military service began resisting war upon their return. Two international veterans' organizations developed in France, both of which were supported by the International Labor Organization and the League of Nations. The aims of the organizations were to secure the well-being of veterans in whatever nation they happened to reside and to ensure that the world would never again experience another catastrophic war. The impact of these international veterans' organizations (and organizations like FoR) was twofold. First, male pacifism loosened the presumed ties binding (male) soldiers to the nation for which they had fought, in effect redefining the term "citizen" as not necessarily requiring armed service. In addition, male pacifists limited the effectiveness—the coercive powers—of the patriotic, masculine soldier ideal.[37]

Efforts by WILPF in the postwar era brought women into the realm of international politics, despite earlier resistance in relation to the 1899 and 1907 Hague Conventions. The 1919 meeting in Zurich demonstrated the sense among WILPF leaders that the war had revealed the ways in which women's concerns were universal and transcended national boundaries. The organization's members were convinced that all women sought political representation via the franchise, that all women were equal victims of catastrophic events such as war, and that all women felt equally shut out of international political events such as the war-ending events held at Versailles. In the face of these interests, they were united in their belief that if women held more political power, both the national and international levels, these injustices could be rectified.

However, at least judging by their public declarations, they believed men to be naturally more violent and less peaceful than women. One of the reasons WILPF considered females less likely to resort to war was what it perceived as women's transnational emotional response to war. "They [women] don't feel as men do about war," commented Aletta Jacobs, a Dutch delegate, in 1915. "Men think of the economic results; women think of the grief and pain, and the damage to the race. If we can bring women to feel that internationalism is higher than nationalism, then they won't stand by governments, they'll stand by humanity."[38] However, while WILPF wanted to demonstrate to the world that women were "naturally" more able to form friendships and work together across national boundaries, its members also continued to harbor nationalistic feelings, and wartime animosity came across at times during their 1919 Zurich congress. For example, despite the clasping of hands in warm welcome that German pacifist Lida Gustava Heymann had extended to French delegate Jeanne Mélin in front of all those assembled, Jacobs noted that the Belgian women she encountered in Zurich could not rise above their hatred of all things German (Germany had invaded Belgium as its second act of war in 1914).[39] Transnational sentiment among female pacifists in the immediate postwar years only went so far. On the other hand, WILPF members obviously worked very effectively with each other in Zurich. They publicly and vociferously rejected the Treaty of Versailles, arguing that it did not reflect Woodrow Wilson's Fourteen Points, which formed the basis of the November Armistice and was to have been the foundation of postwar reconciliation among nations. They passed the Women's Charter, which demanded universal suffrage for women, the ability to determine their nationality equal to men, women's right to own and dispose of property in marriage, and opportunities for women to participate in international political events such as the peace conference that ended the Great War. Finally, they planned for their organization's future as they established Geneva as WILPF world headquarters.[40]

Geneva was also the host city of the International Committee of the Red Cross, founded in 1863. The field of international humanitarian aid has obvious transnational elements. People who came to the rescue of those rendered needy by the war understood these transnational elements of combat. Bullets fired in battle rent human bodies no matter what nation those bodies happened to come from; the pain inflicted and the need for aid were the same. The Great War witnessed the beginning of the use of lethal gas as a weapon of war. This substance moved beyond battle lines and into civilian populations, and it changed responses to future war. In addition to medical forms of aid, organizations also offered assistance to displaced persons in need of shelter and temporary housing. While the call for aid was sometimes pointed at particular groups of people, such as the victims of the 1915 Armenian genocide, at other times the aid offered was meant to be based on need, not nationality. Particularly in the latter case, humanitarian aid clearly fostered the transnational interpretation of the war. Aid organizations such as the International Committee of the Red Cross actually were quite impartial when they dispensed help to persons in need, regardless of national origin. Nation-based organizations, on the other hand, were not as impartial and, indeed, often aided the belligerency of the nations they represented.[41]

The link between humanitarian aid and resistance to war derives from the pacifists who dispersed relief during war. Perhaps the two best-known such pacifists working in humanitarian aid in the Great War era were Jane Addams and Vera Brittain. Indeed, for Brittain, working as a Voluntary Aid Detachment nurse awakened her pacifist feelings. In addition, humanitarian aid has an obvious connection to nursing. Field nurses bound up soldiers' wounds, provided basic needs such as water and medication, and offered comfort to suffering and dying uniformed men. Aid workers, in the context of war and postwar, provided similar services, but more often to civilians adversely affected by war. American Red Cross workers, for example, provided food, shelter, and medical assistance to refugees and other noncombatants.[42] While certainly not exclusively female, humanitarian aid was an arena where women's reputation for nurturing fit the context. Indeed, US physician Alice Hamilton, touring London, Paris, Berlin, and Brussels in 1915, commented that she had a feeling of déjà vu as she watched Belgian women in Brussels providing relief to those in need, noting, "And in Paris, and in London, it was the same," women dispensing humanitarian aid.[43] Providing relief brought out the physical impact of war on the providers, but also upon societies as a whole when reporters and writers such as Hamilton filed accounts of the destruction of war on soldiers' bodies and on the havoc wreaked upon civilian populations by invading armies, including the rape of civilian women. Once this was brought home to civilians not directly impacted by the war, the enormity of war's destructiveness encouraged a pacifistic response.

However, some caregivers began to sense a conflict between aid and war. Florence Nightingale, who worked as a nurse in the Crimean War, began to fear that the caregiving she offered only made the war worse by prolonging it. In other words, while she dutifully bound up soldiers' wounds, she began to realize that the effect of this was merely to send them back out into battle, where they either might suffer again from a more serious wound or, of course, might die. Not unreasonably, Nightingale questioned whether the aid she dispensed actually did more harm than good.[44]

Meanwhile, in addition to actually offering relief to victims, women participated indirectly in binding up wounds by organizing aid efforts and, more indirectly, by symbolizing those needing aid. Women successfully organized and orchestrated humanitarian aid from their homes, but also overseas. Two US pacifists, Jane Addams and Alice Hamilton, distributed $30,000 worth of food and twenty-five tons of clothing during their American Friends Service Committee tour of Europe in 1919. Addams's experience left her feeling gravely disappointed in the League of Nations, which did very little to alleviate Europe's postwar food and health crises, as it remained mired in old-fashioned, nationalistic diplomatic methods that did little to help those in need. Quaker women were quite active as well, along with other women who answered the call to send relief to European countries from already-established organizations. These included the Red Cross and YMCA, and those established in response to Great War conditions, including the California Thanksgiving Offering for Germanic Widows and Orphans, and the German and Austrian Relief Society.[45]

In addition to organizing and dispensing aid, women were nearly universally seen as the victims of postwar suffering, alongside wounded (male) soldiers. Thousands of war relief posters featured drawings of starving women and children to encourage viewers to donate money and time to aid efforts. The text of such posters drew viewers' attention to the numbers of women and children left needy by the war. Victimized women, usually paired with children, reinforced the sense of women's relative powerlessness in relation to men, and of their dependent condition, similar to the dependency of children and older people on others—usually conceived of as male.

Given women's roles as caregivers, one might expect to see women leading the dispensing and managing relief efforts. However, US State Department records containing correspondence between officials and relief administrators demonstrate that men did not easily relinquish their leadership positions in society, and aid societies were no exception. In addition to the previously named organizations, State Department officials corresponded with church leaders and private individuals, almost all of whom were male and who were anxious to help postwar efforts to alleviate suffering.[46] Historians can only speculate on why this particular set of correspondence reflects primarily male relief providers. It may be that men simply felt more comfortable writing to government officials, whereas women did not.

GENDER AND RESISTANCE

Historians of the First World War have always been aware of resistance to that war in particular and to all wars. For example, much has been written about the US Congress's debate over President Wilson's war declaration, and historians have considered the institutionalization of conscientious objection to serving in the military. Until recently, however, they had not considered the ways that gender, especially masculinity, may have persuaded congressmen and the sole female US representative,

Jeannette Rankin, to vote either in favor of the declaration or against it. A reading of the debate provides plenty of evidence that congressmen did indeed believe that American men had grown weak due to the lack of military engagement since the Spanish-American War of 1898 and that they needed to fight in order to reinvigorate themselves and the nation for which they would fight.[47] This notion, of course, also provides evidence of the ways in which the nation itself was conceived by the congressmen making this argument as a masculine entity. Rankin's "no" vote, as we have seen, was motivated in part by her belief that she represented women who were opposed to intervention in the conflict.

Traditional ways of thinking about gender during war were both adhered to and disrupted by the Great War. If convention held that men's prerogative was to do their duty and take up arms to protect their homes and homelands, while women waited for them patiently, then during the First World War, women were asked to leave those safe havens and support the war effort in public; this transformed the understanding of their labor. Industrialized warfare, for example, required a multitude of new kinds of weapons produced on a massive scale to be used by millions of armed soldiers who were unavailable to make them, so female power was used in arms manufacturing.[48] Women's traditional dress was even altered to accommodate this new role.[49]

Men who resisted the war by refusing to fight countered the gender ideal of armed masculinity. Those who fled the draft or their units and those who become conscientious objectors often paid a heavy price for their resistance. Fifty British resisters, early in the war, were forcibly inducted into the army and sent to France. There, they were told that if they did not fight, they would be shot. None of the fifty relented, and only heavy lobbying in the British Parliament spared their lives.[50] These men's act of refusal testified to the fact that if people decline to fight, there would be no war. While it is difficult to measure the impact of resistance (in part because it often goes unpublicized; to tell these men's story would be to undercut the ability of the nation to prosecute the war), 200,000 Britons signed a petition to negotiate an end to the war in 1916, and by the end of the war some 20,000 men refused to join the British military.[51] This incident demonstrates the power of individuals' resistance to war and the limitations of the masculine ideal of manly warrior. In addition—given the Parliament's forgiveness of the resisters' actions—it demonstrates the ways that war is negotiated between and among citizens and their governments.

Precisely because of this greater focus on gender, historians began considering women's and men's lives transnationally, above and beyond the construct of the nation. Despite so much focus on suffrage in this period—or perhaps because of it—historians understood that because women had lacked political rights, they had felt themselves less connected to the nations in which they lived. But women perceived that lack as an injustice. Given their sense of marginalization from the nation, and their belief that their marginalized status was unfair, they were more able to see the injustices of war more acutely and more profoundly. This prompted feminist pacifists to use their understanding of women and femininity in resistance to gender conformity, and to the war itself. Men who resisted the war by refusing the draft or by deserting, too, felt less connected to the nation than the hegemonic soldierly ideal presumed, though that ideal itself was open to negotiation, since at least in the United States, those legislators who wrote the draft law requiring men's military service exempted themselves from it. The British Parliament, too, undercut its reliance on the soldierly ideal when it forgave resisters for not conforming.

Future research may open up new avenues to understanding the role played by emotion in people's responses to war and to the resistance of war. While gender played into how and why people participated in or chose not to participate in war, emotion was used as a way both to entice citizens to support and join the war effort and to urge resistance and refusal to participate. Human societies have attached certain emotional responses to men, women, and transgender people. Future research may explore how those assumed emotions encouraged both participation in and resistance to war.

NOTES

1. Jason Crouthamel, *An Intimate History of the Front: Masculinity, Sexuality, and German Soldiers in the First World War* (New York: Palgrave, 2014), 6.

2. Kimberly Jensen, *Mobilizing Minerva: American Women in the First World War* (Urbana: University of Illinois Press, 2008), 62.

3. George L. Mosse, *Fallen Soldiers: Reshaping the Memory of the World Wars* (New York: Oxford University Press, 1990), 166.

4. Tammy M. Proctor, *Civilians in a World at War, 1914-1918* (New York: New York University Press, 2010).

5. Jensen, *Mobilizing Minerva*, 124.

6. Linda Polman, *The Crisis Caravan: What's Wrong with Humanitarian Aid?*, trans. Liz Waters (New York: Metropolitan Books, 2010), 5–6.

7. Jensen, *Mobilizing Minerva*, 120.

8. Christine E. Hallett and Alison S. Fell, "Introduction," in *First World War Nursing: New Perspectives*, ed. Alison S. Fell and Christine E. Hallett (New York: Routledge, 2013), 1–4.

9. Erika Kuhlman, *Petticoats and White Feathers: Gender Conformity, Race, the Progressive Peace Movement, and the Debate over War, 1895–1919* (Westport, CT: Greenwood Press, 1997), 27.

10. Kuhlman, *Petticoats and White Feathers*, 35–37.

11. Jeanette Keith, *Rich Man's War, Poor Man's Fight: Race, Class and Power in the Rural South during the First World War* (Chapel Hill: University of North Carolina Press, 2004), 61, 72.

12. Keith, *Rich Man's War, Poor Man's Fight*, 14–15.

13. Alexander Watson, *Enduring the Great War: Combat, Morale, and Collapse in the German and British Armies, 1914–1918* (Cambridge: Cambridge University Press, 2008), 40–41, 142.

14. Leonard V. Smith, *Between Mutiny and Obedience: The Case of the French Fifth Infantry Division during World War I* (Princeton, NJ: Princeton University Press, 1994), 18–19.

15. Laura E. Nym Mayhall, *The Militant Suffrage Movement: Citizenship and Resistance in Britain, 1860–1930* (Oxford: Oxford University Press, 2003), 11, 6.

16. Katherine H. Adams and Michael L. Keene, *Alice Paul and the American Suffrage Campaign* (Urbana: University of Illinois Press, 2008), 175.

17. Erika Kuhlman, *Reconstructing Patriarchy after the Great War: Women, Gender, and Postwar Reconciliation between Nations* (New York: Palgrave, 2008), 110.

18. Kevin S. Giles, *Flight of the Dove: The Experience of Jeannette Rankin* (Beaverton, OR: Touchstone Press, 1980), 90.

19. Sarah N. Cleghorn, *Four Lights* (February 6, 1917), n.p., SR reel 23.01, Women's International League for Peace and Freedom Collection, DG043, Swarthmore College Peace Collection, Swarthmore College, PA. See also Kuhlman, *Petticoats and White Feathers*, 1.

20. Margaret Higonnet et al., eds., *Behind the Lines: Gender and the Two World Wars* (New Haven, CT: Yale University Press, 1987), 43, 209.

21. Nicoletta F. Gullace, *The Blood of Our Sons: Men, Women, and the Renegotiation of British Citizenship during the Great War* (New York: Palgrave Macmillan, 2002), 8.

22. R. Claire Snyder, *Citizen-Soldiers and Manly Warriors: Military Service and Gender in the Civic Republican Tradition* (Lanham, MD: Rowman and Littlefield, 1999), 55–56.

23. Crouthamel, *Intimate History of the Front*, 2–6.

24. Crouthamel, *Intimate History of the Front*, 73.

25. Volker Depkat, "Remembering War the Transnational Way: The U.S.-American Memory of World War I," in *Transnational American Memories*, ed. Udo J. Hebel (New York: Walter de Gruyter, 2009), 185–186.

26. Norman Rich, *The Age of Nationalism and Reform: 1850–1890* (New York: Norton, 1976).

27. Leila Rupp, *Worlds of Women: The Making of an International Women's Movement* (Princeton, NJ: Princeton University Press, 1997), 19, 210–211.

28. Heymann quoted in Jane Addams, Emily G. Balch, and Alice Hamilton, *Women at The Hague: The International Congress of Women and Its Results* (New York: Macmillan, 1916), 145.

29. Glenda Sluga, "What Is National Self-Determination? Nationality and Psychology during 'The Apogee of Nationalism,'" *Nations and Nationalism* 11, no. 1 (2005): 1–20.

30. "Women's International League" statement, May 29, 1919, SR 12.4, Woman's Peace Party Papers, Swarthmore College Peace Collection, Swarthmore, PA.

31. Jane Addams, "Why Women Should Vote," *Ladies' Home Journal* 27 (January 1910): 21–22.

32. Mayhall, *Militant Suffrage Movement*, 120; Jensen, *Mobilizing Minerva*, 45–46.

33. Ann Kramer, *Conscientious Objectors of the First World War: A Determined Resistance* (Barnsley, South Yorkshire: Pen and Sword Books, 2013), 14.

34. Robert Weldon Whalen, *Bitter Wounds: German Victims of the Great War, 1914–1939* (Ithaca, NY: Cornell University Press, 1983), 107–129.

35. Depkat, "Remembering War the Transnational Way," 185.

36. Jay Winter, *Sites of Memory, Sites of Mourning: The Great War in European Cultural History* (Cambridge: Cambridge University Press, 1995), 27–28.

37. Julia Eichenberg and John Paul Newman, eds., *The Great War and International Veterans' Organizations* (Basingstoke: Palgrave Macmillan, 2013), 1–18.

38. Quoted in Catherine Foster, *Women for All Seasons: The Story of the Women's International League for Peace and Freedom* (Athens: University of Georgia Press, 1989), 16–17.

39. Kuhlman, *Reconstructing Patriarchy after the Great War*, 115; Annika Wilmers, "Zwischen den Fronten: Friedensdiskurse in der Internationalen Frauenfriedensbewegung, 1914–1919," in *Frieden—Gewalt—Geschlecht: Friedens und Konfliktforschung als Geschlechterforschung*, ed. Jennifer A. Davy, Karen Hagemann, and Ute Kaetzel (Essen: Klartext Verlag, 2005), 129.

40. Kuhlman, *Reconstructing Patriarchy after the Great War*, 116–117.

41. Heather Jones, "International or Transnational? Humanitarian Action during the First World War," *European Review of History* 16, no. 5 (2009): 698.

42. Julia Irwin, *Making the World Safe: The American Red Cross and a Nation's Humanitarian Awakening* (New York: Oxford University Press, 2013), 6.

43. Alice Hamilton, "At the War Capitals," *Survey*, August 7, 1915, 418.

44. Polman, *Crisis Caravan*, 5–7.

45. Kuhlman, *Reconstructing Patriarchy after the Great War*, 114–115.

46. Erika Kuhlman, *Of Little Comfort: War Widows, Fallen Soldiers, and the Remaking of the Nation after the Great War* (New York: New York University Press, 2012), 109–122.

47. Kuhlman, *Petticoats and White Feathers*, 90.

48. Jensen, *Mobilizing Minerva*, 14.

49. Maurine Weiner Greenwald, *Women, War, and Work: The Impact of World War I on Women Workers in the United States* (Ithaca, NY: Cornell University Press, 1980), includes many photographs of women industrial workers wearing trousers instead of dresses.

50. Adam Hochschild, *To End All Wars: A Story of Loyalty and Rebellion, 1914–1918* (Boston: Mariner Books, 2011), xvii.

51. Hochschild, *To End All Wars*, 188.

3

Gender and Work

Deborah Thom

∾——

WAR HAS BECOME a kind of social laboratory for testing theories about gender. War changed the workplace and the work process as Europe went onto a war footing. For some, this conflict challenged the sexual division of labor, giving women new roles and calling into question their exclusion from some kinds of work and their inequality at work. In other places, war emphasized their marginality and weakness in the labor market. The history of women and war work in its various forms has continued to test these theories. Debates on gender and war work focused around two main questions—what the sexes did and what it meant for them, often assuming that war brought positive social change for women and challenged male power. However, women such as the trade unionist Mary Macarthur saw war quite differently, noting in 1918 that it may have changed perception but not reality: "Of all the changes wrought by the war none have been so great as the change in the status and position of women, yet it is not so much that woman herself has changed as that men's view of her has changed."[1] War emphasizes gender difference as men's work becomes predominantly to enlist and to fight and women become increasingly recruited to replace them or supplement their work. The assumption of the male breadwinner and the female homemaker remained unchallenged despite the lived experience of war work.

Questions about class and gender during the war keep returning to haunt any historian looking for progressive change in wartime workplaces. Men's work remained gendered, especially in combat, but most commentary naturalized men as workers, focusing on novel experiences for women. Gender defined work and pay in arrangements designed to introduce new workers to war production. Work expanded greatly in places where gender had not been an issue of power in the same way—shops, offices, farms, theaters and music halls. Histories of women's work in Europe have changed since 1980s debates about progress or exclusion, raising new questions about performance and gendered bodies. Yet old arguments about power remain pertinent. The history of work can be seen in relation to politics, trade unions, state power, feminist interest in motherhood, and the ways in which work "performed" gender. These questions are reminders of the persistent significance of discussions about social divisions in the First World War.

The year 1914 saw social dislocation as refugees fled combat zones in European theaters of war, and manufacturers adjusted to new demands for industrialized war material. On the one hand, women's work had, before the war, been an object of pity and condemnation in discussions on "sweating," low wages, poor industrial conditions, sexual exploitation, and problematic conditions for women's health; on the other, pronatalist women's movements had celebrated domestic work and demanded resources to increase women's highest service to the state—the production of more children. At the same time, educated middle-class women increasingly demanded entry into professional work from which they were excluded by law or custom.

Work and labor had multiple meanings for women. Domestic labor debates emphasized women's contribution to the health of the nation in terms of whether mothers were good enough at raising children. Nations where welfare policies were coming into view tended to treat women's work as primarily for homes and children. Paid work was often necessary for poor people but still considered to be undesirable. In this context governments expressed concern over women's economic dependence and lack of resources as armies mobilized and volunteers geared up for war in 1914. Trade unions condemned exploitation by employers who hired women to replace those volunteers, since women, they argued, would be prepared to work for lower pay because they did not know or understand the world of industrial work and lacked the strength or knowledge to organize to defend rates of pay. In most European nations, women organized in voluntary bodies, and trade unions campaigned to protect women's working conditions while also wanting to make a contribution to the war effort. In predominantly rural countries involved in the war such as Ireland, Austria-Hungary, Russia, Finland, Serbia, Montenegro, Turkey, Romania, Bulgaria, Greece, Italy, Portugal, France,[2] the majority of women worked in agriculture and often in concert with family members, thus leaving little formal record of their exact contributions. These workers were unlikely to receive wages as such, and to some extent they remained dependent on their families for support. In those countries, agricultural work fell increasingly to women as men left to fight.

War raised profound questions of gender by celebrating masculine valor and women's separateness from fighting. Russian activist Alexandra Kollontai, touring the United States and speaking against the war, wrote of this phase in 1915 as entirely negative for women. They were, she said, made miserable by deprivation, hunger, and loss, meeting returning soldiers in the countryside. She described women doing emotional work despite not being directly involved, showing war's effects on their bodies: "The women have been run off their feet. They are haggard and starved, worn out with weeping."[3] In mainland Britain, Belgium, the Netherlands, and Germany, in contrast, large numbers of women were already involved in the waged workforce, laboring in the main in roughly equal proportions in industry, domestic service and shops, catering, and offices. For them, war was beginning to seem an opportunity to show off women's capacity, especially for those who had argued that women's virtues as economic contributors had been ignored.

Historians who have framed the war within longer narratives of modernization and industrialization have often focused on men when they look at new skills, especially those involving mechanization. Industrialized mass production of armaments spread new technology faster. The metaphor of a double helix in which the two genders have separate but linked histories reflects earlier arguments that men and women have different chronologies—men's affected by war and politics, women's by longer transitions involving birth rates, family size, and cultural shifts.[4] Certainly discussing gender has been much more about women than men, although political narratives of independence and autonomy do apply equally to both. One of the main types of war work—soldiering—has rarely been considered as work at all. Yet for four years of the war, most men labored in uniform in jobs related to combat, since most belligerent nations used conscription.

Labor history echoed trade unions at the time, and historians ever since, in seeing the war as separate from the world of waged work. For some the history of women's labor has, like the leftist politics of Lenin's day, been about the "woman problem," the idea that women were part of a reserve army of labor driving wages and conditions down. These scholars described women as helpless, inert tools in the hands of employers. There were traces of this in Sylvia Pankhurst's condemnation of her mother, Emmeline, and sister, Christabel, for welcoming a women's war register in 1915. Sylvia worried that this attempt to mobilize females to intensify the war effort would make all women vulnerable to low wages and exploitation in the workplace, and that it would affect the working lives of the men they replaced. This historical narrative occasionally reappeared in 1970s arguments about men's trade unions keeping women out of wartime work, then kicking them out again brutally once the war was over.

More recent histories of wartime workplaces have investigated far more productively the words and arguments of workers themselves. The rise of oral history and autobiography encouraged this form of history from the bottom up.[5] Participants' attitudes and imagery reflected a challenge to wartime administration that made all women seem the same. Oral history was done in victorious countries very early on in commemorating the war, much later in those that had been defeated, but this too began to challenge the notion of a universal war changing all lives in the same way.

Records of sensibility and sentiment began to create a new story of war work, in which historians objectively counted workers and the shells they produced but also asked what their subjective impressions of war had been, what they had thought about it at the time and later. Histories of material objects began to focus on the work process, the clothing women wore, and the labor process itself. The history of the body looked at gender for soldiers, sex workers, and nurses but also examined work again, thinking more about physicality. Cultural historians and critics noted the new visibility of previously marginalized groups in their attempt to recognize the diversity of contributions to a newly industrialized war, which both raised hopes and dashed them in arguing about a newly inclusive citizenship. Women were "doing things / They had never done before" wrote Nina Macdonald in 1918. "All the world is topsy turvy / since the War began."[6]

The First World War saw a temporary shift from deploring women's need to work as a required but undesirable supplement to male breadwinners to celebrating waged work as constructive for families, desirable for the nation, and healthy for women. Those who pondered women's roles often wrote as if they had not noticed their contribution at all before the war. Journalists ventured into factories, often with photographers, and women's organizations exploited the publicity of wartime to promote their own political agenda. Political claims now reflected women's work as much as their domestic contribution. For example, Alexandra Kollontai, writing in 1919 Russia, echoed August Bebel's *Women under Socialism* and the writings of Klara Zetkin, a German Social Democrat, in arguing that women in trade unions had limited ambitions because they experienced a double burden:

> The woman is not only an independent worker and citizen—at the same time she is a mother, a bearer of the future. This gives rise to a whole series of special demands, in areas such as women's labour protection, security for maternity and early childhood, help with the problems of children's upbringing, reforms in house-keeping and so on.[7]

She further elaborated that this meant that women had been disabled in protecting their own interests as well as those of society: "Whether in politics, in the family, in relations between the sexes (prostitution, double morality), or in the work situation, the woman is always allotted 'second place,' her lack of rights is underlined by her life itself."[8]

Kollantai summarized the existing labor organization in Europe, demonstrating pronounced disparities between countries in her study in terms of the numbers of women in labor unions and political parties. While her figures are partial, describing a mixture of social democratic and trade union organizations, they demonstrate the variety of levels of employment and organization among nations just before the war. She found that in 1911, there were about 300,000 women in trade unions and socialist parties in Germany and the United Kingdom, while France had 80,000, Austria-Hungary 60,000, Italy 50,000, and Holland 45,000. Her argument that women might make a new world in which both their labor and their maternity were important and could work together was very radical at the time.

Finding statistical evidence to address questions about war work is not simple. Governments tended to exaggerate women's contribution and its novelty when they sought to allow women entrance into workplaces. They were after all encouraging employers to take a risk in using a sort of labor that they had not been used to employing and often did not want. However, government officials and employers were then just as likely to say that women were not that good and did not do as much as men when they wanted them to leave after the war. There was a timeline for celebrating women's work that peaked in most European countries from early 1915 until 1917. The places where the most propaganda in support of women's employment occurred—Britain, France, and Germany—were also countries where labor shortages and some level of democracy or welfare provision meant that laborers could not simply be coerced into war work. Thus, these were the nations with the most extensive government records of women's contribution, including discussions of how it might be increased, and what it meant for the future. Even in these states, however, such data tend to be a bit of a problem. They overstate the importance of large firms and of the war work itself because that is what governments wanted investigated. Despite this, we can identify trends in women's employment in war industries.

INTRODUCING WAR WORK

In the first phase, lasting in Europe for about eight months from August 1914 to May 1915, government records reveal ground rules about how and when factories and offices began hiring new workers in industry or clerical work. To some extent, women's factory work started with the idea of deficiency, namely, that women were the least desirable option out of the other alternatives being used, which included prisoners of war, refugees, or imperial subjects. Narratives about female deficiency reflected recent history and, in part, recent campaigns for protective legislation meant to shield women from workplace dangers, especially in Britain and Germany. Women were seen as physically weaker, likely to produce less; they were unwilling, unreliable, and untrained. Thus women's organizations, feminist and trade unions alike, had to challenge the idea of the inherent weakness of the unorganized, the inexperienced, and the domesticated, to convince their allies as well as their opponents.

Despite this opposition, feminists and feminist organizations did promote women as an alternative source of labor. In particular, suffragists agitating for the vote in Britain, the United States, and Scandinavian countries became adept publicists of women's labor potential, already waging a battle in which they successfully argued for women as contributors to the national war effort. In France and Germany, maternalist politicians idealized motherhood and tended to emphasize women's domestic contributions to the nation as support for granting political representation.

EXPANDING WAR WORK

By spring 1915, it was apparent that the war had settled down to fighting on a large scale. From the trenches on the Western Front in the winter of 1914 to the fighting over the Dardanelles from February 1915, there is ample evidence of extended supply lines and soldiers, which required large quantities of armaments as well as uniforms, boots, and food supplies. Private companies were able to sustain most of these demands in the combatant belligerent powers, but they could not produce an adequate volume of the armaments needed. As a result, nation-states mobilized industrial workers as well as clerical and transport workers to sustain war at a distance. When facing the twin dislocations of war and mobilization, especially in circumstances that involved invasion or flight, families had to rely on members, especially women, who had not worked before. This was seen by some as an opportunity to escape the home and develop new skills or new levels of economic support.

In some areas such as Russia and Finland, women actually fought in the war.[9] Irish nationalist women participated in the Dublin uprising in 1916 in communications, as snipers, and as supply officers.[10] Here, women doing something completely new were seen as legitimate only defensively or as part of a campaign of liberation from alien oppression. Contemporaries divided on celebrating war as opportunity or, more rarely, condemning it as antagonistic to women's interests.

Phase two signaled the visibility of women's work in new ways in spring 1915, when the war settled down to the trenches and new battlefields emerged. Government and industry began to collaborate to maintain and increase the supply of armaments, build ships as warfare became more nautical, and develop some new technologies of warfare such as tanks, airplanes, TNT, airships, and poison gas.[11] As new products encouraged some new enterprises, or expanded old ones, all labor was reconceptualized as war service and celebrated and recorded.

The labor of women was more and more required. In Germany, for example, the number of women in larger workplaces rose from 1.5 million in 1913 to about 2.3 million in 1918.[12] However, the newly expanded labor requirements largely redistributed female workers in existing factories. The number of women in metalwork rose eight times, and those making machines increased thirty-five times, while textile workers halved.[13] In France, there were 430,000 "munitionettes" by 1918, whereas in Britain, there were about 1 million.[14] Similarly, in Austria, about a million women entered wartime factories, and half the workers in state factories were female, but women gained little in terms of new opportunities because the work was still paid on gendered grounds. Women found poor working conditions, and their rates of pay came out at about one-third that of men.[15] Russia saw an enormous increase of women in industry. Half a million women worked in industry in 1914, and by 1918 they made up 45 percent of the industrial workforce.[16] By comparison, in France, there were about a million women in commercial jobs and half a million in professions and public service.[17] All over Europe, women went into wartime factory work in larger numbers and proportions than before the war, but they also entered offices and shops as workers, and here they stayed after the war.

This new visibility meant that contemporary commentators became more and more interested in women's labor, yet the proportion of the workforce that was female did not necessarily change much despite the rhetoric. Thus, while commentary on women's nature and capacity became more and more complimentary, it was often double-edged in its effects. Women were increasingly seen as capable of great sacrifice, likely to threaten their own well-being and that of their future children, because they were too prone to believe in their mission to join in the war effort.

The exigencies of war production meant that records of factory workers are largely quantitative, not qualitative. Typically, industrial workers who were managers or forewomen appeared more frequently in the record than the nameless masses of anonymous factory workers who came and went. The fullest records tend to be from parts of the world that did not experience land warfare on their own soil such as Canada, the United States, and Australia. However, we have documentation from the United Kingdom, France, Germany, and Austria, as well as Finland, where there were bombs from the air and artillery damage. Some of the evidence for levels of work is contradictory, and the official statistics leave only a partial record of what was actually happening. Change occurred for women laborers, but not as much as the critics or the celebrants claimed. By 1918, France's metalworkers were a quarter female, compared with one-twentieth in 1914, and workplace patterns could be very regional. In the south of the country, the numbers of women at work rose slowly, nothing like the rise in the industrial cities of the north.[18]

Albert Thomas, the socialist minister of munitions in France in 1917, saw the role of women in the labor force as existing solely for the duration of war, in part because they were needed to create the next generation. Long-standing French fears of a falling birth rate meant that the dual demands of production and reproduction were even mentioned in assessing the pragmatic considerations of how many workers could be enlisted and the extent of their mobilization. Thomas argued: "National interest demands that women's labour be used rationally and with great care for it represents a reserve for the future which must be safeguarded in its entirety."[19]

Opportunities to participate fully in industrial work remained constricted. Unionization was limited and severely policed in most European countries, and workers mostly lacked the kind of factory inspectors who protected laboring women in Britain and France. In France, there was much less movement between different types of work, partly because large numbers of women were already working in factories before the war. French female wartime workers were actually called replacements—placeholders there for the duration only, implicitly temporary—this despite the fact that the female workforce during war rose by about 20 percent. As in the United Kingdom, employers opened up industrial jobs reluctantly and slowly, and women were constantly told that war work was only for the duration. This was not true of women working on the land, who were urged to replace men all over Europe and in North America.

Some states encouraged women to volunteer for war service. None dared conscript women, although they could manipulate policies of family support to encourage women to work. Some female workers came to war factories by migrating from rural areas to towns in Italy, France, and Germany. In Britain, women went across the Irish Sea to work in factories as they had done before the war for jobs in domestic service. Throughout Europe, large numbers of servants left domestic jobs for war service in factories. Some served in uniform, cooking, cleaning, and tending to officers and men alike near the battlefront, though that happened less on the Eastern Front. Most women war workers were young, aged eighteen to twenty-five, just like the men who served as soldiers, although high soldier death rates in France and Belgium in the early years of war meant that there were many widows who went into factories. Married women worked in factories, and day cares were set up to provide for their babies.

Probably the largest numbers of novice factory workers were former domestic servants who either volunteered or were "let go" by middle-class households trying to reduce expenditures in the first year of war. In most combatant countries, the first six months of war saw high female unemployment, but this quickly reversed. By 1916, the reserves of factory workers were running low, and several governments encouraged married women to work or, as in Germany and Austria, to increase turnover of men back from the front. In most countries the sick, the old, the injured, and the young were drafted into industrial work, and there were debates about boy labor and the problem of management it presented.

WOMEN AT WORK

There were few jobs women did not do during the war. The manual jobs women did still included factory work in clothing trades, which had been largely dominated by women before the war. But the big expansion was in armaments production and in services like transport and catering that kept armies on the move and supplied. In Italy, for example, women drove trams from 1916 to 1919.[20] Private manufacture continued internationally more or less regulated by the state. Women labored in conventionally male jobs in some countries. In Russia, for example, women were still working in mining, which had mostly stopped in Western Europe. Across many nations, they continued to work in food processing and cloth making. Many employers carried on with women directly replacing men in breweries, in dockyards, and on the railways. Women dug, carried, hauled, and filled. However, the biggest change, and the most noticeable one, was in producing war materials.

In Britain, France, and Germany, state factories expanded the production of armaments. The manufacturing of ships and big guns largely stayed in private hands and was thereby less affected by attempts to substitute women for men. Trade union power was strongest in the United Kingdom, where the unions involving skilled men accepted the need to "dilute" skilled labor with that of semiskilled or unskilled workers. They controlled the process on the factory floor through the use of shop steward committees. This meant that jobs that before the war could be performed only by skilled men, who had served apprenticeships and managed their own tools, were retooled with adapted machinery or subdivided so that many unskilled workers could be taught how to do components of them. This process of subdividing work into smaller jobs for unskilled workers was known as "dilution." The new milling machines and lathes enabled skilled tasks to be done by workshops full of "dilutees." A few skilled men remained central to production; they set, ground, and mended tools for unskilled workers. Young women quickly mastered the new technology, and production levels soared.

The largest group of female factory workers were not dilutees but workers in new war factories or substitutes, doing jobs that had not been performed by skilled workers before the war. Many of these jobs were classified as women's work and paid at lower rates. Mass production dominated in shells and bullets, but guns and ships remained largely the preserve of the skilled and the unionized. In France, factory managers and employers, along with the trade unions representing skilled men, refused to allow women to learn new skills, going instead to considerable lengths to pull back skilled men from the front or recruit boys who could be trained to be the workers of the future.[21]

In some respects, the war encouraged a global labor market that spread new technology partly through an army of women industrial workers who took levels of production to new heights. Women themselves did not move about the world as did men from China, Africa, and India. Such laborers traveled from far away to dig ditches or service white troops. Women tended to move within their own nations, which encouraged more generalized patterns of work and more standardization of machinery. Payment systems using modifications of the premium bonus system spread throughout Western Europe.

The mobilization of women into industry helped to modernize factory work during the war in ways that then reappeared after the war, with, as trade unionist Mary Macarthur crisply said, "old faces in new places."[22] For the individual worker, of course, the experience of factory work in a modern mechanized mass-production system was usually new, and she lacked the power to effect change in how the work was organized and run either during or after the war. Labor discipline in war factories was tight and highly controlled. Most war work consisted of arduous manual labor in uncomfortable conditions. It was endurable because it was not going to go on for long and because it was, comparatively speaking, better paid than most factory (or other female) work before the war.

New physical technologies and new management of workplaces were both directly tested on women. One of the ways that women helped modernize the factory was by opening a major new skill, arc welding. This was used in mechanical engineering during the war, and it required strength and dexterity. Oxyacetylene torches or lances were used to seal joints for bombs, torpedoes, and pipes. Women were also employed to build airplanes, which were just going into mass production, made out of stiffened cloth that was glued and sewn by women, who also worked on their engines. The great airships used by Germany for bombing raids were also glued together by female workers.

Women developed and used new technologies during the war. Women worked on the new electrical substations and trains while female scientists worked with chemicals. However, because professional organizations refused to admit women who did these jobs, they usually had to establish their own associations. Telephones and typewriters were the main implements used by women in offices and reflected certain gendered assumptions about women's precision and docility, enabling them to relay information without interposing their own ideas in the process. But women of property were also able to use old technologies such as horses and new ones—motorbikes—in getting goods and information around the front. The new woman and her bicycle were also in evidence in large cities, but few women had the capital to buy such expensive pieces of equipment, and women consistently remained closer to home than men.

The war also offered new opportunities in skilled jobs dealing with the public or receiving public attention, like the workers driving buses and trams and running the expanded European railway network. There were, however, limits to this innovation. Women did not start going to sea in ships except as nurses serving on the hospital ships in the Mediterranean. They had been aviators before the war, but only a few women were able to apply those skills in transporting aircraft to and fro. Winston Churchill described the activities of the Ministry of Munitions in Britain and its allies as "a revolution in the workplace," by which he appears to have meant the speed-up and production levels of shells, projectiles, and bullets in state-run factories. One of the most spectacular examples of war as opportunity and even fun was the rise of women's sport. Again, this was particularly noticeable in Britain, where teams of workers were encouraged to play football in public on men's grounds to improve morale and keep workers fit. Matches were shown on newsreels and recorded in popular cigarette cards.

In industrialized parts of the world, women also began to appear in shops, offices, food outlets, and places of entertainment. Much of this work occasioned little comment and showed less dramatic contrasts with peacetime. Here there was some of the feminization that popular and official history celebrated in the 1920s and again in the 1960s. More controversially, the sex trade increased substantially where soldiers and sailors gathered. In France, for example, prostitutes learned English or German depending on which side of the front they were found.

War workers were often much better paid than prewar factory workers in prosperous Britain and North America. In France, Austria, and Germany, household income increased with rising employment levels, and wages were better than before the war, but the simultaneous shortage of food and fuel as well as higher rents meant that living standards in wartime were neither evenly distributed nor adequate. Goods were in short supply, and prices rose faster than money wages so that, even though there was full employment, there was little benefit from it. In Austria and Germany, women earned one-third or one-half of men's wages, despite promises of equal pay. Even women replacing skilled men received lower pay.[23] As Ute Daniel put it, "The slight improvement in women's nominal wages did not translate into any actual improvement in their material situation."[24]

Discontent among workers grew in late 1917, with strikes occurring on both sides of the conflict. In Germany, workers protested a poor food supply, while in Russia women joined in bread riots. In Italy, farmworkers refused to work first as a means of agitating for peace, then in protest over war conditions. In the United Kingdom and France, workers went on strike to protest low wages, bad working conditions, and dilution. In Britain, some unrest focused around air-raid warnings.[25] Working in factories did not seem to create any strong sentiment of loyalty or sacrifice beyond a short period at the start of conscription in Britain or after invasion in France and Belgium.

However, women workers, like servicemen, did develop strong bonds with their fellow workers. Some factories provided social facilities, and many had canteens and entertained workers or organized civic events to urge them on to greater production levels and improved efforts. In Ireland, where there were few munitions factories despite the English government's promise to bring them there, those that were there had gramophones playing music at meals and flowers on the tables, organized by "lady volunteers." Class collaboration in the factory was much more limited than newspapers and propaganda allowed, even in Britain, where it was most publicized. However, the sense of recognition and respect that lady volunteers who did the occasional shift at weekends could give was valued, as oral history showed sixty years later.

CLOSING WAR WORK DOWN

There was a backlash in 1917. Women workers began to be laid off as shell production decreased. The media increasingly stigmatized male workers as noncombatants and both sexes as increasingly prone to strikes. The closure of the Russian front meant that one destination for shells was out of the war. The Land Army, the Forage Corps, and the horse stations that rehabilitated horses for the front began to recruit women in Britain, keeping uniformed war service at the fore in addition to the new women's services—such as the Queen Mary's Army Auxiliary Corps, and the Women's Royal Navy Service. There were also very large numbers of volunteers in the Voluntary Aid Detachment, mostly nurses and aides, who operated beside professional nurses. The French Service de Santé Militaire had 100,000 women serving, of whom only 30,000 were professionals.[26] Other combatant nations mobilized fewer women in uniform, and the bulk of women's war work was still in factories or white-collar clerical jobs. Nearly all the armies had women working as telephonists, telegraph clerks, typists, and messengers, and the British had women dispatch riders. In France, war was the zenith for women's employment, not the start of a rise as elsewhere. So while women were celebrated and photographed, recruited through posters and advertisement, most factory workers continued to function as replacements—placeholders—for the men of the family.

Working conditions in wartime factories were widely studied, initially because of anxieties about production levels, women's health, and concern for employees working twelve-hour shifts. Researchers found that long hours of work meant more wastage and mistakes, so they recommended eight-hour shifts instead. They investigated factory lighting, seating, and ventilation. They also instructed supervisors in management practices and urged intensive welfare supervision on reluctant factory managers. Although emotional well-being was also included in discussions on worker management and soldiers' loyalty, few factory managers paid much attention to whether their workers were happy. They also monitored women workers in particular. This was more than just social control; it was also intensive policing. Factory workers who were found with matches or lighters in their pockets would be sent to six months hard labor. The extent to which paternalist social control could stretch can be seen in the pamphlets that urged workers to change their underwear regularly, to go to bed early, and to wash frequently.

Paternalism extended to family life as well. Many young workers living in hostels away from home did find wartime difficult, and the national factories in Britain or the secret factories making planes and bombs in Germany were deliberately placed away from established cities so isolated workers were often quite lonely, without much to do in the evening. Here the work of the war worker was very like the training period of a conscript soldier. Discipline was strict in order to control youth. But war workers' lives were very different in old, established centers of metalworking, where they often had family members nearby, may have had trade union links, and were much less likely to accept tight patterns of regulation.

MEMORY AND PERCEPTION

Certainly, women workers were encouraged to see themselves as members of the nation in a new way. Medical investigators of women's work increasingly argued that physical work, however arduous, was good for women. Because it was regulated, experts argued, factory labor was actually healthier than much housework. Opinions varied about sex or age affecting psychological suitability for manual labor. In France, women were commended for their capacity to work long hours on repetitive tasks— seen by some as their essential nature as women but by others as a demonstration of the sacrifice women would make for the nation. In Germany, similar arguments were used to justify a parallel policy of not training women but concentrating on providing training for wounded soldiers, skilled workers, and boy laborers. Again and again, officials told women to expect to leave once the war was over and that they, too, should privilege motherhood as their main task. Motherhood was only temporarily suspended during wartime.

Popular memory has tended to emphasize this idea of war service and exaggerate the differences of war from peace for industrial workers. But popular memory also reflects war workers' own understanding of themselves and the way war service was written up at the time. They were particularly encouraged to have a sense of achievement in the victorious countries, but less in those nations where defeat brought criticism of those who may have been seen as not having done enough to win the war. Women war workers had shown they could manage repetitive physical movement. These women also demonstrated the stamina to produce and fill shells, the acumen to gauge and inspect them, and the gross motor skills to drive the cranes that lifted them. Finally, women were able to prepare volatile raw ingredients, shell casings, and paper for cartridges.

However, women were also seen not just as workers but also as mothers of the future. Those who were already mothers were less likely to get the better-paid jobs replacing men. They were far more likely to be the general workers running trolleys, filling bullets, or making paper cases, and they were paid less. In addition, across combatant nations, the educated middle classes were also encouraged to enter new areas of work but discouraged from assuming they could keep them. However, for many in this category, voluntary work became professionalized. War encouraged this as volunteer organizations expanded their scope in order to support soldiers, refugees, and women and children. Their work, like military service, became a contribution to the nation.

Women's work made for excellent patriotic propaganda. Most of the images of working women were quite technical, showing them next to the machines they used. Occasionally they were also sexualized, especially in published images during the war.

There is a gender politics in such images much more than a sexual politics. Some photographers or graphic artists found women in trousers particularly interesting, although the trousers were very modest, being baggy and extending down to the ankle (Figure 3.1).

Yet some observers found no justification for women's work in war industries. One soldier told his girl not to go into men's work, rejecting both patriotic and industrial narratives:

Whatever you do, don't go in Munitions or anything in that line—just fill a Woman's position and remain a woman—don't develop into one of those

Female workers pull trolleys of shells on the grounds of the National Shell Factory at Parkgate Street, Dublin, during the First World War. The photo demonstrates how women took on traditionally male labor and played a significant role in wartime production. © *Imperial War Museum (Q 33212)*

"things" that are doing men's work, as I told you in one of my letters, long ago. I want to return and find the same loveable little woman that I left behind— not a coarse thing more of a man than a woman—I love you because of your womanly little ways and nature, so don't spoil yourself by carrying on with a man's work—it's not necessary.[27]

The idea that the end of war should see a return to life as it was before clearly carried powerful emotional arguments, some of which some women shared. In the defeated countries of middle Europe, war brought famine and consistent ongoing domestic difficulty. Elsewhere, the work of keeping the nation fed and cared for encouraged a new appreciation of women's unpaid work at home. However, women changed domestic labor too.

Canada provides a good example of shifting ideas of "domestic" labor. Large numbers of soldiers fought overseas, but the women of the country mostly remained on farms and in the countryside. They set up one new organization—the Women's

Institute—that multiplied all over British dominions as well as in the United Kingdom itself. Another organization was the Farm Service Corps, which modernized and expanded agricultural production. Women participated successfully in providing for soldiers, replacing men on the farm. The work they were encouraged to do was an extension of domesticity. For example, the Canadian Department of Public Works saw the following areas as appropriate for women: "On fruit or vegetable farms. In the camps to cook for workers. On mixed and dairy farms. In the farmhouse to help feed those who are raising the crops. In canneries, to preserve the fruit and vegetables. To take charge of milk routes."[28] This mixture of old and new tasks, extensions of domestic work but essential to managing the supply of food, reflected a distrust of existing knowledge and expertise and partly reflected the fact that many in agriculture were inexperienced because they were young.

LONG-TERM CONSEQUENCES OF WARTIME WORK

Wartime work had an impact, beginning with those women who talked reluctantly about hands too roughened for respectable needleworking after the war. Munitions workers believed that exposure to explosive materials such as cordite had damaged their health, though there is no medical evidence that it did. Factories were dangerous places with poor lighting, inadequate ventilation, and excessive hours of work. In Germany, conditions became more dangerous, and as one diarist showed, her factory was risky partly because women's other work made them tired: "The nightshift was particularly dangerous. All of us had other duties at home. Indeed, many women took on night shifts so that, during the day, they could take care of their children. There was little time for sleep."[29] Zeppelins and airplanes had also made factories frightening places when bombing started in 1915 and continued through the duration.

The explosive TNT had been invented in Germany and was produced on both sides of the war effort. It was effective, and it was less likely to catch fire than cordite or dynamite and thus was much easier to control as well as more powerful. But it damaged the liver if manufactured without protective clothing and caused death by toxic jaundice. It was the biggest single cause of death for British war workers, with about 400 dying from its effects.[30] And, it could and did blow up. The largest explosion on US soil was the 1916 Black Tom Island explosion, possibly an act of sabotage. Two thousand tons of TNT exploded near New York in a blast heard 100 miles away. Munitions workers wore war service badges, but their jobs were also written on their skin as the chemicals caused yellowing on the hands and face as well as the hair. Workers' pride in their war service could enable them to endure the risks of war work, but it became more difficult when people began to condemn their extravagance and high spending as public opinion began to change slightly late in 1917. But war work did not just expand. It was also organized in new ways, with new technologies of labor management and, in particular, a new attention to the body of the worker as a working machine.

Women contributed to the war in many different ways. They developed skills in forms of manual work and were able to demonstrate strength and stamina in doing so. They did uniformed work, most extensively in Britain as police officers, nurses, service personnel, bus and tram drivers and conductors, and train guards. They developed professional work, replacing men as civil servants, clerks, and teachers in jobs that were needed after the war as well. The volume of wartime administration did not die down after the war, given the need for pensions and other postwar reconstruction concerns. But they also did womanly work as nurses and carers, in catering and cleaning. In fact, the "five Cs" of women's work were dominant then as a century later—catering, caring, cleaning, clerking, and cashiering. And in a move that magnified anxiety about the future of the nation, they did sex work as well.[31]

What changed in the aftermath? Trade unions grew just after the war as most organized skilled men's unions reclaimed the new wartime jobs for their members. The engineering workers, electric workers, transport operatives, and factory workers in trades like clothing and footwear were all evicted from their factories. Many of them were pleased to go; others faced hunger, especially in the defeated countries of Central Europe. The rhetoric of a common female interest was supported by some pacifist organizations whose volunteers tried to feed the starving, but any idea of international "work" to challenge war as a solution to problems remained limited to very few people. Women's war contributions were widely recognized, but the popular press began to criticize women for hanging on to work or power, especially in France and Britain. Most representatives of working women were anxious to avoid any impression of women wanting to take work from men.

CONCLUSION

The challenge of comparative history is to assess whether there can be a general history of women's war work at all. The British case differs slightly because strong trade union and feminist movements challenged inequality and political exclusion in all sorts of commentary, helping to keep the question of women's interests in view throughout the war and making it evident in postwar commemoration; something easier after victory. Feminists helped construct a historical record of achievement and success.[32] Elsewhere in Europe, feminist movements had been part of social democracy. In Germany and Scandinavia, they focused especially on prostitution and motherhood—women's wrongs rather than rights perhaps. In Russia, the middle classes concentrated on equal opportunities for women in education and the professions. Thus the history of women's wartime contribution was much more problematic because people saw the war as causing more losses than gains. Working-class movements organized by and for working women were similar in Australia, Canada, and the United States in seeing war as a terrain on which old arguments could be renewed. But the postwar slump meant that organizations to defend women workers could not push for further reform. Reliance on state documents tends to show little of the workers' attitudes or expectations—increasingly criticized by government and employers and male members of their own political movements. The problem articulated by Kollontai of fighting on both fronts—the home and the workplace—became particularly difficult after the war.

Visual sources provided some of the most powerful history of women's work in the war. They fed into public history very early on. Before the war, Albert Kahn, a French banker, had created a photographic catalog with his Archives de la Planète. He aimed with this visual record to recognize unity in diversity and to overcome division by recording the similarity in work experiences across nations.[33] Photojournalism was used extensively in newspapers and on film and generated both an instant history and materials for the archives. The most extensive use of images was in the British Imperial War Museum, which included a women's work section from its founding in 1917. Other exhibits of the war while it was going on tended to concentrate on soldiers and battle, but this one included women's contribution as well as civilian life.[34] After the war, new recording and film technologies featured famous women rather than those with ordinary lives.

Archives did collect autobiographies and memoirs as well as letters and diaries, all of which have been a valuable source for television and film accounts of living through the war. But there are not many from war workers for obvious reasons of shortage of time, limited privacy, and exhaustion.[35] The lesson of these records was that women had served gladly but that, often, the gains of full employment, regular wages, and patriotic rhetoric were seen by many as temporary. War work as such was often considered desirable only for those for whom it was an improvement, and for many it was not. Exaggerating women's exclusion before the war and ignoring the varieties of work experience resulted in contemporaries reducing the war too far into one experience for all women.

Finally, we need to consider the link between work and politics. Women's war work did not bring the vote to all or most females. In the United Kingdom, only women over thirty gained suffrage in 1918, and in France, women did not have the vote until 1944. Short-lived revolutions brought votes to women in Russia, Austria, and Hungary. There was a new sense of strength and recognition, but in most countries the end of war brought demobilization for women faster than for soldiers, and women saw few benefits immediately. Support for soldiers' dependents encouraged the extension of prewar welfare state policies in the richer combatant nations.[36]

Historians have begun to recognize that, as Gail Braybon has pointed out, women were *both* winners and losers in the First World War.[37] Profound national differences existed in war work and women's capacity to improve work during the war. Men have generally been seen as gaining in the factory, losing on the battlefield. Centenary celebrations continue to encourage debate about the war and whether the achievements of women can be summed up at all. At least the rediscovery of the argument gives a chance to use the words and images of participants themselves. Yet for many witnesses from the war, the sense of a topsy-turvy world mattered much less than the sense of a war as separate from the rest of their working lives. For many it was more regretted than celebrated. They measured themselves less against the male workers and more against the soldiers who had served. In the compound noun "women war workers," every part matters. Recent labor history has, by putting the war itself back into the history of work, made it possible to recognize that the work done in wartime was not as separate from the soldiers' experience of the work of war as has been argued.

Despite the limited evidence of women's view of themselves, we can still see that Mary Macarthur did, in some ways, get it wrong because it was far more that women's view of themselves had changed than that men's view of women had changed. The double burden of paid work and housework, including child care, remained. Real change had to wait for a different war where the extent to which work made women free was also limited. To some degree, however, the history of women's work in the First World War continues to be seen through the lens of the Second; further research may finally change this.

NOTES

1. Mary Macarthur, "The Women Trade-Unionists' Point of View," in *Women and the Labour Party*, ed. Marion Phillips (New York: B. W. Heubsch, 1918), 22.

2. I have listed all countries participating directly in the war, including Ireland, which was not yet a nation.

3. "Who Needs the War" (1915), in Alexandra Kollontai, *Selected Articles and Speeches* (New York: International Publishers, 1984).

4. Margaret Higonnet et al., eds., *Behind the Lines: Gender and the Two World Wars* (New Haven, CT: Yale University Press, 1987); Françoise Thébaud, *La femme au temps de la guerre de 14* (Paris: Stock, 1986).

5. Particularly noticeable for soldiers' letters, diaries, and memoirs is Michael Roper, *The Secret Battle: Emotional Survival in the Great War* (Manchester: Manchester University Press, 2009). The Library of Congress, the Historial at Péronne, and the Imperial War Museum all have extensive collections of interviews with combatants and civilians.

6. Nina Macdonald, "Sing a Song of War-Time" (1918), quoted in *Scars upon My Heart: Women's Poetry and Verse of the First World War*, ed. Catherine Reilly (London: Virago, 1981), 69.

7. Alexandra Kollontai, *Women Workers Struggle for Their Rights* (1919; Bristol, UK: Falling Wall Press, 1973), 14.

8. Kollontai, *Women Workers Struggle for Their Rights*, 14.

9. Laurie Stoff, *They Fought for the Motherland: Russia's Women Soldiers in World War I and the Revolution* (Lawrence: University Press of Kansas, 2006).

10. Margaret Ward, *In Their Own Voice: Women and Irish Nationalism* (Dublin: Attic Press, 2001).

11. As photography increased its presence on the battlefield, although it was behind the lines, it also began to celebrate the battle for production. It was even a tool in mobilizing a new labor force. Manufacturers of metalwork and armaments recorded their employees' work and reproduced the images in newspapers, posters, and eventually historical archives and museum displays.

12. Ute Daniel, *The War from Within: German Working-Class Women in the First World War* (Oxford: Berg, 1997), 38.

13. Matthew Stibbe, "Women's Mobilisation for War (Germany)," in *1914–1918-Online— International Encyclopedia of the First World War*, ed. Ute Daniel et al. (Berlin: Freie Universität, 2014), DOI: 10.15463/ie1418.10025.

14. Peggy Bette, "Women's Mobilisation for War (France)," in *1914-1918-Online*, DOI: 10.15463/ie1418.10027.

15. Susan R. Grayzel, "Women's Mobilization for War," in *1914–1918-Online*, DOI: 10.15463/ie1418.10348.

16. Wendy Z. Goldman, *Women at the Gates: Gender and Industry in Stalin's Russia* (Cambridge: Cambridge University Press, 2002), 10.

17. James McMillan, "The Great War and Gender Relations: the Case of French Women and the First World War Revisited," in *Evidence, History and the Great War: Historians and the Impact of 1914–18*, ed. Gail Braybon (New York: Berghahn, 2005), 134–53

18. Jean-Louis Robert, "Women and Work in France during the First World War," in *The Upheaval of War: Family Work and Welfare in Europe, 1914–1918*, ed. Richard Wall and Jay Winter (Cambridge: Cambridge University Press, 2005), 256.

19. Robert, "Women and Work," 260.

20. Allison Scardino Belzer, *Women and the Great War: Femininity under Fire in Italy* (Basingstoke: Palgrave Macmillan, 2010), 59.

21. Laura Lee Downs, *Manufacturing Inequality: Gender Division in the French and British Metalworking Industries, 1914–1939* (Ithaca, NY: Cornell University Press, 1995).

22. Deborah Thom, "The Bundle of Sticks," in *Unequal Opportunities: Women's Employment in England, 1800–1918*, ed. Angela John (Oxford: Blackwell, 1986) 261-289.

23. Holger Herwig, *The First World War: Germany and Austria Hungary, 1914–1918 Modern Wars* (London: Bloomsbury Academic, 1996)

24. Daniel, *War from Within*, 282.

25. Barbara Engel, "Not by Bread Alone: Subsistence Riots in Russia during World War 1," *Journal of Modern History* 69, no. 4 (1997): 696–721; Belinda J. Davis, *Home Fires Burning: Food, Politics, and Everyday Life in World War I Berlin* (Chapel Hill: University of North Carolina Press, 2000); Simonetta Ortaggi, "Italian Women during the Great War," in Braybon, *Evidence, History and the Great War*, 216-238.

26. McMillan, "The Great War and Gender Relations," 145.

27. Letter quoted in Janet S. K. Watson, "Khaki Girls, VADs, and Tommy's Sisters: Gender and Class in First World War Britain," *International History Review* 19, no. 1 (1997): 49.

28. Canada, Department of Public Works, Women's Work on the Land (Ontario, Tracks and Labour Branch) www.collectionscanada.gc.ca/firstworldwar/025005-2100.005.07-e.html.

29. Kate Kestien, "A Night in a German Munitions Factory," in *Women's Writing on the First World War*, ed. Agnès Cardinal, Dorothy Goldman, Judith Hattaway (Oxford: Oxford University Press, 1999), 114–115.

30. Coroners' reports are still inconclusive, and many doctors were reluctant to certify in the early days. Antonia Ineson and Deborah Thom, "TNT Poisoning and the Employment of Women Workers in the First World War," in *The Social History of Occupational Health*, ed. Paul Weindling (London: Croom Helm, 1985), 89–102.

31. Susan R. Grayzel, "Mothers, Marraines, and Prostitutes: Morale and Morality in First World War France," *International History Review* 19, no. 1 (1997): 66–82; Julia Laite, *Common Citizens and Ordinary Prostitutes: Commercial Sex in London, 1885–1960* (Basingstoke: Palgrave Macmillan, 2012), chap. 7

32. Diana Condell and Jean Liddiard, *Working for Victory: Images of Women in the First World War* (London: Routledge, 1987), demonstrates the power of this popular and public history in the British context; there is no comparable national archive like it elsewhere.

33. Paula Amad, *Counter-archive: Film, the Everyday, and Albert Kahn's Archives de la Planète* (New York: Columbia University Press, 2010).

34. Stefan Goebel, "Exhibitions," in *Capital Cities at War: Paris, London, Berlin 1914–1919*, vol. 2, *A Cultural History,* ed. Jay Winter and Jean-Louis Robert (Cambridge: Cambridge University Press, 2007), 143-187.

35. Gabrielle West, *War Diary* (Alexandria, VA: Alexander Street Press, 2005).

36. Pat Thane and Gisela Bock, eds., *Maternity and Gender Policies: Women and the Rise of the European Welfare States* (London: Routledge, 1991).

37. Gail Braybon, "Winners or Losers? Women's Symbolic Role in the War Story," in Braybon, *Evidence, History and the Great War*, 86–112.

4

Gender and Race

Richard S. Fogarty

ᴏɴ ᴊᴜʟʏ 25, 1919, two black deputies from Guadeloupe and a white deputy from Réunion presented a text to their colleagues in the French Chamber of Deputies declaring that the body, "faithful to the immortal principles that inspired the Declaration of the Rights of Man and Citizen, censuring and condemning all prejudices of religion, caste, or race, affirms and proclaims the absolute equality of all men, without distinction of origin or color, to the benefit and protection of all the laws of the nation."[1] The declaration, unanimously approved and applauded by all deputies present, called on the French government to uphold the rule of law in the face of any crime committed on French soil, regardless of the identity of the perpetrator or the victim. The episode clearly highlighted the salience of race in France during and immediately after the war, since the clear impetus for the declaration was the presence of men of color in France, presumably in need of a renewed and explicit guarantee of equality before the law.

But also at issue were women, sex, and gender, and the potentially explosive intersections between these and race in the transnational space that France had become. What collided that day in the French Chamber of Deputies were differing national understandings of race and the importance of what Americans called "the color line"; colonial, national, and international politics; and ideas about the place of women, notions of gender, and attitudes toward sexuality. The story of how the French legislature came to reaffirm its commitment to universalism and equality before the law that day is illustrative of how important the interactions of gender and race are to understanding the history of the First World War, and how central the French national and colonial contexts, as well as other and larger transnational and global contexts, are to these interactions.

One of the Guadeloupian deputies who rose that day in 1919 to question the government was Achille René-Boisneuf, who since entering the legislature in 1914 had become a consistent defender of colonial subjects who served in France's army. Some half a million of these men of color defended the metropole during the war, and many remained stationed in France and occupied Germany for months after the Armistice. These men played an important role in helping to set the context of this global war of empires, which saw the mixing of peoples from around the world over vast spaces in the war's many theaters. France, where most of the decisive Western Front was located, was the site of a particularly intense multicultural mixing, as men from all over France's worldwide empire arrived as soldiers and workers and joined Americans both black and white, Europeans from Russia to Portugal and nearly everywhere in between, Indians from the British Empire, black African laborers from South Africa, Native Americans from Canada and the United States, workers from China, and more. Indeed, though interacting with British soldiers and Belgian civilian refugees had from the first days of the war exposed the people of France to the mixing of peoples and cultures as a salient experience of the conflict, what struck many even more forcefully were the ways in which the war was a multiracial experience. And the mixing of races raised the possibility, and as it happened the fact, of men and women interacting in a variety of ways that challenged notions and hierarchies of both race and gender. Some of these interactions brought Deputy Boisneuf to the podium to ask his government and his colleagues to make a statement about what kind of racial, gender, sexual, and legal orders prevailed in France.

Part of the impetus for the discussion in the Chamber of Deputies that day was a circular written in August 1918 by Colonel J. A. Linard, French liaison to the American Expeditionary Force in France. In it, Linard advised his colleagues that the racism of white Americans, which he asserted the French did not have the right to question, meant that French civilians should be warned against "intimacy," especially in public, with black American soldiers. For instance, an illustration on the cover of a recent issue of *La Vie Parisienne*, "The Child of the Dessert," showing a black soldier and a white French woman dining together and flirting, had deeply offended white American soldiers.

Linard suggested that French officers refrain from praising black American troops overly warmly, and from treating them with too much respect.[2] What incensed Boisneuf was not just the advice to bow before the most odious aspects of American racism, but the ways Linard seemed to justify white Americans' attitudes, for instance, by noting the greater dangers of "degeneration" through sexual contact presented

In this cover image, "The Child of the Dessert," from *La Vie Parisienne*, a white French woman dines with a black African soldier. This depiction particularly upset white American soldiers in France, who saw such interactions as undermining both racial and gender hierarchies. *Bibliothèque nationale de France, La Vie Parisienne 07/27/1918 (A56,N30), ark:/12148/bpt6k1258420n*

by the United States' very large and permanent black population. Boisneuf linked this offensive document to another series of outrages, these too (not coincidentally) linked to interracial intimacy: he demanded that the government condemn several acts of violence on the part of white US troops toward France's own soldiers of color, targeted as they enjoyed the liberty to socialize with whomever they pleased, even white women, in the nation they served. Noting that he spoke not as a "black" but a "Frenchman...a French Deputy" (but who could fail to note that a black man could rise to a powerful political position in the national legislature, hardly a realistic hope for a black American in the United States), Boisneuf singled out for particular contempt Linard's contention that "black American troops in France have, by themselves, been the source of as many reports of attempted rape as the entire rest of the [US] army," asking if lynching was now to be the law of France as well as of the United States. Then he expressed neatly the ways that racial, gender, and sexual anxieties had mixed historically to poison social relations and provoke hatred and violence, pointing to the "abominable legend of the negro satyr, especially crazed for white flesh."[3]

American racism struck such a nerve with Boisneuf and many others in France because so many regarded France's extensive use of colonial subjects in the army as the fulfillment of the promise of republican egalitarianism and color-blindness. Reactions inside and outside Parliament highlighted the ways contemporary notions of proper relations between people of different races and between men and women could combine in volatile ways. Race and gender were both critical sites of change and contestation during the war, and never more so than when they came together. Careful attention to these intersections is important for making sense of this history, as it is in studying the history of gender more generally. Indeed, one of the most vibrant, if not uncontested, areas in women's and gender history has been the study of "intersectionality," the ways the multiple forces of sex, gender, race, class, sexual orientation, disability status, and others develop and work together and simultaneously to shape experiences and identities.[4] During the First World War, intersections between and interactions of gender and race were clearly significant, but these in turn also intersected with sex, masculinity, femininity, and colonialism. It is important, in other words, to examine where women, men, race, gender, masculinity, femininity, sex and sexuality, empire, and nation come together to inform lived experiences during wartime. Though the history of women is critical, this cannot be women's history any more than men's history, or even subalterns' history.[5] All of these histories are critical to the full range of wartime experiences, and this is clear in the many instances in which men of color, usually as soldiers or workers, interacted with European men and women.

Intersections of race and gender helped to drive the construction of gender norms during the war. Understandings of sexual desire and practices informed and shaped gender identities when contemporaries—European women and men, and colonial subjects both in Europe as soldiers or workers and at home in the colonies—considered interracial sex, both the possibility and the fact of it. For example, white soldiers' anxieties about "black" men on the home front interacting with white women clearly evoked this construction, as European men asserted their roles as white males but at the same time admitted anxieties about their potency and serious threats from unruly women and potent and unconstrained colonial men. Also, when colonial subjects crossed the color line for sex and love, and when they wrote and talked about it with other colonial subjects, they reconfigured their roles as men and as members of subject "races." These and other examples show how notions of gender and race came together and influenced each other, often in combustible ways. Intersection and construction were not separate processes but were linked and mutually supporting.

Joan Scott has observed of feminist approaches to history, "It is this critical activity—the relentless interrogation of the taken-for-granted—that always moves us somewhere else, from object to object, from the present to the future."[6] Taking seriously the intersections and interactions between gender and race during the First World War contributes to a broader rethinking of the history and significance of the event, so critical and so opportune as we mark the centenary of the conflict. This is already unfolding in increasing recognition of the event as genuinely global and transnational in its causes, course, and consequences.[7] Relentlessly interrogating the taken-for-granted narratives of the war through the lenses of both gender and race recasts and enriches metanarratives of the war as a whole, national (even nationalist) narratives, colonial and racial narratives, women's and men's narratives, gendered narratives, and more to allow us to write about and understand the Great War in new, more detailed, more nuanced, and more richly textured ways.

CONTEXTS: GLOBAL AND TRANSNATIONAL WAR, GENDER,
AND SEXUALITY

Gender and race mattered, and mattered together, so much during the First World War because the war was global, and its combats, supply, and movements were transnational. And the war was global and transnational because the war was one of empires: the principal combatants of 1914—Great Britain, France, Russia, Germany, and Austria-Hungary—as well as Belgium, all possessed significant and diverse imperial holdings. Later entrants such as the Ottoman Empire, Italy, Portugal, and

Japan were avowedly imperial and imperialistic, while the United States fit the mold in many, though less acknowledged, ways. All these empires clashing and cooperating in locations around the world mobilized, moved, and mixed human resources on an unprecedented scale. As people traveled and came together in the fraught circumstances of war, ideas and practices came under pressure and confronted change and difference in new contexts.

Imperial war brought race and gender together in new ways. Most dramatically, the war brought more than a million nonwhite people from all over the world to Europe, generating interracial contacts on an unprecedented scale. France deployed some 500,000 colonial subjects from North and West Africa, Southeast Asia, and Madagascar, as well as smaller numbers of men from the Caribbean, the Pacific, and East Africa, as soldiers in the French army in Europe between 1914 and 1918.[8] Another 200,000 colonial subjects came to France to labor in support of the war effort, along with some 37,000 laborers recruited from China.[9] The British employed approximately 100,000 Chinese workers on the Western Front and in 1914–1915 deployed 135,000 men from India as infantry, with a few thousand cavalry remaining in France for the duration.[10] More than 20,000 black South Africans served in France as part of the South African Native Labour Contingent, while Britain's other dominions fielded men of color as soldiers in Europe: 4,000 Native Americans from Canada and hundreds of indigenous people from Australia and New Zealand.[11] Some 10,000 West Indians from British possessions in the Caribbean fought in the British army on the Western Front.[12] And among the American Expeditionary Forces troops who arrived in France in 1917–1918 were 200,000 African Americans.

Men of color served as workers and soldiers in all of the many theaters of the war beyond the Western Front, including in eastern and southern Europe, Africa, Asia Minor, and the Middle East, where Ottoman, Russian, and British forces all included diverse ethnicities. Most notably, the majority of Indians who served the British outside India during the war, some 1 million men, served in the Middle East. Fighting in Africa involved tens of thousands of indigenous troops, and more than 1 million porters carrying supplies. The interaction of race and gender—for instance, relationships between local women and foreign workers and soldiers in the Middle East, and the effects on family life and indigenous gender roles and hierarchies of mobilization and service in Africa—clearly had important effects, but the situation was clearer in Europe. The decisive Western Front might seem the most conventionally European aspect of the war, with the armies of the Great Powers facing each other in France and Belgium. Yet the Western Front was in fact a microcosm of the global war. France in particular became the largest multicultural space on the planet, bringing into contact peoples from all over the globe, and bringing these peoples into contact, or collision, with European concepts of masculinity and often racialized expectations of gender roles, and above all with white European women.

Like so many aspects of Europe in the early twentieth century, gender roles and ideas about sexuality were undergoing transformation under the quickening pressures of modernity. Even before the war began to accelerate these, destabilization of gender roles generated fears that women were increasingly both unruly and unfeminine, and that men were suffering a crisis of masculinity. The troubling specter of an emasculated future appeared in the guises of women's entry into previously male spheres in employment and politics, and demands for further integration and rights combined with the quickening pace of technological change, urban living, and fears of "degeneration" and impotence in a modern life lived so far away from the eugenically salutary, natural struggle for existence.[13] Women not just in politics but in the workplace only heightened bourgeois concerns about a future turned upside down and belonging to the degenerate masses. The Great War acted to stimulate further existing trends, which seemed all the more destabilizing because they were now manifest in the violent, existential struggle of world war. Scholars have shown that the older conventional wisdom that women entered the workforce in large numbers for the first time is incorrect. Many women worked outside the home before the war, and wartime increases were not in fact so dramatic. However, what did change, and what was authentically dramatic for everyone involved, is that women moved in very large numbers from previous "traditional" occupations—low-paid textile work, for instance, and above all domestic service—into more skilled, higher-paying, and higher-status jobs.[14] Meanwhile, millions of men were away from home at the front, leaving women not only working in new ways—it is important to remember that the majority of women in Europe lived in rural areas, and so new work meant continuing their usual tasks while adding those of the absent men and even animals, some having to go so far as to harness themselves to plows—but also doing this work and living alone and more independently.[15]

As if there were not already enough specters haunting Europe before and during the war, female independence could not fail to work with other factors to conjure changing ideas, practices, and anxieties related to sexuality. By 1914, sex had become "political." Prostitution and venereal disease, developments in medical and theoretical understandings of sex, contraception and abortion, eugenics, and increasing public discussion of same-sex relations all deeply affected Europeans' practices, expectations, and experiences.[16] Sexuality was already intertwined with questions of race, most notably because many viewed it as the critical site of both generation and degeneration. The public, and even the state, seemed to have an unprecedented need to intervene in and police boundaries and behaviors. Not only eugenics but also public hygiene and natalist movements aimed explicitly at the health and future of "the race."[17]

But gender, women and men, and sexuality were all also wrapped up very tightly with what might be called Europeans' external-facing preoccupations with race. This era was the height of European imperial expansion and colonialism, and gender and sex were never very far away from the processes of and thinking about empire. Colonies had always been places where European men could imagine and participate in illicit, exotic sex, particularly since they made and ruled empires as more or less exclusively masculine European domains.[18] By the turn of the twentieth century, European nations were increasingly sending women to the colonies, hoping to "civilize" male colonists as well as indigenous lands and peoples.[19] Moreover, European colonists, both male and female, were not merely attempting to export bourgeois notions of sex and sexuality, but were forming notions of these in the colonies to bring back to Europe.[20] Now, between 1914 and 1918, Europeans confronted a new situation in which the colonies, in particular colonial men with their dark skins and apparently menacing sexual potency and deviancy, had come home to Europe, and even into European homes.

GENDER, RACE, SEX, AND WAR IN EUROPE

Notions of gender played a role in the ways Europeans thought and talked about colonial subjects during the war, from recruitment and training to working and fighting. For instance, ideas about masculinity, aggression, and prowess informed recruitment and even deployment that rested on conceptions of "warlike" and "unwarlike" races" (*races guerrières* and *races non-guerrières*) for the French army and "martial races" for the British. This meant that certain groups among West Africans and North Africans were heavily represented in the French army and served in combat, while other groups such as Indochinese and Madagascans served in lower numbers and as support troops. The British declined to recruit heavily among "effeminate" Bengalis, preferring instead to send into combat men from the Punjab, Sikhs, and Gurkhas.[21]

Gendered notions also showed up clearly in the habit many had, especially in France, of talking about colonial subjects in familial terms. Official rhetoric claimed both white French troops and colonial subjects in uniform as "sons" of the French nation, but the notion was more infantilizing when applied to colonial men. In fact, in 1915 Senator Henry Bérenger made a fairly typical distinction when in a report he celebrated "our sons of the metropole and our children of the colonies." In the sons' veins "old Gallic blood" flowed, while the veins of "these young races" contained "new blood." The text certainly celebrated unity and solidarity, but distinctions with a hierarchical flavor remained.[22] Rhetoric within the French army also emphasized how childlike colonial subjects, or *indigènes* (soldiers were known as *troupes indigènes*), looked to their officers as "fathers." A manual for officers serving with West Africans asserted that "the captain is the head of the family, the father of his indigènes."[23] Sometimes, in a highly symbolic if perhaps puzzling twist, officers acted as "mothers" to the colonial subjects in their charge. A prewar treatise by an experienced officer serving in Indochina explicitly advocated this maternal role, and a Madagascan soldier serving in France reported in 1917 that the captain commanding his company told his men, "Know that in me you will find a father and a mother."[24]

Yet the most salient way gender and race intersected during the war was through sex and love across the color line. Men of color and white women encountered each other in a variety of contexts, not all of them charged with sex. Indian troops billeted with French civilians. West African troops encamped in the south of France to avoid the debilitating winters of the north entered into the home of a local woman to learn proper French. Chinese and North African laborers often worked alongside French women in factories. West Indian soldiers encamped with their British army units befriended and did odd jobs for local French women.[25] These are just a few of the wide variety of everyday contacts and interactions that were inevitable with so many men of color living, working, fighting, convalescing in hospitals, and so on, among Europeans. Of course, contacts and interactions also included sex, romance, love, and in some cases even marriage and children. A number of factors help explain the frequency of these developments, a frequency that was clearly elevated enough to cause consternation for postal censors and other officials. These officials were particularly sensitive on these subjects, given the implications for the "white prestige" so important to European self-conceptions and to the maintenance of colonial order and authority. But it is clear that their fears were not exaggerated. That young men in homosocial environments, far from home, would seek intimate companionship is not surprising, and many women were alone because fathers, husbands, brothers, and other men were dead or away fighting at the front. Also, it is clear that colonial men discovered in metropolitan France a white population far less conscious and obsessed with race and the color line than were Europeans living in the colonies. Plenty of racism and color prejudice existed in Europe, but the commonness of intimate relations, sexual and otherwise, makes clear that many Europeans on their own soil displayed a degree of openness that was not possible for Europeans striving in the colonies to maintain their "prestige" and authority. Colonial men saw this clearly. One Madagascan noted the radical difference between the attitudes of white women in France and in the colony: "What to tell you of white women? Down there, we fear them. Here they come to us and solicit us by the attraction of their charm."[26]

Soldiers who served in Europe from all parts of all the European empires took these unprecedented opportunities to approach white women. Umed Sing Bist wrote home to India in 1915, "If you want any French women, there are plenty here, and they are very good looking."[27] Balwant Singh was even more explicit, writing, "The ladies are very nice and bestow their favors on us freely. But contrary to the custom in our country, they do not put their legs over the shoulders when they go with a man."[28] In some cases, colonial men's encounters were casual, or with prostitutes. D. N. Sricar wrote from a hospital in Brighton, England, "The girls of this place are notorious, and very fond of accosting Indians and fooling with them. They are ever ready for any purpose, and in truth they are no better than the girls of Adda Bazar of Indore."[29] Secretary of state for India, Lord Crewe, had the same impression of the behavior of Indian men and English women in and around this hospital: "Brighton seems to me a bad place," because with their men enlisted, the women were "all the more at a loose end and ready to take on an Indian warrior."[30] A Madagascan soldier wrote in September 1917, "Upon arriving or walking on French soil, one is obliged to partake of, or one is attracted by something: prostitution."[31]

But some soldiers were very clear that their interests were more pure. Risaldar Anjamuddin Khan wrote that "married ladies, and young unmarried women, attend to our wants and tidy our beds, and eat at the same tables as we do. They are as beautiful as fairies, but for us they are like mothers and sisters. I assure you that by the grace of God my faith will remain unbroken [i.e., he will resist the temptation to have sex with these Christian women]."[32] Other soldiers struck up relationships that were sometimes amorous and sometimes more platonic, but clearly serious enough to impress bourgeois European women and their families. A West African soldier, Mbaye Khary Diagne, recollected after the war that he and his comrades had their own versions of the *marraines de guerre*, French women who contributed to the war effort by writing letters to men at the front: "They were not prostitutes. They were girls from good families," who met the soldiers in everyday social settings and "said to you she wanted to take you home and present you to her parents. And you got a French family that way."[33] A Tunisian, a driver stationed in Montpellier, married the daughter of a lawyer in that city.[34] Jacques Ngon, an Indochinese nurse who had taken up with the daughter of a captain in the artillery, wrote that he ate lunch each day at the home of the father, who also provided the couple with an allowance.[35] Another army officer, a lieutenant, had agreed to the marriage of his daughter to an Indochinese interpreter, promised to help his future son-in-law obtain naturalization, and consented to the couple moving to Indochina after the war.[36] Indochinese soldier Dinh also benefited from parental benevolence, as he paid frequent visits to a young, twenty-two-year-old widow, "in full view," censors noted, "of her father and mother."[37]

The opportunities for non-European workers to mix with white women and their families were at once more plentiful and more restricted. Though not enlisted in the military, laborers even from places such as China that were not formally colonized by Europeans were subject to military discipline and carefully segregated both in the workplace and in barracks outside working hours.[38] Still, it was impossible to seal these men off hermetically from the surrounding society. One aspect that struck visitors from the colonies was the labor of European women. This was true of soldiers, such as Dayal Singh, who wrote to his wife in India that "women are doing all the work of their houses; and they are even engaged in war and in ploughing the land. In short, women are doing work which men find it impossible to do."[39] But colonial workers witnessed firsthand women laboring in industry. A Madagascan working in a factory in Toulouse wrote, "Would you believe that white women, who at home love to be served, here work as much as men? In the factories they are very numerous and work with the same ardor as men."[40] And colonial workers, despite segregation and discipline, clearly interacted with women in other settings. One Tunisian wrote, "The city where we are stationed is full of women, and fornication here is as abundant as grains of sand. As for me, I have four women, two young girls and two widows. I am awash in sensuality." His countryman Tayeb Gananchi was even more explicit: "If you wish I will send you a *wagon* of young *French girls*, because here we have large quantities at our disposal. A kilogram of *vaginas* is worth five cents, as is a pound of *breasts*."[41]

It is not hard to imagine that these and other interactions across the color line provoked reactions among Europeans as they considered the gender, racial, and sexual orders. Initial responses to the new multicultural wartime environment were often fearful and sometimes hostile. Even Lucie Cousturier, who eventually welcomed West African soldiers into her home as language students and even friends, noted that when the soldiers first arrived in the area, she and others regarded the men with "horror," expecting "drunkenness, theft, rape, disease" and fearing what would happen if one encountered in person "these savages . . . these gorillas."[42] Some women resented colonial workers in particular because the arrival of these men made possible the dispatch of French male workers to the front to fight. Labor activists in France suspected that the use of colonial labor would degrade working conditions and pay for French workers, and they even feared that *troupes indigènes* would serve as a praetorian guard for the reactionary capitalist class and the state, breaking strikes and firing on workers. But the greatest tensions swirled around matters of sex and love. French soldiers at the front sometimes worried about the fate of their women at the hands of colonial men, such as men in a unit of the French army who declared during the 1917 mutinies, "We don't want the blacks in Paris and in other regions mistreating our wives."[43]

Sentiments like these often lay at the root of violence against nonwhite workers, of which there were many important examples. In Great Britain, the most significant violence took place after the war, but in the period immediately following the Armistice and clearly as a result of circumstances created by the war. Between January and August 1919, race riots erupted in nine British port cities. Wartime shipping demands had by this time drawn more than 20,000 men of color from India, Africa, the Middle East, the Caribbean, and China to reside in Britain and work as sailors and longshoremen. The roots of this violence were clear even in earlier, smaller precursors. For instance, in July 1917 in East London, local men and women had attacked several black sailors, aggressions the police explained by noting that "some of the inhabitants are greatly incensed against the coloured man" because of "the infatuation of the white girls for the black men."[44] Events in 1919 were equally obviously linked to fears of interracial sex and miscegenation, with British men fearing and resenting not only sexual competition and race pollution from men of color but also a loss of masculinity after a disillusioning war and in the face of a postwar economic slump. Adding insult to injury, British women seemed to betray both race solidarity and their feminine duties through surrendering willingly to the allegedly greater, even if depraved, potency of "black" male sexuality. The *Liverpool Post* declared, "One cause of the trouble was said to be that certain white women in the district had stated that blacks were *better* than whites."[45]

Violence marked race relations in France, too, where the non-European population was far greater. To be sure, many factors were at work propelling racial violence in this context, and correspondence between race riots and a general crisis of wartime morale in France during 1917 and 1918 shows the importance of economic crisis, political discontent, troubling news from the front, and increasing tension between labor and capital.[46] Yet tensions over sex and the color line were also at work. After a race riot in Toulouse in January 1918, Madagascan worker Emmanuel Rasafimanjary wrote about how he personally encountered violence when three Frenchmen called him and a friend "dirty niggers" for walking with French women, and a fight ensued. He went on to say that "such incidents are frequent, French men being very jealous of the favors women show the Malagasy." An official report supported this contention in a general way, explaining attacks on Indochinese workers by asserting, "Jealousy concerning women is usually the cause of these aggressions."[47]

Despite the very real significance of tensions over sex and love in fueling interracial violence during the period, it is important to remember that a willingness to cross or ignore the color line was equally present in some segments of European societies. Sexual tension would not have played as large a role in violence if this were not the case. Simply put, some women and men had no problem with intimacy with men of color. Tunisian soldier Khamaci Mohamed impressed a French family with his knowledge of French over dinner in their home and noted that they accepted him "as a true child of the family."[48] Other colonial men raised the issues of children and family in a different way. At least 250 Indochinese men married Frenchwomen during the war, with 231 living together in the metropole in 1918, and scattered evidence suggests that at least dozens of men from other areas, particularly North Africa, also married into French families during the war.[49] These unions carried with them the possibility of the permanent residence of colonial men and mixed couples in Europe, or the migration of French women to the colonies, of naturalization and citizenship for colonial subjects, of employment in the metropole after the war for colonial subjects, and of mixed-race offspring. Postal censorship reports tallied each month the number of engagements, marriages, and births stemming from liaisons between Indochinese men and French women. In December 1917, a woman named Andrea wrote to her Indochinese husband, Mai, that she had had a baby who was "very cute, but rather white."[50] If interactions with prostitutes troubled British and French authorities in part because they risked colonial subjects considering these women of dubious morals as typical European women, more serious, stable, and perhaps permanent relationships resulting in marriage and children could be even more troubling for different reasons. A wartime problem could thus become a long-term one, both at home and in the colonies.

Colonial control in the empire itself was a question because of the ways news of crossed and blurred color lines inevitably leaked out of Europe. Colonial men wrote home during the war and would certainly go home after it. Postal censors in particular worried over both problems. They noted letters such as that from Ky Sum, an Indochinese worker, who wrote, "My dear parents, I would like to inform you that I have already found a girlfriend here. I enclose her photograph. She is a worker who is employed in the same factory as me. When I was sick she often visited me at the hospital, and that is why I cannot do without her now."[51] Both the mention of a committed relationship and the inclusion of a photo were problematic from an official point of view. Images were a particular nuisance for authorities, since they seemed to offer concrete proof of relationships that were strictly taboo in the colonies. In 1915, British censors withheld a letter from Tura Baz Khan, writing from the Brighton hospital to his comrade in France. Accompanying the letter was a cigarette card featuring a print of Sir Joshua Reynolds's painting of the Duchess of Gordon. Giving a perhaps rather odd erotic interpretation of this image, Khan wrote, "This is the woman we get. We have recourse to her. I have sent you this and if you like it, let me know, and I will send her. We get everything [we want]. If you do not, let me know and I will try to procure it for you."[52]

Soldiers could be creative in both sending and interpreting images of European women. In 1917, Fang, an Indochinese worker, wrote to a friend from the hospital that he could not get any more pornographic photographs as requested because the sale of them was forbidden, but, "In order to simplify, I will draw some myself and send them to you."[53] Ultimately, any image of a European woman, whether a portrait of an eighteenth-century aristocrat, a photo of a sweetheart, or a freehand sketch, could be threatening if sent back into a colonial context where white women were untouchable symbols of the hierarchical racial order, examples of bourgeois propriety, and vehicles for the civilizing mission. Pornography was, of course, worse. This could take the form of many of the categories under which in 1918 censors of Indochinese mail categorized the nearly 10,000 images they had seized in two years of operation: nudes, undressed, bathers, kissing, mixed-race children, photographs of French women, photographs of Franco-Indochinese couples.[54] Or it could take the form of an ostensibly nonpornographic image with a pornographic message, such as Khan's remark about the Duchess of Gordon, or a North African soldier's Arabic caption on a photograph of a Muslim soldier with his arm around a very young French girl: "I ask you, my brother, to tell me if this young girl pleases you, in which case I will procure one for you [and] you can then do with her what you like." Other men sent pictures of French women with obscene captions such as, "One can have this young thing for a few francs."[55]

All of this—the relationships, the images, the sincere and amorous sentiments, and the disrespectful and lecherous behavior—upset European authorities in two respects. First of all, these white men, representatives of imperial states, were concerned about the future of empire. The British, traditionally even more prickly than the French about the importance of racial prestige in upholding the colonial order of things, in part because of the importance of this prestige in an Indian context where a tiny white minority ruled over vast millions of indigenous people, were most aggressive in policing the color line through segregation and prohibition. Hospitals and encampments in Britain remained tightly secured and segregated, for reasons that were self-evident to men like mail censor E. B. Howell, who wrote: "The troops in hospital rather resent their close surveillance, but it is obviously better to keep a tight hold on them than to allow them to conceive a wrong idea to the 'izzat' [honor] of English women, a sentiment which if not properly held in check would be most detrimental to the prestige and spirit of European rule in India."[56] This was all the more interesting coming from an official who admitted that it was virtually impossible to prevent French women from treating Indian soldiers with dangerous respect and familiarity, because British and Indians alike were guests in France. To the British authorities, the French seemed to have an exceedingly lax attitude toward white prestige, which highlighted for Indians very different British attitudes and treatment. As one official put it, "As regards Marseilles, the main cause of discontent seems to be that the French allow their African troops the same privileges as the Europeans: [he] is as good as a Frenchman, whereas the Indian is kept under various restrictions."[57]

It is true that the traditions and laws of French republicanism, as well as humanitarian concerns, placed limits on the lengths to which French officials were willing to go to police the color line. As the author of one report asked near the end of the war, "Should we respect these consensual unions, especially when they are consecrated by a birth?" The author went on to articulate an open and optimistic vision of the assimilationist impulse that putatively lay at the heart of French republican colonialism: "Assimilation increases day by day, to such an extent that this stage could be easily reached by a rather large number of *indigènes*, if their stay in France is prolonged for many more months." In other words, perhaps these unions would perform the ideological work of French imperialism, civilizing colonial subjects.[58]

Yet picturing the differences between British and French approaches to the issue as one pitting a hierarchical and conservative tradition of indirect rule against an egalitarian, liberal republican tradition of assimilation does not capture the complexity of the French response. First of all, French officials did repeatedly intervene to discourage or prevent relationships and sought to segregate colonial men, especially workers, from French society when they could. Republican scruples may have sometimes placed limits on these responses, but they did not prevent authorities from imprisoning an Indochinese man for fifteen days for "daring to fall in love with a French girl."[59] Officials also often sought, albeit episodically and with seemingly little real effect, to warn women of the potential dangers they faced when courting colonial men, or to reduce reliance on female nurses in hospitals that treated nonwhite men.

And regular procedures of cantonment, discipline, and segregation among workers (the uniform and status as defenders of the nation gave soldiers marginally more room to maneuver) easily rivaled Britain's approach to its Indian soldiers. Moreover, race consciousness and racism were never absent from the consideration of most officials, and it was clear that they often wanted to "do" something about these relationships. "What can we do?" asked one report on Indochinese soldiers and workers. "To protect the French woman for us is an urgent duty, but stopping a few letters is a palliative which loses all of its value when the writer remains in the country." The report did cite republican misgivings about overly draconian restrictions on individual liberty but fretted over "unfortunate French women led astray in obviously grotesque liaisons."[60] In the end, broader currents of European and Western racism shaped French officials' attitudes and approaches to sex across the color line, in particular the racism that, as Benedict Anderson puts it, "dreams of eternal contaminations . . . an endless series of loathsome copulations."[61]

Ultimately, the nations that recruited the nonwhite workers and soldiers who served in Europe during the war—Great Britain (including its dominions), France, and the United States—were all concerned in their own way about the color line. In France, the state's efforts to limit contacts across this line, one scholar has argued, established "the very idea of a color line in France, particularly one governing relations between members of the opposite sex."[62] That color and race really are what mattered, not just colonial subjecthood and politics, is clear when one considers that French officials were just as keen to police Chinese workers' behavior and encounters with French people as to regulate those of Africans and Asians from France's colonies.[63] This is ironic, given that the Great War helped establish in some quarters France's reputation as color-blind. African Americans in particular had experiences while serving in France that convinced them that the country was free of the virulent racism that shaped their lives in the United States. Addie Hunton and Kathryn M. Johnson, two African American women who went to France in 1918 to work for the YMCA with African American troops, recorded the liberating atmosphere they found in France. They noted the "most cordial and friendly" relations all African Americans had with French people, in whom they found "sympathy and understanding." The two women marveled at the "most unusual and welcome experience" of entering public spaces, using public transportation, and entering private homes not to encounter "some humiliating experience" but to be greeted with "hospitality and kindliness of spirit." Despite the very real hardships of life in a nation at war, their arrival in France "furnished to some of us the first full breath of freedom that had ever come into our limited experience."[64] An African American soldier put it more simply, writing home to his mother, "These French people don't bother with no color line business. They treat us so good that the only time I ever know I'm colored is when I look in the glass."[65] Hunton and Johnson reported that white Americans deeply resented this egalitarian treatment, attempting to spread the idea among the French that African Americans were uncivilized brutes. When this did not work, white Americans were especially incensed to see that "French women were particularly kind and hospitable to their dark-skinned allies."[66] Indeed, African American experiences in France began a long tradition of admiration in this community for France and of expatriation to that country, which established a significant cultural presence in French life through jazz, literature, and other cultural forms.[67]

Of course, white Americans' attempts to bring their own version of the color line to France and to enforce it, even with respect to France's own colonial subjects in uniform, provoked outraged reactions from Frenchmen such as Deputy Boisneuf. The irony of the situation is not just in France's possession of and efforts to police its own version of a color line, but that in a general sense the preoccupations of white Americans and white French officials were the same: both worried that the precedent of egalitarian treatment, especially access to white women, would undermine white prestige, respect, and political control. White Americans wanted to maintain control over a large domestic population of black citizens, while French authorities wanted to preserve control over a large overseas population of nonwhite colonial subjects. But in both cases, control was at issue. What a colonial official in Tunisia wrote after the war could easily describe the fears and sentiments of many white Americans in the same period: men were coming back from Europe "with ideas clearly turned around as far as French prestige, and European prestige in general, are concerned," and in particular, "the license of certain *milieux* and the impropriety of too many women have succeeded in destroying the respect they had for us, and all of the countryside now knows about the amusing adventures" these soldiers had while in France.[68]

Standing alongside these concerns with racial and colonial control were fears about the control of women. When one French officer claimed that Algerians were apprehensive about "contact with our women, who in their eyes are all prostitutes and whose conduct unfortunately, in many cases, only confirms them in their opinion," he was voicing not only his concern over the effect of French women's behavior upon the mentality of colonial subjects but also his disappointment as a French male with the failure of these women to conform to sexual mores and social expectations.[69] And perhaps worst and most dangerous of all, these women were introducing the possibility, and often enough the fact, of blurring the color line and lines of racial and colonial authority in the most fundamental and irrevocable way by producing mixed-race offspring. What Americans and the British called miscegenation and the French called *métissage* was an express route to degeneration, which so preoccupied the racial imagination of the era, as well as a "sexual affront." Behind ostensibly biological concerns about "contamination" lurked the larger and more unsettling questions about the permeability of political and cultural boundaries between European and "other," between colonizers and colonized, between white and nonwhite. Crossing and blurring these lines destabilized the separation of people into categories upon which white supremacy depended, and confused questions of national identity in troubling ways.[70]

British, French, and American authorities also feared that women would "spoil" men of color by exalting their bravery, their necessity for the defense of civilization, their sexual prowess, their (equal and full) manhood. Racist and sexist thought often converged in infantilizing its targets, and convergence also occurred when racists painted "inferior" races as effeminate, since the feminine was by definition inferior. If these two groups themselves converged to engage in relationships and validate their mutual humanity, authentic personhood, and full citizenship, the war would appear very destabilizing indeed.[71] In light of these circumstances, it is not surprising that the postwar period saw reactionary calls for a return to "normalcy," reestablished gender roles and boundaries, a harder and more violent policing of the color line (in the United States), and a more conservative and exploitative approach in the colonies (particularly those of the French empire).[72]

CONCLUSION

Gender and race intersected in so many ways during and as a result of the war that there is abundant opportunity for further research and exploration. For instance, fear of unrestrained non-European sexuality played a role in discussions of citizenship for Algerian soldiers who fought for France. Efforts resulting from a sincere republican commitment to the linkage between military service and citizenship foundered on largely mythical beliefs that Muslims were inveterate polygamists and so unfit for republican citizenship. This citizenship was constructed as entirely male, with a certain relationship to sexuality that only non-Muslim, white European men were capable of maintaining.[73] What influence did understandings of non-European sexual practices and family structures have on attitudes and policies in other areas, with regard to other peoples?

Even more in need of exploration are the sometimes surprising and contradictory developments in issues having to do with gender and race. To take one important example that brings together two key questions, during the infamous "Black Shame" controversy that roiled societies throughout the Western world in the immediate aftermath of the war, questions of rape and of the role of women were central. The controversy arose over France's use of troops from the colonies to occupy defeated Germany's Rhineland territory. Women played a prominent role in the international outcry over France's introduction of "savages" into the heart of white European civilization, and the placement those savages in charge of vulnerable civilian populations. Almost entirely specious claims of black men raping German women propelled other women in many Western countries to highly public activism. Here, women played their expected role as defenders of the racial order, but how did this square with women's prominent role in subverting that order through very different attitudes and practices during the war? Scholars certainly have not ignored the Black Shame or its gendered aspects, but the topic is not yet exhausted.[74] Nor is the question of why rape became a symbol indelibly associated with men of color in this instance, in ways that are similar to the prominence of rape accusations in maintaining the racial order in the American South, when rape seems to have been largely absent from even racialized discourse about colonial men in Europe during the war. The exception of course is the Linard circular's mention of African Americans' propensity to rape, but the connections there with the American and emerging postwar contexts may make this the exception that proves the rule.

A final area for further research is the context of gender and sexuality in the colonies themselves. Considerable work has focused on events in Europe, given the racial mixing there that was so much a part of the story of the war. Often this work focuses on anxieties among Europeans about the implications of the war experience for colonial subjects' behavior when they returned home. Some excellent scholarship has addressed the effects of the war on the colonies and colonialism, and among colonial subjects who lived in Europe during the interwar period.[75] But more remains to be done to explore, for instance, the postwar careers of workers and soldiers who had been to Europe or elsewhere, to discover what differences the war experience might have made in attitudes and behaviors with respect to gender and sex, and to understandings of racial hierarchies that intersected with these.[76] Perhaps even more important is exploring the effects of the war on gender not in Europe but in other theaters. For example, if ideas about race were among the most important motivating factors in building and maintaining empire in places like Africa, then race was implicated in the war there even in the absence of the spectacular mixing of peoples that took place in Europe. The war directly affected millions of Africans through service in armies as soldiers and porters, hardships created by recruitment and combat, and economic mobilization of resources. All of these had effects on gender, not least because African women did what European women did, taking over out of necessity labor and other tasks that absent men could not do. Scholars of African history have long recognized the important social effects of the war on the continent, but the full exploration of these issues and their integration into the global history of the First World War remain an ongoing project.

Attentiveness to the ways gender, race, and sex come together helps paint a fuller picture of the war, showing how even a focus primarily on the Western Front can still reveal key aspects of the worldwide conflict. This was clear long before Deputy Boisneuf stepped to the tribune to speak that day in 1919 about equality in the home of the Rights of Man. His concerns brought together France and colonial subjects in uniform recruited from across France's worldwide empire, the United States and its army of white and African American soldiers, French women who felt themselves free to consort with men of color in a nation that was at once race conscious and color-blind, acts of violence and racism committed by both a Frenchman and Americans, and the rule of law. But this convergence was but one of the culminations of a global war of empires, moving and mixing peoples, crossing and blurring boundaries of nation, race, gender, and sex.

NOTES

1. *Journal Officiel de la République Française* (JORF): Chambre des Députés-Débats (CD-D), 25 juillet 1919, p. 3732.

2. Service Historique de la Défense (SHD) 6N97: Colonel J. A. Linard, Mission militaire française près de l'armée américaine, "Au sujet des troupes noires américaines," 7 août 1918.

3. JORF, CD-D, 25 juillet 1919, p. 3731.

4. See Cornelia H. Dayton and Lisa Levenstein, "The Big Tent of U.S. Women's and Gender History: A State of the Field," *Journal of American History* 99, no. 3 (2012): 793–817. See also Crystal N. Feimster's response, "The Impact of Racial and Sexual Politics on Women's History," *Journal of American History* 99, no. 3 (2012): 822–826. On intersectionality, see Kimberle Crenshaw's seminal article, "Mapping the Margins: Intersectionality, Identity Politics, and Violence against Women of Color," *Stanford Law Review* 43, no. 6 (1991): 1241–1299; and also Jennifer C. Nash, "Re-thinking Intersectionality," *Feminist Review* 89 (2008): 1–15.

5. For treatments that move beyond a history of women during the war to consider a broader range of gendered wartime experiences, see the following essays: Susan R. Grayzel, "Men and Women at Home," in *The Cambridge History of the First World War*, ed. Jay Winter, 3 vols. (Cambridge: Cambridge University Press, 2014), 3:96–120; Joanna Bourke, "Gender Roles in Killing Zones," in Winter, *The Cambridge History of the First World War*, 3:153–177.

6. Joan Wallach Scott, "Feminism's History," *Journal of Women's History* 16, no. 2 (2004): 23.

7. See in particular Hew Strachan's concise case, "The First World War as a Global War," *First World War Studies* 1, no. 1 (2010): 3–14, as well as Olivier Compagnon and Pierre Purseigle, "Géographies de la mobilisation et territoires de la belligérance durant la Première Guerre mondiale," *Annales* 71, no. 1 (2016): 39–63. See also Andrew Tait Jarboe and Richard S. Fogarty, eds., *Empires in World War I: Shifting Frontiers and Imperial Dynamics in a Global Conflict* (London: I. B. Tauris, 2014); Robert Gerwarth and Erez Manela, *Empires at War, 1911–1923* (London: Oxford University Press, 2014); Tyler Stovall, *Paris and the Spirit of 1919: Consumer Struggles, Transnationalism, and Revolution* (Cambridge: Cambridge University Press, 2012); Lawrence Sondhaus, *World War One: The Global Revolution* (Cambridge: Cambridge University Press, 2011); William Kelleher Storey, *The First World War: A Concise Global History* (New York: Rowman and Littlefield, 2010); Michael S. Neiberg, *Fighting the Great War: A Global History* (Cambridge, MA: Harvard University Press, 2006); John H. Morrow Jr., *The Great War: An Imperial History* (New York: Routledge, 2004); and Hew Strachan, *The First World War*, vol. 1, *To Arms* (Oxford: Oxford University Press, 2001).

8. Richard S. Fogarty, *Race and War in France: Colonial Subjects in the French Army, 1914–1918* (Baltimore: Johns Hopkins University Press, 2008); Jacques Frémaux, *Les colonies dans la Grande Guerre: Combats et épreuves des peuples d'outre-mer* (Saint-Cloud: Éditions 14–18, 2006); Marc Michel, *L'Appel à l'Afrique: Contributions et réactions à l'effort de guerre en AOF, 1914–1919* (Paris: Publications de la Sorbonne, 1982); Joe Lunn, *Memoirs of the Maelstrom: A Senegalese Oral History of the First World War* Portsmouth, NH: Heinemann, 1999); Gregory Mann, *Native Sons: West African Veterans and France in the Twentieth Century* (Durham, NC: Duke University Press, 2006); Gilbert Meynier, *L'Algérie révélée: La guerre de 1914–1918 et le premier quart du XXᵉ siècle* (Geneva: Droz, 1981); Driss Maghraoui, "Moroccan Colonial Troops: History, Memory and the Culture of French Colonialism" (PhD diss., University of California, Santa Cruz, 2000);

Mohammed Bekraoui, *Les Marocains dans la Grande Guerre 1914–1919* (Rabat: Publications de la Commission Marocaine d'Histoire Militaire, 2009); Chantal Valensky, *Le soldat occulté: Les Malgaches de l'Armée française, 1884–1920* (Paris: L'Harmattan, 1995); Jacques Razafindranaly, *Les soldats de la grande île: D'une guerre à l'autre, 1895–1918* (Paris: L'Harmattan, 2000); Mireille Favre-Le Van Ho, "Un milieu porteur de modernisation: Travailleurs et tirailleurs vietnamiens en France pendant la première guerre mondiale," 2 vols. (Thèse de doctorat, École nationale des chartes, 1986); Henri Eckert, "Les militaires indochinois au service de la France (1859–1939)," 2 vols. (Thèse de doctorat, L'Université de Paris IV, 1998); and Kimloan Hill, "A Westward Journey, an Enlightened Path: Vietnamese Linh Tho, 1915–30" (PhD diss., University of Oregon, 2001).

9. Tyler Stovall, "The Color Line behind the Lines: Racial Violence in France during the Great War," *American Historical Review* 103, no. 3 (1998): 737–769; John Horne, "Immigrant Workers in France during World War I," *French Historical Studies* 14, no. 1 (1985): 57–88; Bertrand Nogaro and Lucien Weil, *La main d'oeuvre étrangère et coloniale pendant la guerre* (Paris: Presses Universitaires de France, 1926); Li Ma, ed., *Les travailleurs chinois en France pendant la Grande Guerre* (Paris: CNRS Editions, 2012).

10. Xu Guoqi, *Strangers on the Western Front: Chinese Workers in the Great War* (Cambridge, MA: Harvard University Press, 2011); Andrew Tait Jarboe, "Soldiers of Empire: Indian Sepoys in and beyond the Imperial Metropole during the First World War, 1914–1919" (PhD diss., Northeastern University, 2013); George Morton Jack, "The Indian Army on the Western Front, 1914–1915: A Portrait of Collaboration," *War in History* 13, no. 3 (2006): 329–362; David Omissi, ed., *Indian Voices of the Great War: Soldiers' Letters, 1914–18* (New York: St. Martin's Press, 1999); Jeffrey Greenhut, "The Imperial Reserve: The Indian Corps on the Western Front, 1914–15," *Journal of Imperial and Commonwealth History* 12 (1983): 54–73; Gordon Corrigan, *Sepoys in the Trenches: The Indian Corps on the Western Front, 1914–15* (Kent: Spellmount, 1999).

11. Albert Grundling, *Fighting Their Own War: South African Blacks and the First World War* (Johannesburg: Ravan Press, 1987); Brian P. Willan, "The South African Native Labour Contingent, 1916–1918," *Journal of African History* 19, no. 1 (1978): 61–86; Timothy C. Weingard, *Indigenous Peoples of the British Dominions and the First World War* (Cambridge: Cambridge University Press, 2012); Timothy C. Weingard, *For King and Kanata: Canadian Indians and the First World War* (Winnipeg: University of Manitoba Press, 2012).

12. Richard Smith, *Jamaican Volunteers in the First World War: Race, Masculinity and the Development of a National Consciousness* (Manchester: Manchester University Press, 2004); Richard Smith, "World War I and the Permanent West Indian Soldier," in Jarboe and Fogarty, *Empires in World War I*, 304–327; Glenford Howe, *Race, War, and Nationalism: A Social History of West Indians in the First World War* (Kingston, Jamaica: Ian Randle, 2002).

13. Daniel Pick, *Faces of Degeneration: A European Disorder, c. 1848–1918* (Cambridge: Cambridge University Press, 1993); Philipp Blom, *The Vertigo Years: Europe, 1900–1914* (New York: Basic Books, 2010).

14. Gail Braybon, "Women, War, and Work," in *The Oxford Illustrated History of the First World War*, ed. Hew Strachan (Oxford: Oxford University Press, 1998), 149–162.

15. On rural women's war experience, see, for instance, Martha Hanna, *Your Death Would Be Mine: Paul and Henri Pireaud in the Great War* (Cambridge, MA: Harvard University Press, 2006); and Margaret H. Darrow, *French Women and the First World War: War Stories of the Home Front* (Oxford: Berg, 2000).

16. Dagmar Herzog, *Sexuality in Europe: A Twentieth-Century History* (Cambridge: Cambridge University Press, 2011), 1–44.

17. The literature is large; for an overview, see Richard S. Fogarty, "Eugenics in Europe," in: James D. Wright, ed., *International Encyclopedia of Social and Behavioral Sciences*, 2nd ed. (Oxford: Elsevier, 2015), 237–245.

18. Ann Laura Stoler, *Carnal Knowledge and Imperial Power: Race and the Intimate in Colonial Rule* (Berkeley: University of California Press, 2002); Margaret Strobel, "Gender, Sex, and Empire," in *Islamic and European Expansion: The Forging of a Global Order*, ed. Michael Adas (Philadelphia: Temple University Press, 1993), 345–375; Ronald Hyam, *Empire and Sexuality: The British Experience* (Manchester: Manchester University Press, 1990); Kenneth Ballhatchet, *Race, Sex and Class under the Raj: Imperial Attitudes and Policies and Their Critics, 1793–1905* (London: Weidenfeld and Nicolson, 1980).

19. See Stoler, *Carnal Knowledge and Imperial Power*; Mrinalini Sinha, *Colonial Masculinity: The "Manly Englishman" and the "Effeminate Bengali" in the Late Nineteenth Century* (Manchester: Manchester University Press, 1995); Nupur Chaudhuri and Margaret Strobel, eds., *Western Women and Imperialism: Complicity and Resistance* (Bloomington: Indiana University Press, 1992); Julia Clancy-Smith and Frances Gouda, eds., *Domesticating the Empire: Race, Gender, and Family Life in French and Dutch Colonialism* (Charlottesville: University Press of Virginia, 1998)

20. Ann Laura Stoler, *Race and the Education of Desire: Foucault's History of Sexuality and the Colonial Order of Things* (Durham, NC: Duke University Press, 1995). See also Stoler, *Carnal Knowledge and Imperial Power*, chap. 6, "A Colonial Reading of Foucault: Bourgeois Bodies and Racial Selves," 140–161.

21. See Fogarty, *Race and War in France*; Joe Lunn, " 'Les races guerrières': Racial Preconceptions in the French Military about West African Soldiers during the First World War," *Journal of Contemporary History* 34, no. 4 (1999): 517–536; Sinha, *Colonial Masculinity*; Heather Streets Salter, *Martial Races: The Military, Race, and Masculinity in British Imperial Culture, 1857–1914* (Manchester: Manchester University Press, 2004).

22. SHD 7N2121: Rapport sur le recrutement d'une armée indigène, présenté à la Commission Sénatoriale de l'Armée par M. Henry Bérenger, Sénateur, 26 novembre 1915.

23. SHD 16N198: *Notice sur les Sénégalais* (Grand Quartier Général, 19 octobre 1918): 20–21.

24. SHD Bibliotèque, D2s428 (18): Auguste Bonifacy, *Conférences faites aux officiers de la garnison de Hanoi par le chef de bataillon Bonifacy, 2ᵉ Conférence, "Principes qui doivent régler l'organisation des troupes indigènes et leur emploi dans l'attaque et la défense, si on tient compte de leur qualités et de leurs défauts ataviques"* (1909); SHD 7N997: Commission militaire de contrôle postal de Marseille, Rapport mensuel, "Les soldats malgaches en France," juillet–août 1917.

25. For West Africans learning French, see Lucie Cousturier, *Des inconnus chez moi* (Paris: Sirène, 1920). On West Indians helping French women with household chores, see Howe, *Race, War and Nationalism*, 144.

26. SHD 7N997: Contrôle Postal Malgache, Rapport du mois de Septembre 1917.

27. Omissi, *Indian Voices of the Great War*, 123.

28. Omissi, *Indian Voices of the Great War*, 114.

29. Omissi, *Indian Voices of the Great War*, 119.

30. Jeffrey Greenhut, "Race, Sex, and War: The Impact of Race and Sex on Morale and Health Services for the Indian Corps on the Western Front, 1914," *Military Affairs* 45, no. 2 (1981): 73.

31. SHD 7N997: Contrôle Postal Malgache, Rapport du mois de Septembre 1917.

32. Omissi, *Indian Voices of the Great War*, 127.

33. Lunn, *Memoirs of the Maelstrom*, 173. On *marraines de guerre* more generally, see Susan R. Grayzel, "Mothers, Marraines, and Prostitutes: Morale and Morality in First World War France," *International History Review* 19, no. 1 (1997): 66–82.

34. SHD 7N2107: Commission Militaire de Contrôle Postal, Tunis: Rapport sur les opérations de la commission pendant le mois de Janvier 1917.

35. SHD 7N997: Contrôle postal indochinois, août 1917.

36. Favre-Le Van Ho, "Un milieu porteur de modernisation," 541.

37. SHD 7N997: Contrôle postal indochinois, août 1917.

38. Horne, "Immigrant Workers in France during World War I," 57–88; Tyler Stovall, "Colour-Blind France? Colonial Workers during the First World War," *Race and Class* 35, no. 2 (1993): 35–55; Stovall, "Color Line behind the Lines," 737–769.

39. Omissi, *Indian Voices of the Great War*, 303.

40. Tyler Stovall, "Love, Labor, and Race: Colonial Men and White Women in France during the Great War," in *French Civilization and Its Discontents: Nationalism, Colonialism, Race*, ed. Tyler Stovall and Georges Van Den Abbeele (Lanham, MD: Lexington, 2003), 305.

41. Stovall, "Love, Labor, and Race," 306, 311.

42. Cousturier, *Des inconnus chez moi*, 13.

43. Leonard V. Smith, Stéphane Audoin-Rouzeau, and Annette Becker, *France and the Great War, 1914–1918* (Cambridge: Cambridge University Press, 2003), 124.

44. Lucy Bland, "White Women and Men of Colour: Miscegenation Fears in Britain after the Great War," *Gender and History*, 17, no. 1 (2005): 34.

45. Bland, "White Women and Men of Colour," 37.

46. Stovall, "Color Line behind the Lines," 739–740.

47. Stovall, "Color Line behind the Lines," 761.

48. SHD 2107: Commission Militaire de Contrôle Postal, Tunis: Rapport sur les opérations de la commission pendant le mois de Février 1917.

49. Hill, "Westward Journey," 168; Stovall, "Love, Labor, and Race," 308; Fogarty, *Race and War in France*.

50. Stovall, "Love, Labor, and Race," 308.

51. Stovall, "Love, Labor, and Race," 308.

52. Omissi, *Indian Voices of the Great War*, 113.

53. Archives Nationales d'Outre-Mer (ANOM) SLOTFOM I,8: Contrôle Postal Indochinois, Juin 1917.

54. ANOM SLOTFOM I,8: Contrôle Postal Indochinois, Décembre 1918

55. SHD 7N1001: Rapport sur les opérations de la commission militaires de contrôle postal de Tunis, pendant le mois de juin 1917; Rapport . . . octobre 1917.

56. Greenhut, "Race, Sex, and War," 73.

57. Greenhut, "Race, Sex, and War," 72.

58. ANOM SLOTFOM I,8: Contrôle Postal Indochinois, Mars 1918.

59. Hill, "Westward Journey," 166.

60. SHD 7N997: Contrôle Postal Indochinois, Novembre 1917.

61. Benedict Anderson, *Imagined Communities: Reflections on the Origin and Spread of Nationalism*, rev. ed. (New York: Verso, 1991), 149.

62. Stovall, "Love, Labor, and Race," 313. See also Stovall, "Color Line."

63. Stovall, "Colour-Blind France?"

64. Addie W. Hunton and Kathryn M. Johnson, *Two Colored Women with the American Expeditionary Forces* (Brooklyn: Brooklyn Eagle Press, 1920), 182.

65. Quoted in Tyler Stovall, *Paris Noir: African Americans in the City of Light* (New York: Houghton Mifflin, 1996), 18.

66. Hunton and Johnson, *Two Colored Women with the American Expeditionary Forces*, 188.

67. See Stovall, *Paris Noir.*

68. SHD 7N2305: Unattributed, "Note sur l'état d'esprit des tirailleurs tunisiens libérés," no date (probably 1922).

69. ANOM DSM6: Observations de M. Reymond Officier Interprète Principal sur le Rapport de M. Flandin Sénateur relatif à la Conscription des Indigènes de l'Algérie, 28 nov 1917.

70. Stoler, *Carnal Knowledge and Imperial Power*, chap. 4, "Sexual Affronts and Racial Frontiers: Cultural Competence and the Dangers of Métissage," 79–111.

71. Philippa Levine, in "Battle Colors: Race, Sex, and Colonial Soldiery in World War I," *Journal of Women's History* 9, no. 4 (1998): 104–130, has explored some of the ways male policymakers in Britain employed parallel and related strategies to contain both colonial men and European women.

72. On the impulse toward restoring the gender order in the postwar period, see Mary Louise Roberts, *Civilization without Sexes: Reconstructing Gender in Postwar France, 1917–1927* (Chicago: University of Chicago Press, 1994). On changes in the colonial order, see Alice L. Conklin, *A Mission to Civilize: The Republican Idea of Empire in France and West Africa, 1895–1930* (Stanford, CA: Stanford University Press, 1997).

73. See Fogarty, *Race and War in France*, 230–269.

74. The literature on the Black Shame is large, but some recent relevant works include Dick Van Galen Last, *Black Shame: African Soldiers in Europe, 1914–1922* (London: Bloomsbury, 2015); Julia Roos, "Nationalism, Racism, and Propaganda in Early Weimar Germany: Contradictions in the Campaign against the 'Black Horror on the Rhine,'" *German History* 30, no. 1 (2012): 45–74; Julia Roos, "Racist Hysteria to Pragmatic Rapprochement? The German Debate about Rhenish 'Occupation Children,' 1920–1930," *Contemporary European History* 22, no. 2 (2013): 155–180; Jean-Yves le Naour, *La Honte Noire: L'Allemagne et les troupes coloniales françaises, 1914–1945* (Paris: Hachette, 2003).

75. Key examples include Mann, *Native Sons*; Lunn, *Memoirs of the Maelstrom*; Jennifer Anne Boittin, *Colonial Metropolis: The Urban Grounds of Anti-imperialism and Feminism in Interwar Paris* (Lincoln: University of Nebraska Press, 2010).

76. Richard Smith, in his *Jamaican Volunteers in the First World War*, has shown the way forward in one area, exploring the war's effect on masculinity in the Caribbean.

5

Gender and Sexuality

Ana Carden-Coyne and Laura Doan

DURING THE FIRST WORLD WAR, the popular cartoonist Douglas Tempest created a number of witty comics that poked fun at both front-line and home-front life. Published as novelty postcards by Bambord and Company, the series was part of the wider British practice of using self-deprecating humor as a patriotic tool to support the war effort and to enhance military recruitment.

Far from harmless fun, its lighthearted humor masks a deeper social critique of the female commuter alighting from a train after a hard day's work and being met by her "wife." In an age when two women kissing raised few eyebrows, the postcard expresses anxiety about the reversal of gender roles in wartime and attempts to assert a political rhetoric that the mobilization of genteel middle-class women in war work was necessarily temporary.[1]

Juxtaposing two couples in different time frames underscores the unnaturalness not of love between women but of the extension of wartime gender arrangements beyond the duration. The temporariness of the phenomenon of middle-class women in the workplace was crucial in gaining widespread acceptance of women as "part and parcel of our great army," for "without them it would be impossible for progress to be made, but with them . . . victory [could] be assured," as Lord Derby, the undersecretary of state for war, exhorted in 1916.[2] That these kinds of women were expected to give up their jobs with the enemy's surrender is driven home by the caption's exclamation point ("This is another job the men will want back when they come home!"). In this way, the illustration both reassures and warns. Not

This humorous postcard responds to concerns that the mobilization of women into the workforce might be permanent rather than temporary. It also highlights wartime anxieties about women becoming entirely independent of men. "Two Women Kissing," Douglas Tempest postcard, "Witty Comics" Series, No. 548. *Glasgow Women's Library Archive (GB 1534 S-S/1-S/1/31)*

everything in wartime has changed: the stance of the daintily clad feminine figure of the woman who has elected not to work matches her stance in the cartoon bubble. Other things, however, have changed—and after the war the norms of prewar life should return.

In recent times, this image has been reclaimed as representing a playful expression of same-sex affection during the First World War.[3] Imagining a lesbian or queer past is as pleasurable as it is purposeful in satisfying the political demands of communities that yearn to connect with others like them across time. However, for the historian of gender and sexuality, this is an anachronistic projection. We, who live in the present, should be wary of projecting current identities in our own image onto historical actors. This chapter will show that the interplay between sexuality and gender during the First World War is fluid, topsy-turvy, and, above all, discursive. The notion of discourse is not easy, but we argue that getting to grips with the "discursive"—that is, the ways in which knowledge is constituted—is indispensable if we want to comprehend fully how sex is not (and never has been) natural, familiar, or self-evident but historically specific and culturally constructed. Our discussion of how the experience of war transformed the gendered and sexual lives of individuals whose knowledge and understanding of sex was not like our own will be attentive to how sexuality in the modern age gradually came to be constructed as a field of "scientific" knowledge.[4]

To understand the postcard, then, we must appreciate it as a witty investment in gender policing rather than any form of titillation. To do this, we need to understand the context of its own time and place. Current hyperawareness of the sexual makes it difficult not to entertain passing thoughts of lesbianism, but for viewers in the era of the First World War there existed a greater range of interpretive possibilities, some much more subtle than can be recognized today. Writing about how sex was understood and talked about by those who lived and worked in any country during the war calls for coming to terms with the profound differences between us and them, which is why we focus as much on the challenges of historiographic methodology as on historical experience itself. We argue that in the First World War, while there was enormous upheaval of the gender order, our modern and ostensibly scientific knowledge of the sexual was not widespread outside of elite groups. This means that sexual identities familiar to us now (such as "straight" or "gay") were not yet attached to individuals.

Present-day notions of sexual identity and gender roles often hinder our ability to historicize the sexual understanding of women and men during the First World War, either on the home front or the front lines of the combatant nations. In the early twentieth century the sexual lives of most ordinary people were regulated and governed not by a powerful ideological system called "normality" but by norms of morality, class-based standards of respectability, and ideals of self-control. To grapple with the cultural meanings of *their* words and phrases, *their* way of making sense of what is now called "sexuality," entails unpacking the circuitries of diverse modes of sexual regulation as well as prising apart overlaps, a method we demonstrate here. From among the vast terrain of sexual experience during the First World War, we want to highlight problems of historiographic method by focusing on two discrete areas. We explore how the "sexual" was known and not known, particularly in relation to the masculinizing and feminizing effects of war and war work on women and men. We then illustrate how wartime intimacies shaped understandings of sex, looking briefly at medical attitudes toward wounded men and social reconstructions of the male body.

SEXUAL KNOWLEDGE BEFORE SEXUAL IDENTITIES

The earliest major study of the First World War's impact on sexual matters appeared in 1930. Entitled *The Sexual History of the World War* and written "from the viewpoint of sexology"—"with no prejudice [on] behalf of any of the warring groups"—this collaborative venture was led by a German at the forefront of his field, Magnus Hirschfeld, who drew on the expertise of several "world-famous physicians, historians, and scientists."[5] Without question, this classic work still provides a useful starting point for practitioners interested in how the war changed public attitudes toward sexuality and sparked anxieties about the pleasures and dangers of sex across Europe and beyond. Rarely has any other single volume on the subject spanned as wide a geographical area or dealt with as many topics: gender, immorality, friendship, prostitution, venereal disease, promiscuity, homosexuality, transvestism, sadism, sexual violence, and genital injury. Yet such breadth and depth notwithstanding, the book's structuring of sexual knowledge as "modern" inevitably tells us more about the thinking of specialists in 1930 than of ordinary people in 1914–1918: like us, Hirschfeld regards sexuality as a scientific system that classifies individual sexual desires based on case histories assessed as abnormal in relation to an imaginary normal.

First World War historians have questioned the reliability of Hirschfeld's account of "war enthusiasm" but have been less engaged with his work on "sexual behavior." Research into sex has examined front-line prostitution as a reward for soldiers, and conversely the military medical effort to treat venereal disease. Sex and power converge in cases of military rape and the "pleasure" derived from killing. Policing sex on the home front also implicated the state and impacted on citizenship. Scholars have highlighted social issues such as "khaki fever," miscegenation and mixed-race babies, and the return of "impotent ghosts from no man's land" and their sexual reconstruction. But this work has been less concerned with interrogating sex as a system of knowledge and discourse.[6] To be sure, historians are faced with tough historiographic questions about how to locate and interpret archival evidence of sex or discern the salient features of particular systems of sexual knowledge. Recognizing our own knowledge of sexuality as "modern" makes it possible to track how sexual acts or desires in the past shaped culture and, conversely, how cultures were shaped by acts and desires. The task of representing the sexual past, then, entails self-reflexivity and acute attentiveness to the entanglements of sexuality, gender, and the sexed body as integrally related to other ideological structures such as race, nation, empire, and class.

After decades of neglect and marginalization, new historical work of the First World War's transformative effects on sex and sexuality has started to emerge. Hence the timeliness in confronting persistent methodological conundrums, in particular the troubling tendency in assuming—as did Hirschfeld—equivalences between how we organize sexual knowledge in the present compared with its organization in the past. Most historians fall into this trap because of the powerful pull toward present ways of thinking about the sexual. A good example of projecting modern formulations onto the past appears in Craig Gibson's discussion of sexual encounters between British soldiers and French civilians.[7] To contest the "myth" that the British officer class was "rife with homosexuality," he contends that "heterosexuality" was "more prevalent than hitherto thought," even as he questions whether "admiration and innocent flirtation" became overtly sexual. This discussion glides between modern formulations of sexual practices and older understandings of sexuality shaped by morality and identity labels that people at the time would have found baffling.

The crucial point is that the current belief that sexual behavior and inclinations determine one's identity as heterosexual or homosexual has come about as a result of historical forces that took place after the First World War. It would have utterly confounded people who lived during this era. For example, most British officers were accustomed to thinking of their sexual behavior as moral choices informed by familial expectations of chastity and class respectability.[8] In a study of masculinity and German soldiers, Jason Crouthamel argues the war allowed "heterosexual men an alternative universe in which to explore their 'feminine' side in order to be a good comrade without disrupting traditional gender dichotomies."[9] This project significantly enhances historical knowledge of the war's disturbing effects on gender, but, even in Germany, which was at the vanguard of sexology, it is unclear if the common German soldier was aware of the research that diagnosed sexual activities as pathological or healthy. In a further example of presentism, Katie Holmes explored the erotic tensions between Australian military patients and female nurses, alluding to the cultural values of a pre-sexological age that demanded sexual ignorance, as evident in the women's reluctance to construct "themselves as sexual subjects" and avoid remarks about the "sexuality of their patients." At the same time, Holmes specifies her main concern as relating to "heterosexual relationships."[10] The assumption here is that people during the war understood themselves as heterosexual when this identity did not exist. Respectability and propriety, underpinned by the boundaries between the classes, were the codes that most affected ordinary people's sexual behavior, before the "science of sexology" was influential. That is not to say people in wartime did not take risks or break those boundaries. Though we regard this body of scholarship as tremendously valuable, these examples show how easy it is in the early twenty-first century to shift from one discursive frame to another. Indeed, there are analytical risks in glossing over profound differences between a modern system that fixes sexual practices as binary identities (homosexual and heterosexual) and an older one associating sexual ignorance with respectability.

These slippages might—initially—look trivial, but we must not forget the values ascribed to sexual knowledge were sometimes radically opposed. For instance, awareness of the most basic facts of life might have tainted the character of a genteel spinster while being empowering for a newlywed couple guided by marital literature. This is why we insist that referring to women or men as heterosexual or homosexual is not merely a matter of terminology; it is an anachronistic projection of present identities onto past agents. Crucially, these concepts obscure the values, beliefs, and norms of the contradictory and yet entwined character of sex and gender operating during the First World War. There is scant evidence in personal papers, correspondence, official reports, and the print media that points to the habit of naming or self-naming the sexual subject. Neither physical acts nor psychosexual feelings constituted a way of knowing one's sexual identity as fixed.

The exception is the discussion of sexuality among a handful of individuals who were engaged with sexology and psychology, such as members of an early sexual emancipation organization called the Wissenschaftlich humanitäres Komitee (Scientific-Humanitarian Committee, founded in 1897) or the British Society for the Study of Sex Psychology (1913). That these elite organizations were conducting quasi-scientific investigations with experimental hypotheses underscores the fact that there was no secure knowledge about different-sex or same-sex desire at this point. Moreover, ordinary people were not seeking to find out who they were through their sexual practice, and there were no available sexual identities around which to shape one's selfhood. In short, between 1914 and 1918, it was not possible to think of people as "straight" or heterosexual. Such identities did not exist. No one was "gay," "trans," or homosexual (not even in buggery trials), and few women identified as lesbian apart from the "sapphic" fashioning of closed progressive or artistic circles.[11] Same-sex desire existed across a wide spectrum and was mediated by a range of acceptable and unacceptable behaviors, with different class and cultural codes that are not easy to read from the distance of the present.

Hence, there is a need to critically differentiate between understandings of sex available to most people and those of a tiny educated elite composed of feminists, bohemians, intellectuals, artists, writers, and social reformers. Modern sexual knowledge was remote among ordinary people, which is why so many men (and women), were often mystified by their own bodies and desires, and those of their partners, as Lesley Hall has shown in the letters written to Marie Stopes for sexual advice. Though she became famous for the publication of *Married Love* (1918), Stopes herself professed to have been ignorant about how to consummate her own marriage.[12] Furthermore, the upheaval of the First World War in which men's bodies and minds were severely affected by what they had been through may well have exacerbated their anxieties when returning to the domestic realm. Wartime rates of venereal disease among troops might suggest either ignorance or indulgence, but rising postwar divorce rates across Europe revealed wider difficulties with the return to intimate life.[13]

Ordinary people's sexual understanding was not informed by the research that sought to "modernize" sexual knowledge, a project forged in the middle to late nineteenth century by sexologists such as Richard von Krafft-Ebing and Havelock Ellis and expanded in the early twentieth century by sex reformers and sex radicals such as Magnus Hirschfeld and Edward Carpenter.[14] However, these new "scientific" modes of sexual knowledge disseminated unevenly and at a different pace, depending on the country—not in treatises or learned journals but in newspapers, magazines, books of popular sexology, marital advice literature, and sex education. As a consequence, it is misleading to assume there was anything like a shared public understanding of sexuality as a system of categories of identity shaped by prevailing ideals of masculinity and femininity. Indeed, recent scholarly interventions in lesbian history argue that, outside the sapphic elites, same-sex desire between women was only hinted at in the 1930s working-class popular press and that it was not until the Second World War that more coherent sexual identities began to emerge.[15]

Therefore, moving uncritically between concepts of sex and sexuality makes it more—not less—difficult to offer historical explanations of erotic practices, attitudes, values, and beliefs of competing systems. This difficulty arises because the logic of older forms of morality and social regulation linger as new ones evolve. In a document produced in the early 1940s, a medical officer gives advice on how to deal with the problem of lesbianism, which references the latest thinking on "homosexual impulses" but also innocence and evil, natural and unnatural desires.[16] Examining the representation of the "masculine woman" in the First World War is a useful case to demonstrate the flexible and unstable sex-gender system under wartime conditions.

MASCULINE WOMEN AND THE "TOPSY-TURVY" GENDER SYSTEM

Wartime manifestations of "muscular femininity" were seldom associated with sexual abnormality, though social historians have frequently misjudged the link. Instead, this was a period in which the "Amazon" female body took up war work; this "topsy-turvy" inversion of gender roles was associated with patriotism.[17] The British press frequently exaggerated the number of women who responded to the nation's call ("quite half the feminine world") and cited the "cult of physical exercise" as the reason for their overwhelming response to the war effort.[18] Sport and outdoor activities were thought to have given British women an edge over their counterparts in France or Germany: "For all their capacity, Frenchwomen do not like doing men's work. . . . A masculine woman in France is as rare as a woman who is without something of masculine intelligence."[19] On the other hand, the British press thought that German women were ill-equipped to contribute to the war effort because their families forbade "their daughters playing tennis," regarding it as "indecent."[20] This was pure propaganda, as there was a strong tradition of feminist "life reform" and female physical culture in Germany.[21]

Occasionally, the Amazonian appearance and strength welcomed by the British press in their own women did not extend to women of other nations. For example, an article on the Russian Women's Battalion of Death described a cross-class unit of women who had shaved their heads and overthrown "every conviction and forgotten everything" they had "been taught" about how to be women.[22] While the sight of uniformed British women clearly captivated the interest of the viewing public at home and abroad, there is little evidence that "people drew links, either consciously or unconsciously, between displays of militarism and masculine women, feminism, and lesbianism."[23] Stretching the boundaries of acceptable gender roles and attributes was as much about nation and class as gender and sexuality—but even the well-educated and well-traveled had limited access to the information about sex that we take for granted now. This is evident in a letter from a former officer in the First Aid Women's Yeomanry to Marie Stopes: "I imagine I was singularly innocent and clean-minded. . . . I did not even dimly grasp things said in front of me."[24] This is not to suggest that all men and women were singularly ignorant; in both Britain and the United States, the vaudevillian tradition of bawdy humor could provoke calls for moral policing of the working classes.[25] This mass-culture genre would be trans-ferred to the military setting in the First World War, with official approval.

Modern sexual knowledge secured power and authority in the social and medi-cal spheres by casting older perceptions and systems as ignorant and unscientific. However, sexual knowledge was constructed differently through marriage and class-based understandings of respectability, honor, intimacy, friendship, romance, virginity, chastity, and courtship. Depending on the constraints and privileges of gender, class, education, and religion, sex talk in wartime brimmed with informa-tion and misinformation, suggestion and hearsay. Front-line exchanges about sex were as likely to convey useful practical advice as anecdotes and gossip. In the mili-tary there was an accepted culture of salacious allusion, cross-dressing entertain-ment, and gallows humor that drew on sexual stereotypes and even jokes about sadomasochistic fantasies.[26] From the vantage point of the historian of sexuality and war, battlefields, military hospitals, and munitions factories were sites in which multiple knowledge practices collided. Such spaces brought together people who possessed different understandings of the sexual, conditioned by their upbringing in cities, towns, and villages and by the cultural frameworks provided by class, reli-gion, and ethnicity.

Between 1914 and 1918, Dr. Letitia Fairfield, a medical inspector for the Women's Royal Air Force (WRAF), would have had ample opportunity to observe the irregu-lar sexual relations between women, but there is nothing in the historical record to suggest she remarked on such behavior. In 1917, she joined the army and served in the Queen Mary's Army Auxiliary Corps, and by 1918 she had transferred to the WRAF. However, it was not until 1943 that Dr. Fairfield, writing a report advising fellow officers on how to deal with this "Special Problem," was able to name these women's relationships as homosexual and even then warned against mistaking "close friendships" as perverted.[27] Therefore, historical investigation of sexuality in war-time entails acknowledging the complex history of defining and structuring sexual knowledge—formulating sexuality into a system and creating identities based upon that system—while developing the analytical skills to make sense of the strange, often incongruous past. This sensitivity is particularly required in the context of total war, when extra demands were placed on society with the expediency of the militarized state, which reinforced certain norms while tolerating a wide range of transgressions.

WOUNDED MEN AND INTIMACY IN WAR HOSPITALS

During the First World War, the extreme maiming of men's bodies and minds funda-mentally challenged military masculinity. Medicine's gendered framework shaped

both the diagnosis and the treatment of physical and mental wounds. Blind, muti-
lated, crippled, and hysterical men, for instance, were often feminized and infan-
tilized. Rehabilitation aimed at transforming men from this abject state to one of
masculine fitness and, therefore, military purpose. The military hospital often had
a coercive atmosphere, as men were pressed to heal quickly and return to the front.
The wounded might internalize the medical view and see themselves as weak and
fragile. Yet their visceral experience of pain and wounding—and the constant prospect of death—also intensified intimacies and sexualized relations that stretched
the boundaries of respectability. The mutilating capacity of industrial warfare made
the ordinary codes of masculinity much more fallible than in civilian life. Female
surgeons disrupted gender norms in war hospitals, where these contradictions were
especially visible. Hospitals operated as both homosocial (soldiers sharing the ward
culture) and heterosocial environments, given the presence of nurses, doctors, orderlies, chaplains, patients, and visitors.

Emotional friendships between wounded men thus took on a greater sense of
urgency when pain was witnessed and death seemed inevitable. Such bonds could
even resemble romantic love. Liddell Hart described how men "lived in such intimacy"; friendship "redeemed" the "sordidness and stupidity of the war."[28] Santanu
Das has described the trope of "the dying kiss" in literature of the period, and in the
intimate, claustrophobic trenches.[29] Recovering from wounds in hospital also created spaces for intimacy. Though the military authorities oversaw the rules of conduct in hospitals, intimate bonds nevertheless developed between people. Patients
looked to each other when their bodies were incapacitated or when they were suffering. One patient poet observed "how fate has formed us together . . . into a regiment of pain," eliding the collective identity of the regiment with that of shared
suffering.[30] Similarly, a Welsh patient with a "fine tenor voice" went "from bed to
bed" singing quietly to each of the moaning, restless patients until they were lulled
to sleep.[31] Nurses could refer to close male friends as "couples." Photographs showed
men holding hands or in bed together, and some men suffered sympathetic pains.[32]
Tenderness was experienced alongside pain. Intimacy among men was thus heightened by their shared fate of front-line redeployment.

Entertainments thus had an important role to play in alleviating the strain of
war and diverting attention from the suffering. Cross-dressing plays were strong
components of hospital and wartime theater. Female and male impersonation was
a theatrical convention that drew in audiences from all classes in Britain, from
university reviews to vaudeville. Vesta Tilley (the stage name of Matilda Alice
Powles) transformed her prewar dandy character into a British Tommy during the
war, performing for the wounded and in recruitment drives. Cross-dressing was
not seen as socially transgressive. Front-line "concert parties" maintained gender

and class hierarchies, though merging homosocial and homoerotic arenas.[33] In Russian POW camps, where men experienced the humiliation and brutality of captivity, drag performances maintained gendered and political hierarchies, while also sanctioning certain homoerotic desires through "the cult of the female impersonator."[34] Similar to cross-dressing performances, the fictional feminized figure of "La Poilue" (a woman disguised as a soldier, or poilu) was an icon of French popular literature. Devised by a female journalist, "La Poilue" was a character used to uphold traditional gendered codes; her courage and virtue were designed to shame men or spur them on to fight.[35] Nevertheless, women all over Europe at this time yearned to be militarized in various ways, whether as French aviatrixes and nurses, or in wearing paramilitary uniforms, which British women associated with patriotism, or serving in Serbian and Russian combat units.[36] In 1920s Poland, photographic postcards were circulated showing women posing as soldiers, embracing and marrying their brides. Inscriptions on these cards were often ambiguous.

One inscription reads: "My father left a legacy for me. To protect my Homeland, my sweet little girl. I can't take you with me, my dear. So stay at home, with God."[37] This verse suggests the humor of a woman replacing a soldier in the marital bed, and thus saying his lines in the poem. But it also takes a somber tone of a folk poem, where the departing male lover cannot take his sweetheart to the front, and that while he must defend the fatherland, she must stay in the village, instructed to remain with God, suggesting female purity and loyalty. Still further, the postcard may also relate to the theatricalization of women disguised as soldiers in the Polish army and yet the reinforcement of the traditional order of the feminine home front and masculine front line.

The complexity of this history and visual culture is thus not as easy to read as we might assume. To be sure, British imperial hospitals imported cross-dressing entertainments into the wards, involving nurses, orderlies, doctors, and patients, such as Australia's "Yellow Dandies" or the British troupe the "Queries," starring A. J. Smith and John Plumridge from the Field Ambulance service. Male actors were expected to be "pretty" and thus convincing, and to be pleasurable for both male and female audiences. But, as Captain Harland of the Royal Army Medical Corps noted, when men "hadn't seen a girl of any sort for months, these shows went like hot cakes."[38]

Gender play in these performances mirrored the gender and class inversion perceived in hospital life and in wounding itself, such as with the feminization of bedridden patients, by wearing the costume of "hospital blues" and dressing gowns, and in the masculinization of nurses as they exerted a degree of power over men's frail bodies. At Beaufort War Hospital, Australian patients even staged a mock wedding

Mam ja po ojcu spuściznę,
Żebym dziewczę, bronił ojczyzny
Z tobą dziewczyno,
        pojechać nie mogę.
Zostań więc w domu z Bogiem

This Polish postcard from the 1920s or 1930s depicts a women soldier romancing her sweetheart. It is captioned, "My father left a legacy for me / To protect my Homeland, my sweet little girl / I can't take you with me, my dear / So stay at home, with God." Images that militarized women used humor and innuendo to comment on wartime gender roles across Europe. *Courtesy of the National Library of Poland*

This patriotic postcard, labeled "Soldier and Bride," shows two women, one in male soldier attire and one in bridal wear, posing for the camera as if preparing for a wedding photo. Gender-bending images were a feature of wartime and postwar popular culture in every nation at war. *Courtesy of the National Library of Poland*

The cross-dressing men on this British postcard remind viewers of the all-male wartime communities of the front and the prisoner of war camps. Many hospital entertainments employed female impersonators, such as this depiction of A. J. Smith and John H. Plumridge in a concert party in 1916, in theatrical plays that parodied gender roles and sexual propriety. *The RAMC Muniment Collection in the care of the Wellcome Library, Wellcome Images*

ceremony—with male patients playing the bride, bridesmaids, mother, and little sister. The ceremony was reported as beginning with the tune "When There Isn't a Girl About," sung by "a large gathering (mostly military)." The (impersonating) "Reverend" "exhorted the couple . . . to 'behave themselves.'"[39] In suffering and recovering from wounds together, men found a little joy in the sex-gender playfulness of the hospital community.

Nevertheless, intimacy between men could also spill over into violence, especially when alcohol intensified emotions and sexual frustrations. Field Ambulance sergeant W. R. Bland recalled an incident with his friend Archie, who got drunk and "started fawning all over me as I lay in my blanket." Bland was "beside myself with rage," resulting in a fight. After calming down, Archie "squeezed my arm" apologizing; then "tears sprang to my eyes as I gripped his hand and he moved silently to his bed."[40] Bland retells the incident with mixed emotions of anger and compassion. Officers also transgressed the codes of conduct. One medical officer found the second lieutenant, having drunk a whole bottle of whiskey, "lying prone and naked on the ground whilst a fellow officer was sucking his buttock." After "dragging the attendant from his prey, I pronounced there was no sign of a [scorpion] wound," the excuse apparently given for the misconduct.[41] No punitive action was taken; the military was mostly pragmatic about disciplinary matters.

War hospitals not only provided spaces for intimacy between men but were also places where men and women shared temporary romances and sometimes found love and marriage. Separation from partners heightened frustrations and raised the prospect of infidelity. Dr. Eric Dark was incensed that his senior colleague was writing to his wife while arranging liaisons with three other women. He ensured the "lecherous, slimy bastard" was found out. Yet Dark also expressed his own sexual frustration—and restraint—in a letter to his wife: "I'm sweating on leave, and when I get home the only scenery you'll have to look at will be the ceiling."[42] Affairs were part and parcel of hospital gossip, but when respectable behavior was stretched too far, complex emotions were aroused.

A wide spectrum of liaisons, fantasies, and longer relationships between men and women effectively sexualized the tight but temporary community of the hospital. Popular stereotypes highlighted the coexistence of suffering and desire. The amorous patient coming around from an anesthetic was one popular image; he demanded kisses from nurses and confused them with his wife. Slurring his speech, patient Jones insisted, "Gimme kish, Betty . . . . Gimme hand. I want hold handsh"—to which she joked, the patient was "making violent love to me."[43] "Ward scandals" poked fun at bold flirtations. Though the authorities disciplined the women of the Voluntary Aid Detachment (VAD), who assisted nurses in hospitals among other duties, the prospect of romance was a motivation for some, as Henriette Donner argues. Affections between men and women could occur despite the rules of rank and class, and thus social propriety. Patients wrote in the girls' autograph albums with undisguised pleasure.[44] To be sure, the husband-hunting VAD was a comical figure accused of making "goo-goo eyes" at the wounded regulars, or "reggies."

However, historians have not recognized that it was not only VADs who married their patients; nurses also fell in love, till after the war to marry while others left the service. At Crescent Hospital in Croyden, trained nurse May Baker met and married patient R. Derry.[45] Sergeant A. Richards of the Lancashire Fusiliers married Dora Coombes, who had nursed him through an above-knee amputation at the Princess Christian Soldiers' and Sailors' Home, Woking. This is significant, as there was anxiety at the time regarding the marriage and employment prospects of disabled soldiers.[46] Nevertheless, nurses who married were required to leave the British and imperial services.[47] Secrecy thus heightened desires and emotions.

Recovering from serious wounds at Leeds Military Hospital, Private Charles Richmond Dobbs fell in love with Sister Ethel Helena Foster. In 1916, she performed in one of the hospital's cross-dressing theater shows. After Charles had been sent back to the front, Ethel sent him a studio-shop photograph of herself dressed as a male character, Bill, posing with (presumably) a VAD or nurse, sitting on her lap. Ethel signed the card as "Bill" on the photo side, and "Lovingly yours, Ethel. Xmas 1916," on the reverse.

Ethel's personal archive also contained a script for a remarkably risqué play in which a childless couple mistakes a professional baby photographer for a "government agent" from the Ministry of Births, sent to "assist" in the siring of children. The unlikely plot contains innuendos about group sex and about public sex in Selfridges department store and in St James's Park, with squirrels "nibbling my equipment." Charles and Ethel's romance was sparked in an atmosphere in which a cross-dressing hospital play was entirely normal. After the war, they married, and she continued to look after him as he suffered from years of chronic pain from his wounds.[48]

Intimacy inside the wards contrasted with the social expectation that the wounded should recover quickly and reclaim their masculinity. Conversely, the public could idealize and sexualize its wounded heroes. "Khaki fever" became "hospital blue" fever, as British and Dominion patients mingled with local women. Hospitals warned patients against venereal disease, and the trade in visitor passes led Wandsworth hospital commanding officer Colonel Porter to restrict "*promiscuous visiting*" by young women.[49]

This wartime British comic, entitled "Ward Sister Detecting V.A.D. handing goo-goo eyes to a wounded Reggies," depicts Voluntary Aid Detachment nurses' aides, who were working in a hospital. The comic pokes fun at the popular notion that these middle-class aides mostly flirted with soldiers rather than nursing them and that such behavior scandalized professional nurses. *Pvt. Stephen Baghot de la Bere, "An Army in Training," Third London Hospital Gazette, February 1916. The RAMC Muniment Collection in the care of the Wellcome Library, Wellcome Images*

A British photographic postcard sent from a nurse (Ethel Helena Foster) to her soldier sweetheart reminds him of her role as a cross-dressing soldier in a hospital theatrical production while he was recovering from his wounds. In the photo she poses as her vaudeville character "Bill" with another woman perched on her lap, suggesting the complexity of wartime romance, fantasy, and sexual identities. *Courtesy of Maurice and Rebecca Dobbs*

Recovering patients were treated as heroes by local people and frequently were invited on outings, some of which led to romantic adventures. Sergeant Archibald Barwick, an Australian patient at a hospital in Birmingham, went to the park with a local girl and described his new experiences with women:

> I done a bit of spooning practicing of course for the time when the right girl comes along. I have been very bashful and shy in the past you know so I am rapidly making up leeway. I only wished I had started before. I can see what a good time I have missed. We took a good few snaps. Some of them should be *quite interesting*, though I wouldn't want Aunties to see them.[50]

Sexual opportunity was so intrinsic to the experience of wounding that it was difficult to ignore the constant female attention. But flirtation was also a source of anxiety. Developing a crush on his nurse was emotionally painful at first: "Oh these English girls, what peace disturbers they are and bad for the heart." Soon, though, Barwick met another girl, confessing: "I can't get her out of my mind."[51] His diary suggests that the hospital created a space in which boundaries of morality and sexuality were stretched.

Mindful of its public image, the army emphasized in its official communications that relationships between patients and nurses were asexual and familial, likening them to brothers and sisters. However, notions of sexual propriety, just like the expectations of masculine stoicism, could shift when men experienced intense physical and psychological pain. Men also found moments of deep emotion and physical intimacy with one another. Nevertheless, the military could also be quite pragmatic and inconsistent in its approach to discipline. Above all, the war brought a huge range of women and men from all walks of life and cultures together under the hospital roof. They lived and worked in an intense emotional and professional environment. The war and wounding shaped men's and women's experiences of gender and sexuality in ways that may or may not have been new to them.

WHERE DO WE GO FROM HERE?

The First World War presented new working and social opportunities for some classes of women and men. The extent to which it changed individual lives and entire societies has been heavily debated, especially whether its impact was short-lived or fundamentally shaped the twenty-first century. To be sure, the war is an important site in which to study the connections and disconnections between gender roles and categories and sexual behavior—but not, as commentators often assert, because of the powerful effect of war in destabilizing and loosening social restrictions governing social, cultural, or moral norms. Rather, the disturbances of war—for civilians and combatants alike—made *more visible* the intrinsically mutable and unfixed character of gender and sexuality. This paradox is best discerned by surveying trends in historiographic work that foreground these analytical categories.

One possible direction for future work is to focus on the construction of the normal, a line of inquiry that invites scrutiny of concepts such as "heterosexual" in the context of the First World War. To illuminate the peculiar discursive nature of this sexual category, it is important to work out its entanglements with ideas of what is natural, instinctive, or even morally righteous. Each of these regulatory systems represents norms that are different from the modern construct of heterosexuality. Reading through hundreds of letters sent to Marie Stopes, the author of *Married Love* (1918), confirms that sexual relations between women and men were uncertain and difficult. Unlike sexological materials that were off limits to ordinary readers, Stopes's marital advice was directed to the "great majority" and stressed the "essential joyousness of sexual union."[52] Her skillful blend of "sober physical and psychological fact with the romance and beauty of love" struck a chord for military men who had endured long absences from their wives. A captain serving in Italy commented that *Married Love* had come "just when it is most required" and would "be read by thousands of men in a similar position to mine": "The strain and hard work of this war has not tended to strengthen one's sexual powers."[53]

Importantly, Stopes was able to move with ease between ideas central to biology, morality, and the new "science" of sexology. These theories helped her to craft a vision of the "normal" woman and man, their healthy sexual desires and behavior, and thus also to define what was "abnormal." Though she never uses the term "heterosexuality," the concept of the normal appears forty-seven times in her landmark and influential text. By associating normality with male-female intercourse, Stopes aimed to legitimize women's desire for sexual happiness and increase their sexual knowledge. This logic may have helped to create a new sexual being that was later transformed into a self-conscious "heterosexual" identity.

Therefore, doing historical work on sex and sexuality is not simple because it requires us to become attuned to listening to what people said as well as what they could *not* say. Future work will need to grapple with how to read the silences of cultural anxieties and fears. Here we find guidance in the work of Foucault, who suggests that when people in the past were silent about sexuality, whether it was by oppressive social forces or self-censorship, silence functioned within wider frameworks of power and class.[54] We would add to this the specific historical contexts in which gendered codes of masculinity and femininity operate. As historians, we must continue to steer through the entanglements of the prewar, wartime, and postwar periods of change and continuity in knowledge, behavior, and cultural expression—and to understand them on their own historical terms.

NOTES

1. In a similar comic by Tempest, "Girls Are Doing *All* the Fellows' Jobs Now!" (Comic Series 49), two middle-class women are kissing, but it is not particularly passionate or romantic as seen in similar cards featuring a man and woman, and could even be perceived as a genteel greeting.

2. This 1916 statement is **quoted** in Helen Fraser, *Women and War Work* (New York: Shaw, 1918), 124.

3. Modern websites claim these images for a different use as with the example of http://outhistory.org/exhibits/show/postcards/item/203.

4. This methodological framework is discussed at length in Michel Foucault, *The History of Sexuality*, vol. 1, *An Introduction* (London: Penguin, 1976). For an excellent introduction to understanding Foucault's discussion of discourse, see Lisa Downing, *The Cambridge Introduction to Michel Foucault* (Cambridge: Cambridge University Press, 2008), esp. 86–96.

5. Magnus Hirschfeld, *The Sexual History of the World War* (Honolulu: University Press of the Pacific, 2006), 275, vii, v. Hirschfeld's work was first published widely in the 1930s. According to the *Oxford English Dictionary*, "sexology" is the "scientific study of sex and the relations between the sexes"; see *Oxford English Dictionary Online*.

6. Susan Grayzel, "Liberating Women? Examining Gender, Morality, and Sexuality in First World War Britain and France," in *Evidence, History and the Great War: Historians and the Impact of 1914–18*, ed. Gail Braybon (New York: Berghahn, 2003), 113–134, esp. 115; Mark Harrison, "The British Army and the Problem of Venereal Disease in France and Egypt during the First World War," *Medical History* 39, no. 2 (1995): 133–158; Lutz Sauerteig, "Sex, Medicine and Morality during the First World War," in *War, Medicine and Modernity*, ed. Roger Cooter, Mark Harrison, and Steve Sturdy (Stroud: Sutton, 1998), 167–188; Ruth Harris, "The 'Child of the Barbarian': Rape, Race and Nationalism in France during the First World War," *Past and Present*, no. 141 (1993): 170–206; Nicoletta Gullace, "Sexual Violence and Family Honor: British Propaganda and International Law during the First World War," *American Historical Review* 102, no. 3 (1997): 714–747; Joanna Bourke. *An Intimate History of Killing: Face-to-Face Killing in 20th-Century Warfare* (New York: Basic Books, 1999); Philippa Levine, " 'Walking the Streets in a Way No Decent Woman Should': Women Police in World War I," *Journal of Modern History* 66, no. 1 (1994): 34–78; Judith Smart, "Sex, the State, and the 'Scarlet Scourge': Gender, Citizenship and Venereal Diseases Regulation in Australia during the Great War," *Women's History Review* 7, no. 1 (1998): 5–36; Angela Woollacott, " 'Khaki Fever' and Its Control: Gender, Class, Age and Sexual Morality on the British Home Front in the First World War," *Journal of Contemporary History* 29 (1994): 325–347; Lucy Bland, "White Women and Men of Colour: Miscegenation Fears in Britain after the Great War," *Gender and History* 17, no. 1 (2005): 29–61; Lesley Hall, "Impotent Ghosts from No Man's Land: Flappers' Boyfriends or Cryptopatriarchs? Men, Sex and Social Change in 1920s Britain," *Social History* 21, no. 1 (1996): 54–70; Ana Carden-Coyne, *Reconstructing the Body: Classicism, Modernism and the First World War* (Oxford: Oxford University Press, 2009), esp. chap. 4. A short critique of Hirschfeld appears in Gail Braybon,

"Winners or Losers: Women's Symbolic Role in the War Story," in *Evidence, History and the Great War: Historians and the Impact of 1914–18*, ed. Gail Braybon (New York: Berghahn, 2003), 101; for a discussion of Hirschfeld's misguided discussion of war enthusiasm, see Eric J. Leed, *No Man's Land: Combat and Identity in World War I* (Cambridge: Cambridge University Press, 1979), 40. According to the Yale historian Joanne Meyerowitz, the history of sexuality—a field that began to evolve in the mid-1970s—continues to be perceived by historians as "fairly new and somewhat marginal"; see Joanne J. Meyerowitz, "Transnational Sex and U.S. History," *American Historical Review* 114, no. 5 (2009): 1276.

7. Craig Gibson, *Behind the Front: British Soldiers and French Civilians, 1914–1918* (Cambridge: Cambridge University Press, 2014), 313.

8. Laura Doan, "Sex Education and the Great War Soldier: A Queer Analysis of the Practice of 'Hetero' Sex," *Journal of British Studies* 51, no. 3 (2012): 641–663.

9. Jason Crouthamel, *An Intimate History of the Front: Masculinity, Sexuality, and German Soldiers in the First World War* (Basingstoke: Palgrave Macmillan, 2014), 8.

10. Katie Holmes, "Day Mothers and Night Sisters: World War I Nurses and Sexuality," in *Gender and War: Australians at War in the Twentieth Century*, ed. Joy Damousi and Marilyn Lake (Cambridge: Cambridge University Press, 1995), 43–59, esp. 45, 57.

11. Laura Doan and Jane Garrity, eds., *Sapphic Modernities: Sexuality, Women and National Culture* (New York: Palgrave Macmillan, 2006).

12. Lesley Hall, *Hidden Anxieties: Male Sexuality, 1900–1950* (Cambridge: Polity Press, 1991).

13. Doan, "Sex Education and the Great War Soldier."

14. For an excellent introduction to sexual science, see Chris Waters, "Sexology," in *Palgrave Advances in the Modern History of Sexuality*, ed. H. G. Cocks and Matt Houlbrook (Basingstoke: Palgrave Macmillan, 2006), 41–63.

15. But there are caveats here, too. As Michaela Hampf writes, few women in the Second World War American Women's Army Corps "used the word lesbian or identified with lesbian culture as we understand it today" (*Release a Man for Combat: The Women's Army Corps during World War II* [Cologne: Böhlau, 2010], 239). For other examples, see Laura Doan, *Disturbing Practices: History, Sexuality, and Women's Experience of Modern War* (Chicago: University of Chicago Press, 2013); Alison Oram, *Her Husband Was a Woman! Women's Gender-Crossing in Modern British Popular Culture* (London: Routledge, 2007); Rebecca Jennings, *A Lesbian History of Britain: Love and Sex between Women since 1500* (Westport, CT: Greenwood Press, 2007).

16. Dr. Letitia Fairfield, "A Special Problem," PH/GEN/3/19, 1943, London Metropolitan Archives.

17. This phrase appeared in *War Budget Illustrated*, September 23, 1915, 173. For an extended critique of historical work on public responses to women's masculine clothing during the First World War, see Laura Doan, "Topsy-Turvydom: Gender, Sexuality, and the Problem of Categorization," in *Disturbing Practices*, 97–133.

18. *Spectator*, June 15, 1918, iv; *Autocar*, May 5, 1917, 463.

19. *The Times*, December 20, 1915, 11.

20. *The Times*, November 6, 1916, 4.

21. See Michael Hau, *The Cult of Health and Beauty in Germany: A Social History, 1890–1930* (Chicago: University of Chicago Press, 2003).

22. *The Times*, July 30, 1917, 7.,

23. Jenny Gould, "Women's Military Services in First World War Britain," in *Behind the Lines: Gender and the Two World Wars*, ed. Margaret Higonnet et al. (New Haven, CT: Yale University Press, 1987), 121.

24. Letter from G.M. to Marie Stopes, May 6, 1926, Papers of Marie Stopes, Add BL 58673, British Library.

25. See Stuart Hylton, *Leisure in Post-war Britain* (Stroud: Amberley, 2013); Mark Whelan, *American Culture in the 1910s* (Edinburgh: Edinburgh University Press, 2010), 52.

26. See Ana Carden-Coyne, *The Politics of Wounds: Military Patients and Medical Power in the First World War* (Oxford: Oxford University Press, 2014).

27. This document is held in the London Metropolitan Archives; see Letitia Fairfield, "A Special Problem," PH/GEN/3/19, 1943. For a substantial entry on this British public health physician, see Fairfield, (Josephine) Letitia Denny (18850–1978), in the *Oxford Dictionary of National Biography*: http://www.oxforddnb.com/index/101054196/Letitia-Fairfield.

28. Sarah Cole, *Modernism, Male Friendship and the First World War* (Cambridge: Cambridge University Press, 2003), 140.

29. Santanu Das, *Touch and Intimacy in First World War Literature* (Cambridge: Cambridge University Press, 2005).

30. "The Sight That Will Rouse a Nation," by a Wounded Soldier, *Cooee*, 1, no. 4, February 20, 1916.

31. May Bradford, *A Hospital Letter-Writer in France* (London: Methuen, 1920), 42.

32. G.Y.P., "Cobbers," *Cooee*, 1, no. 11, September 18, 1916; John Edward Squire, *Medical Hints for the Use of Medical Officers Temporarily Employed with Troops* (Oxford: Oxford War Primers, 1915), 111–113.

33. David A. Boxwell, "The Follies of War: Cross-Dressing and Popular Theater on the British Front," *Modernism/Modernity* 9, no. 1 (2002): 1–20.

34. Alon Rachamimov, "The Disruptive Comforts of Drag: (Trans)Gender Performances among Prisoners of War in Russia, 1914–1920," *American Historical Review* 111, no. 2 (2006): 362–382, esp. 364.

35. Libby Murphy, "Trespassing on the 'Trench-Fighter's Story': (Re)-Imagining the Female Combatant of the First World War," in *Gender and Conflict since 1914: Historical and Interdisciplinary Perspectives*, ed. Ana Carden-Coyne (New York: Palgrave Macmillan, 2012), 55–68.

36. See Margaret Darrow, *French Women and the First World War: War Stories of the Home Front* (Oxford: Berg, 2000); Susan Grayzel, "'The Outward and Visible Sign of Her Patriotism': Women, Uniforms, and National Service during the First World War," *Twentieth Century British History* 8, no. 2 (1997): 145–164; Melissa K. Stockdale, "'My Death for the Motherland Is Happiness': Women, Patriotism, and Soldiering in Russia's Great War, 1914–1917," *American Historical Review* 109, no. 1 (2004): 78–116.

37. See the National Library of Poland collection. Thanks to Agnieszka Leszyńska and Dorota Sajewska at the NLP for this research.

38. Diary of Captain W. C. F. Harland, RAMC (T), 72 Field Ambulance, 24th Division, 14, Royal Army Medical Corps Archives, 1590.

39. W. L. P. F., "Beaufort Hospital Notes," *Cooee*, 11, no. 11, September 18, 1916.

40. W. R. Bland, "Memoir," IWM collection, n.d., Imperial War Museum.

41. The Memoirs of Martin Littlewood, 18, Wellcome Trust Archives, MS5415.

42. Dr. Eric Payten Dark, "Military Memoirs of the First World War (9th Field Ambulance Unit)," State Library of NSW, MLMSS 5049.

43. Malcolm Savage Treacher, "On Coming Round," *Happy Though Wounded*, 74. [it is an article in a hospital gazette—you could have if you want . . . Country Life, London, published on behalf of the 3rd London General Hospital, 1917]

44. Henriette Donner, "Under the Cross: Why V.A.D.s Performed the Filthiest Task in the Dirtiest War: Red Cross Women Volunteers, 1914–1918," *Journal of Social History* 30, no. 3 (1997): 687–704.

45. R. Derry, "One Man's War, 1914–1918," n.d., IWM collection.

46. See Carden-Coyne, *Reconstructing the Body*.

47. Ian Martin, "'When Needs Must'—The Acceptance of Volunteer Aids in British and Australian Military Hospitals in WWI," *Health and Society* 4, no. 1 (2002): 88–98, esp. 90.

48. Thanks to Rebecca Dobbs and Maurice Dobbs for access to the family archive.

49. "Concerning Visitor Passes," *Third London Hospital Gazette*, October 1915, 24; Woollacott, "'Khaki Fever' and Its Control," 325–347.

50. Archibald Barwick, WWI war diary, State Library of NSW, MLMSS 1494/3; emphasis in original.

51. Barwick, WWI war diary.

52. Sec. Lieut. D.A., Cairo, to Marie Stopes, December 31, 1918, PP/MCS/A/15, Papers of Marie Stopes, Wellcome Library for the History of Medicine.

53. Letter from Captain H. to Marie Stopes, November 10, 1918, and Lieut. Col. H.W.A.C., B.E.F., April 15, 1919, Papers of Marie Stopes, Add BL 58670, British Library.

54. Foucault, *History of Sexuality*, vol. 1, *Introduction*, 27.

6

Gender and Age

Tammy M. Proctor

YOUNG MEN GO to war. That central concept pervades most accounts of the war generation. Yet the image of fresh-faced uniformed "boys" marching off to the sound of drums and bugles obscures the complicated mix of young and old, male and female who served in time of war. Male conscripts and volunteers represented a broad range of ages and experiences, sometimes spanning nearly forty years. In nations that required a mandatory draft, men were often called to service in age cohorts or classes. Even in countries that relied on voluntary enlistments, groups of friends joined up together. However, these groups fragmented as the war progressed, with substitution of older and younger men into units that were decimated by wartime casualties. Like men, women also understood and experienced the war differently depending on their age, their marital status, and their location. Young women volunteered for service as auxiliaries, workers, and medical personnel. In occupation zones, whole towns of elderly men and women lived in isolation, and they often had fewer reserves of energy and resources than those in their twenties, for instance. For populations at war, age and gender intertwined to shape lived experience as well as perception of the war.

Although scholarly works do focus on the experiences of children and youth at war, less attention has focused on the broader question of age and the war, and particularly the intersections of gender and age. Indeed, age defined the lives of men at war, men at home, and women in a variety of settings.[1] Too often a mention of age in historical scholarship equates in readers' minds only with the experiences of young people, especially children. While social scientists and researchers in education have studied age as a social construct especially as it relates to the transition from youth to adulthood, historians have developed fewer theoretical models for studying age and its effects on social history.[2] The notion of a war generation is one that has received important attention from scholars, but the Great War generation is framed more by the type of wartime experiences than by the actual age of the participants. Yet a gendered concept of age categories was a significant factor in governmental wartime policies and propaganda. Military officials made determinations about soldiers' placement based on age, while civilian governments wrestled with pensions and payments for soldiers, their children, their wives, and their widows. Different groups within a nation at war responded uniquely to calls for service, so propaganda and war service opportunities for teenage girls and boys differed considerably. Posters aimed at recruiting adult men for war had to address service differently than posters whose purpose was to convince women to conserve food or supplies. Propaganda emphasized qualities that appealed to the gender and age assumptions of the period. For instance, a poster recruiting females for munitions or agriculture work always showed an attractive young woman who looked as if she could change out of her work clothes and attend a soirée.

In multiple ways, age was woven into the fabric of wartime ideology and realities. However, the powerful narrative of war as a young man's game not only hides the gendered nature of modern warfare and its complexities but often erases the generational chasms that existed in the war period. It was never as simple as the trope of old men at the home front pushing their young sons off to war, although this scenario did play out in 1914–1918. An alternate reality can be found in the cases where fathers and sons both served in the war as did mothers and sisters. One way to understand both the lived experience of the war and its popular representation is to examine the ways in which age and generation, particularly of adults, shaped gendered expectations in wartime.

SOLDIER BOYS

Popular descriptions of soldiers often describe "our boys" going off to war, and media depictions of the time linger on the images of young men marching to the fight. Jason Jingoes, a labor battalion recruit from Swaziland, describes his cohort and echoes this image: "We were young, scared and excited, and we got up to some amazing high jinks."[3] This idea of young men going off to a grand adventure emerged as a central theme of wartime recruitment, propaganda, and media coverage. Soldier-poets sang of the waste of a generation of youth as they realized the sacrifice they faced.

In his poem "August 1914" (1916), British soldier Isaac Rosenberg provided such an example by describing his comrades using terms of age and experience: "Iron are our lives, molten right through our youth."[4] In most wartime accounts, there is at least some tacit sense that the men waging war are young, which adds to the pathos of their sacrifice. Propaganda posters reinforced the notion that war is for the young, again emphasizing the loss of youthful vigor in the battlefields of the war.

This sense of young men going off to war was certainly true of the realities of the First World War, but it does not tell the whole story. National statistics suggest that the armies of the 1914–1918 conflict mobilized men of different generations as a norm, not an exception. In the German and Austro-Hungarian armies, large numbers of older men (late thirties on up) found themselves in *Landwehr* or *Landsturm* units assigned not just to battle zones on the Eastern Front but also to occupied countries and to domestic police work within the empires, especially by the end of the war.[5] Other countries gradually expanded their age categories as the war progressed. Australia, for instance, maintained an official minimum age of eighteen, but it raised its upper age for volunteers to forty-five in 1915. Germany's draft cohorts ranged from seventeen years old to forty-five, and by the end of the war Austria was taking volunteers who were in their fifties.[6] As has been demonstrated quite compellingly for the Second World War, a key feature in socialization, decision-making, and camaraderie in militarized units was age.[7] Yet it is difficult to find analysis of statistics breaking down war service by age in each country unless it is a study of demographic trends such as marriage and childbirth or an attempt to calculate casualties.[8]

No historian has yet studied the effect of age and generation on trench life and socialization in the First World War, yet there are rich primary accounts that could be mined for such analysis. In his diaries, Louis Barthas, a French corporal and barrel maker who was thirty-five years old when he was called up in 1914, talked of his resentment of the older men in the territorial reserves: "How we envied these grandfathers! How we wanted to be their age, with their white hair, to be exempt from attacks."[9] Barthas himself was conscripted into the third-line reserve, but the high rate of French casualties in 1914 meant that by late fall 1914, he had already been moved to active duty, where he remained until 1918. As a mature, married man, Barthas sought out comrades like himself, and in his diary he wrote compellingly about the importance of regional and familial networks in his unit friendships; he was delighted to find a man who had done compulsory military duty with him years earlier. They shared news of their wives and children, but they also reminisced about civilian life before the war, especially politics and work. Barthas built networks in the trenches with men of a similar age, class, and region. As his diary illustrates, an area of future study for scholars might be a closer look at age and masculinity as they shaped trench sociability, connections between home/front, and understandings of war-induced trauma such as shell shock.

A further area that might prove intriguing to study is the issue of how men coped with injury at various life stages, such as what being wounded at age seventeen versus age forty-five meant. In Britain, for instance, a small debate arose in 1918 about the medical inspections conducted for older men versus those for young men by Medical Boards of the Ministry of National Service. The debate centered around the question of whether standards of physical fitness should differ by age and, if so, at what age the standards should change. As the *British Medical Journal* noted in a brief essay, "It would not be possible to establish different systems of grading for men of different ages as no scientific or medical basis could be found." Yet the problem remained—men of eighteen and men of forty-five often had quite different levels of physical fitness and stamina, and medical boards faced a difficult task of determining for older men "the full normal physical fitness to be expected of their age."[10] Added to this concern were the different levels of nutrition and physical fitness based on social class and environmental factors, with the result that local draft boards in each belligerent state struggled to determine what a fit man needed to be able to do, regardless of age.

The generational diversity of men at war would have yielded varied understandings of masculinity, courage, nurturing, and hierarchy among units. Scholars have examined some of these issues, but there is a fruitful opportunity for someone to explore further how gender and age defined men's experience of war and how their war service was perceived at home.[11] At the fronts themselves, the question of how men interacted based on age and generation is likewise an important one. For instance, how did older working-class men interact with younger middle-class soldiers and officers? Did men assume roles in military units based on their age? How did age and generation shape understandings of sexuality and masculinity? Behind the lines, recreation huts run by organizations such as the Salvation Army or the Young Men's Christian Association faced a problem in entertaining men of different backgrounds and ages. When men were home from the front for visits, age played a role as well. Furloughs meant different things to older married men with children than to youngsters just leaving school. Scholarly work on "war neurotics" demonstrates the complexity of notions of comradeship, masculinity, and courage among German men at war, yet age is not a factor that emerges.[12] Did a "war hysteric" of nineteen receive different treatment than one who was forty when the Armistice was signed?

During any war utilizing conscripted troops, one would assume that all able-bodied men would be fighting. For those who did not, how was masculinity defined? Did men of a certain age get a "pass"? Of course, ten-year-old boys or seventy-five-year-old men were not expected to serve as soldiers in 1914, but what of a forty-year-old man? In Vera Brittain's acclaimed war memoir, *Testament of Youth*, she commented on her thirty-six-year-old uncle's sense of shame about spending his war out of uniform and behind a desk in London. In a letter to Brittain, her uncle confided: "I am getting more and more ashamed of my civilian togs . . . and I shrink from meeting or speaking to soldiers or soldiers' relatives, and to take an ordinary walk on a Sunday is abominable. . . . the contemplation of the future if one has to confess never to have fought at all is altogether impossible."[13] Other men tried to join up and faced the problem of being denied for medical reasons. Pacifists and men outside the military age faced pressure at home to explain why they were not at the fronts. Still others were funneled into military desk jobs or labor corps, challenging their masculinity in more subtle ways. Those who were tied to so-called essential occupations such as mining, government work, or transport found themselves explaining that they were working for the war, just not in uniforms in a combat zone.

Occupied zones presented different sorts of challenges for men, who either faced having no army to join or were trapped and unable to join their comrades in arms. In Belgium, many men, especially older males, could not participate militarily without considerable risk and a small chance of a successful escape to neutral territory. Some men sought to prove their patriotism in other ways, through resistance to the occupiers, through espionage, or by refusing work. Still others sought to use the war to create political traction for their vision of the future by collaborating with German occupiers in the creation of pro-Flemish educational institutions and language laws.[14] Another group of men who had lost their livelihoods during war were deported to work in Germany, but an analysis of the ages of these men and the impact on their work and family lives remains to be written.

All-male wartime communities in prisoner of war camps are a good laboratory for studying masculinity and belonging, but here again, the question of age is hidden from sight. In officers' camps, for instance, female impersonators commanded huge audiences at theatrical performances within the camps. Not only did young male officers assume female roles onstage in the camps, but they retained their female personas offstage, attracting fan clubs and providing a missing feminine element in the all-male camp culture.[15] Youth and beauty attracted older male protectors and admirers. In these camp cities, both civilian and military prisoners of war often experienced a sense of disempowerment and loss of masculinity. Therefore, the creation of alternate societies and families in the camps provided comfort and a new sense of identity, and evidence suggests that age determined largely where men might fit into these pseudofamilies behind barbed wire. Information on age differentiation exists in the guides to camp libraries and canteens, which had to cater to different generational tastes as well as to differences in class, rank, language, and education.

While it is not yet well understood in this context, age played a vital role in POW memoirs—older men with established careers and families recounted that they sometimes mentored younger men in the camps, hiring them as apprentices or batmen (personal servants). Age also made these older men more vulnerable to disease and harsh conditions, and cemeteries near former internment and prison camps bear witness to the often disproportionate casualties occurring among older male prisoners. Young men, on the other hand, banded together to form sport associations or clubs. Some flourished in camp as they took starring roles in musical ensembles, acquired education, or formed lifelong friendships. Age constituted an important hierarchy in camps. Older men served as leaders in the camp's social and political life, such as at Ruhleben camp in Germany, where they often became barracks captains. Age also helped determine how men adjusted to life in a prison camp. Henri Pirenne and Paul Fredericq, well-known Belgian historians, were confined to camps as civilians in Germany in 1916 for their resistance to war. Pirenne (aged fifty-four) and Fredericq (aged sixty-six) found the loss of their creature comforts difficult to take. Each wrote frequently to family members and friends to catch up on news and to ask for food, warm clothing, books, and other things. Fredericq noted his weight loss in his diary, and Pirenne longed for his wife and children. At one point in April 1916, after days of maudlin reflections on his lack of contact with home, he rejoiced in his diary that he received a package demonstrating that his wife has not forgotten him.[16] Loneliness, homesickness, and isolation all featured in men's prison diaries and letters, but these seem particularly acute issues for older men.

Pirenne's distress over his separation from home speaks to another aspect of war and masculinity worth mentioning. How did a man who was used to the comforts of family life and to a wife who cared for his needs adjust to war? Life in the trenches must have been different for the young men of eighteen who interacted with mothers but usually did not have wives and largely had no children at home. Twenty-two years old and away from home for the first time, American Walter Arthur Richter asked repeatedly for letters from his mother during his first few weeks in France. However, his homesickness was partly assuaged by the kindness of a French couple who assumed the role of parents (or grandparents) for Richter and his friends. In Richter's letter to his parents in early November 1918, he explained: "I am writing this letter at an old french [sic] couples home. They treat me like a son every time I go there they want to make me some thing [sic] to eat and we drink a bottle of their old wine and it costs me allmost [sic] nothing. I have a hard time to make them take anything. They are very old the woman is about 65 years and the old gent is about 70 years old but they are preaty [sic] spry for their age."[17] These intimate glimpses of homesickness, kindness, nurturing, and familial relationships expose perhaps the biggest area of intersection between age and gender in wartime. These stories also suggest an area of research into the postwar period that would provide new insights.

KHAKI-MAD GIRLS, OLD WOMEN, MOTHERS, SISTERS

As with men, age functions as an extremely important category when considering women's lives during wartime. For women, age played a more significant role in the possibility of conceiving children than for men, and generational views of women were tied less to educational attainment or workplace than to familial status (married, widowed, or single). Married women faced different challenges than single women with the outbreak of war, and of course, mothers expressed an outpouring of grief, pride, and worry with the conscription or enlistment of their sons for the conflict. The war challenged women's roles in serious ways, with the need for female work in agriculture and industry, with the rise in poverty and rates of casual prostitution in areas devastated by war or occupied by foreign armies, and with women's sense of their own war service and its claims on the privileges of citizenship. World War I left approximately 3 million war widows as well, and widowhood too varied according to age.[18] In short, the notion of generation fundamentally shaped understandings of femininity and female roles, both during the war and in its aftermath.

For women, official paid war service often fell to younger females, especially because wartime officials established age categories for this employment. In some cases, age restrictions were advertised up front, as in the case of women hired to work at MI5 (the counterintelligence bureau) in London, with youth being privileged. Most of the 800 or so women hired in MI5 were between aged twenty and thirty; older married women had to possess special skills or experience to qualify.[19] Female auxiliary services, nursing, and other women's war work also included age restrictions in many countries. In one study of US women war workers, the average age of YMCA canteen workers and nurses was around thirty-one to thirty-two. Most of the women recruited were between twenty-four and thirty-nine years old, although younger women joined in 1919 when the age restriction was lowered.[20] Indeed, a majority of the auxiliaries and medical personnel stationed in war zones were women younger than fifty. For instance, American women physicians who served overseas were on average younger than those who worked stateside during World War I.[21]

One of the most celebrated roles for women in the war was that of replacement workers in munitions, transport, and other industrial occupations. Portrayed in propaganda photos as fresh-faced young women who were doing their bit, female workers came from diverse ages and backgrounds, depending on country and skill level. While Britain's wartime industrial workforce trended toward younger, single female workers, in France, many older married women in their thirties and forties worked in war industries.[22] Anxieties about women working in so-called men's jobs also tapped into the question of age and marital status; single young women were widely seen as workers "for the duration," but the question of continuing women's work after the war for widows raised more difficult questions. The redistribution of women's labor from domestic service into factories or agriculture also caused concern among middle- and upper-class households that depended on paid female servants. Women's experiences of war and patriotism changed according to their age, class, and marital status; clearly for some women, war was an opportunity for work and patriotic service, but for others it was a profoundly unsettling experience that challenged their sense of their place in society.

The invisible women in histories of this war are often elderly women, despite the fact that they played a variety of roles in society and contributed to the war effort. Older females were vulnerable to wartime exigencies in different ways than younger women. They served as farmworkers and estate managers at home fronts. For elderly women at home, the war could also provide meaningful service opportunities, often in unpaid voluntary work. Older women of all classes took the lead in such voluntary work, staffing soup kitchens, hosting refugees, knitting and sewing for comfort boxes, visiting the wounded, and running large voluntary agencies. Some of these women left compelling memoirs about their war service, suggesting that war offered a level of personal service and patriotic expression for older women that they could not claim during peacetime. In Richmond, Virginia, elite older women even tried to begin a "Service Legion" for women to parallel the American Legion for men; many older women submitted applications detailing their work fabricating surgical dressings, running canteens for departing soldiers, or working for their local Selective Service Board.[23]

For older women in occupied and front-line zones, war service sometimes acted as an extension of their regular paid occupations or familial duties. They conserved resources and cooked without supplies; they served food in soup kitchens and organized local relief; they worked in the absence of husbands and sons. In Belgium, older women worked as laundresses for the armies and staffed cafes to serve occupation forces. Older women were also the primary people responsible for billeting soldiers. For instance, in her wartime diary, eighty-year-old Virginie Loveling in Ghent (Belgium) describes the strangeness of hosting a young man in her home as a single older woman.[24] Elderly women could also be seen on the roads as refugees. In fact, because of wartime needs for younger men and women as soldiers and laborers, a disproportionate number of older women were refugees. While no study of the ages of those receiving war assistance has been done, older women featured prominently in the group impoverished and displaced by war. In Germany, special attention was paid to the food and fuel needs of sectors of society that were perceived to be weak; older women (and men) and young children were considered to be particularly at risk.[25] A study of old women at war would be a fascinating addition to the literature, and it would fill an important gap in understanding not only the emotional work of war but also the physical work of maintaining households, communities, and societies during wartime.

One area where young women were particularly vulnerable was in active combat zones and occupied regions, where sexual assault and forced prostitution became problems. While detailed accounts and clear numbers are hard to ascertain, recorded episodes during World War I highlight the danger women of all ages, but particularly young women, faced. In Lille, France, German occupying authorities deported roughly 25,000 people for agricultural labor, about one-third of them adolescent girls and young women. Many in this subgroup of Lille deportees were forced to have gynecological examinations, others feared assault, and some appear to have been lured or forced into sexual encounters with their German guards. However, the story often recounted is a highly sensationalized and gendered account that focuses on rape and atrocity, thereby emphasizing the roles young women played as victims in the larger war narrative.[26] Women's sexuality assumed even more significance in the setting of an occupied country, where collaboration was perceived as being highly gendered. This significance was apparent in France, for instance, where young women faced trials for "relations with the enemy" or for infanticide of babies conceived as a result of rape. These trials became gendered media circuses highlighting both the threat to women during wartime and their treachery.[27]

During the war, the protection of female virtue became an important tool for recruiting men to the colors. This role as a symbol of all that was pure and noble in national life required a certain vision of womanhood that not only was inscribed with womanly qualities such as tenderness, loyalty, and innocence but often relied as well on a generational vision of a young woman. The flip side of this vision—the evil or unpatriotic woman—was not coincidentally depicted as young as well. A useful example of this dichotomy was the execution of two middle-aged women, Edith Cavell and Mata Hari. Cavell, a forty-nine-year-old British nurse in Belgium who was shot by the Germans for her role in running an Allied escape network, was most often shown in print and memorials as a young, innocent woman.

In a similar way, Mata Hari, a Dutch-born exotic dancer before the war who was executed by the French for espionage, was usually depicted in her prewar dance routines not as the forty-one-year-old aging courtesan whom she was at her death in 1917.[28] In fact, the International Spy Museum in Washington, DC, used a large photograph of young Mata Hari in a skimpy dance costume as an entrée to its exhibits on women spies when the museum opened.

This widely distributed postcard pictures British nurse Edith Cavell as an innocent victim of German oppression after she was executed for taking an active part in an escape network for Allied soldiers. Cavell was one of the most important Allied propaganda icons of the war and is often shown as an innocent young victim despite being nearly fifty years old in 1915. Laureys, Paris, ca. 1915; artist Georges Carrey. Collection of Tammy Proctor

Women's relationship to war is a difficult story to tell because their roles are so varied and because protection of women is so crucial to recruitment of men to arms. Despite often being treated as a monolithic category, especially in military histories of the First World War, women faced the war in very different ways depending on their maturity, their age, and their generational expectations. This diversity in experience is one deserving of further study by scholars who can take the existing corpus of excellent work on gender in wartime and overlay it with a sensitivity to age and generation.

WAR ORPHANS AND LITTLE CITIZENS

Children left few contemporary accounts of their war experience, but they featured prominently in adult memoirs, newspaper stories, photographs, and propaganda. Despite the notion that war is an adult endeavor, children inhabited all the spaces of war—homes, combat zones, occupied regions, and even some POW camps. Children confronted the violence of this war, from the trauma of armed invasion to the random attacks from aerial bombing to the ravages of diseases such as tuberculosis or typhoid. In addition to the threat of disease, injury, or death, children and youth experienced targeted propaganda and re-education from states. Campaigns to educate young people in appropriate nationalism launched in virtually every belligerent country. In the most extreme cases, regimes attempted to transform young people, especially war orphans, into new kinds of citizens and nationalists. One example of such a policy was the attempted "Turkification" of Armenian war orphans by the Young Turks, which led to very young children being adopted into Muslim families and re-educated.[29]

War and education were deeply intertwined, and schools at all levels were reshaped by war. Universities emptied of men throughout the nations at war, and some institutions shut their doors for the duration of the conflict. The University of Paris saw a drop from 14,000 students to 3,000 during the first year of the war, and by October 1914 Cambridge enrollment was down by 50 percent.[30] For younger schoolchildren, the destruction of their homes and schools as well as heightened work obligations made it difficult for them to attend classes at all in some areas. Many older children took over child care duties for absent fathers and mothers who had taken up paid work. Other states enlisted the work of children in formal ways. The Habsburg Empire devised the Pupils' Volunteer Corps, which became a teen work brigade for use in agriculture, transport, and other necessary occupations. Younger children did their war work at school by knitting, rolling cigarettes, or making bandages.[31] In both Germany and France, children conducted scrap drives, foraged for food, collected money for the war effort, and learned about wartime cooking and conservation.[32] Children and young people often longed to provide war service. They learned about the sacrifices of soldiers and then wanted to do their part to demonstrate patriotism. Youth organizations mobilized members around the notion of war service, and numbers soared. The British Girl Guides, for example, had approximately 10,000 registered members in 1914; by 1920, the number was more than 180,000.[33] One teenage Guide in Britain captured the excitement of war for young people living far from the battles, and her comments help explain the attraction of war service organizations: "One did realize that it *was* War-time—and yet somehow it was rather jolly tearing about and managing everything for oneself. It gave you such a ripping feeling of independence."[34]

Shortages of teachers also exacerbated the problem of effective wartime schooling. In France, for instance, roughly 30,000 teachers left classrooms for war service.[35] Schools faced requisition for military and municipal requirements, and classrooms became soup kitchens, hospital wards, and billets in support of the war machine. When children went to school, the wartime curriculum emphasized patriotic service, which militarized many of their exercises. French children learned arithmetic by adding war loan amounts and worked on memorization of the "Ten Commandments of Victory."[36] The disruptions of school days, the need for adolescent labor, and the general social disintegration of structures for youth led to increases in rates of petty crime among young people in many nations. Added to this problem were high rates of sick and underweight children, so states became increasingly concerned about the future of their youth. In Vienna, for instance, officials worried about a new "generation of war-damaged degenerates," especially since clinics were admitting underweight children and documenting a high incidence of nervous conditions, such as bed-wetting.[37]

Babies in all the belligerent countries were the focus of concern because of rationed food supplies, absent mothers and/or fathers, and wartime destruction. The infant had been the object of political debate prior to the war with the rise of social welfare movements designed to combat infant mortality and to clean up working-class homes. With the advent of war, babies became even more important as symbols of the nation's future and as propaganda. Images of sickly children were used to raise money for war charities, and in the United States, Baby Week campaigns were held to help finance Belgian food relief. The future of the nation's children, as symbolized by the babies born in war, would become a central concern of postwar societies.

Children and youth served another important role in the war as the focus of propaganda. Gender and age were important markers in national propaganda efforts— young girls, for instance, immediately signaled innocence in need of protection. In a famous British poster from the war, a young girl asked her father, "Daddy, what did you do in the Great War?"[38] A US poster displayed a cherubic blonde girl clutching a Liberty Bond and asking, "My Daddy bought me a Government Bond of the Third Liberty Loan, did yours?"[39] Clearly, young girls functioned as motivational images in these posters aimed at their fathers. On the other hand, teen boys alternated in the popular media as potential fodder for recruitment drives and as symbols of societal degeneration. An increase in juvenile crime (especially with schools closed in many areas) made adolescent boys a target for reform efforts in the cities and in the propaganda efforts of moral reform proponents.

Perhaps the most potent figure in official propaganda was the teenage girl, who featured prominently in fearful accounts of war's effect on societies by 1917 and 1918. In Warsaw, for example, the press targeted female students as a problem, describing one such creature as having "one leg on top of the other, the essential cigarette in her mouth, hair short and closely cut . . . in her soul the absence of 'healthy' values."[40] Other belligerent nations worried about teen girls becoming "khaki-mad" or embracing the lifestyle of a "flapper." In occupied and front-line zones, military officials collected reports of girls and young women who were suspected of engaging in casual prostitution, lending credence to broader fears that girls' morals were being corrupted. As teenager Piete Kuhr noted in her war diary of life in Germany, her mother chastised her for playing piano during afternoon dances at a classmate's house that featured local girls and billeted soldiers. Her mother worried that Piete would be seen as immoral.[41] Older teenage girls did live under threats of sexual assault and rape in occupation and battle zones, so the propaganda depicting teen girls as victims was based in part on the realities of wartime life for adolescent girls.

World War I not only affected children and youth during the years of conflict but also had a long-lasting impact on their lives. The injury and/or death of their parents, disruption of education and work opportunities, new freedom of movement, and political awakenings often meant the war functioned as a watershed in the lives of those who were young in 1914–1918. The children of the First World War reached adulthood when the Second World War was fought, and as such they brought their preconceptions and memories of warfare to that second conflict, which proved to have significant differences from the war they experienced as children. A fascinating area of possible scholarship is comparative work linking the two world wars through the lives of children of the Great War.

CONCLUSION

With the cessation of hostilities in November 1918, it was immediately clear that physical destruction and personal grief dealt a blow to families who had experienced war. It was also apparent that many of the most vulnerable populations by age— the elderly and the very young—continued to experience the deprivations of war through the extended blockade of Germany and Austria-Hungary until 1919. Civil wars, population exchanges, and other postwar dislocations also disproportionately affected certain age groups. Military losses varied considerably across nations, but each belligerent saw an enormous decrease in its birth rate during the war and demographic decimation of young men. Death rates varied according to the nation, but grief was a present force. In Britain, about 12 percent of men who were mobilized died in the war, while in Serbia, the death rate was 37 percent. In France and Germany, one man died for every five mobilized, while in the Ottoman Empire, that figure was more than one in four.[42]

Certain generational groups demonstrated the impact of war very clearly. For instance, more than a third of all German men who were of university age (nineteen through twenty-two) in 1914 died before the Armistice.[43] These mortality rates, when combined with high levels of physical and psychological trauma, wreaked havoc on workplaces, societies, and family units. Age cohorts were distorted by war, which was apparent in university populations and workplaces in the 1920s. Emotionally and physically wrecked men sometimes returned home, upsetting family life and disrupting age and gender norms. For example, many of the Australians who did not return at all were young, under twenty-five, so the grieving parent became a potent political symbol and force in postwar Australia.[44]

The conflict of 1914–1918 highlighted new patterns of sexuality and marriage. Newly formed states in Austria, Hungary, Poland, and other regions joined with more established nations to develop policies for managing domestic life while encouraging women to rebuild postwar societies. Anxious policymakers worried about birth rates and passed legislation to encourage families to have more children. Women were important to the nation both as active participants in wartime mobilization and demobilization (as caretakers and laborers) and as ideological boosts to men (as those in need of protection). In the postwar period, their importance only increased, as women were responsible for reproducing the nation. Balancing all these roles, while also reining in women's sexuality and independence, proved difficult for social welfare organizations and government officials alike.

Even those who were relatively protected from the violence and dislocation of war at so-called home fronts found their families affected by shifts in marriage and divorce patterns. Britain and France serve as good examples of some of the demographic changes the war wrought. In France, marriage patterns shifted to account for wartime losses, with higher marriage rates for widowers and divorced men, as well as a trend toward women marrying men who were their own age or younger. Britain, however, saw little change in its marriage patterns into the 1920s except for a tendency for marriage across geographical and social divides. What did change in Britain was a higher rate of divorce by the 1920s.[45] Birth rates also fluctuated as a result of war, with a steep decrease between 1914 and 1918, followed by spikes in births in the immediate aftermath. Throughout Europe, however, the trend for a falling birth rate continued into the 1920s, especially in industrialized nations such as Germany and Britain.

For families, the longed-for reunion with demobilized soldiers could be both joyful and traumatic, especially given the number of men suffering from physical and psychological ailments as a result of war. Throughout Europe, widows were omnipresent; in Germany and France, the war widowed more than 600,000 women in each country.[46] Government officials tried to alleviate the suffering of widows and orphans through pensions and family allotments, but postwar inflation and unemployment made it difficult for many women to make ends meet. For war orphans and refugee children, the postwar world could be an even harsher place as social service networks struggled to find suitable accommodation and funding for these wartime victims. Of those men who did return, millions were disabled for life, and countless others suffered from psychological and physical symptoms in the years that followed the war.[47] Men returned to wives who had worked in new jobs in the war and to children who did not know them. For many, this altered reality of home and workplace called into question their masculinity and led to depression, domestic violence, and other social adjustment issues. Reforming the home became a priority for individuals and governments, and the postwar backlash against independent women was widespread.

The question of how age shaped the ability of men and women to cope with these private upheavals is one worth understanding fully. Was it easier to cope with a return to normalcy if one had experienced normal family life prior to war, as many older men had? Some scholars of masculinity have suggested that young men who "grew up" at war had trouble readjusting to family and society, but it was this generation of young men that shaped the interwar period. British author A. E. Housman encapsulated in his poem "Here Dead Lie We" a generational cry of young men who felt their youth had been wasted, a sentiment that shaped the postwar era:

Here, dead lie we because we did not choose
To live and shame the land from which we sprung.
Life, to be sure, is nothing much to lose;
But young men think it is, and we were young.[48]

With their new and sometimes competing visions of the world, the young became a moving force in interwar politics and society.

Age matters in historical experience and memory. It framed the way individuals interacted with each other, and it shaped how each person made sense of the trauma of war. As we move into a new century of scholarship focusing on the impact and significance of the Great War, scholars should pay closer attention to the ways in which actual age, age perception, and subtle differences in generation may have framed war experiences and their legacies.

NOTES

1. For work on children and youth in World War I, see, for example, Stéphane Audoin-Rouzeau, *La guerre des enfants, 1914–1918* (Paris: Armand Colin, 1993); Andrew Donson, *Youth in the Fatherless Land: War Pedagogy, Nationalism, and Authority in Germany, 1914–1918* (Cambridge, MA: Harvard University Press, 2010); Susan Fisher, *Boys and Girls in No Man's Land: English-Canadian Children and the First World War* (Toronto: University of Toronto Press, 2011); and Rosie Kennedy, *The Children's War, Britain 1914–1918* (Houndmills: Palgrave Macmillan, 2014).

2. A recent article provides a good overview of some of the social science literature on age transitions: Justin Allen Berg, "Subjective Age Identity during the Transition to Adulthood: Psychological and Sociological Perspectives," *Social Thought and Research* 28 (2007): 145–163. Another excellent sociology article bringing gender and generation together in

historical perspective is Susan A. McDaniel, "Born at the Right Time? Gendered Generations and Webs of Entitlement and Responsibility," *Canadian Journal of Sociology* 26, no. 2 (2001): 193–214.

3. Quoted in Norman Clothier, *Black Valour: The South African Native Labour Contingent, 1916–1918, and the Sinking of the Mendi* (Pietermaritzburg, South Africa: University of Natal Press, 1987), 27.

4. The poem and a biography of Rosenberg can be found at http://www.poetryarchive.org/poet/isaac-rosenberg.

5. Richard G. Plascka, Horst Haselsteinger, and Arnold Suppan, *Innere Front: Militärassistenz, Widerstand un Umsturz in der Donaumonarchie 1918* (Munich: R. Oldenbourg Verlag, 1974), provides a detailed chronicle of the use of army units (especially these older male units) for policing domestic problems in the crumbling Austro-Hungarian Empire by the end of World War I.

6. For a comparative chart showing ages of men mobilized for war, see Tammy M. Proctor, *Civilians in a World at War, 1914–1918* (New York: New York University Press, 2010), 22.

7. See Christopher R. Browning, *Ordinary Men: Reserve Police Battalion and the Final Solution in Poland* (New York: HarperCollins, 1992).

8. Two useful studies that analyze age of servicemen are J. M. Winter, "Some Aspects of the Demographic Consequences of the First World War in Britain," *Population Studies* 30, no. 3 (1976): 539–552; and Louis Henry, "Perturbations de la nuptialité resultant de la guerre 1914–1918," *Population* 21, no. 2 (1966): 273–332.

9. The English edition is Edward M. Strauss, trans., *Poilu: The World War I Notebooks of Corporal Louis Barthas, Barrelmaker 1914–1918* (New Haven, CT: Yale University Press, 2014), 39.

10. "The Work of the National Service Medical Boards," *British Medical Journal* 1, no. 2999 (June 22, 1918): 704.

11. Stéphane Audoin-Rouzeau, *14–18 Les combattants des tranchées* (Paris: Armand Colin, 1986).

12. Jason Crouthamel, *The Great War and German Memory: Society, Politics and Psychological Trauma, 1914–1945* (Exeter: University of Exeter Press, 2009).

13. Vera Brittain, *Testament of Youth* (New York: Penguin, 1989), 307.

14. See Lode Wils, *Honderd jaar Vlaamse beweging* (Leuven: Davidsfonds, 1977).

15. Alon Rachamimov, "The Disruptive Comforts of Drag: (Trans)Gender Performances among Prisoners of War in Russia, 1914–1920," *American Historical Review* 111, no. 2 (2006): 362–382.

16. Paul Fredericq, Wegvoeringsdagboeken, 1916, HS 3708A, Universiteit Gent; Bryce Lyons and Mary Lyons, eds., *The Journal de guerre of Henri Pirenne* (Amsterdam: North-Holland, 1976), 51.

17. Letter to Mother, November 3, 1918, Walter Arthur Richter Collection, National World War I Museum, Kansas City, MO.

18. Erika Kuhlman, *Of Little Comfort: War Widows, Fallen Soldiers, and the Remaking of the Nation after the Great War* (New York: New York University Press, 2012), 3.

19. Tammy M. Proctor, *Female Intelligence: Women and Espionage in the First World War* (New York: New York University Press, 2003), 66.

20. Susan Zeiger, *In Uncle Sam's Service: Women Workers with the American Expeditionary Force, 1917–1919* (Ithaca, NY: Cornell University Press, 1999), 35.

21. Kimberly Jensen, *Mobilizing Minerva: American Women in the First World War* (Urbana: University of Illinois Press, 2008), 87.

22. Laura Lee Downs documents this national difference in metalworking industries in her book *Manufacturing Inequality: Gender Division in the French and British Metalworking Industries, 1914–1939* (Ithaca, NY: Cornell University Press, 1995), 47–50.

23. Membership Applications (Folder 7), Box 280 Service Legion, Series XV Margaret Ethel Kelley Kern, Virginia War History Commission Files 1915–1931 (RG66), Library of Virginia, Richmond.

24. Ludo Stynen and Sylvia Van Peteghem, eds., *In Oorlogsnood: Virginie Lovelings Dagboek, 1914–1918* (Gent: Koninklijke Academie voor Nederlandse Taal-en Letterkunde, 1999).

25. Belinda J. Davis, *Home Fires Burning: Food, Politics, and Everyday Life in World War I Berlin* (Chapel Hill: University of North Carolina Press, 2000), 160–161.

26. Margaret H. Darrow, *French Women and the First World War* (New York: Berg, 2000), 117–122.

27. For a full discussion of these issues, see Susan R. Grayzel, *Women's Identities at War: Gender, Motherhood, and Politics in Britain and France during the First World War* (Chapel Hill: University of North Carolina Press, 1999), esp. chaps. 2–4.

28. Proctor, *Female Intelligence*, 100–110, 126–131.

29. Uğor Ümit Üngör, "Orphans, Converts, and Prostitutes: Social Consequences of War and Persecution in the Ottoman Empire, 1914–1923," *War in History* 19, no. 2 (2012): 175–176.

30. Martha Hanna, *The Mobilization of Intellect: French Scholars and Writers during the Great War* (Cambridge, MA: Harvard University Press, 1996), 70; "Cambridge Gone to the War," *The Times*, October 26, 1914, 3.

31. Maureen Healy, *Vienna and the Fall of the Habsburg Empire: Total War and Everyday Life in World War I* (Cambridge: Cambridge University Press, 2004), 241–243.

32. Roger Chickering, *The Great War and Urban Life in Germany* (Cambridge: Cambridge University Press, 2007), 500–507; Manon Pignot, "French Boys and Girls in the Great War: Gender and the History of Children's Experiences, 1914–1918," in *Gender and the First World War*, ed. Christa Hämmerle, Oswald Überegger, and Birgitta Bader Zaar (Basingstoke: Palgrave Macmillan, 2014), 168.

33. Tammy M. Proctor, *Scouting for Girls: A Century of Girl Guides and Girl Scouts* (Santa Barbara, CA: Praeger, 2009), 26.

34. Quoted in Tammy M. Proctor, *On My Honour: Guides and Scouts in Interwar Britain* (Philadelphia: American Philosophical Society, 2002), 69.

35. Joseph F. Byrnes, *Catholic and French Forever: Religious and National Identity in Modern France* (University Park: Pennsylvania State University Press, 2005), 168.

36. Stéphane Audoin-Rouzeau, "Children and the Primary Schools of France, 1914–1918," in *State, Society and Mobilization in Europe during the First World War*, ed. John Horne (Cambridge: Cambridge University Press, 1997), 45.

37. Healy, *Vienna and the Fall of the Habsburg Empire*, 249–250.

38. War Office poster (ca. 1914–1915). ART.IWM PST 0311

39. US Printing and Lithograph Co. (ca. 1917) in Library of Congress collection.

40. Robert Blobaum and Donata Blobaum, "A Different Kind of Home Front: War, Gender and Propaganda in Warsaw, 1914–1918," in *World War I and Propaganda*, ed. Troy R. E. Paddock (Leiden: Brill, 2014), 259.

41. Piete Kuhr, *There We'll Meet Again,* trans. Walter Wright (Gloucester: Walter Wright, 1998), 186–189.

42. Exact numbers are hard to pinpoint, but these are accepted approximations. Stéphane Audoin-Rouzeau and Annette Becker, *14–18: Understanding the Great War* (New York: Hill and Wang, 2000), 21; Ian F. W. Beckett, *The Great War, 1914–1918* (Harlow, UK: Longman, 2001), 310–312.

43. Leo Van Bergen, *Before My Helpless Sight: Suffering, Dying, and Military Medicine on the Western Front, 1914–1918* (Farnham, UK: Ashgate, 2009), 409.

44. Joy Damousi, *The Labour of Loss: Mourning, Memory, and Wartime Bereavement in Australia* (New York: Cambridge University Press, 1999).

45. J. M. Winter, *The Great War and the British People* (London: Macmillan, 1985), 250–264.

46. Kuhlman, *Of Little Comfort*, 3.

47. Van Bergen, *Before My Helpless Sight*, 493.

48. Quoted in Michael Copp, ed., *Cambridge Poets of the Great War: An Anthology* (Madison, NJ: Fairleigh Dickinson University Press, 2001), 96. With gratitude to The Society of Authors as the Literary Representative of the Estate of A. E. Housman for their permission to quote this poem.

7

Gender and Occupation

Jovana Knežević

ᕲ───

OCCUPATION WAS A central experience of World War I. In addition to Belgium and northern France, the Central Powers occupied nearly 400,000 square kilometers of territory inhabited by 20 million people in the East, including Serbia, Montenegro, Albania, Poland, Romania, Italy, and Russia.[1] However, despite the wide expanse of territory in Europe that was occupied and the significant number of people for whom occupation was the primary wartime experience, scholars have only recently turned their attention to the phenomenon of occupation in the study of the First World War. One reason is that occupation was predominantly an Eastern experience, and so much of the scholarship has focused on the Western Front.[2]

The widespread encounter with occupation during the Great War has been overshadowed not only by the story of the Western Front but also by the Nazi occupations of World War II. The conceptual framework and categories developed in reference to the Second World War, such as those of collaboration and resistance, serve as almost inevitable points of departure for the study of World War I occupations. The question of whether we can see the precursors of Second World War occupations in the experience of occupation in the Great War seems inescapable. Scholars of German occupations in the East explicitly pose this question of continuity. Moreover, in the East, the history of the First World War writ large has been relegated in importance to the experience of the Second World War, in particular because this latter conflict played a central role in the foundational myth of the state in the Soviet Union and the socialist countries of Eastern Europe.

The relative lack of attention may be attributed as well to the fact that the experience of occupation could prove problematic for telling the tale of the war in a country. Occupation challenged the canonical wartime image of the brave man fighting at the front, being supported by faithful and patriotic civilians, primarily women, who were making their own sacrifices on the home front. The harsh economic circumstances of occupation made compromise of this ideal on the part of the occupied population next to inevitable. In almost every choice civilians made or every action they took, they risked committing acts of betrayal that could border on treason. Civilians under occupation had to be wary not only of the occupiers' policies but also of their own duty to the nation. Not only did occupying regimes deem actions of civilians as suspect, but compatriots and the exiled national regime often joined the chorus of recrimination. This is why, in accounts of the wartime experience in France, for example, the occupation received less attention than the figure of the French soldier, the poilu, being supported by the civilians at the home front.[3]

In the East, the situation was further complicated by the fact that many national groups did not yet have independent states and thus found themselves fighting on the side of empires from which they would be "liberated" at the end of the war. In these cases, national histories remained largely silent about soldiers or civilians who had served the "wrong side" during the war, according to victorious nationalists in the postwar period. For example, in German-occupied Warsaw, thousands of Polish young men and women voluntarily served in the Russian war effort as soldiers or nurses.[4] Also omitted from these postwar depictions were figures who did not support the Polish national government or the conservative doctrine of the Polish Roman Catholic Church.[5]

While the term "collaboration" is most associated with World War II, fellow citizens raised accusations of cooperation with or accommodation of the enemy when it appeared that civilians did not adequately defy occupiers during the First World War. In the case of women, accusations of accommodation most often employed moral terms and reflected national anxiety about the conquest or co-optation of women as being symbolic of the broader conquest of the nation. Such apprehension was rooted in the perception both of the enemy as brutal and barbaric and of women as vulnerable and weak, physically and morally. These views found their full and vivid articulation in war propaganda, which morally justified the nation's war effort and continually mobilized the population for war by persuading it of the need to defend the nation against a barbaric enemy as well as by morally justifying the nation's war effort. Many propaganda themes invoked "gender fear," the anxiety of men that they would not be able to defend their homes and nations.[6] Here, women were portrayed mainly as helpless victims. Much of this propaganda emerged during the period of invasion, which was marked by extreme violence. Under occupation, violence generally abated and conditions gradually normalized, as did the population's interactions with the enemy forces. Under these circumstances, the members of the occupied population could not remain simply victims. They became agents who made a range of choices to survive the harsh everyday conditions of war and occupation.

INVASION, CONQUEST, AND OCCUPATION

Occupation was gendered in terms of both numbers and symbolism. It was a condition that made it particularly difficult for women and men to behave in accordance with society's expectations of them. Women were typically overrepresented in an occupied population. In the Habsburg-occupied Serbian capital of Belgrade, for example, women constituted 63 percent of the population as compared with 43 percent before the war.[7] Thus, the national experience of occupation was largely the experience of the nation's female population. On the other hand, the occupying regime was composed predominantly, if not exclusively, of men, particularly in military occupations where troops were not accompanied by their families, and civilian "colonizers" did not settle in the territory. This resulted in a gendered power dynamic with the rulers being mostly male and the ruled mostly female. While their numbers were smaller, men were certainly present in occupied societies. However, their failure to satisfy the ideal image of the powerful protector by having succumbed to conquest caused them to be ignored in the gendered accounts of occupation that emerged. At best, it was thought, these men were not capable of fulfilling their masculine duty to fight for their countries; at worst, they were shirking this duty.

Women, in contrast, were central to the occupation narrative, not merely because of their numerical predominance but more significantly because of their symbolic value to the nation. This was evident in the propaganda that emerged in the first year of the war, in which the image of women as victims and martyrs played a pivotal role. In all cases, invasion and conquest, which were marked by extreme violence against civilians, preceded occupation. Various international commissions investigated and documented the acts of violence committed by invading armies in reports that were widely and deliberately circulated to mobilize populations for war. One such report was the *Official Report of the Committee on Alleged German Outrages*, or the Bryce Report, named for the former British ambassador to the United States Lord James

Bryce, who led an inquiry into actions of the German army in Belgium in 1915. Similarly, the Swiss criminologist R. A. Reiss issued the *Report upon the Atrocities Committed by the Austro-Hungarian Army during the First Invasion of Serbia* in 1916. These reports described incidents of violence in European theaters of war, particularly against noncombatants. The kind of violence that was reported to have been committed against women was gendered or sexualized, especially rape and the mutilation of the female body.[8] Such documented atrocities then formed the basis for wartime propaganda.

Propaganda was important in the First World War to mobilize popular opinion in support of the war effort, especially in Britain, where conscription was not introduced until 1916. In places like France, propaganda served to continually re-energize the population behind the war effort. It was also aimed at gaining support in neutral countries that had not yet entered the war, such as the United States. This atrocity propaganda helped to justify the Allied war cause by offering proof of the enemy's extreme and limitless brutality. Atrocity accounts also highlighted enemy violations of international law. These violations, historian Nicoletta Gullace has argued, "carried a particular potency when depicted in terms of women, children, and the safety of the home."[9]

The graphic images of violence committed against women were particularly effective in the propaganda effort and became widespread in public discourse. The depiction of suffering women in propaganda drew on existing conceptions of them as innocent and vulnerable.[10] Even though women were often reluctant to recount the violence they experienced and chose to do so with minimal detail, propagandists opted to represent this violence in a manner that struck at the heart of the public's anxieties about the dangers women faced in war.[11] Images of violence against women and children conveyed a sense of a threat to home that even those most removed from international politics could understand as a call to arms. This is why the portrayal of rape "as a rape of *mothers*" was particularly potent.[12] In propaganda, individual victimized women came to represent a feminized nation fighting a defensive war to liberate itself from barbaric brutes, the sort that would commit atrocities against the most vulnerable.[13] Thus, vulnerability of the invaded nation found its embodiment in the vulnerability of the violated woman.

Understanding the violent invasion and its rhetorical representation remains deeply relevant to any consideration of occupation because these experiences prefigure to a great extent the period of occupation and the encounter between occupier and occupied. Although invasion and conquest needs to be differentiated from occupation, the former being more chaotic, unbridled, and marked by more extreme violence, in the propaganda materials of the time, invasion and occupation often were seen as part of a seamless continuum. Popular accounts articulated both invasion and occupation in gendered terms, as narratives about occupation cast the invaded zones as violated women.[14]

Indeed, violence against women continued under occupation, albeit to a lesser extent and in less radical forms than during the invasions. Two well-known stories of martyrdom in occupied Belgium and France are that of Edith Cavell, the British nurse who served in Belgium and was arrested, court-martialed, and executed for helping Allied soldiers escape the occupied territory, and that of the deportation of young girls from Lille to the countryside for forced agricultural labor during Easter week in 1916. The French government seized particularly on this targeting of women to indict of the German mistreatment of the occupied population more generally. In *The Deportation of Women and Girls from Lille*, a collection of documents published in Britain, the United States, and Canada in 1916, addressed a note to "the Neutral Powers and to the public opinion of all nations," supported by documentary evidence of the German authorities' transgressions of international conventions in its treatment of the occupied French population. Its grievances centered on the incident in which "about 25,000 French—consisting of girls between 16 and 20 years of age, young women, and men up to the age of 55—without regard to social position, were torn from their homes at Roubaix, Tourcoing, and Lille, separated ruthlessly from their families, and compelled to do agricultural work in the Departments of the Aisne and the Ardennes."[15] The "moral impact" of this document, according to Gullace, "lies wholly in its rhetorical use of women and the family."[16]

Georges Gromaire, a French historian writing in the immediate postwar period, condemned female forced labor and criticized the Germans for demanding the same kind of labor from women as they did from men, stating with irony, "They showed themselves to be perfect feminists, not making any differentiation between men and women."[17] Another practice that caused outrage was the physical inspections to which the French women were subjected, including gynecological examinations. Contemporaries experienced the deportation as "a reversal of the sexual order" and this new social order to be one in which "women work like men, bourgeois are treated like prostitutes."[18]

The realities of the hardships experienced by civilians under invasion and occupation often were obscured by the symbolism ascribed to them. While the deportees included both men and women of various ages, the story of martyrdom that emerged focused particularly on the image of enslaved young girls, which invested the narrative with added layers of meaning—atrocity, oppression, sexual violence.[19] Similarly, although women represented a little more than 3 percent of those condemned to death, it was the story of Edith Cavell's execution that elicited international indignation. Thus, even though in both cases women statistically were less targeted than men, contemporaries nonetheless seized on these incidents of the victimization of women by the occupier to make them symbols of the trauma to further a national end. Moreover, an attack on women was also experienced as an emasculation of the nation, a demonstration of the impotence of men in protecting their collective home. Propaganda depicted accounts of rape in a manner that could humiliate men for not acting as society expected of them, as defenders of their nations.[20] By treating actual victims as symbols of victimhood, propaganda thus overshadowed actual experiences of violence.[21] As the war progressed, the growing perception of atrocity reports as propaganda even led to the discrediting of actual accounts of later abuses.

THE LIVED EXPERIENCE OF OCCUPATION AND ITS REPRESENTATION

How, then, did the lived reality of occupation compare with the image of the occupation experience that came to dominate national propaganda? To understand occupied populations, one must consider where occupation fits into the broader experience of the war. An occupied territory was not a military fighting front, but neither was the experience of occupation one of peace. Occupied territories were not home fronts mobilized in support of the war effort of their own countries. Instead, the occupying regime mobilized populations into hinterlands for the benefit of their own countries, with greater or lesser success.[22] The occupied zones in France and Belgium had extraordinary strategic importance as the territory immediately behind the lines of the German front. Occupiers exploited territories under their control for their natural resources and labor. These circumstances led contemporaries and later scholars to describe an occupied country as "imprisoned in its own borders,"[23] or as being under a state of "internal siege."[24] Occupied populations were at once embattled, living with the enemy in their midst, and excluded from the national experience of war.[25] Occupied territory was to a great extent cut off from the rest of the nation; it was difficult to travel in and out, and contact was limited. This gave rise to rifts in the national community and even led to the questioning of the sacrifice and patriotism of the occupied population.

The hardships of life under occupation were manifold, and they presented daily, immediate challenges. War in general, but occupation in particular, produced conditions in which liberties and choices were severely curtailed. Occupation policies imposed laws and regulations that governed the minutest aspects of everyday life. These were enforced through a pervasive system of surveillance and policing. Occupiers placed restrictions on cultural and social life out of proclaimed military necessity, in an effort to thwart subversive activity and maintain peace and order. Occupation by definition was an asymmetrical power relationship, and the occupied population was ultimately at the mercy of the occupying authorities. Even in contexts in which there was extensive interaction and even cooperation of locals with the occupiers, such as in German-occupied Romania, there were constant reminders that the members of the occupied community were subordinate and subject to arbitrary use of power. For example, although Romanians were significantly represented in the administration of the occupying regime, the German authorities held ultimate control, especially in strategic ministries. They closely monitored Romanian employees, censored them, and reduced their pay. The population was also subject to repression in the form of politically motivated arrests and the taking of hostages. Moreover, fraternization and cooperation between occupier and occupied did not save Romania from devastating economic exploitation.[26]

Under these conditions, occupied populations waged a daily battle for their security, to avoid imprisonment, internment, deportation, and in some cases execution. They struggled for physical subsistence against food scarcity. They fought a battle for spiritual subsistence against the persistent uncertainty created by lack of information that resulted from censorship and propaganda. Some engaged in individual or organized acts of subversion against the occupying authorities and their policies. Doing so challenged the status of these civilians as noncombatants, both figuratively and in some cases legally.

At the same time, as the period of invasion gave way to the condition of occupation, there was a normalization of life, even of relations with the enemy. With this shift, questions of victimhood also ceded to questions of patriotism. Getting on with life under occupation exposed the population to an entirely new set of questions that revolved around how much they were sacrificing or contributing to the national war effort, and whether their actions were proper, moral, and patriotic. People felt vulnerable not only at the hands of their occupiers but also in the eyes of their fellow citizens. Thus, occupied populations also fought internal battles with their neighbors.

As life returned to a normal routine under occupation, occupied populations were placed in a "damned if you do, damned if you don't" situation. The experience of women under occupation was particularly reflective of this dynamic. Atrocity propaganda had depicted women primarily as objects of violence and symbols of the nation—victims and martyrs. These images of violence and abuse were grounded in reality, as women *had* been victims of rape and other forms of violence. However, women were not merely objects of occupied rule. They were also agents and actors, who made decisions and choices in navigating very difficult and constrained circumstances. Material scarcity, more so than any other condition brought on by war and occupation, shaped the lives of women in occupied territories. Supporting their families fell on women's shoulders to an unprecedented extent during the First World War. To feed their families and themselves, women had to assume the role of provider, which their husbands had solely or predominantly performed before the war. In occupied Serbia, women worked in the offices of the Habsburg Military General Government as administrative assistants or translators, as well as serving as teachers in schools. If they were able to secure concessions, some ran small businesses. Because it was not forced labor, such work was considered "voluntary," and some compatriots deemed it to be an undesirable accommodation to the occupier, even unpatriotic. In occupied France, the number of women who worked voluntarily for the German occupiers was higher than that of men, which may be understandable in light of the fact that women had fewer means to make a living. Somewhat patronizingly, a contemporary French historian stated, "One must remember in order to judge them fairly that the majority of these women were ignorant and, in the majority of cases, did not realize the effects of their actions."[27]

Women moving out of the "domestic sphere" and into traditionally masculine roles was not unique to occupied territories. This phenomenon generated anxiety everywhere due to its potential to upend the social order, which rested on the preservation of gender roles. Many viewed this change as undesirable, but necessary for the war effort. Under occupation, this anxiety was heightened because moving out of their traditional domestic roles brought women into closer contact with the occupier and increased the opportunity for transgression and treason. Such behavior could call into question the idea of a suffering civilian population.

Official accounts of occupied territories focused on stories of endurance and survival of daily hardships. At the same time, speculation and accusations that women were taking advantage of their newfound freedom to act in a morally unconstrained manner also emerged. When it came to women, the issue of sexual (mis)conduct was a central trope through which contemporaries, and even some historians, viewed the experience of occupation. In the context of the humiliation of defeat and loss of sovereignty, of penetration of the country by the enemy, the honorable comportment of women under occupation acquired national significance. National security had already suffered its worst blow—military defeat and loss of sovereignty, so honor was all that was left to save the nation from total conquest. Women were the mothers of the "nation," and their honor and morality was fragile because it was tested every day in their struggle to survive and subsist under occupation. Women's fragile moral constitution not only could threaten the social order but also could prove a national liability in such close proximity to the enemy.

Self-appointed social and national watchdogs unofficially monitored public morality, and women, in particular, were judged by how they related to the occupier. Their choices in response to the circumstances of war and occupation fell under this scrutiny. Women who deviated in any way from what was considered appropriate behavior, from the image of a woman as a faithful wife and mother, could be, and often were, accused of being prostitutes. In the north of France, a moral-patriotic framework dominated the dialogue in the occupied community. Those who transgressed this code were dubbed *mauvaise conduite* (misbehaved), which was a fundamentally female phenomenon.[28] In Serbia, members of the occupied community employed a similar term, *nevaljalice* (naughty women), to chastise such women for degrading or reinforcing the negative image of Serbs that the occupiers already held. While there were women who worked as prostitutes in the narrow, formal sense of the term, under occupation the rhetoric of prostitution was broadened to include the actions of women who had liaisons with members of the occupying regime, whether out of necessity or love. A notion of "informal prostitution" or "soft prostitution" gained currency and broadened the scope of those who could be condemned for this offense.[29]

This was not unique to occupied areas, but under occupation, prostitution was not just a question of morality or social stability; it was one of patriotism and treason. By fraternizing in any way with the enemy, a woman was tainting not just her own honor and that of her family but also that of her nation at a time of vulnerability when the nation not could bear any such blows to its image. Other occupied civilians considered sexual misconduct to be akin to denunciation or providing intelligence to the occupier.[30] In German-occupied Belgium, communities considered the prostitute a "double traitor" both morally and patriotically.[31] In fact, due to the perceived connection with espionage, many prostitutes were suspected of being spies.[32] Thus, the anxieties of the nation were borne particularly by women, whose actions, if anything short of defiance, could be construed at best as accommodation of the occupier or at worst as a betrayal of the nation.

Fraternization with occupying troops was not always a choice and was usually born of the necessity to fight those daily battles of survival and endurance. Occupied civilians had to balance the need to survive with their desire to maintain a patriotic stance. Women suffered tangible consequences of perceived transgression. Local authorities in Belgium refused assistance to soldiers' wives "suspected of dalliance with Germans."[33] Food relief agencies also tried to withhold food from civilians engaged in "unpatriotic behavior."[34] In their treatment and view of women, occupiers were yet again at odds with the occupied nation. The sexual misconduct and its potentially damaging implications, which caused so much anxiety among the members of the occupied nation, were a concern for the occupier as well, but for entirely different reasons.

The policies of the occupying authorities toward prostitution are illustrative of this point. In Serbia, the Habsburg Military General Government primarily concerned itself with the role of prostitutes in spreading venereal diseases, which threatened to seriously curtail the strength of its troops and their capacity to carry out their duties. Venereal diseases were indeed among the most common and widespread diseases recorded in Belgrade during the war, less prevalent only than malaria and whooping cough.[35] Like other militaries, the Habsburg army saw the potential benefits of prostitution in raising the morale of its troops. Thus, prostitution in occupied Serbia was permitted but regulated, with prostitutes regularly given medical examinations. In the hands of occupying authorities, the relationship between prostitution and patriotism was also turned on its head, as officials of the Habsburg Military General Government in Serbia believed that "some female individuals . . . consider it their patriotic duty to infect soldiers of the Imperial and Royal Army, and thus reduce their effectiveness."[36]

In German-ruled Ober Ost, occupied territory that included present-day Lithuania, Latvia, Belarus, and parts of Poland, a similar fear of venereal disease led to the strict regulation of prostitution. Indeed, public health was a major concern for the occupiers, who perceived the East to be "diseased and contagious." One official source reported an infection rate of 70 percent for the prostitutes of the town of Wilna.[37] For the leaders of Ober Ost, who already were fearful of epidemics from the East spreading to Germany, venereal disease "loomed up . . . as a special nightmare."[38] Their significant worry about fraternization with locals stemmed not only from the fear of infection and subsequent incapacitation of their troops but also from the possibility that it would lead the soldiers to " 'go native,' " thus losing their own identity and culture.[39]

Therefore, in addition to the daily battles women waged under occupation for subsistence, they faced the burden of defending the integrity of their nations, and often without the help of their compatriots. Women were not alone in being judged. Men were also taken to task for actions that were perceived as accommodation of the occupying regime, as in the case of some prominent writers and intellectuals who contributed to the occupier's official newspaper, *Beogradske novine* (Belgrade News), in Habsburg-occupied Serbia. In Belgium also, writers faced a dilemma over whether to submit their works for censorship or simply to stop producing at the risk of not earning a living. This issue caused a rift between Belgians living in the occupied territory and those who had managed to escape. While these tensions lessened over the course of the war, the issue of publishing continued to be fraught with implications of civic treason.[40] Women's transgressions, however, were articulated in terms of morality and proper conduct and judged based on accepted conceptions of their femininity and place in society. Women had to uphold national virtue by upholding their own, even in the most threatening and trying of circumstances.

OCCUPIED TERRITORY AS A NATION APART

These anxieties stemmed in part from the position of the occupied community as being apart from the nation at war. While their fellow citizens were fighting at the front or supporting the war effort from a place of refuge, occupied civilians were at best viewed as powerless to act in support of their national war effort and, at worst, considered to be as supporting that of the occupier. Moreover, the occupied territory stood as a persistent reminder of the failure to protect the home and a symbol of the shame of defeat. The occupied nation was a nation divided. Contemporary historian Henri Pirenne characterized the population of occupied Belgium and Belgian refugees who had escaped occupation as "two Belgiums," and described relations between the two as resentful, with "each party claiming it was shouldering the brunt of the war hardships. The refugee press repeatedly referred to the occupied Belgians' supposedly snug accommodation with German rule. The Belgians who were 'stuck inside,' as the claustrophobic expression went, felt abandoned by those who had fled to safety abroad."[41] Similarly, one could speak of three Serbias—arguably four if the Bulgarian occupied zone was considered separately from the Habsburg. There was occupied Serbia, the exiled government and military on the island of Corfu and at the Salonika front, and refugees and émigrés settled in various neutral and Allied countries, especially Switzerland, Britain, and France.

The estrangement of Serbs living in the different Serbias is demonstrated in a very intimate way by the rift that developed between an officer and his wife, Natalija Aranđelović, who lived in occupied Belgrade with their four children. Because the officer had also served in the Balkan Wars of 1912–1913, the spouses had experienced long periods of separation, but occupation had limited their contact even more significantly. Natalija's perception that her plight was worse than her husband's and her consequent resentment are evident in the thoughts she confided in her diary: "Why should I safeguard my husband's honor! . . . why should these years pass in vain for me—while you seize [the day]—worry to an extent about your children, but still continue your fun?!"[42] While Natalija's picture of a carefree life at the front was certainly unrealistic, it was reciprocated by her husband's unrealistic picture of life on the occupied home front. In one of his infrequent letters, he instructed Natalija to teach their children "merriment and music," in response to which Natalija wrote in her journal, "Under this pressure . . . to be merry and to sing?...Do you really think that we are well-off here, when you write such things??—or do you think that I am surrounded by company, merriment, song?— the kind of company in which you find yourself determines how you think. Here there is only sorrow, misery, and the hope that I will see you again soon."[43] Even when she acknowledged, "you too live in despair over there," she qualified the statement with "but at least you are free!"[44] This exchange reveals not only a rift between man and wife, possibly men and women, but also a rift between two different Serbian national experiences of war.

In both cases, that of divided Belgium and divided Serbia, the estrangement resulted from the occupied territory being cut off from the rest of the nation. The lack of information about the other part of the nation spurred the imagination about both the suffering and the lack of sacrifice. This contributed to the emergence of two extremes in the conception of occupied populations as victims or traitors. In the silence created by the absence of information, people imagined realities. Thus, populations living under occupation were suspect not only to the occupying regime, which treated them as potential enemies, but also to their "free" compatriots. Questions of patriotism and heroism abounded during the war, as did those about the magnitude of sacrifice. Occupied populations ran the risk of seeming unpatriotic, immoral, and unheroic both because they were not actively engaged in battle in a manner that was formally recognized and because their proximity to the enemy and their efforts to endure and survive occupation caused them to engage in interactions that could be construed as self-serving or unpatriotic.

In Belgium, males who joined intelligence and resistance organizations, such as La Dame Blanche, did so out of fear of being seen as unpatriotic or cowardly.[45] Women also joined the service to prove their patriotism.[46] Perceiving the need to show themselves as patriotic and loyal, members of the occupied community took it upon themselves to monitor each other. In doing so, they were sometimes the most extreme in their indictments. Indeed, in the postwar period, the members of the occupied population in the north of France were dissatisfied with local and national officials who refused to prosecute the transgressions of the moral-patriotic order they had established during the war.[47] In Serbia, in the years immediately following the war, there was a politically motivated campaign in the press against prominent intellectuals accused of accommodating the occupiers by writing for the Habsburg daily, *Beogradske novine*. The accusers were outraged when these cases either never came to trial or were dismissed.[48] In Belgium, the tendency to force women into stereotypes of victims or sexual collaborators meant that the legacy of women intelligence agents was obscured in the postwar period.[49]

CONCLUSION

Gender was a lens through which contemporaries made sense of the invasion, conquest, and occupation of countries throughout Europe during the Great War. Propaganda depicted invaded and occupied countries as violated women, and the victimization of women, more so than other members of the population, was highlighted with moral outrage to exhibit the lack of humanity of the enemy and the moral authority of a nation's war cause. The actions of women in occupied communities were the focus of much of the national discourse about proper conduct and patriotism during the war.

But gender is a lens that can also obscure. While it may have served the purposes of propaganda or postwar nationalism, constructing the narrative of occupation along these lines stripped occupied civilians of their agency. This was not a realistic depiction of how they lived, experienced, endured, and survived occupation. One need not talk of active resistance in order to see that occupied populations were not entirely passive. One need only look to daily acts of endurance and survival, which were complex in their motivations and constrained by the reality of occupation. Women suffered real hardship under occupation and the violent invasions that preceded it. They were subjected to rape, forced labor, deportation, economic privation, upheaval in their home lives, and anxieties born of uncertainty. But in the hands of governments, local authorities, and intellectuals, among both their compatriots and the enemy, their plights were appropriated and ascribed symbolic value that served a national purpose. This was true even when one moved out of the realm of propaganda, where hyperbole might be expected, into the rumors and judgments exchanged in everyday life on the streets. The lived experience of occupation represented a wide range of actions, shaped by constraints, opportunities, and individual inclinations. Far more research into this experience of ordinary people living under occupation needs to be done before we can understand the dynamics of occupation, including gender dynamics, in occupied communities. More research into everyday life under occupation can bring to light individuals and groups who have remained invisible because their experience of war challenged the predominant national story, and analyzing their choices, actions, and motivations beyond stereotypical paradigms can challenge and reshape the vision of the occupation experience that persists.

The study of gender provides a good framework for comparative and transnational history of the occupations. To be certain, there were national distinctions in the occupation experience. These stemmed from the state administering the occupation and whether the occupying regime was military or civilian. There were also distinctions based on the degree to which national and local institutions and elites remained intact under occupation. Within the nation there were differences based on socioeconomic standing and the urban versus rural experience. Finally, occupations were memorialized differently in different national contexts. In France, for instance, the experience of occupation was not commemorated as part of the official memory of the war experience as it was in Belgium. The experience of women under occupation lends itself particularly well to analysis across national boundaries. There are many similarities in their experiences and the way in which they were perceived and treated by both the occupying regimes and their compatriots. In pursuing these avenues of investigation, however, it is important to remember that women under occupation in Europe during the Great War were not just mothers, wives, and Mariannes.[50] Those elements were present in women's identities, but women were foremost people who had to make difficult, sometimes impossible, choices to survive an imposed, constricting, belligerent situation. They were not just the embodiment of the symbols externally ascribed to them. They were humans enduring one of the greatest forms of hardship that can be imposed by war.

NOTES

1. Oskar Regele, *Gericht über Habsburgs Wehrmacht: Letzte Siege und Untergang unter dem Armee-Oberkommando Kaiser Karls I. Generaloberst Arz von Straussenburg* (Vienna: Herold, 1968), 132, cited in Jonathan E. Gumz, *The Resurrection and Collapse of Empire in Habsburg Serbia, 1914–1918* (Cambridge: Cambridge University Press, 2009), 9.

2. Existing studies of occupation are most extensive for the western occupied territories, although new works have been published in recent years on occupation in the Baltic States, Poland, Serbia, Montenegro, and Romania. English-language works include Gumz, *Resurrection and Collapse of Empire*; Jesse Kauffmann, *Elusive Alliance: The German Occupation of Poland in World War I* (Cambridge, MA: Harvard University Press, 2015); Vejas Gabriel Liulevicius, *War Land on the Eastern Front: Culture, National Identity, and German Occupation in World War I* (New York: Cambridge University Press, 2000). German-language works include Tamara Scheer, *Zwischen Front und Heimat: Österreich-Ungarns Militärverwaltungen im Ersten Weltkrieg* (Frankfurt am Main: Peter Lang, 2009); Lisa Mayerhofer, *Zwischen Freund und Feind—Deutsche Besatzung in Rumänien 1916–1918* (Frankfurt am Main: Peter Lang, 2010).

3. Laurence van Ypersele, "En guise de conclusion, Les résistances belges et françaises en 14–18," in *La résistance en France et en Belgique occupées 1914–1918: Actes de la journée d'études, bondues, 30 Janvier 2010,* ed. Robert Vandenbussche (Villeneuve-d'Ascq: Institut de recherches historiques du Septentrion, 2012), 215.

4. Robert Blobaum, "Warsaw's Forgotten War," *Remembrance and Solidarity Studies* 2 (2014): 203.

5. Blobaum, "Warsaw's Forgotten War," 204.

6. Alan Kramer, *Dynamic of Destruction: Culture and Mass Killing in the First World War* (Oxford: Oxford University Press, 2007), 245–246.

7. *Ortsverzeichnis für das von den k.u.k. Truppen besetzte Gebiet Serbiens. Zusammengestellt auf Grund der Ergebnisse der Volkszählung vom 31. Dezember 1910* (Belgrade, 1917).

8. Interestingly, these propagandist accounts of violence have little parallel in non-European zones where violence was so central to the experience of colonial conquest.

9. Nicoletta F. Gullace, "Sexual Violence and Family Honor: British Propaganda and International Law during the First World War," *American Historical Review* 102, no. 3 (1997): 735.

10. Michael J. Shover, "Roles and Images of Women in World War I Propaganda," *Politics and Society* 5:4 (1975): 485.

11. Gullace, "Sexual Violence and Family Honor," 716; Ruth Harris, "The 'Child of the Barbarian': Rape, Race and Nationalism in France during the First World War," *Past and Present*, no. 141 (1993): 179.

12. Susan Grayzel, *Women's Identities at War: Gender, Motherhood, and Politics in Britain and France during the First World War* (Chapel Hill: University of North Carolina Press, 1999), 50.

13. Harris, "The 'Child of the Barbarian,'" 179–180.

14. This trend is discussed in works such as Margaret H. Darrow, *French Women and the First World War: War Stories of the Home Front* Oxford: Berg, 2000), and Tammy M. Proctor, *Female Intelligence: Women and Espionage in the First World War* (New York: New York University Press, 2003)

15. *The Deportation of Women and Girls from Lille* (London: Hodder and Stoughton, 1916), 3–4.

16. Gullace, "Sexual Violence and Family Honor," 742.

17. Georges Gromaire, *L'occupation Allemande en France (1914–1918)* (Paris: Payot, 1925), 247.

18. Annette Becker, *Oubliés de la Grande Guerre: Humanitaire et culture de guerre, 1914–1918: Populations occupées, déportés civils, prisonniers de guerre* (Paris: Noêsis, 1998), 72.

19. Darrow, *French Women and the First World War*, 117.

20. This dynamic is observed by Ruth Harris and Susan Grayzel in "The 'Child of the Barbarian'" and *Women's Identities at War*, respectively.

21. Kramer, *Dynamic of Destruction*, 245.

22. This characterization of occupation is offered by Sophie De Schaepdrijver in "Military Occupation, Political Imaginations, and the First World War," *First World War Studies* 4, no. 1 (2013): 1.

23. Henri Pirenne, *La Belgique et la guerre mondiale* (Paris: Les Presses Universitaires de France, 1929), quoted in Darrow, *French Women and the First World War*, 227.

24. Annette Becker, *Les cicatrices rouges, 14–18, France et Belgique occupées* (Paris: Fayard, 2010), quoted in De Schaepdrijver, "Military Occupation," 1.

25. This dynamic has been observed by scholars of various occupied territories, including De Schaepdrijver, "Military Occupations," 1, and van Ypersele, "En guise de conclusion," 207.

26. Mayerhofer, *Zwischen Freund und Feind*, 92.

27. Gromaire, *L'occupation Allemande*, 247–248.

28. James E. Connolly, "*Mauvaise conduite*: Complicity and Respectability in the Occupied Nord, 1914–1918," *First World War Studies* 4, no. 1 (2013): 16.

29. "Informal prostitution" is used by Connolly in "*Mauvaise conduite*," and "soft prostitution" by Jovana Knežević in "Prostitutes as a Threat to National Honor in Habsburg-Occupied Serbia during the Great War," *Journal of the History of Sexuality* 20, no. 1 (2011): 312–335.

30. Connolly, "*Mauvaise conduite*," 9.

31. Benoit Majerus, "La prostitution à Bruxelles pendant la Grande Guerre: Contrôle et pratique," *Crime, Histoire Sociétés* 7, no. 1 (2003): 5–42.

32. Proctor, *Female Intelligence*, 140.

33. van Ypersele, "En guise de conclusion," 209.

34. Sophie de Schaepdrijver, "Occupation, Propaganda, and the Idea of Belgium," in *European Culture in the Great War: The Arts, Entertainment, and Propaganda, 1914–1918*, ed. Aviel Roshwald and Richard Stites (Cambridge: Cambridge University Press, 1999), 276.

35. Archives of Serbia, MGG/S, IV-8, 1917, Sanitärer Jahresbericth des k.u.k. Kreiskommandos Belgrad-Stadt für das Jahr 1917 (K.u.k. Gouvernement-Druckerei in Belgrade).

36. Österreichisches Staatsarchiv-NFA-MGG/S-K, 1680, Leistungen der Verwaltung des kuk MGG/S in sanitärer Hinsicht 1916.

37. Wilna was the German name for the city of Vilnius, the capital of Lithuania.

38. Liulevicius, *War Land on the Eastern Front*, 105.

39. Liulevicius, *War Land on the Eastern Front*, 133.

40. De Schaepdrijver, "Occupation, Propaganda, and the Idea of Belgium," 274.

41. De Schaepdrijver, "Occupation, Propaganda, and the Idea of Belgium," 271.

42. Istorijski Arhiv Beograda (IAB), Zbirka Gradje (ZMG), Dnevnik Natalije Nikole Arandjelović (NNA), K. 1/I, 2b, January 6, 1918.

43. IAB, ZMG, Dnevnik NNA, K. 1/I, 2b, September 20, 1917.

44. IAB, ZMG, Dnevnik NNA, K. 1/I, 2b, October 30, 1917.

45. Tammy Proctor, "*La Dame Blanche*: Gender and Espionage in Occupied Belgium," in *Uncovered Fields: Perspectives in First World War Studies*, ed. Jenny Macleod and Pierre Purseigle (Leiden: Brill, 2004), 238.

46. Proctor, "*La Dame Blanche*," 239.

47. Connolly, "*Mauvaise conduite*, 16.

48. Marko Pejović, "Beogradska štampa o sudjenjima za saradnju sa okupatorima u Srbiji 1918–1920 godine," *Godišnjak za društvenu istoriju* 12: 1–3 (2005), 85–109.

49. Proctor, *Female Intelligence*, 143–144.

50. Marianne is a symbol of the French Republic, an icon of liberty, whose image figured prominently in France's World War I propaganda.

8

Gender and Everyday Life

Karen Hunt

"POTATO WAR IN West Cumberland. Women's Organised Boycott," shouted a newspaper headline in January 1917.[1] This was a different kind of war from the one being fought in the battlefields of Europe, Asia, Africa, and the Middle East, involving different people, different weapons, and different spaces. It too was part of the conflict zone of the First World War. Although the British had been hearing for some time about shortages and food riots in the other belligerent nations, this report of "action" far from London was new. Yet what was happening in the extreme northwest of England had many of the characteristics of the unrest in Germany and Austria caused by significant shortages of basic foodstuffs.

In the small industrial towns of Cumberland, housewives organized a boycott of farmers and food dealers by refusing to pay more than the government's fixed price for potatoes, despite the farmers' demanding twice as much. According to the *Manchester Guardian*, "The women surged round the carts and sought to storm and capture them. Potatoes and turnips were used as missiles." Some farmers took their wares home unsold, while others conceded to the crowds and reduced their prices. The women appealed to the mothers and wives of soldiers to join the boycott, angered not only by what was seen as profiteering but also by their belief that the farmers were not sharing equally in the sacrifices of war. There was a widespread feeling, not just in Cumberland, that farmers and their sons were often unfairly exempt from military service. All the terminology used in the newspaper report was significant and gendered: housewives, wives of soldiers, profiteers (usually represented as men exploiting women), and avoiding military service.[2] In a nearby village, house-holders "cleared" (stole) a field of potatoes that a local farmer said he had not had enough labor to lift, and then celebrated with "jovial hot-pot suppers." They were in turn raided by the local police, who made four arrests. It was all reported in a rather jokey tone.

On other home fronts, similar events took place when housewives, often the wives and mothers of soldiers, challenged "unfair" prices, fought over goods, and even took them from farmers' fields. However, the situation was often much more des-perate in Germany and Austria, where even the most ordinary aspects of everyday life became harder and harder to sustain. By the last years of the war, the challenge of daily survival for civilians involved the relentless search for enough food to feed themselves and their families on the other front in this new "total war," the home front. The struggle for food made explicit the gender relations that underpinned a novel kind of warfare and in so doing created both challenges and opportunities for women, as what had previously been a private domestic matter became a public political one, central to the survival of individual home fronts.

Histories and memorialization of the First World War usually center on the sol-dier and the war front rather than the civilian and the home front. But whatever the focus, the tendency is to concentrate on the extraordinary, the memorable, and the apparently distinctive. Yet we understand much more about the experience of war, particularly this new kind of total war that the First World War exemplified, if we reach behind the extraordinary stories of war to everyday life. An innovative study of wartime Vienna has shown that "the refraction of the everyday" is a particular feature of total war: "Everyday matters previously considered private or sub-political were refracted through the . . . lens of war, and, like a ray of light, came out 'bent' on the other side." The everyday matters reinterpreted through the experience of war included food, fashion, shopping, child-rearing, leisure, and neighbor relations.[3]

However, it is not just that these ordinary aspects of daily life were significantly affected by a war being fought many miles away. The disinterring of everyday life on the diverse home fronts of the First World War gives us a new way of understanding the war itself. This is particularly the case when we turn to the most basic necessity of daily life—food. During a crisis, almost everything else in everyday life could be allowed to suffer, such as the cleaning of the home, person, or clothing, as contrasted to the requirement for daily food. What was at stake was survival. Indeed, everyday life, specifically the acquisition of food, was crucial to the winning or losing of a total war. Without understanding this aspect of modern war, and the world's first experience of it, we miss the significant role that civilian morale and its interdepen-dence with military morale have for the practice of warfare. This all begins with the mundane and relentless task of feeding oneself and one's household as the rising prices, poor distribution, and even dearth of basic foods and fuel made shopping and cooking an exhausting struggle for those whose responsibility this had always been: women, specifically housewives.[4]

In this new kind of warfare, food became a weapon of war. The economic blockade was used systematically by both sides in the First World War. The purpose was to starve out the enemy, particularly civilians, as part of a modern total war that involved everyone—the military and civilians, men and women, the young and the old. Such a strategy was designed to undermine civilian morale: the thinking was that hunger would drive the population to demand an end to the war. This in turn would have a catastrophic effect on military morale. Soldiers fought to defend their homes and families, and if they knew that their families were suffering at home, they might mutiny or desert. And if economic blockade worked, they too would be hungry, ill-equipped, and thus less efficient soldiers.

Enforced at sea, this blockade was particularly effective in what was by 1914 a world economy where raw materials, manufactured goods, and particularly food were regularly transported across the world's oceans to equip and feed the urban populations of Europe. As an island, Britain was particularly vulnerable to economic blockade and to the new German U-boat (submarine), which was very efficient at

Official British war artists such as C. R. W. Nevinson depicted not only scenes of battle but also the gendered experience of women on the home front, as in this 1918 drawing, entitled *The Food Queue.* One of the omnipresent sights of everyday life during the war was the line of women and children waiting for rationed food. © *Imperial War Museum (Art.IWM ART 840)*

sinking merchant shipping that brought food as well as military supplies to British ports. Between the destruction of merchant shipping and the competing demands of the military, all the belligerent nations and most neutral countries were affected by the suspension of the norms of world trade and the blockading of nearly all shipping within the world's ports—albeit in different ways and to different degrees.

Contemporaries understood this argument about the home front. For example, in November 1916, Lady Cornelia Wimborne told a Dorset society recently formed to bring agricultural producers into closer touch with retailers and consumers that

> the agricultural and food question was one of the weapons by which we must hope to win in the terrible war which was going on . . . . She did not think that in the past the people of England . . . had realised the importance of the food question. They had been so accustomed to get their food cheaply and easily that they did not trouble to enquire where it came from, but now at last, they were awake to the fact that more than half of their food came from abroad, and that there were very serious dangers in securing that food supply.[5]

A year later, Mrs. Pember Reeves of the Ministry of Food was unequivocal:

> The war was now one between the two civilian populations of . . . [Germany and Britain]. If the war were lost it would be due to the civilian population. . . . This country appeared to be unprepared for compulsory rationing, but we must be as heroic about this as were the men at the front. They could not win the war unless they had behind them the support of the civilian population.[6]

This was why, as a British First World War poster put it, "The Kitchen Is the Key to Victory." This battle was understood to be women's responsibility in a sexual division of warfare in which the language and iconography deployed were always gendered.

To conduct a total war, a belligerent had to organize itself to feed an army at the front and to sustain a healthy civilian population to maximize war production to equip that army, while maintaining the support of the people. Otherwise there might be food queues, riots, and worse. The various regimes fighting the First World War, or caught up in its widespread effects, as the neutral nations were, could not afford to be destabilized in this way. It became increasingly clear that the war front could not succeed without a sustainable home front. In terms of food, this posed a real challenge. Although in many ways Britain was not a typical example, the scale of the problem is evident in its growing food crisis. Britain relied very heavily on imported food in 1914, producing only 20 percent of the wheat it required,

40 percent of the butter and cheese, 60 percent of the meat and bacon, and none of the sugar.[7] These commodities were essential to the diet of the majority of the population. This inevitably led to shortages, which were exacerbated by a significant rise in the cost of living. By mid-1917, the average price of food was double that of 1914. This mattered when the working class spent about 60 percent of their income on food.[8] There was little room for maneuver, as even when goods were available, supply was erratic. Distribution suffered because of domestic fuel shortages and the priority given to the needs of the military on the railways and in shipping. Nevertheless, there is still surprisingly little recognition of how significant food was to the progress of the war as a whole; how food shortages and the different responses to them (individually, collectively in homes and neighborhoods, and by the local and national governments) were experienced in everyday life; and how this significantly affected civilian and army morale, and thus the conduct of the war.

Most histories of First World War home fronts do not center on everyday life, particularly the increasingly relentless struggle to find sufficient food. They are more concerned with government policies and the war economy than with the banality of daily life. In contrast, there are studies of Berlin and of Vienna that concentrate on ordinary urban women's attempts at daily survival.[9] Here the conduct of the war is seen not through high politics and decisions about how civilians should behave but in terms of how the construction of the home front was negotiated in everyday life in these cities.[10] Their focus is primarily on the women who bore the brunt of this daily struggle. They plot how daily shopping created opportunities for women "to act and interact in the public sphere: in the streets, before shops, and in market squares."[11] "Women of little means," as they were termed in Germany, engaged with those in power without being formally political. These women, despite not being citizens, had agency and used it.

Women's actions were not limited to the Central Powers. Violent cost-of-living riots fomented by crowds of unorganized urban housewives broke out in cities across the world in 1917 and 1918.[12] Spurred by the extreme challenges of everyday life in wartime, these protesters were motivated by something that has been termed "female consciousness." It was their roles as housewives and mothers that made desperate women feel entitled to demand as their right the minimum subsistence needed to carry out their crucial part in sustaining the home front.[13] However, large, violent riots were not the only way in which a woman's politics of food might emerge from the daily struggle to deal with the wartime food crisis. Britain did not experience such dramatic events, yet here too women made a politics of food. This was a quieter and arguably more sustained attempt to break down the barriers between everyday domestic life and what was understood more widely as politics.[14] If the wartime food shortages are seen only through the lens of protest, it is possible to overlook the actual experience of women dealing with the food crisis, particularly the range of innovative ways that they found to respond to the daily challenge of trying to feed their families. Using everyday life as a means to view the First World War can give a new perspective on how civilians experienced the home front and how it in turn was inextricably linked to the war front, thus creating a total history of the new phenomenon of total war. This history must necessarily plot how gender roles were mobilized, challenged, or reinforced in the daily experience of this new kind of war, because everyday life is saturated with gender.

Mapping the wartime food shortages and rapidly increasing cost of living reminds us that this was a global war. Wherever in the world it occurred, a range of factors affected the experience of the food crisis and thus the nature of and the degree to which the ordinary tasks of everyday life became increasingly challenging. A key context for understanding individual, everyday experiences of food shortage is the extent of a country's food self-sufficiency at the outbreak of war and the degree to which the country was integrated into the world economy. For instance, Britain was highly dependent on imported food, while Germany imported 25 percent of its grain and 40 percent of the fats it consumed.[15] Further, Germany's agricultural sector also relied on imported fertilizers and feeds. This helps explain why both sides seized upon the economic blockade as a crucial part of their strategy to win the war. A combatant state's capacity for food production was equally important. Yet less than 10 percent of the British population participated in agriculture at the outbreak of war, in contrast to more than 37 percent for Germany and more than 40 percent for France.[16] Equally, those countries that were highly dependent on agricultural exports, such as Denmark and New Zealand, suffered. Whether a belligerent, a neutral, or just a country located far away from the main theaters of war, there was no escaping the wider effects of the European economic blockade. Severe dislocation to everyday life could be found across the world, with tragic consequences: 1 million people died in the Punjab in 1918 because of a decrease in domestic food production in order to export supplies for the Allied war effort.[17] Colonial societies in many parts of the world felt the pinch of shortages, and in some cases famine, because of the requisitioning demanded by their imperial leaders.

Moreover, the effects of economic blockade were not uniform. A significant difference emerges when ones takes into consideration what kind of regime was in power (from liberal democracies to autocracies to states under colonial control) and its willingness and capacity to intervene not only in the market but also in what hitherto had been understood to be the private behavior of individuals. Central to the overall experience of everyday life at home was the degree to which the state was willing or able to implement elements of food control such as price-fixing or rationing and, as important, the extent to which they had popular support.

The most immediate challenge to the continuance of people's daily routine of acquiring and preparing an adequate diet for the family lay in the increase in the cost of living and how rapidly this took place. Whether a country had conscription or relied on volunteers, the loss of men to the military necessarily had an impact on household incomes. Wage earning was affected by the new demands of a war economy, and there were various systems of separation allowances paid to the families of soldiers. This brought new challenges for the working-class woman, the traditional manager of household income. Prices for necessities rose sharply, albeit at different rates both between and within countries. Where systems of rationing were especially ineffective (such as Germany), the black market fueled the upward spiral of prices. For all nations, the second half of the war was the hardest, when extensive food shortages were exacerbated by inadequate distribution and poor harvests. However, the pace of the crisis and the responses of local and national governments varied across the belligerent nations.

Nor could the neutrals stand apart from what was becoming a world food crisis. For instance, from 1914, the United States, the Netherlands, and Spain worked together to feed the civilians in occupied Belgium and northern France to alleviate the suffering of the captive population. Moreover, neutral nations were not exempt from food shortages themselves. For example, the United States' entry into the war in 1917 had a significant effect on neutral countries such as the Netherlands. Despite pressure from both Britain and Germany to trade with only one of the belligerents and to limit transit trade from third parties to "the enemy," American exports guaranteed a continuous supply of foodstuffs and raw materials. Once the United States became a belligerent, neutral states lost their access to these supplies, and the blockade became total.[18] This necessarily put pressure on Dutch domestic consumption and thus on everyday life.

The timing of the food crisis within each country was another crucial factor in shaping the daily challenge faced by the woman consumer. For example, the late entry of the United States into the war affected its population, who were asked only in 1917 to engage in the kind of voluntary restraint in food consumption that Britain had been relying on since 1916. The British finally introduced formal rationing in 1918 after issuing sugar ration cards in 1917, but the American government never faced widespread hardship or the domestic unrest that so often followed it. The New York food riots of 1917 did not spread very widely, although there were also violent protests by immigrant women in Boston and Philadelphia.[19] The US Food Administration's wartime campaign to turn American housewives into an army of "kitchen soldiers" seems to have had some effect on what was a problem of a different order than that experienced in continental Europe and parts of Africa and Asia.[20]

Rationing was introduced in belligerent and neutral countries, but at different rates and with varying effects. These effects become particularly apparent in the case of bread, as there were a number of possible responses to the ubiquitous shortage of wheat. In Britain, the free market prevailed for the first two years of the war, but not without protest. From the outset of the war, there were calls to nationalize food. Prices kept rising, and there were intermittent supplies of a range of necessities. Government put increasing moral pressure on civilians to limit their consumption. Bread was a particular focus of these campaigns. Posters, the example of the king limiting his own bread consumption, and the activities of local food economy committees proselytizing against waste were all used to persuade people to eat fewer slices of bread so that the country would consume less wheat. This, it was suggested, would mean more bread for the troops and free space in ships for war materials.

The government decided that the political costs of rationing bread would be too high, so instead it took a number of steps that other belligerents also deployed. These included adulteration, adding other grains and even potato, to stretch available wheat supplies that had also not been ground so finely. From 1917 on, Britons could get only rougher "war bread." In addition, the sale of bread was prohibited until it was twelve hours old. Both steps allowed bread to remain available but ensured it was much less palatable and therefore unlikely to be squandered. This all took time to develop in Britain. Supplying bread took on a slightly different form elsewhere in Europe. For instance, in Germany, state action about the food supply occurred more quickly so that adulterated "war bread" appeared in 1914, and it was rationed the following year. This was particularly important as in 1914, the average German household spent nearly 12 percent of its income on bread.[21] By the summer of 1918, German Elfriede Kuhr noted in her diary that bread was made from flour mixed with potatoes, beans, peas, buckwheat, and horse chestnuts. It only became palatable a few days after it was baked.[22] The French introduced "national bread" in 1916, and by the following year they too ordered that it should only be sold when stale. Although various constraints were placed on restaurants and cafes in different countries, it remained possible for those who could pay to get cakes and other luxuries when the less well-off were struggling for necessities. Michel Corday, a middle-aged civil servant who worked in Paris throughout the war, recorded in his diary in January 1918 that cakes had now been "abolished," with tearooms selling only pastries.[23]

State-imposed rationing was a way of sharing limited resources and dissipating protests at the injustices created by an unregulated market. However, its effectiveness depended on how well it was designed and how firmly it was policed. Critically, its success rested on widespread public support—if that ebbed away, then what the Germans termed "self-help," particularly the black market, took hold. The Central Powers implemented rationing before the Allies, but the system was often subverted and could not guarantee adequate supplies to those who held ration cards. In Britain, there was strong official resistance to rationing but increasing popular demands for it. Local municipal schemes were devised in some towns and cities before a national system was finally rolled out in the last year of the war.

The British Ministry of Food was all too well aware of the failings of the German and Austrian systems. In public discussions of the need to ration, it was the eradication of the "evil of the queues" that it stressed. British rationing, Ministry of Food officials claimed, would achieve everything that their enemies' systems had failed to do. One detail that precluded the endless search for particular foods was that in the British system, individual cards were valid only at a specific shop, which allowed for more effective distribution of unpredictable supplies and made speculative queuing pointless. How one rationed could define how successful a home front might be. There was a fundamental connection between a system of rationing that civilians had faith in and their susceptibility to war-weariness.

The other key factor shaping the degree to which wartime food shortage impinged upon and reshaped everyday life was the geographical and social location of an individual, as no home front was homogeneous. Age was one factor that divided the wartime population and its access to resources. However, the biggest divide was that between urban and rural communities, particularly in countries that had a large peasantry, as in most of continental Europe and especially Russia. The standard of living remained higher in rural areas, and food shortages had a less detrimental effect. One reason for this was that the social contract between the food producers and urban consumers broke down as each suspected the other of failing to share. In Britain, the polarization between urban and rural populations was less stark, but there remained real differences between metropolitan and provincial experiences, as well as between highly urbanized areas and smaller towns and villages. Such experiences were sufficiently differentiated that it is plausible to speak of plural local home fronts.

In all these settings, social class was one of the most significant determinants of the experience of food shortage and shaped the strategies that people adopted to cope. Class also helped shape the extent to which the routines of everyday life of any one individual or family were disturbed or even overturned. This helps explain how restaurant and cafe life continued alongside food queues and cost-of-living protests across all the belligerents. Hoarding (the focus of much attention in Britain) and participating in black markets in countries as diverse as Austria-Hungary and Sweden were not just the province of the better-off. Increasingly, the everyday lives of the middle classes were also affected by widespread food shortages. Not only were servants instructed not to waste, but middle-class housewives themselves took to keeping a close eye on price movements and the availability of goods within local markets. They even shopped themselves, which was a novelty for many.[24]

However, when it came to the effect of food shortages on daily routines, gender was particularly significant. This was not because women were the only occupants of the home front: there were always male civilians, not just the very young and the very old. Diaries of men on the home front show that despite privations, the sexual division of domestic labor was never seriously upset.[25] It was customary across the home fronts that women had the responsibility for ensuring that households were adequately fed.

Gender was central to the way in which everyday life was affected by the war. The demands of the home front meant mundane aspects of daily life that had previously been seen as domestic matters now became a public and state concern. This had many implications for women. Their invisible domestic work could no longer be overlooked. Indeed, their labors were crucial to winning or at least not losing the war. In Britain, those responsible for food control noted in 1922 that "the food question was largely a domestic one upon which the views of women were entitled to full expression."[26] It was increasingly recognized by the public and politicians alike that accepted daily practices of shopping for necessities, the cooking and sharing of food within families, and the management of household resources were no longer private matters. As the *Win the War Cookery Book* (1917) had it: "Every meal *you* serve is now literally a battle."[27]

The language of war penetrated the private space of the home and particularly women's domain: the kitchen. What food was eaten, who got the lion's share, how well the food was cooked, and how much was wasted had until that point been largely private choices. A notable exception was for the poor, whose poverty deprived them of privacy. In Britain, prewar concerns about high infant mortality had prompted surveys and interventions based on the assumption that working-class women needed to be taught how to feed their children properly. Maud Pember Reeves, the author of one such survey, *Round about a Pound a Week* (1913), was to become one of the two women responsible for the Women's Department of Britain's wartime Ministry of Food. What was new in wartime in a variety of national contexts was the idea that the state could at first advise and then directly interfere in private decisions within respectable households across the classes. However, what was not being questioned, indeed was being robustly shored up, was the sexual division of labor. Whatever else the war economy demanded of her, a woman's principal task was to keep the household going. This included domestic work undertaken outside the home, particularly the acquisition of food through any means necessary.

To some contemporaries the home front seemed feminized. This was partly because so much that had previously been hidden within the home was now being pursued outside it in a range of public spaces, particularly streets and marketplaces.

Women were increasingly visible and out of context, for example, urban women foraging for food in the German and Austrian countryside.

The food queue or the food riot dramatized what was already taking increasing amounts of women's time. It was not that everyday shopping for food had suddenly become women's responsibility in wartime, but now where and how they shopped and how successful they were at acquiring an adequate diet for the family mattered on all home fronts. Yet women's increasing presence in the public sphere in the daily pursuit of food is too easily seen as another marker of a simplistic separation of the war into gendered fronts: masculine war versus feminine home front. Thus, although the German city of Freiburg was by 1916 considered to be a feminized space as women constituted 64 percent of the nonmilitary population, men were very much present and crucially still held power.

Everyday life on the home front was challenged by the extreme circumstances of the war, although the extent and nature of that experience depended on where and who you were. By looking at a number of aspects of the daily acquisition of food, it is possible to explore how they were gendered and the extent to which they prompted a shift in gendered power dynamics in the short or longer term. The phenomenon

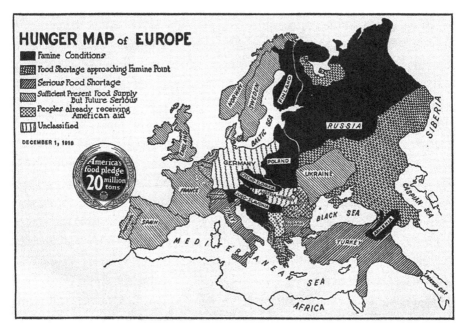

This so-called Hunger Map of Europe, dated December 1918, appeared in *Current History*, the weekly magazine of the *New York Times*. The Allied blockade of enemy ports led to widespread food shortages, hunger, and malnutrition, which turned into a global problem in the postwar period. *The New York Times, Current History, May 1919*

that became most emblematic of the food crisis and the power of it to disturb the balance of power within a nation was the food queue.

The food queue was "a habit unknown in this country except at bargain sales," observed the *Manchester Guardian* in early 1918, yet descriptions of "ever-growing queues of beshawled women and poorly-clad children patiently enduring the bitter cold of hours of waiting in the hope of obtaining a moiety of what they need, and often enough not getting it after all," had already become ubiquitous.[28] Food queues took longer to appear in Britain than in Germany and Austria, but by 1917 and 1918, they were being reported all over the world. In Vienna the first queues for flour and bread had appeared in the autumn of 1914, closely followed by those for milk and potatoes in early 1915, sugar in April 1916, soap in July of that year, followed by cigarettes, plums, and cabbage two months later.[29] It was the extent of food queues, wherever they were, that drew comment. Margarine queues of at least a thousand people, lined up five or six abreast, were reported to be gathering from 6:00 a.m. in Manchester and Salford just before Christmas 1917, with one queue estimated to be a quarter of a mile long.[30] Police reports from Vienna showed that on a typical day in 1917, some 350,000 people waited in 1,100 queues, with 47,000 sent away empty-handed.[31] The mood varied, depending on how everyday the queue had become. The relative novelty of British queues meant that "unruffled good humour" was noted to begin with, but the implied threat was always there, partly because Britons knew what food queues had led to elsewhere, hence the phrase "the evil of the queues."[32] The German *polonaises* (queues) shared similar characteristics but in a more extreme form: the crowds were predominantly women, who waited through the night with policemen walking up and down to keep order, and many left empty-handed, searching for another queue to join.

The practices employed for waiting in queues varied, with some women coming with chairs or bringing knitting "to shorten the leaden hours."[33] Queues demanded new codes of behavior. Because holding one's place in the queue could mean the difference between eating and going hungry, the Viennese abandoned the prewar courtesy of letting the elderly or infirm move to the front of the queue. Shoppers were equally intolerant of pregnant women, who received special passes from the state to avoid waiting, to the point where the police had to revise this system because it led to public disorder.[34] New forms of etiquette, and means of enforcing these modes of behavior, evolved in the food queues of Vienna. The police found it increasingly difficult to keep order as they were subject to derogatory remarks as men still on the home front.

Crucially when it came to food, women also disciplined one another. For example, a woman who arrived fifteen hours before a butcher's shop was due to open in order to get prime position in the queue was chased away by other women.[35] A margarine queue in Bournemouth in early 1918 faced a particular example of "queue-jumping" that dramatized wider social tensions. A lady was driven up in her coach. Her maid went to the head of the queue and directly into the shop. The police who made no effort to prevent this were criticized by the "poor people" in the queue, who were also heard to make strong remarks about rich people. The queue was reported to be incensed even when it was made clear that the lady was collecting hospital supplies, as it was also revealed that the maid had emerged from the shop with a separate parcel of two pounds of margarine destined for the lady's house.[36] As in Vienna, the food queues undermined any pretense of a unified home front, demonstrating "the millions of daily fissures that divided the Viennese from one another."[37] In Berlin, various measures that were set up to allow pregnant women to go to the front of queues at dairy shops and for special milk rations to be issued to children and the ill proved hard to implement. As the crisis worsened, the crowds did not accept the justice of this special treatment. By the winter of 1916–1917, milk had largely disappeared from general public access in the city, so jumping milk queues was no longer an issue.[38] Increasingly queues had given way to uncontrollable crowds and to riots when women seized goods and looted shops or market stalls.

The food queue could also become the space that acted as the seedbed for further protest, specifically the move from individual to collective action. The queue might be seen in press reports as a unified whole, but it consisted of individual women and children whose focus was on their immediate needs. They were often willing to stand for many hours in the cold on the basis of a rumor. In December 1915, in the Russian town of Kamennyi Zavod, 200 soldiers' wives stood in line to receive their benefits. They fell to talking, sharing their anger over the rising cost of daily life, and they decided to take matters into their own hands by going to the nearest shop and demanding that the price of flour be lowered. When the merchant resisted, the women threatened to take the flour without any payment. He then agreed to lower the price. The women repeated this performance at shop after shop.[39]

The markets and shops where food queues assembled were often already the hubs of community networks where housewives gathered not only to shop but also to socialize and gossip and even, occasionally, to organize.[40] It was here that some queues became crowds and then food riots. When an orderly queue became a crowd, the mood changed: now there was pushing, shoving, and cursing.[41] In Freiburg, patience had eroded by the spring of 1916 because of worsening shortages and bureaucratic turmoil, a situation rife with rumors and resentments. The ritual of waiting became "undignified," according to those in the queues. The situation thus became much more volatile: now hundreds of women stormed stores, and there were street battles with the crowds appropriating urban space. The police were instructed to suppress photographs of the long queues.[42] Even images could now be provocative.

In most countries, it was taken for granted that the food queue was largely a space occupied by women and to a lesser extent children, who were usually there as proxies for their mothers. This assumption is underlined by the threat by male workers in some British cities to take time off war work to keep places in queues so that their wives could take a break.[43] Women munitions workers, some of whom were soldiers' wives, protested that after their long working day, they could not get food because "the people who had been standing in queues had the advantage."[44] There were even examples of women mill workers in Darwen, Lancashire, abandoning their looms to join margarine and meat queues. The local Trades Council threatened that if something was not done about the queues, "the employers' time will be used for waiting in food lines."[45] In Berlin, from the end of 1915, some women gave up paid work entirely so that they had more time to queue as the relentless struggle to find extremely scarce foods became more important than earning a little money.[46] In the sexual division of the home front, it was clear who had the task of queuing. This further explains why the food queue was so potentially explosive not just for social order but also for gender relations.

There was an existing tradition in popular protest of food riots and violent cost-of-living demonstrations, but during the First World War there was an important difference: the extent to which these actions involved unorganized housewives. In countries where the food crisis became extreme, such as Germany, Austria, and Russia, food riots were not only prompted by the stresses of the daily search for food but themselves also became everyday events. Their ubiquity meant that increasingly riot seemed the only way to respond to profiteering, short supplies, and the inadequacies and perceived injustices of food control systems. This was not the case in countries where the situation was less severe, such as Britain, the United States, or the neutral nations. Here, food riots were more unusual although still prompted by the demands of everyday shopping for necessities. There were also other ways to protest, particularly in Britain.[47]

What made these wartime food riots different from those of earlier centuries was that now the sexual division of labor was much more firmly entrenched. It was clear that it was women's responsibility to find the food to feed their families.[48] Thus women resorted to food riots because they had no alternative. In contrast, for men, everyday shopping was not considered to be part of their responsibilities, and more significantly, they also had other avenues for registering grievances. In this sense, the First World War food riot was gendered in several ways. We can see this in terms of motivation but also in terms of who populated it and how it arose from the sexual division of labor that affected all the practices of everyday life.

The issues raised by food in everyday life had the capacity to challenge the public/private divide, which the experience of war only exacerbated.[49] This was particularly apparent with the communal kitchens that appeared on a range of home fronts and within occupied regions. Communal or public kitchens and restaurants became an important way to subvert the focus on queues, as they provided one of the only ways to get scarce food, particularly cooked food when fuel was short. They were seen as feminized spaces, carrying over this status from the domestic sphere. However, communal kitchens muddied the boundary between the private and public because despite their association with domesticity, they were argued for, organized, and operated in the public domain. Some people were alarmed by the apparent whiff of charity the kitchens represented, while others resisted collective solutions, and still more were disturbed by the ruffling of the gender status quo. Domestic issues crashed through into political processes, although not without considerable challenge, and in so doing often empowered the women involved. Although tried on most home fronts, such communal provision was not always seen in the same way and had different levels of success. In Berlin, women seemingly resisted this provision as inherently less respectable because of its association with charitable soup kitchens.[50] However in Freiburg, its adoption proved less problematic, with close to 8,000 people a day taking their meals at the city's communal kitchens.[51] In Vienna by mid-1917, there were forty-seven "people's kitchens" providing warm, inexpensive meals and 131 "dining rooms" where food was free. However, many on the home front resisted the extension of these municipal services to all Viennese civilians as some at least dismissed this mass dining as humiliating because of its scale, charitable flavor, and the poor food. In the end the plan was finally scuttled by the fact that the city did not have public spaces large enough to accommodate 2 million diners per day.[52]

In Britain, however, there were women who became strong advocates of central kitchens, even in rural areas. "No woman working on the land ought to be expected to cook on her return home—no man would, why should the woman with less surplus energy?," wrote the suffragist Ernestine Mills in 1916.[53] Women workers petitioned local Food Control Committees to provide communal kitchens, and it was often women who made this facility happen; Florence Laney, for instance, was the energy behind the three successful national kitchens in Bournemouth. She was adamant that these should have a cross-class appeal. "In saving food at this juncture," she said, "we are all 'needy' people."[54] Exporting domestic activities from the home to what were usually municipal spaces remained controversial, but some people shared the hope of Marion Phillips, a leading member of the Labour Party, that wartime communal kitchens "would lead to many reforms and comforts in the working woman's life in the future."[55]

Foraging was another activity that became part of everyday survival on some home fronts. In Britain this meant supplementing purchased or homegrown food with hedgerow plants. Schoolchildren undertook extensive competitive blackberrying in 1917 and 1918 to provide fruit for the enormous quantities of jam required by British troops.[56] Where the food crisis was most severe, as in Germany, Austria-Hungary, and Russia, foraging was a much more desperate activity in which urban dwellers invaded the surrounding countryside to supplement meager rations with food bought on the black market or even stolen. This was greatly resented by the rural population, which felt government food control already exploited them. One Bavarian farmer's wife wrote in 1917, "They take from us and give to the urban people. Now they've taken our entire harvest. I'm doing no more, even if we end up starving."[57]

Despite the rhetorical claims of united home fronts where all were "doing their bit," civilian populations were divided. Food shortages made these tensions far more explicit. Urban populations were convinced that the peasantry not only were better fed but also were holding back supplies from their fellow citizens on a polarized home front. In Germany, the policing of this "self-help" became increasingly difficult. Foraging expeditions, particularly at the weekend, became part of the everyday pursuit of food in the second half of the war. Workers even took leave from their jobs to acquire food in this way: an investigation of 8,000 shipyard workers in October 1917 revealed that 7,000 of them had stocked up on enough potatoes through foraging trips to last until the next harvest. Whether it was they, or more likely their wives, who were the successful "squirrels" is less clear.[58] Largely because of the time these illegal activities took and because in the end they were about supplementing the family's rations, most were dominated by women aided by children. This is reflected in German crime figures. The number of women convicted of petty larceny doubled in 1917 from 1913; their crimes were mostly stealing food from stores or potatoes and other crops from the fields. However, as society broke down, increasingly squirreling ceased to be regarded as criminal. Some rural women benefited from this trade, selling or bartering from the fields as well as journeying in the opposite direction to sell goods on the urban black market.

There is little surviving evidence of how the urban population's practice of squirreling affected rural women's domestic responsibilities of providing daily meals for themselves and their families. As a result of these foraging expeditions, entire areas of the countryside were picked over, leaving farmers unable to fulfill their food-delivery obligations and further reducing the food allocations to the cities. On a June day in 1918, it was estimated that 30,000 city dwellers were in the potato region around Vienna. They were mostly women and children joined by soldiers on leave. As a result of this "great potato robbery," the government restricted travel to the area, and there was even an attempt to ban the carrying of rucksacks.[59]

By 1917, it had become clear on many home fronts that food shortages were too severe to be combated merely by the skills of an economical housewife. The power of dominant ideas about appropriate gender roles meant that women, no matter what their social and geographical location, were tasked with maintaining daily domestic life whatever the circumstances. In wartime, their ingenuity and resilience had ramifications for the success of whichever home front they formed a key part.

CONCLUSION

One of the new conflict zones of the first total war was everyday life on the home front. Here food was used as a weapon of war, deployed in different ways over each successive year of the war, in the spaces where the tasks of everyday life were carried out: homes, streets, marketplaces, and shops. In such skirmishes, the language and the practices of the relentless daily challenge of acquiring enough food for a family were gendered. We know more about how this played out in the mundane practices that constituted everyday life in particular parts of the First World War home front: the Central Powers more than the Allies; cities more than other urban spaces; urban more than rural areas; belligerents more than neutrals; and women more than men. An area of fruitful research for the future might be to expand work on everyday life and gender to areas not yet studied in detail.

What we already know is that underlying the resourceful and persistent strategies of the women most affected by food shortages and escalating food prices was a robust sexual division of labor whose foundations were never really shaken by the crisis. Despite all the other demands on her time, few questioned that it was a woman's responsibility to find the food to feed her family. However, the gender order was open to challenge as previously private matters became public ones, reframing what was understood as "political." The actions taken by a woman in pursuit of an adequate diet for her family often revealed the inadequacies of governments and gave voteless women greater leverage with those in power. The crisis of war opened up new possibilities to empower the woman in the food queue or in the various formal and informal food committees created to solve the food crisis. Once that crisis ebbed in the years after the Armistice, it became clear just how resilient gender power remained.

NOTES

1. *Manchester Guardian*, January 15, 1917.
2. Jean-Louis Robert, "The Image of the Profiteer," in *Capital Cities at War: Paris, London, Berlin, 1914–1919*, ed. Jay Winter and Jean-Louis Robert (Cambridge: Cambridge University Press, 1999), 104–132.

3. Maureen Healy, *Vienna and the Fall of the Hapsburg Empire: Total War and Everyday Life in World War I* (Cambridge: Cambridge University Press, 2004), 3. See also Belinda J. Davis, "Food, Politics and Women's Everyday Life during the First World War," in *Home/Front: The Military, War and Gender in Twentieth-Century Germany*, ed. Karen Hagemann and Stefanie Schüler-Springorum (Oxford: Berg, 2002).

4. Karen Hunt, "A Heroine at Home: The Housewife on the WWI Home Front," in *The Home Front in Britain: Images, Myths and Forgotten Experiences since 1914*, ed. Maggie Andrews and Janis Lomas (London: Palgrave Macmillan, 2014).

5. *Western Gazette*, November 17, 1916.

6. *Bournemouth Daily Echo*, December 4, 1917.

7. Derek J. Oddy, *From Plain Fare to Fusion Food: British Diet from the 1890s to the 1990s* (Woodbridge: Boydell Press, 2003), 71.

8. For the Ministry of Labour's statistics for the range of price rises broken down across commodities and between large towns and villages, see Ian Beckett, *Home Front 1914–1918: How Britain Survived the Great War* (Kew: National Archives, 2006), 111.

9. Belinda Davis, *Home Fires Burning: Food, Politics and Everyday Life in World War I Berlin* (Chapel Hill: University of North Carolina Press, 2000); Healy, *Vienna and the Fall of the Hapsburg Empire*. See also Ute Daniel, *The War from Within: German Working-Class Women in the First World War* (Oxford: Berg, 1997).

10. Tammy M. Proctor, *Civilians in a World at War, 1914–18* (New York: New York University Press, 2010), 76–112.

11. Belinda Davis, "Food Scarcity and the Empowerment of the Female Consumer in World War I Berlin," in *The Sex of Things: Gender and Consumption in Historical Perspective*, ed. Victoria de Grazia and Ellen Furlough (Berkeley: University of California Press, 1996), 289.

12. For example, Judith Smart, "Feminists, Food and the Fair Price: The Cost of Living Demonstrations in Melbourne, August–September 1917," *Labour History* 50 (1986): 113–131; Barbara Engel, "Not by Bread Alone: Subsistence Riots in Russia during World War," *Journal of Modern History* 69, no. 4 (1997): 696–721.

13. Temma Kaplan, "Women and Communal Strikes in the Crisis of 1917–22," in *Becoming Visible: Women in European History*, 2nd ed., ed. Renate Bridenthal, Claudia Koonz, and Susan Stuard (Boston: Houghton Mifflin, 1987), 429.

14. Karen Hunt, "The Politics of Food and Women's Neighborhood Activism in First World War Britain," *International Labor and Working-Class History* 77, no. 1 (2010): 8–26.

15. Alexander Watson, *Ring of Steel: Germany and Austria-Hungary at War, 1914–1918* (London: Basic Books, 2014), 341.

16. Jose Harris, "Bureaucrats and Businessmen in British Food Control, 1916–19," in *War and the State: The Transformation of British Government, 1914–1919*, ed. Kathleen Burk (London: Routledge, 1982), 136, 137.

17. Matteo Ermacora, "Rural Society," in *1914-1918-Online—International Encyclopedia of the First World War*, ed. Ute Daniel et al. (Berlin: Freie Universität, 2014), DOI: 10.15463/ie1418.10530.

18. Marc Frey, "Bullying the Neutrals: The Case of the Netherlands," in *Great War, Total War: Combat and Mobilization on the Western Front, 1914–1918*, ed. R. Chickering and S. Förster (Cambridge: Cambridge University Press, 2000), 23.

19. Dana Frank, "Housewives, Socialists, and the Politics of Food: The 1917 New York Cost-of-Living Protests," *Feminist Studies* 11, no. 2 (1985): 255–285; Paul A Gilje, *Rioting in America* (Bloomington: Indiana University Press, 1996), 132–133.

20. Christopher Capozzola, *Uncle Sam Wants You: World War I and the Making of the Modern American Citizen* (Oxford: Oxford University Press, 2008), 95–103.

21. Keith Allen, "Sharing Scarcity: Bread Rationing and the First World War in Berlin, 1914–1923," *Journal of Social History* 32, no. 2 (1998): 373.

22. Kuhr's diary (July 28, 1918) quoted in Peter Englund, *The Beauty and the Sorrow: An Intimate History of the First World War* (New York: Vintage, 2012), 470.

23. Corday's diary (January 27, 1918) quoted in Englund, *The Beauty and the Sorrow*, 428.

24. Hunt, "A Heroine at Home."

25. Thomas Livingstone, *Tommy's War: A First World War Diary* (Hammersmith, UK: Harper Press, 2008).

26. H. W. Clemesha, *Food Control in the North-West Division* (Manchester: Manchester University Press, 1922), 22.

27. Quoted in Gerard DeGroot, *Blighty: British Society in the Era of the Great War* (London: Longman, 1996), 208.

28. *Manchester Guardian*, January 17, 1918; December 24, 1917.

29. Healy, *Vienna and the Fall of the Hapsburg Empire*, 40.

30. *Manchester Guardian*, December 24, 1917.

31. Healy, *Vienna and the Fall of the Hapsburg Empire*, 82.

32. *Manchester Guardian*, December 24, 1917; *The Times*, December 31, 1917.

33. Daniel, *War from Within*, 191.

34. Healy, *Vienna and the Fall of the Hapsburg Empire*, 79.

35. Healy, *Vienna and the Fall of the Hapsburg Empire*, 80.

36. *East Dorset Herald*, January 10, 1918.

37. Healy, *Vienna and the Fall of the Hapsburg Empire*, 81.

38. Davis, *Home Fires Burning*, 160–169.

39. Engel, "Not by Bread Alone," 703.

40. Lynne Taylor, "Food Riots Revisited," *Journal of Social History* 30, no. 2 (1996): 492.

41. Roger Chickering, *The Great War and Urban Life in Germany* (Cambridge: Cambridge University Press, 2007), 235–236.

42. Chickering, *The Great War and Urban Life*, 406.

43. Beckett, *Home Front*, 116.

44. *Manchester Evening News*, January 18, 1918.

45. *Liverpool Daily Post*, January 18, 1918.

46. Davis, *Home Fires Burning*, 42.

47. See Hunt, "Politics of Food

48. Taylor, "Food Riots Revisited," 491.

49. See Karen Hunt, "Negotiating the Boundaries of the Domestic: British Socialist Women and the Politics of Consumption," *Women's History Review* 9, no. 2 (2000): 389–410.

50. Davis, *Home Fires Burning*, 152, and chap. 7.

51. Chickering, *Great War and Urban Life*, 224.

52. Healy, *Vienna and the Fall of the Hapsburg Empire*, 71–72.

53. Ernestine Mills, "Real Food Economy" (1916), in *Women's Writing in the First World War*, ed. A. K. Smith (Manchester: Manchester University Press, 2000), 233.

54. *Bournemouth Graphic*, January 19, 1918.

55. Marion Phillips in *Labour Woman*, March 1917. For wartime British communal kitchens, see Karen Hunt, "Gendering the Politics of the Working Woman's Home," in *Women and the Making of Built Space in England, 1870–1950*, ed. E. Darling and L. Whitworth (Aldershot: Ashgate, 2007), esp. 112–114.

56. *Manchester Guardian*, September 2, 1917.

57. Benjamin Ziemann, *War Experiences in Rural Germany, 1914–23* (Oxford: Berg, 2007), 158.

58. For "squirreling," see Daniel, *War from Within*, 197–207.

59. Healy, *Vienna and the Fall of the Hapsburg Empire*, 55.

9

Gender and Warfare

Susan R. Grayzel

IF TOTAL WAR can be interpreted as "war without limits," then one of the truly innovative features of the Great War was that it was the first war whose use of modern technology challenged participants' perceptions of where war took place and whom it involved. By so doing, the war further complicated assumptions about gender, heroism, and even citizenship. For example, was flying planes into combat something that made a man a heroic figure, as the appellation "ace" might imply? Or was the aerial bombing of civilian populations the act of effeminate cowards, since no real warrior or true man would attack defenseless women and children from the safety of the sky? If dying or being willing to die for the nation at war was one of the hallmarks of male claims to citizenship, then what did it mean when women did so? The increased use of new modes of warfare had profound implications for gendered understandings of the spaces in which war was waged, puncturing the borders between "home front" and "front line." Further, the First World War's blend of older modes of warfare (invasion, occupation) and newer ones (especially air power and chemical weapons) had a powerful impact on gender identity in both cultural and political terms.

The varying means of waging war during this conflict took place in, and adapted to, terrains as varied as those found in sub-Saharan Africa and the Middle East (a concept that was itself a legacy of the war). Across Europe, war raged from the snow-covered Alps to the rain-soaked, devastated fields of northern France and Belgium. This war allowed for deeply modern ways to die—via aerially delivered shells in regions far beyond the so-called front lines. And it permitted deeply familiar and traditional ones—via starvation and disease regimes, bullet wounds to the gut, and blood loss and shock. If we accept new chronological parameters for the war as beginning with conflicts in 1911 and lasting until the final peace settlements of 1923, then the war zones also expand to include rebellion and revolution, violent engagements that involved civilian populations across the globe.

Because warfare was being transformed, in practical as well as cultural terms, this meant a newly calibrated role not only for civilians (gendered feminine) but also for those waging war in more traditional battle zones, members of armed forces (gendered masculine). The forms of modern warfare that characterize the First World War included the growing use of industrialized weapons: aircraft; chemical munitions; submarines; tanks; machine guns; large-scale artillery, enhanced bullets and ballistics, and antiair batteries. But this war also utilized mounted cavalry, bayonets, and trenches. Defense mechanisms could encompass air-raid shelters, and the war gave us evidence of the shift in war's borders via modern bomb craters in ancient city centers. All of this called into question the neat demarcation of populations into the gendered spheres of combatant and noncombatant. This chapter draws on the insights offered by gender historians of war in light of the transformations in the nature of war that emerged during this conflict in order to demonstrate that warfare itself shaped and reshaped gender during and in the long afterlife of the conflict. It is one of its most important legacies.[1]

MEN AT WAR FACE NEW MEANS OF WAR

How did the Great War's incorporation of new forms of warfare alter wartime ideas and debates on masculinity? Combat-induced trauma could affect participants' views of the ideals of masculinity and sense of themselves as men.[2] One of the most well-documented of such medical conditions resulting from the war can be found in what contemporaries labeled "shell shock." The creation of this diagnosis and its use to explain a range of war-induced psychosomatic disorders has been ascribed to a number of factors. These range from the emotional toll of warring men's immobility and inability to take action because of trench warfare to the need to repress emotions like fear, anger, and grief among a population of men who had largely never been exposed to military violence. In one line of analysis, the men of this war found themselves in the position of the previous complainants of "hysteria"—namely, bourgeois women forced to deny their most basic needs. At the time—as the very term indicates—soldiers suffering from mental traumas were presumed to be suffering precisely because of the size and thus devastation of new and modern artillery shells. Some new studies of post-traumatic stress disorder suggest that concussive injury could have produced the kinds of symptoms found in the sufferers of the Great War.[3] This suggests a need to focus on what effect new weaponry—or even the combination of new and indeed old modes of warfare—had on soldiers' sense of themselves as men at war both during the conflict and in its aftermath.

There is ample evidence that troops actively disliked the use of these new weapons, especially chemical arms, and that disturbing soldiers' emotional and psychic equilibrium was part of these weapon's so-called success. Those witnessing the first use of poison gas in 1915 commented that its efficacy lay in part in its ability to induce widespread panic. British officials reported on troops who tried to tear off protective devices or otherwise acted "as though they have temporarily lost their reason." German commanders complained that they lost control of their men when gas entered a trench. Terms such as "gas hysteria" or "gas neurosis" arose to describe the behaviors induced by chemical attacks that persisted after the physical effects had subsided or healed.[4] Even when relatively effective protective devices against chlorine, phosgene, or mustard gas came into regular use, medical officers continued to note the emotional trauma of such weapons. After exposure to a poison gas cloud, British medical officer Captain Waugh reported: "A few men lost their heads, took off their [antigas] helmets and ran back, being severely gassed in consequence." A medical officer of the London Scottish recalled treating men who believed they had been gassed, with no evidence of their exposure, who all apparently responded to treatment with a placebo.[5]

The estimated 1 to 1.3 million men exposed to poison gas did not respond uniformly.[6] Yet particular kinds of fears—especially of blindness after exposure to mustard gas—and the witnessing of men "breaking down" after being subjected to such weapons captured attention at the time.[7] The visual specter of clouds of gas as well as its suffocating qualities provoked a different kind of anxiety than did other weapons. As a Canadian medical officer noted: "Men do not fear to stand up and face an enemy . . . but they do hate dying like so many rats in a trap, when death is due to gas against which they cannot contend."[8] According to an account in *Le Filon*, the newspaper of France's Thirty-Fourth Division, waves of poison gas affected "all around us, all who lived, all who breathed," and even if one had seen "the most horrifying wounds," nothing was "comparable to this fog, which, during hours that seemed as long as centuries, veiled from our eyes the radiance of the sun, the light of the day, the purity of the snow."[9] Underneath such poetic language lay a genuine evocation of what made gas warfare particularly unbearable—it removed sight, scale and time, reminding men of their own insignificance.

In addition, because there was no immediate way to fight back, no offensive measures that could be taken against a tangible enemy, the impact of gas on "nerves" seemed higher than its physiological effects. German infantryman Arnold Zweig powerfully evoked the feeling of being gassed: "Subjectively speaking, I was dead. So long as a man can feel fear, it's awful . . . you gasp for air and breathe in more and more of the poisonous muck, your gullet burns, and there's a roaring in your ears; but oblivion was deliverance."[10] Nor were such views restricted to European troops. Daya Ram of the Second Lancers wrote to his teacher in the Punjab that "the war is on entirely new lines and is full of surprises . . . . A new kind of smoke [gas?] has been invented which is let loose in the trenches and . . . it does not matter whether you are armed or not, as you lose all your senses."[11] The language here is telling—to be gassed is to lose all of your senses or is to feel fear and to feel dead. To inflict such death was to ignore codes of military behavior and engagement. In the words of one historian, the gas wounded of the Great War "were collectively martyred."[12] Moreover, nothing in the military ethos, with its emphasis on offense, equating action with virility, could prepare men for a weapon that incapacitated them by contaminating the very air they breathed.

This helps explain the development of the chemical weapons taboo as civilians too reacted with horror to the accounts of these attacks and to the kinds of injuries they left.[13] Noncombatant eyewitnesses, such as nurses, responded with as much frustration and horror as the men. A nurse's account that appeared in the *Nursing Times* shortly after the first use of poison gas summed up her reaction to seeing wounded men, "all these poor black faces struggling, struggling, for life, what with the groaning and noise of the efforts for breath," as leading to the conclusion: "It is without doubt the most awful form of scientific torture." Australian nurse Ellen Cuthbert wrote of witnessing gas wounds as leading her to realize "it is not war—just murder."[14] Instead of accepting poison gas as a legitimate weapon, such language conveys that contemporaries saw it as beyond the scope of customary warfare, as "torture" or "murder." The men and the regimes using such weapons, then, had to grapple with the toll of engaging in practices so widely condemned, portrayed not as heroes but as villains.

Unease with the use of poison gas did not limit its scope, and armies made use of chemical weapons in regions beyond the Western Front. While Germany initiated lethal chemical warfare in 1915, the Allied side quickly followed suit. Yet when the British government decided to introduce chemical arms in its war with the Ottoman Empire in January 1917, the language employed by the cabinet to justify its use reveals a continued discomfort with the weaponry and desire to use it only in retaliation. Gas here can almost be seen as suitable punishment for not waging war appropriately: "Atrocities perpetrated on subject races by the Turks and . . . maltreatment of Allied prisoners during the present war [led us to feel] . . . no hesitation in reversing the decision not to use gas against the Turks unless the latter employed it first."[15]

When British forces unleashed poison gas, commanders did so with the stated aim of lowering enemy morale and kept its use secret. Some participants even believed that the appearance of an array of troops wearing their dehumanizing gas masks in the Palestine theater would "terrify" the enemy. Yet with little evidence to support claims of lowering morale either by the toxic chemical fumes or the appearance of troops in devices to protect against them, poison gas was short-lived as a weapon of war in what came to be known as the Middle East.[16]

What is clear from a variety of contexts is that both the chemical weapons and the gas masks utilized to defend against them caused profound reactions. The training that ordinary men who filled the ranks of the armies of this war received to prepare them to fight did not necessarily prepare them well for the kind of war they then experienced. Chemical arms would seem to epitomize this new form of warfare that caught forces by surprise.[17] Poison gas wounded and killed men not only in novel but also in terrifying ways, transforming the basic task of breathing into something that annihilated rather than sustained. The comparison to the poisoning of vermin and to a sense of its being "dishonorable" echoed in accounts by militaries on both sides of the conflict. Claims to heroic wartime masculinity failed beside the reality of choking to death. Gas became indefensible in part, perhaps, because it so clearly undermined the interdependent notions of masculine valor and traditional combat.

In contrast to the considered lack of enthusiasm for chemical weapons shown by troops during and in the aftermath of the conflict, accounts of the Great War in the air suggest that the pilot—especially the "ace"—could epitomize a new kind of idealized male, a modern version of the heroic warrior. Air power came into its own during this war, first used for reconnaissance and quickly transformed into an offensive weapon. Air raids coincided with the outbreak of war, and Zeppelin attacks in 1915–1916 were then followed by more sophisticated airplane attacks in 1917–1918. At the same time, celebrated pilots in smaller planes had a new mission: to take out enemy aircraft before they could damage targets on the ground. From 1916 onward, such aerial pioneers increasingly engaged in air-to-air combat, the dogfight, and in France, such pilots could become "aces" after downing five hostile aircraft. Unlike his hapless compatriots below, the fighter pilot flew alone and became, as one French pilot put it, "the absolute master of his destiny . . . free to seek out the adversary, to accept combat or decline it."[18]

The mythic heroic "ace" who dominated much of the media coverage of the air war may be one of the reasons that the link between aerial warfare and the chivalric ideal was challenged so strongly in other wartime media. One visually arresting piece of British propaganda that reflected such views was a poster featuring Kaiser Wilhelm II in conversation with General von Hindenburg, who bestows the title

"Knights of the Air" on pilots who have clearly bombed a hospital, marked with a Red Cross in the background. The use of the word "knight" mocks any pretense to chivalry when the actions of air men so fully destroy innocent lives.[19]

Air power used beyond conventional front lines animated calls for civilians of all ages and both sexes to exhibit stoic bravery in the face of unprecedented destruction. It also led (as was the case with unrestricted submarine warfare) to calls to denounce the bravery and indeed to ascribe a deviant masculinity to those who would wage war with such means. For instance, among many responses to air raids against French civilians during the war, this critique emerges graphically in the lyrics of songwriter Jean Bastia. In 1915, Bastia tried to gain the censor's approval for a new song, "Zeppelinade," later resubmitted as "Nuit de Mars." During the first attempt to gain approval for the song, the censor marked its second verse with a large red X objecting to particular phrases. The censor signaled out as objectionable the lyrics that described a Zeppelin over Paris as a "fat phallus raping the virginity of the stars." As the lyrics elaborated, this phallic Zeppelin (standing in for German masculinity) was a "demon" capable only of dropping "sterile seed" that "far from creating new sons only serves to depopulate the world."[20] While other lines in the song spoke mockingly of the Zeppelin's power and of the cowardice of its attacks, the second verse both sexualized and emasculated those who would wage war in this manner.

Jean Bastia did not take the censorship of his song quietly, and he wrote a letter to the prefect of police defending his words in April 1915. He claimed that the censor only thought of the "pornographic sense" of the word "phallus" without "comprehending the character" of the word in this poetic context, one that would "not scandalize those that knew this sense." Bastia lost his argument with the censors, but his imagery nonetheless provides an example of one powerful way in which the air raid would come to be represented—as being the act of cowards (infertile rapists) rather than true warriors.[21] Rather than effeminizing the French men who could no longer defend their women and children from attack, such interpretations questioned the masculinity of the German attackers. It was their deviant manliness—that of eunuchs, sterile, cowardly men—that marked the German airmen. Far from calling into question wartime gender roles and the gender system itself, such images maintained the status quo by presenting aerial bombardment as violating the codes of chivalric warfare that separated out "real" men (combatants) from civilians, symbolized by women and children.

One can see this as well in the widespread training for hand-to-hand combat with bayonets that became a staple of combatants' versions of the war, and in the sense that civilians, especially women and children, should remain a protected category.[22] Yet, when confronted with the frustrating immobility of trench warfare combined

"KNIGHTS OF THE AIR"

LOOK HINDENBURG! MY GERMAN HEROES!

This piece of British propaganda portrays Kaiser Wilhelm II (right), in conversation with General von Hindenburg, bestowing the title "Knights of the Air" on his pilots. The use of the word "knight" is clearly ironic, as attacking the defenseless was the opposite of demonstrating chivalric valor. The poster thus questions the masculine honor of those willing to use innovative warfare against undefended targets. © *Imperial War Museum (Art.IWM PST 13561)* with the sense of an unseen enemy engaging in fierce artillery barrages along the Western Front, men in combat there had to stifle their "flight or fight" inclinations with profound effects.

Neurological studies at the time suggested that being unable to express the "instinctual activity" that should result from the "fear and anger" wartime conditions produced led to soldiers' incapacitation.[23] To survive such circumstances, soldiers during this war depended on things other than strategy, tactics, and devices; this could mean relying on long-distance emotional sustenance from home and the emotional labor of fellow men in arms.[24] Combining studies of the new mechanisms to injure male bodies and of the myriad ways in which men coped with new and often horrifying weaponry such as poison gas may open avenues to link emotions to the history of warfare. An expanded notion of survival that included a consideration of the role played by emotional sustenance might further transform our understanding of the new ways in which men experienced military conflict. By so doing, we may illuminate how societies and individuals understood how gender affected the capacity to wage as well as to endure war.

WOMEN AT WAR AT HOME

When thinking about gender and warfare as it pertains to women and the First World War, it helps to locate the multiple ways in which the inhabitants of the so-called home front (typically gendered feminine) experienced violence overtly. When foreign armies invade and occupy territory, those living in such battle zones always experience war directly. The wartime circumstances of invasion and occupation reveal multiple examples of day-to-day violence. Nor were abuses of the civilian population, including sexual violence, restricted to Allied populations.[25] Yet, while the sexual violence accompanying this war was not new, the ability to depict the brutality and sexualized elements of such modes of warfare was greatly enhanced by new communication methods and technologies. One of the innovations of warfare during the conflict was the state-sanctioned role of information warfare—a war of words, sounds and images largely, but not exclusively, directed at those at home. The ability to circulate publicly, and on a mass scale, exaggerated depictions and accounts of sexualized violence becomes another avenue to analyze the ways in which a new kind of war might affect how gender operated.

Propaganda in its modern incarnation was one of the innovations of this war. Understood as the promotion of certain ideas regardless of their veracity, this was something that states invested in, as well as being orchestrated by both official and nonstate entities. Britain provides a key case for studying propaganda because it alone among the major powers at the start of the war had to raise a volunteer army rather than rely on conscription. Government efforts aimed to shape the behavior of both men and women as seen in the images used in the Parliamentary Recruiting Committee's mass-produced posters. In several well-known posters, a range of female figures appeal to their men: a young mother proclaims that "Women of Britain Say Go!"; a young girl sitting on her father's lap asks, "What did you do in the Great War Daddy?"; and a white-haired grandmotherly figure points the way to a younger man, saying, "Go! It's Your Duty!"[26] In all these instances, femininity is associated with women at home imploring male protection, but the external threat to home life and homeland is offstage. Age features here as well, suggesting different versions of the mobilization of the female population.

In other British propaganda efforts, the external and gendered violence of war was more overt. Parliamentary Recruiting leaflet number 23, *Women and the War*, chastised women who had deliberately held back their men. While acknowledging "it is natural that mothers and wives and sweethearts" should be reluctant to send their men, they were putting themselves in danger "of our homes being ruined and laid waste." Women were urged to "think of what has happened in Belgium. Towns and villages have been destroyed by fire and sword, women and children outraged and killed, mothers separated from their children, and wives from their husbands, not knowing whether they are dead or alive." Explicitly asking British women if they wished "to share the unhappy fate of Belgian women," this propaganda played upon the previously circulated images of Germans as savage rapists, reminding them that the saying "Your country needs You" meant not that the king or government needed them but that "British cottage homes, British women and children, peaceful fields and villages"—a particular vision of home—needed to be defended.[27]

Such efforts also involved censorship through the Defence of the Realm Regulations and the use of the press in more informal ways. Propagandists also utilized organizations devoted to promoting the British cause at home and abroad, including throughout the empire. In India, for example, the Central Publicity Board produced more than 300,000 posters in addition to 4 million leaflets, 2.5 million war journals, and 275 communiqués, all part of a sustained program to ensure that the war effort garnered and retained public support.[28] The sheer scale and amount of resources utilized to persuade colonial populations to enable the British Empire to continue to engage in the conflict reflect a commitment to cultural mobilization as an additional means of waging war, and in this sense, Britain was hardly unique.[29]

Images helped other states to wage their war. In Russia, hundreds of posters from the early years of the war helped convey a message that the Russian empire should be viewed as a "military family," with father-commanders benevolently leading their men. Such metaphors had a dual purpose, to foster a common bond among men across class lines and to show how men from various ethnic and regional groups could unite. If such images worked to promote Russian mobilization, they could not be sustained in light of the war's toll on the home as well as on men.[30] In France, too, posters and other visual media sought both to mobilize and remobilize France and its colonies and to show connections between the fronts, across a range of locales.[31]

The mass production and distribution of such imagery and language represent a departure from previous wars. As the enormous wartime ephemera of posters, pamphlets, postcards, and placards across participant states reveals, ideas about the war could be spread by new methods of mass communication and mass culture. This leaves aside the oral power of songs, which could again be quickly printed up as sheet music and sung both in performances and in private, and the visual power of cinema, a new and powerful means of "showing" the war.[32] For example, a short film by Wladyslaw Starewicz, *Lilya Belgii* (Lilly of Belgium; 1915), illustrates the threat of the war's violence to innocent lives at home. Its opening scene features a tiny girl gathering mushrooms and flowers in an idyllic landscape, where she finds a "pale tragic dead flower"—a lily. When she returns home, she asks her grandfather to explain what happened to the lily. The resulting scenario depicts the war as a battle between animated insects—those who sing sweetly to the lily and the aggressive beetles, who in their pursuit of land and power attack their neighbors. When the lily [Belgium] stands in their way, they trample and destroy her, until nature wreaks havoc via a flood against the invaders. In this allegory, the stricken and innocent nation (one of the casus belli) was both feminized and eroticized.[33]

Other cinematic efforts showed the damage done far less obliquely and highlighted the need for war to audiences far removed from the initial battle zones. Cecil B. DeMille's film *The Little American* (1917) demonstrated how the danger to women from ruthless enemy actions could be spread far beyond the borders of war zones. It starred Mary Pickford as the embodiment of patriotic female innocence and pictured her in its introductory sequences, among other things, saluting against the backdrop of the American flag. This was the film that helped make her "America's Sweetheart."[34] As the story opens, Angela (an appropriate name for the pure American) is being wooed by Jules, a French aristocrat, and Karl, a German with an American mother. She is drawn to her German suitor and has accepted his proposal, when both men are called home by the outbreak of war. The turmoil prevents Angela from hearing a word from her beloved, so she accepts an invitation to join her aunt in her French chateau. Angela journeys across the ocean on the *Veritania*, which is torpedoed, although she survives and reaches France. Here she discovers the Germans advancing on the chateau of her now dead aunt. There are scenes showing the Germans as capricious occupiers who violate basic laws of humanity (let alone war) by raping women and shooting unarmed civilians, and they suggest such actions merit a forceful response. Karl, who thinks his fiancée dead and thus turns to alcohol and the influence of his odious compatriots, sexually menaces America's sweetheart, but in the end, he helps preserve her virtue and is overcome with remorse. When Angela helps to arrange an attack on the Germans and is about to be executed, Karl comes to her side and the two face death together, only to be saved by a timely artillery shell that takes out the Germans. The end finds Karl sentenced to a prison camp, the enemy redeemed by the love of a good woman. In a film suffused with traditional gender dynamics, perhaps it is the American maternal inheritance that redeems one man from a portrait of otherwise deviant German masculinity. Still, the film's ability to showcase depictions of German depravity and thus justify American participation makes it an effective example of using a new technology for propaganda.

Despite new methods for conveying the horrors of invasion, the targeting of enemy populations as a wartime strategy was not itself new, nor was deliberately cutting off lines of supply to enemy populations, but the Allied naval blockade extended the severity of a technique with ancient roots.[35] The blockade of German ports by Allied ships (mainly the British navy) was ostensibly aimed to prevent war materiel from reaching the Central Powers, but it also prevented foodstuffs and fertilizers from reaching civilian populations. Both Germany and Austria-Hungary used the term "hungerblockade," to describe this process, one they viewed as deliberately trying to starve their populations. Whatever the motives, the impact of the blockade can be seen in the experiences of hunger, malnutrition, and deprivation, all of which took a toll on women and on women's lives in the intimate spaces of the home. The inability not merely to feed children but also to provide them with the foods associated with a nurturing home deeply affected the women of Berlin, and presumably elsewhere in the Central Powers. This profoundly shaped the war experiences of women, who could add foraging for food and negotiating the new state systems of rationing to their wartime tasks.[36]

Ottoman Beirut offers another site where the politics of managing food and new opportunities for women took center stage. Once it entered the war in 1915, the Ottoman Empire tried to shape the increasingly complicated feeding of civilians in outposts like Beirut by using female volunteers as a cornerstone of relief efforts. Despite women's increased participation in public relief programs providing food and material aid, male politicians could view these efforts as "exceptional" and only appropriate during the war. They saw women as nonpolitical actors extending care in the home externally and thus did not recognize them as needing a public voice. That this took place in a region where famine became a weapon of war meant that using female volunteers helped secure both the existing patriarchal state (since it restricted women to an appropriate sphere of providing food and assisting with domestic life) and its "modernity"—modern in its willingness to support women's taking on an extradomestic role. Yet such actions often had the unintended consequence of contributing to women's political agency—here and elsewhere.[37] If food could be (and was) deployed as a weapon of war then the home could certainly became a battleground with direct consequences for women.

The destruction of homes via invasion and occupation further expanded with the new use of aerial warfare, an innovation that dramatically shifted the scope of who could now be considered at war. Air raids were an invention of the war, affecting some populations more than others but shocking many when they led to death and destruction in zones far removed from official battlefields. For reasons of both technology and geography, civilians in the capital cities of London and Paris experienced air raids over the course of the war in ways that those in Berlin and Vienna (and Petrograd) did not.

Perhaps the most profound effects of this new way of waging war can be seen in Britain, where domestic spaces long assumed to be immune from attack because of Britain's island status and naval supremacy instead became battle zones. The effect of using air power against civilian targets and populations troubled many contemporary British commentators. Public accounts of such attacks consistently and throughout the duration of the war condemned these as criminal acts, and they did so by emphasizing the unacceptable damage done to young and/or female victims. In Britain, Zeppelin raids that intensified in 1915, and even more deadly airplane raids by the summer of 1917 all brought damage and death to young and old, men and women, on British soil, but the popular media repeatedly emphasized the suffering of female victims and survivors.[38]

In many ways the late May 1915 Zeppelin raid on London provided the British public with quintessential victims who vividly illustrated how war had changed. On the night of the raid, Elsie Legett and her sister Elizabeth were asleep in bed with three other siblings; when a bomb fell directly upon them, their father tried to rescue all the children but failed, receiving severe burns in the process. Elsie was three years old when she died that night; Elizabeth was eleven when she subsequently died from injuries sustained in the raid. As a headline in one of the major daily newspapers put it, this was the "tragedy of the Zeppelins."[39] By late November 1917, housewife Ethel Bilbrough was quick to condemn the latest onslaught of airplane attacks: "The cowardly wickedness of such raids is almost incredible . . . . But as someone said the other day, 'There are no civilians now, we are all soldiers.' Still, soldiers have the power to *hit back*, but what chance have poor frightened folk in their beds?"[40] This demonstrates an awareness by a non-combatant woman that while the home front was now a war zone, those at home had no way to take action, which underscored the new stakes of warfare even for women far removed from the official battle zone.

Writing in the aftermath of raids that occurred during the celebration of Britain's first ever National Baby Week, feminist Ida O'Malley articulated what this new mode of modern warfare meant: "Things which used to be separate in fact, or in our minds, have been violently thrown together . . . . In former days . . . [o]ne could still, if one wished, think of the state as separate from the home, of men as separate from women. Now it is much less possible to do so."[41] This mixing up of the state and home, the worlds of men and women, resulted not only from the aerial attacks on homes far beyond a front line but also from the resulting militarization of the domestic sphere.

The deployment of lethal chemical munitions in April 1915 also changed the scope of modern war. Governments had to improvise rapidly to provide antigas devices for troops. Thus, a week after the Second Battle of Ypres that introduced chlorine gas as a weapon on the Western Front, the British War Office called on the women of the country via the national media to turn cotton wool, cotton gauze, and strips of elastic band into respirators for the troops. Within forty-eight hours, the number of handmade respirators deluging the Royal Army Clothing Depot in London was so high that the War Office called off the effort. An article in the *Irish Times* thus complained: "Irishwomen had no real chance to help, so short was the time which it took to produce the requisite number of respirators."[42] Indeed, the *Daily Mail*, one of the papers that took credit for the entire enterprise, used the headline "Women Foil the Poisoners," suggesting that the "magnificent" response of women throughout England mattered to the war effort.[43] In this redirection of female domestic skills toward the service of the military, turning ordinary household materials into a military object to protect a soldier in the face of modern industrial warfare, we can see the altered stakes of total war.[44]

The danger that poison gas posed to civilian populations closer to battlefields also prompted the use of gas masks that appear in photographs taken by the Service Photographique de l'Armée from regions most directly under threat from such weapons and published in January 1916 in the French pictorial *L'Illustration*. In a series of startling and poignant images, young schoolchildren in gas masks pose, both as individuals and then in a group portrait with their teacher.[45] Such mass-circulated visuals reveal a genuinely new result of World War I—putting a civilian population at risk from something that could not be confined to the battle zone. That the patrimony of the nation and those caring for these children could not be protected called upon women to act in new ways. The expression on the face of the female teacher in the photos is remarkably calm, exhibiting the "pluck" that the British women making gas masks were meant to exhibit in the face of air power. Expecting resilience from women now potentially threatened at home was one of the gendered legacies of the war.

Historical amnesia about the alterations created by the Great War has eclipsed the damage that modern weaponry inflicted at home. The damages sustained from air raids and from the shelling of urban (civilian) spaces like central Paris from long-range artillery have faded from a historical memory that highlights the suffering and accomplishments of men at the front. To take seriously the insights offered by gender historians of war in light of the transformations in the nature of war itself that emerged during this conflict means to see contested ideas about military masculinity and domesticated femininity with new eyes. The toll that new forms of warfare took on female as well as male bodies and lives is also something that future studies of gender and the war need to analyze more fully. One insight that arises from existing scholarship is that ideas about how men and women could and should behave and respond both supported and challenged assumptions about masculinity, femininity, courage, and survival in the face of sustained and widespread violence that incorporated new as well as traditional modes of warfare.

For one thing, by looking closely at the connections across "home" and "war" fronts, we can see shared experiences of new technology cross the borders of time (war and postwar) and space (geographical and psychic). The extent to which this held true throughout participant states can only be determined by new research in settings beyond the major powers. Further studies of the Ottoman Empire and war zones outside Europe may tell us about the limits of technological innovations or reveal the reach of new forms of warfare, perhaps especially information warfare, in "remote" settings such as the United States, Canada, Australia, and New Zealand as well as Asia.

What happened during the Great War had a significant afterlife. To come to terms with the new means of waging war, we can see, for example, states investing considerable resources in the technology that would enable them to attack enemy populations from the air. At the same time, many governments also created structures and policies to prepare civilian populations to become full participants in future conflicts. This can be seen in the widespread and transnational creation of civilian antigas protection in the 1930s and the emergence of the policies and procedures associated with civil defense. Given the new stakes of modern warfare, a key strand of postwar feminism expanded a commitment to antimilitarism and disarmament and to the removal of threats that new weaponry (poison gas shells, aerial bombs) now posed directly to women and their children.

As all of these new military practices continued—especially air raids—commentators, and particularly feminists, began to highlight another aspect of this new warfare. If the men who attacked innocent targets became "less than men," then the women who carried on despite these threats had the potential to prove themselves as heroic or even as worthy of belonging to the wartime state *as* men, even men in uniform. This shaped new discussions of women's global citizenship, and their efforts to see the home and the state, the realms of women and men, as "mixed up" in ways that merited their attention and activism.

In addition, if we take seriously how changes in warfare transformed wartime spaces and lives, we can see two things emerging. One is the militarization of the domestic and the home, of the full incorporation of women into the waging of modern war. The second is the domestication of war making so as to incorporate civilians into its calculations and spheres, something that was a central legacy of the Great War. By attending to the concurrent transformations in warfare and in the roles that men and women played during the war, we will learn more not only about how closely this shaped wartime and postwar politics and culture but also about the nature of modern war.

NOTES

1. There has been little work that attempts to analyze the impact of the new means of waging war beyond operational military history. One recent attempt to address this in terms of international law can be found in Isabel V. Hull, "Germany and New Weapons," in *A Scrap of Paper: Breaking and Making International Law during the Great War* (Ithaca, NY: Cornell University Press, 2014).

2. See Elaine Showalter *The Female Malady: Women, Madness and English Culture 1830–1980* (London: Virago, 1987); Ben Shephard, *War of Nerves: Soldiers and Psychiatrists in the Twentieth Century* (Cambridge, MA: Harvard University Press, 2003); Tracey Loughran, "Shell Shock, Trauma, and the First World War: The Making of a Diagnosis and Its Histories," *Journal of the History of Medicine and Allied Sciences* 67, no. 1 (2012): 94–119; Jason Crouthamel, "Male Sexuality and Psychological Trauma: Soldiers and Sexual 'Disorder' in World War I and Weimar Germany," *Journal of the History of Sexuality* 17, no. 1 (2008): 60–84; and Laurinda Stryker, "Mental Cases: British Shellshock and the Politics of Interpretation," in *Evidence, History and the Great War: Historians and the Impact of 1914–18*, ed. Gail Braybon (New York: Berghahn, 2003) 154-171.

3. Jacques Dayan and Betrand Olliac, "From Hysteria and Shell Shock to Posttraumatic Stress Disorder: Comments on Psychoanalytic and Neuropsychological Approaches," *Journal of Physiology-Paris* 104, no. 6 (2010): 296–302.

4. Edgar Jones, "Terror Weapons: The British Experience of Gas and Its Treatment in the First World War," *War in History* 21, no. 3 (2014): 356.

5. Waugh quote from Committee on Treatment of Gas Cases, Medical Evidence, 2nd Army, May 18, 1916; Lt. G. L. Grant, "Report on Gas Casualties," September 26, 1915, TNA, WO 142/100, and TNA, WO 142/99 both cited in Jones, "Terror Weapons," 363–364.

6. Estimates of numbers are from L. F. Haber, *The Poisonous Cloud* (Oxford: Clarendon, 1986), and are also cited in Tim Cook, "Against God-Inspired Conscience: The Perception of Gas Warfare as a Weapon of Mass Destruction, 1915–1939," *War and Society* 18, no. 1 (2000): 52.

7. For a discussion associating fear of blindness with fear of emasculation among British gas wounded, see Julie Anderson, *War, Disability and Rehabilitation in Britain: Soul of a Nation* (Manchester: Manchester University Press, 2011).

8. Cook, "Against God-Inspired Conscience," 48; R. J. Manion, *A Surgeon in Arms* (1918) quoted in Cook, 49.

9. "Les gaz, à ceux qui les ont vus," *Le Filon*, 1917, quoted in Olivier Le Pick, "Des gaz et des hommes," in *Gaz! Gaz! Gaz! La guerre chimique 1914–1918* (Péronne: Historial de la Grande Guerre, 2010), 25-53; Quote on 25. Translation my own.

10. Arnold Zweig, *Education before Verdun* (New York, 1936), quoted in Cook, "Against God-Inspired Conscience," 50.

11. Daya Ram, Letter to Rohlu Ram, June 12, 1916, in *Indian Voices of the Great War: Soldiers' Letters, 1914–18*, ed. David Omissi (Manchester: Manchester University Press, 1999), 195.

12. Cook, "Against God-Inspired Conscience," 55.

13. Richard M. Price, *The Chemical Weapons Taboo* (Ithaca, NY: Cornell University Press, 1997).

14. Anonymous, "Gas Poisoning," *Nursing Times* 11, no. 524 (1915): 585; and Sister Ellen Cuthbert, Nurses' Narratives, Butler Collection, AWM41/958; both quoted in Christine Hallett, "'This Fiendish Mode of Warfare': Nursing the Victims of Gas Poisoning in the First World War," in *One Hundred Years of Wartime Nursing Practices, 1854–1953*, ed. Jane Brooks and Christine Hallett (Manchester: Manchester University Press, 2015).

15. "Gas Shells against the Turks," Cabinet Minutes, January 19, 1917, TNA CAB 23/1, quoted in Yigal Sheffy, "Chemical Warfare and the Palestine Campaign, 1916–1918," *Journal of Military History* 73, no. 3 (2009): 811.

16. Sheffy, 815, 825, 837.

17. This is emphasized in most accounts of chemical warfare during the First World War. See, for instance, Frederic Brown, *Chemical Warfare: A Study in Restraints* (1968; rpt., New Brunswick, NJ: Transaction, 2006), Marion Girard, *A Stange and Formidable Weapon: British Responses to World War I Poison Gas* (Lincoln, NE: University of Nebraska Press, 2008) and Haber, *Poisonous Cloud.*

18. See the discussion in the aptly named chapter "A New Breed of Heroes," in Lee Kennett, *The First Air War 1914–1918* (New York: Free Press, 1991), 164, quotation from pilot on 166.

19. "Knights of the Air," poster design by Howard Van Dusen, Imperial War Museum [IWM] ART PST 13561 [n.d.].

20. "Zeppelinades," words and music: Jean Bastia, Archives de la Préfecture de Police (APP) Ba 736. I owe this reference and am indebted for parts of my own translation to Regina Sweeney, "Harmony and Disharmony: French Singing and Musical Entertainment during the Great War" (PhD diss., University of California at Berkeley, 1992), 157–158, which forms part of her enlightening discussion of First World War musical culture and censorship. See also her *Singing Our Way*

to Victory: French Cultural Politics and Music during the Great War (Middletown, CT: Wesleyan University Press, 2001).

21. Jean Bastia, letter to the Prefect of Police, April 6, 1915, APP Ba 697.

22. See the discussion of this in Joanna Bourke, *An Intimate History of Killing: Face-to-Face Killing in Twentieth-Century Warfare* (New York: Basic Books, 1999), esp. chaps. 2 and 3.

23. Arthur C. Hurst, *Medical Diseases of the War* (1916, 2nd ed., London, 1940), cited in Joanna Bourke, *Fear: A Cultural History* (Emeryville, CA: Avalon, 2006), 205.

24. Michael Roper, *The Secret Battle: Emotional Survival in the Great War* (Manchester: Manchester University Press, 2009).

25. See John Horne and Alan Kramer, *German Atrocities 1914: A History of Denial* (New Haven, CT: Yale University Press, 2002). See also the evaluation of why those living in the aftermath of the war continued to invest heavily in the idea of exaggerated atrocities in Nicoletta F. Gullace, "Allied Propaganda and World War I: Interwar Legacies, Media Studies, and the Politics of War Guilt," *History Compass* 9, no. 9 (2011): 686–700; see also Vejas Gabriel Liulevicius, *War Land on the Eastern Front: Culture, National Identity and German Occupation in World War I* (New York: Cambridge University Press, 2000).

26. For these images, see ART.IWM PST 2763, ART.IWM PST 0311, and ART.IWM PST 12456, IWM, London.

27. Parliamentary Recruiting Committee, "Women and the War: Leaflet No. 23" (London, 1915); discussed in Susan R. Grayzel, *Women and the First World War* (Harlow: Longman, 2002), chap. 2.

28. Stephen Garton, "The Dominions, Ireland and India," in *Empires at War: 1911–1923*, ed. Robert Gerwarth and Erez Manela (Oxford: Oxford University Press, 2014), 167.

29. For more on British propaganda efforts, see Matthew Hendley, *Organized Patriotism and the Crucible of War: Popular Imperialism in Britain, 1914–1932* (Montreal: McGill-Queen's University Press, 2012); J. Lee Thompson, *Politicians, the Press and Propaganda: Lord Northcliffe and the Great War, 1914–1919* (Kent, OH: Kent State University Press, 1999). The term "cultural mobilization" derives from John Horne, with various case studies addressed in John Horne, ed., *State, Society and Mobilization in Europe during the First World War* (Cambridge: Cambridge University Press, 1997).

30. Karen Petrone, "Family, Masculinity, and Heroism in Russian War Posters of the First World War," in *Borderlines: Genders and Identities in War and Peace 1870–1930*, ed. Billie Melman (New York: Routledge, 1998) 95–120; see also Hubertus F. Jahn, *Patriotic Culture in Russia during World War I* (Ithaca, NY: Cornell University Press, 1995).

31. See Laurent Gervereau and Christophe Prochasson, eds., *Images de 17* (Paris: BDIC, 1987). See also Horne, *State, Society*.

32. On wartime songs, see Sweeney, *Singing Our Way to Victory*.

33. The film *Lilya Belgii* is now available on YouTube. https://www.youtube.com/watch?v=ZnYM8-7R--U. For introducing me to this film, I am grateful to Lora Mjolsness "Animated Propaganda: Visualizing the Great War in Russia" (paper presented at the conference "Europe and the World: World War I as Crisis of Universalism," University of California at Irvine, December 2014).

34. Leslie Midkiff DeBauche, *Reel Patriotism: The Movies and World War I* (Madison: University of Wisconsin Press, 1997), 61. See also Robert S. Birchard, *Cecil B. DeMille's Hollywood* (Lexington: University Press of Kentucky, 2004), chap. 26. For wartime cinema in other

national contexts, see Karel Dibbets and Bert Hogenkamp, *Film and the First World War* (Amsterdam: Amsterdam University Press, 1995).

35. See Hull, *Scrap of Paper*; Alan Kramer, *Dynamic of Destruction: Culture and Mass Killing in the First World War* (Oxford: Oxford University Press, 2007). Kramer makes the point that some of the most denounced acts of cultural destruction came not from innovative technology but from willingness to destroy by fire and looting such monuments as the library at Louvain.

36. Belinda Davis, *Home Fires Burning: Food, Politics, and Everyday Life in World War I Berlin* (Chapel Hill: University of North Carolina Press, 2000). See also Maureen Healy, *Vienna and the Fall of the Habsburg Empire: Total War and Everyday Life in World War I* (Cambridge: Cambridge University Press. 2004), and Hull, *Scrap of Paper*, on the legality of the blockade, as well as Mary Elisabeth Cox, "Hunger Games: Or How the Allied Blockade in the First World War Deprived German Children of Nutrition, and Allied Food Aid Subsequently Saved Them," *Economic History Review* 68, no. 2 (2015), 600–631.

37. Melanie Tanielian, "Politics of Wartime Relief in Ottoman Beirut (1914–1918),"*First World War Studies* 5, no. 1 (2014): 77.

38. Susan R. Grayzel, *At Home and under Fire: Air Raids and Culture in Britain from the Great War to the Blitz* (Cambridge: Cambridge University Press, 2012), chaps. 2 and 3.

39. *The Times*, June 2, 1915; *The Times*, June 10, 1915; *Daily Chronicle*, June 3, 1915.

40. IWM Department of Documents, Papers of E. M. Bilbrough (90/10/1), Ethel Bilbrough, Diary, November 4, 1917 (emphasis in original).

41. Ida O'Malley, "Babies and Bombs and Reconstruction," *Common Cause*, July 1917, discussed in Grayzel, *At Home and under Fire,* chap. 1.

42. "Respirators," *Irish Times*, April 30, 1915.

43. "Women Foil the Poisoner," *Daily Mail*, April 30, 1915.

44. Just as a sampling, see appeals in *Western Times*, April 29, 1915; *Hull Daily Mail*, April 29, 1915; *Manchester Evening News*, April 28, 1915. The most frequently cited source for the appeal is the *Daily Mail*. See Susan R. Grayzel, "Defence against the Indefensible: The Gas Mask, the State and British Culture during and after the First World War," *Twentieth Century British History* 25, no. 3 (2014): 418–434.

45. *L'Illustration*, January 29, 1916.

10

Gender and Violence

Michelle Moyd

∽ ───

THE VIOLENCE THAT occurred during the First World War needs little introduction. Yet for the most part, in the century that has passed since the war began
in 1914, our understandings of the scope of the war's violence have been limited
by several factors. First, historians have only recently begun to grasp the extent to
which European actors mobilized their empires to fight, opening up new ways of
thinking about the First World War as a truly global war. Second, in thinking about
the events of 1914–1918 as part of a longer global crisis that unfolded between 1912
and 1923, historians have realized the limitations in imagining the conflict as having
lasted a mere four years.[1] Third, we have tended to think about violence in fairly
narrow ways—as something that occurs on battlefields, and which primarily affects
soldiers—that ignore the different ways that men, women, and children experienced
this period.[2]

As historians rethink the war's meanings and effects, a gendered approach to
engaging the issues outlined here offers potential for reassessing the scope and magnitude of violence related to the war. Gendered analysis directs historians' attention toward excavating how men and women may have experienced and interpreted
events differently. It also reveals how wartime needs reshaped gender identities—
different versions of masculinity and femininity—to suit wartime contexts and
needs. Gendered analysis of the violence between 1914 and 1918, as well as in the
years immediately before and after this devastating period, shifts focus toward areas
of historical inquiry that reveal commonalities across global human experiences

of the war. This method diverts attention somewhat from diplomatic, political, and military narratives of the war. But it does so with an eye to exposing how a wider range of ordinary people—beyond diplomats, politicians, generals, and even soldiers—could have experienced certain similar forms of violence despite their living in places that might not appear obvious sites of comparison.

Gendering the First World War's history of violence entails removing battlefields—especially European ones—from the center of analysis in trying to understand the war's violent impact.[3] These sites must, of course, remain focal points for studying the First World War and its effects. But horrendous as it was, battlefield violence on Europe's Western and Eastern Fronts represents only a fragment of the story.[4] To better understand the magnitude and scope of violence, an expansive definition is required. Violence thus includes the infliction of physical pain and death, as well as assaults on the psychic, socioeconomic, and cultural dimensions that dramatically affect peoples' lives and personhoods. These elements might not stand out as part of wartime "violence" in prevailing narratives of the war.[5] But an expansive definition, which foregrounds victims' perspectives, exposes the many ways that ordinary people experienced wartime violence.[6] More specifically, this kind of definition throws into stark relief the gendered dimensions of the First World War's violence, revealing possibilities for thinking about gendered wartime violence in ways that might challenge and expand our understanding of the war a hundred years on.

The history of the East African campaign of the Great War illuminates how gender and violence were intertwined before, during, and after 1914–1918 in one colonial setting. The internal, everyday gendered violence that characterized the columns of the German East African colonial army (*Schutztruppe*), as well as the gendered violence these colonial military formations generated as they marched through eastern and southeastern Africa, reflect larger colonial trends.

The history of Africa and Africans in World War I is complex—and essential to understanding the global war. Some 2 million Africans were involved in the war as soldiers or workers, and about 200,000 of them died.[7] Using mainly African soldiers, the Allied powers fought four ultimately victorious campaigns against German colonial armies in Togo, Cameroon, German Southwest Africa, and German East Africa. The former German territories were divided up among the victors at the 1919 Paris Peace Conference, with Britain, France, Belgium, and South Africa all emerging from the war with more colonial possessions than had been theirs before the war began, even if they were technically known as "mandates," not colonies. African soldiers fought in all four theaters, in all the colonial armies, and African porters and other laborers handled these armies' logistical needs during difficult campaigns that relied on mobility through difficult, sometimes harrowing, environmental conditions. The East African campaign lasted the longest, required the most manpower and resources, and generated the most interest in the postwar period. In addition to Africans' service within Africa, however, hundreds of thousands were also deployed to Europe and the Middle East to bolster military manpower needs in these other theaters. Soldiers from French West Africa (*tirailleurs sénégalais*) fought on the Western Front and in the Dardanelles. Members of the South African Native Labour Corps (SANLC) worked as manual laborers at European ports, railways, and quarries. The war's effects on Africa and Africans included massive loss of life, as well as political and economic upheaval, famine, and disease. Yet most people have little idea of the scale of African involvement in the war. Taking a gendered approach to understanding the war in eastern Africa suggests new approaches to thinking about how gender structured wartime violence, and how wartime violence also structured gender, in different parts of the world.

RETHINKING GENDER AND VIOLENCE DURING THE FIRST WORLD WAR

New historical frameworks for thinking about the history of the First World War have made it possible to expand how gender helps to highlight the war's violence differently from past representations.[8] Gendered analysis elicits key insights into the diverse ways people experienced and perceived the war, and how they later interpreted it within their households, communities, nations, and beyond. For example, considering experiences of military occupation allows us to see immediately that violence directed at civilian populations was integral to war, not accidental.[9] When we focus on civilians, the gendered nature of wartime violence reveals itself more clearly. Young men tended to dominate combatant ranks, while women, the elderly, and children dominated the "home front," although in the case of the East African campaign, this division was less fixed than one might imagine at first glance. Still, this social fact often made military occupation zones sites of intensified violence, in which soldiers acted out militarized masculinities against enemy populations perceived by the soldiers as feminized, and therefore inferior.

Perhaps the best-known and best-researched example is the German invasion and occupation of Belgium and northern France in 1914. Historians' interpretation of the available evidence reveals several things. When German soldiers invaded Belgium and northern France in 1914, their realities were shaped by their imaginations. In particular, German collective memory of irregular, harassing warfare waged by soldiers the Germans called "francs-tireurs" (snipers) during the 1871 Franco-Prussian War shaped how they imagined the populations they administered under occupation during the First World War.[10] Many German soldiers viewed enemy civilians as a threat to be controlled only through violence. German soldiers condemned the irregulars' style of warfare, which relied on ambushes against unsuspecting German troops, as well as sniping and other tactics they found difficult to defend against. Such irregular fighters also blended into the civilian population, making it difficult to discern who was a combatant and who was not. German officers and soldiers judged this mode of fighting as cowardly, and cowardice, in turn, was coded as unmanly.[11] In an army conditioned to view direct, disciplined confrontation in battle as the manly ideal form of warfare, the specter of fighting against irregulars during the Belgian and French invasion in 1914 conditioned German soldiers to view the occupied populace as one that had to be controlled through extreme violence. They committed numerous atrocities and abuses against civilians in the process.[12]

Second, German soldiers' rapes or attempted rapes of Belgian women during the invasion and occupation profoundly affected how Belgians understood their wartime experiences and the German occupiers.[13] Women who experienced such violence felt the immediate effects of rape, including physical injury, shame, psychological trauma, pregnancy, and sexually transmitted disease, most acutely. To better discern the scope of violence that occurred in occupation zones, a gendered reading is thus absolutely vital. Without it, acts of sexual violence perpetrated by soldiers are treated as a mere side effect of war rather than as an expression of a particular form of masculine violence.

Third, Belgian and French people who lived under enemy occupation constructed the German soldier as a subhuman,[14] evoking bestial imagery that conveyed a brutish and oversexed German masculinity in contrast to an emasculated and feminized occupied population.[15] Similar patterns are also visible in other theaters such as Poland and Serbia.[16] We cannot fully understand the violence of occupation without also recognizing and exploring how gender shaped military practices that occupiers purposefully employed throughout the global conflict.

Gendered analysis refines our understandings of violence during the war in other ways as well. For example, recruiting propaganda generated by Entente and Central Powers drew on powerful images designed to stoke fears of enemy brutality, to inculcate values of service and heroism, or to promote social conformity in the interest of winning the war. In some cases, these graphic illustrations are also striking examples of how gender and race intersected to mold public perception of the enemy and social roles at home. The social and cultural effects of wartime violence on men's bodies also become clear when we use a gendered lens. Images of wounded or disabled soldiers being cared for by women nurses on the Western Front in Europe became a staple of postcards, an important means of mass communication. These sometimes reinforced notions of ideal gender roles and sometimes challenged them. Images of white soldiers being nursed by white nurses clad in white uniforms invoked accepted

European ideas about relations between men and women, with the nurses in their accepted roles as caregivers to wounded men. On the other hand, images of African men receiving care from white nurses unsettled these ideas, raising the prospect that white men might no longer be able to lay exclusive (however illusory) claim to white femininity. When disabled veterans returned to their homes after the war, their presence unsettled supposed boundaries between battlefield and domestic life, forcing societies to grapple with the relationship between violence and "civilization" on an unprecedented scale.[17]

Colonial and imperial experiences—especially those that occurred outside of Europe—offer distinctive vantage points from which to consider how gender and violence shaped each other during the war.[18] Thus, while our understanding of the experiences of African and Asian soldiers and laborers on the Western Front has expanded over the last two decades, we lack substantive work that links perspectives from overseas imperial territories to the war in Europe.[19] Such work is essential for testing the extent to which the very categories we use to analyze the conflict are the right ones for understanding this global war.

The East African campaign provides an especially useful window into the question of how gender and violence shaped each other. Everyday interrelationships between gender and violence become acutely visible within the standard military formations used by colonial armies in the East African campaign, known as columns. These columns generated particularly intense forms of gendered violence as they churned through eastern and southeastern Africa, especially in the last two years of the war.

GENDERED VIOLENCE WITHIN THE EAST AFRICAN COLUMNS

On November 25, 1918, General Paul von Lettow-Vorbeck, the commander of the colonial army (*Schutztruppe*) in German East Africa, surrendered his remaining forces—some 1,500 men—to the British.[20] A reporter for the *Bulawayo Chronicle*, a Rhodesian newspaper, gave a detailed description of the surrender scene, which captures a key element of the East African campaign of World War I: the presence of families of the askari (African soldiers of the *Schutztruppe*) as part of the colonial army's formation, the column.[21] He wrote:

> It was a most impressive spectacle. The long motley column, Europeans and Askari, all veterans of a hundred fights, the latter clothed with every kind of headgear, women who had stuck to their husbands through all of these years of hardships, carrying huge loads, some with children born during the campaign,

carriers coming in singing in undisguised joy at the thought that their labours were ended at last. All combined to make a sight that was unique.[22]

This "shabby cavalcade" numbered 4,500 people, including porters, women, and children. Only 1,200 to 1,300 of these were askari. The scene was described by one historian as resembling a "carnival procession" that stretched several miles, with the women carrying their families' belongings on their heads, babies slung on their backs.[23] The presence of women and children at the surrender struck British observers as quite remarkable, and the supposed uniqueness of this scene surfaced again and again in postwar historiography for years after the conflict ended. Interestingly, Lettow-Vorbeck's war memoir is conspicuously silent on the presence of women at the surrender: he notes that "1156 Askari and 1598 carriers" were present at the scene, but he does not mention women or children. Lettow-Vorbeck's omission of women from the surrender scene stands out all the more given the steady presence of the askari women as actors in his and other war memoirs.[24] Already, then, we can see that gender played a part in how British and German observers represented the surrender: British writers reported on a feminized remnant of the German army, while some German writers emphasized the stalwart masculinity of those who had survived the long campaign to surrender at Abercorn.[25] The German representation of the scene became the foundation narrative in interwar public calls for the return of Germany's former colonies, which it had lost during the postwar Versailles settlement. German arguments for the return of its colonies relied on scenes like the one at Abercorn as an assertion of the loyalty of Germany's former colonial subjects and Germany's capacity as a "model colonizer."

However, the festive, feminized description of the Abercorn surrender scene also hints at other dynamics at work in the *Schutztruppe* columns, the standard organizational units used in Germany's East African campaign. One observer of the surrender noted, "The women were kept in order by a European assisted by a few askaris."[26] Sir Hugh Clifford, who commanded the Gold Coast Regiment in East Africa beginning in 1916, unfavorably characterized the women of the columns as "a commando of women under military escort, [which] was marched about the country" to serve the needs of both the askari and the Germans.[27] Thus observers perceived the column's women variously as unruly, in need of supervision, or as unwilling participants in the "campaign communities."[28] Certainly much of this commentary might be attributed to the writers' inabilities to escape stereotypical representations of Africans as uncivilized. Still, a gendered reading of the surrender scene also helps us recognize that violence against women was central to the column's functioning.

In addition, what are we to make of the porters' "undisguised joy" at the surrender? Ludwig Deppe, a *Schutztruppe* doctor who had marched with Lettow-Vorbeck's column, noted in his diary that upon hearing news of the Armistice on November 13, 1918, the column's porters immediately began celebrating, singing. and dancing "as [he] had never heard them in over two years" of being on the march.[29] "Tireless" call-and-response songs echoed back and forth between the caravan leader and "the choir" of porters, expressing jubilation among the "youths" that "the hard work had come to an end."[30] Deppe's memoir registers disappointment in the porters' behavior, but it also alerts us to the possibility that not all men in the columns experienced the end of the campaign in the same way.

These multifaceted representations of the column's composition highlighted the presence of soldiers, women, and porters, and thus provide us with access to the shifting and varied masculine and feminine identities the columns encompassed. In turn, such representations help us see how the columns harbored particular kinds of gendered violence within them. A German memoirist described the noncombatant members of the column—"boys, porters, war wives and war children"—as "the colorful people of the askari," thereby capturing the many different kinds of people in the formation.[31] The column women, often referred to as "askari wives,"

German photograph taken in East Africa during World War I shows 'askari women' crossing a river. The image shows the harsh landscape and terrible conditions that African laborers faced as they carried food, supplies, and munitions for the armies at war. More than a million African carriers faced high levels of violence and privation in their dangerous wartime work. *Koloniales Bildarchiv, Universitätsbibliothek Frankfurt am Main. Used with permission*

joined the columns through different means. Some likely accompanied askari on the march from the outset, since their presence within the columns had long been part of the *Schutztruppe*'s way of war. These women occupied a higher place in the column status ranking than did others who joined the columns later in the war. Many women and children who lived along the columns' paths ended up being forcibly incorporated into askari and porter households (and therefore the *Schutztruppe*'s labor pool) while on the march. During the campaign, such vulnerable populations had little ability to resist the dangers the columns posed to their freedom and well-being. Some may have joined the columns because they provided nourishment and protection under difficult conditions.[32] Women coerced into joining the columns either through capture or through economic hardship had no prior connections to the columns. As was the case with young men who worked as servants to the askari (referred to as "askariboys"), such women were subordinate to senior women whose positions within the columns were secured through marriage or other forms of companionate relationships. To some degree, then, women inside the columns helped maintain the labor and status relationships that characterize all armies at war.[33] These relationships were also shaped by the gender roles men and women assumed within the columns.

This meant that women also participated in and experienced the violence of everyday column life. Such violence could include physical abuse for not keeping pace or otherwise frustrating askari and German officer efforts to keep the formations moving. Clifford's observation about women needing to be kept in order by an askari illustrates one aspect of this violence, but it reveals only part of the story. Women of the columns were also subject to sexual violence, and when resources became scarce, they received fewer rations and supplies than others.[34] In the latter phases of the war, commanders often decided to leave the women behind (along with the sick and wounded), while the men continued marching—a decision that exacerbated these groups' vulnerabilities. Further, while we tend to think of women as noncombatants, the blending of home front and front line in colonial warfare, and the ever-present possibility of ambush or of falling victim to long-range or aerial technology meant that the columns could never guarantee their safety from the war's violence.[35] Whether they were there because they "belonged to the army," or because they had been forcibly added to the columns, women and children incurred many of the same risks as soldiers.[36] Distinctions drawn between "combatant" and "noncombatant" are fuzzy at best in such a context.

Similar processes were at work in defining where different men fit into column composition. The askari had the highest social status within the formations, owing to their positions as armed soldiers, protectors, and provisioners for the columns' members.[37] Many of them were also heads of households, which garnered them additional privilege (along with additional complications of having to provide food, clothing, and care) in comparison to others who did not have families along on the march. They were frequently described as ruthless and brutal soldiers but also as doggedly loyal to the German cause. It is hardly surprising that these portrayals paint the askari in overly simplistic terms, given who most often provided the descriptions—German and British colonial military men and administrators. Yet most askari directly experienced combat, thereby assuming the inherent risks of its violence. They did so in part because their positions as soldiers guaranteed a certain degree of prestige and respectability within the colonial context. Their fates were very much tied to the military successes of the *Schutztruppe* columns. Therefore, it was in their interest to ensure that the columns functioned properly, and one means of enforcing compliance was through violence meted out against other subordinate column members, especially the askariboys and porters.[38] In so doing, they reaffirmed colonial rank and race hierarchies.

However, the askari themselves were subordinates to their white officers and noncommissioned officers and thus were subject to physical and psychic violence that rested on an intertwined and mutually reinforcing military rank structure and racial order that kept African soldiers subordinate to white superiors at all times. Most notably, askari who deserted, demonstrated cowardice, or otherwise fell afoul of *Schutztruppe* orders could be flogged or executed.[39] This kind of racialized rank structure, and the punishment regimes it fostered, characterized the British and French colonial militaries as well. Such structures shaped the wartime experiences of hundreds of thousands of colonial troops who took part in campaigns in Africa, Europe, and the Middle East. Among the best researched of these soldiers of empire are the *tirailleurs sénégalais*, the African soldiers who made up the French colonial army in West Africa. Recruited through various methods, including forced conscription as well as voluntarism, these soldiers fought in West Africa to force the Germans from their colonies there. Some 140,000 of them also fought on the Western Front in France, helping fill the French ranks as the war dragged on. Many recruits to the *tirailleurs sénégalais* were drawn from particular areas perceived by French officers to be producers of men skilled at soldiering. French commanders used soldiers from these "martial races" as shock troops beginning in 1916, which contributed to disproportionately high casualty rates compared with their white French counterparts.[40] In these ways, race and gender intersected to influence how and when soldiers might come to experience especially lethal moments of combat violence. Like the askari, the *tirailleurs* were subject to brutal punishments for nonconformity or perceived cowardice.[41]

The military hierarchy also subordinated logistical and support workers to military organizational hierarchies, which meant that they too were subject to the hardships of military life. Porters, servants, and prisoners all occupied subservient positions to the askari and thus were also subject to the soldiers' abuses, as well as the vagaries of campaign hardships and combat violence that women also experienced.[42] Yet as men, they also fostered community and camaraderie among themselves by asserting dominance over women in their day-to-day banter. The memoir of *Schutztruppe* doctor August Hauer recounts a campfire conversation between porters and servants he claimed to have overheard one evening at the end of a day's march. The group of men listened as one of their number described women's fears of being brutally raped by troops of "baboons" as they tended their fields. Two men claimed they had witnessed such an attack with their own eyes. Hauer concludes the section by noting that "Negro women who need to watch [their] fields will often reportedly wear men's clothing, because then the baboons have more respect for them and do not risk stealing [crops]." Caution in using this source is certainly warranted: Hauer's memoir, first published in 1921, offered up this salacious and violent story to a German readership steeped in racist representations of Africans as apelike. The presence of baboons as rapists in the story calls to mind the worst kind of racist stereotypes present in European cultural production at the time. But this disturbing story about East African women's fear of being raped by baboons while engaged in domestic agricultural labor also relied on men's knowledge of the sexual violence that placed women at risk in their everyday lives, not to mention during wartime.[43]

Within the campaign communities, men and women engaged in constant struggles for status and access to resources based on a variety of factors, including seniority, the circumstances under which individuals became part of the columns, and their proximity to men like the askari who could offer some form of protection during wartime. If the column that surrendered at Abercorn in November 1918 appeared carnivalesque to some observers, we should remember that this was merely a snapshot that only partially captured the confusion and violence that underwrote the column's day-to-day functioning while on campaign.

GENDERING THE EAST AFRICAN CAMPAIGN COMMUNITIES'
PREDATORY VIOLENCE

The *Schutztruppe*'s way of war must be understood as part of longer eastern African historical processes in which home fronts and front lines were linked through officers', soldiers', and laborers' households, so that they cannot be easily disentangled. The columns typically marched with white European officers and noncommissioned officers in front, followed by ranks of askari. Porters and others were positioned in the middle of the column, with more askari following. This spatial arrangement offered practical benefits for protecting valuable supplies and general security, creating at least a symbolic divide between soldiers and others. But for considerable portions of the East African campaign, there was no spatial divide between home front and front line. This style of campaign, with precursors in eastern African warfare both before and during colonialism, was the norm for the *Schutztruppe*.

Its opponents, including the British King's African Rifles, the Belgian Force Publique, and South African forces, used similar practices. In fact, Africans drawn largely from British protectorates in eastern and southeastern Africa were formed into carrier corps that made up the bulk of the porters used by all of the Allied forces operating there in the last two years of the war. Like the *Schutztruppe*, these columns incorporated women and children. As the Allies pursued the *Schutztruppe* across vast tracts of East African land, they too contributed to the destruction of the countryside. Thus, large-scale patterns in wartime violence during the East African campaign can be tied directly to the way that all the armies operated in this theater.

The conceptual limitations of "home-front" and "front-line" distinctions during war have long been evident; the two fronts were inextricably entangled.[44] Previous research on this topic has focused on European contexts. The example of German East Africa advances points made by these scholars yet also demonstrates a level of intensity in this enmeshment not visible in other theaters of the war. More can be done to highlight the entangling of home front and front line in the historiography.[45] Recent research also shows that combat in East Africa resembled operations in some Middle Eastern theaters.[46] The tight links between households, labor needs, combat, and the shaping of femininities and masculinities during the East African campaign offer a vantage point from which to reconsider the gendered nature of violence elsewhere in the Great War.

The violence of military formations in the Great War required the participation of men, women, and children. Nurses, cooks, laborers, drivers, communications operators, and others occupied essential positions in the vast logistical support structures that made it possible for armies to stay in the field. These positions were placed "behind the lines," constructing them as feminized zones in subsequent historiography and memory. It did not matter that both men and women worked in these zones in different capacities. One hundred years after the war's end, soldiers' experiences feature as quintessential to understanding the war. Without diminishing the importance of understanding how soldiers lived and died in the war, it is equally important to recognize all the ways that those who worked behind the lines created the conditions by which soldiers could continue to fight. The feminization of "behind the lines" enabled the making of heroic military masculinities, in which combat defines our understanding of the war a century later.

In a study of women in European warfare in the early modern period, John Lynn describes military formations very similar to those used in the East African campaign and other theaters, which were characterized by a high degree of mobility and lack of logistical infrastructure. He uses the phrase "campaign community" to refer to these military formations, describing how they created their own moral logics and practices as they marched:

> Soldiers in the field did not march alone, but as part of communities in which they lived . . . with male and female noncombatants. Armies on the march resembled cities in complexity and size, exceeded in population only by the largest European urban centers. While campaign communities understandably imported some standards and practices from civilian life, they established many of their own, some consciously antithetical to civilian values. Moreover, in order to survive, campaign communities preyed upon those unfortunate populations that lay in the path of the armies, creating a vicious dynamic between civilians and campaign communities.[47]

Lynn's depiction of these early modern military formations as "vicious" agents of destruction holds for the *Schutztruppe* in German East Africa as well. The very mobility of the columns, and the logistical requirements of an army on the march, guaranteed that their encounters with the communities they encountered on the march would be predatory on several different levels.

The columns were consumptive social units that operated according to the logic of "military necessity" while on the march.[48] They seized food stores and livestock whenever and wherever they could find them, and without regard to how local populations who had depended on those sources of sustenance would feed themselves.[49] Able-bodied men, women, and children were captured and forced to fill the columns' logistical labor needs. Alongside their voracious consumption, the columns were also immensely destructive. Their use of scorched earth practices, in which they denied enemy forces any supplies and materials they could not themselves consume or carry, also denied local populations their subsistence. *Schutztruppe* soldiers burned or destroyed goods to keep them out of the hands of Allied columns that pursued them across the southern half of the colony, into Portuguese East Africa and Northern Rhodesia, especially in the last two years of the campaign.[50] These practices had long characterized colonial wars of conquest in German East Africa and elsewhere. The East African campaign amplified these practices, exacerbating harsh conditions for populations that could not escape the destruction the columns caused. Askari also stood to benefit from these practices, since any goods or livestock they could keep for themselves helped them survive. Such seizures of goods also helped askari bolster their claims to respectability as men of consequence, which in turn helped them attract new household members.

Hundreds of soldiers, porters, and others marched through areas where inhabitants could not support the needs of the marauding armies, even in the rare instances when these armies provided compensation for requisitioned goods. Moreover, the volume of troops, porters, and others on the march contributed to the spread of diseases to areas that might otherwise have been protected by virtue of their distance from highly trafficked areas or large population centers. People also fled their homes, abandoning whatever they could not carry with them, to avoid suffering the depredations that accompanied these armies on the march. In this way, communities were dispersed, leading to long-term and sometimes permanent disconnection from ancestral lands and kinship ties. People subjected to such disruption could not easily recover their livelihoods and communal structures, which often led to political and socioeconomic vulnerability in the postwar period.[51]

The full extent of the violence perpetrated by the columns becomes more visible when we use gender as an analytical lens. We can see this by focusing on two kinds of gendered violence that occurred during the East African campaign. First, sexual violence perpetrated against women who lived in proximity to the columns' routes is illustrated through two examples that explicitly address sexual relations between column members and local women.[52] Studying these examples offers opportunities to think "the wartime body" as an important theme in the emergent First World War historiography.[53] Second, a focus on the long-term repercussions of violence done to communities during the war exposes how violence affected the eastern African communities in particularly gendered ways, for example, in their abilities to reproduce themselves, biologically and socially, during and after the war. Examining these two kinds of gendered violence opens paths to understanding wartime experiences in eastern Africa in relation to experiences that took place elsewhere. In turn, such analysis may help reveal new transnational histories of the Great War.[54]

German officers often groused about their day-to-day immersion in the household affairs of column members. Askari and porters added women and children to the columns at a pace that the Germans sometimes found bewildering because they did not fully grasp why askari and others wanted to have their families with them. In Portuguese East Africa in the latter stage of the campaign (March/April 1918), a German naval officer named Richard Wenig found himself overwhelmed with managing askari relationships not only with the women who had trekked with them from German East Africa but also their encounters with a new population of women at their camp in Nanungu. In fact, he referred to this period humorously as being "under the sign of the women," emphasizing that his time was consumed with managing the soldiers' and porters' domestic affairs. According to Wenig, many of his soldiers had not "had a woman in months." Upon reaching "this densely populated land, full of friendly natives, who have more than enough pretty women and girls," his men set about making up for lost time.[55] Fearing that the askari would "marry" local women in great numbers, thus increasing the size of the train and provisioning requirements, Wenig gave an order that "any marriage must have [his] blessing and approval," adding that he would be parsimonious in granting such permission. He realized that he would not be able to control "what happened in two hundred huts concealed by the night's darkness," and wondered why he should bother trying to "restrain the appetites of these primitive children of nature," but insisted that "marriage must be impeded because an expansion of the ladies' colony [*Damenkolonie*] with the expected arduous marches would be a great evil."[56] Wenig's priorities as a *Schutztruppe* officer, and his racist-paternalist worldviews, led him to try to limit column members' liaisons with local women.

His story is also one of askari and other column members building, rebuilding, or expanding their households, and asserting or reasserting their masculinity through sexual relations with local women. While such relationships provided the men domestic comfort and sexual connection, coercion and violence against women were also built into the processes of occupation. A paucity of evidence makes it difficult to know the degree to which women chose such relationships during this period of great privation and stress. But we can glean from the sources that finding security, either through flight or through establishing new kinship links, was paramount.[57] Sexuality, grounded as it is in cultural norms of respectability and morality, is often difficult to interpret and reconstruct.

The conditions of privation generated by the war meant that communities living in the *Schutztruppe*'s path struggled to find ways to limit the negative effects of the column members' presence. Their efforts to come to terms with military occupation included negotiations and exchanges that help explain the columns' tendencies to grow in numbers of women and children. Wenig's descriptions of his column's time encamped at Nanungu illustrate this point. He reported that local men had brought women to have sex with the porters in exchange for meat and cloth, noting that although he was "slightly astonished" at this arrangement, it all seemed to be happening in a "comfortable" way.[58] In another instance, though, he was compelled to order his senior askari to administer the *hamsa ishirini*—twenty-five lashes with a hide whip—to four porters who admitted that they had raped three local women in their home. Two men—a father and son—were forced to watch the rapes, having been tied up by the porters. Two days later, the same porters asked Wenig's orderly to request his permission to marry the women they had allegedly raped. In the intervening two days between the porters' floggings and their request for permission to marry, the porters had reached an agreement with the women and their families: the local leader told Wenig, "Yesterday they all ate *ngali* together, [and] now they are friends!—They love each other!"[59] Wenig wished them well, saying that he did not care what they did while they were still in Nanungu. However, he would not allow them to marry, telling them in no uncertain terms, "When we leave, the women stay here."[60]

The incidents at Nanungu represent a series of negotiations between men—the porters accused of rape, on the one hand, and the male representatives of the women they had raped, on the other. The source provides no indication of the degree to which the women influenced the negotiations, privileging a German masculine perspective on interactions between different groups of Africans. Wenig described the sharing of *ngali* between the porters and the women's representatives as an act of reconciliation. Yet Wenig is also recounting a scenario in which men seem to exert significant control over the fates of the women. The porters likely had to placate the families of the women concerned for having sexual relations with the families' daughters without having secured the permission of the father or guardian beforehand. The porters then incorporated the women into their own households. The shared consumption of *ngali* symbolized the families having reached agreement with the porters. Having compensated the families for the "theft" of their daughters, the porters shared a meal with their new kin.[61]

Hoping to retain some autonomy, or at least to ameliorate the level of extortion the *Schutztruppe* columns practiced, local peoples negotiated with askari and porters to the extent they could. Women's bodies appear as a medium of exchange in these negotiations, though again, we should not assume that women played no role in these negotiations. Wenig read these events in terms of "marriage" and the negative effects such relationships would have on his ability to maneuver and provision the column. Yet such daily interactions and confrontations between the members of the columns and local peoples were the norm over the four-year campaign, as askari and other column members performed their masculinities against the backdrop of war. Men in the columns acted out these violent performances on women's bodies under the watchful eyes of German officers and administrators, as well as local African patriarchs. In addition, Wenig's order to an askari to flog the guilty porters, described in minute detail over several pages in his memoir, renders visible the ways that different men within the columns perpetuated established masculine gender roles, as well as the violent behaviors that often accompanied the construction of these identities.[62] Thus the gendered violence perpetrated by the columns damaged individuals, kinship groups, and communities outside of the columns, and simultaneously reinforced gender rankings among men within the columns.

The columns also embodied forms of violence that had long-term effects on the ability of eastern African communities to sustain themselves and reproduce, whether

in biological or social terms. Protracted lack of access to food among communities
that had the misfortune of living anywhere near the routes the columns traversed
rendered them vulnerable to illness and exhaustion. Destruction of food stores contributed to famine conditions in certain districts. In Ugogo, for example, relentless
requisitioning of grain and livestock and systematic conscription of young men as
soldiers and porters by German and British troops between 1914 and 1916 convinced
many to escape with their livestock and to flee to safety, sometimes at great distances
from their homes.[63] Between 1917 and 1920, famine in Ugogo killed some 30,000 (of
150,000) people and caused many more to flee the area.[64] Belgian askari operating in
northwestern Rwanda in July 1918 also pillaged these areas so badly that local farmers
"declined to plant food crops [that would] immediately [be] looted from them, thus
causing famine."[65] In September 1918, a *Schutztruppe* doctor observed, "We leave
behind us destroyed fields, completely plundered magazines, and for [the immediate future] famine. We are no longer the pioneers of culture; our trail is marked by
death, plunder and deserted villages."[66] "Unseasonable drought" at the end of 1918
caused crops to fail, resulting in a "general shortage of foodstuffs throughout the
territory" and exacerbating famine conditions that existed in some districts.[67] The
influenza pandemic of 1918–1919 intensified the hardships experienced by many as
the war ended and a new British colonial regime assumed authority over the former
German colony. Some 50,000 to 80,000 Tanganyikans died in the pandemic, and
the official, probably conservative, estimate for British East Africa on the whole was
160,000.[68]

The demographic catastrophe that resulted from military requisitioning practices, environmental conditions, and the influenza pandemic produced a range of
new challenges that affected men and women in different ways. The mass conscription of able-bodied younger men to serve as soldiers and porters especially during
the last two years of the war meant that domestic and agricultural labor tasks fell
even more disproportionately on women than they had prior to the war, and that
children and the elderly also had to participate in domestic labor more than they
might have before. Older gendered divisions of labor were transformed by the relative absence of men in some communities. In places like Ugogo, where people fled to
avoid conscription, no one was available to tend crops, undermining the production
of robust harvests.[69] After the war ended, colonial labor needs directed men into
migrant work on plantations, in mines, and in urban areas. Conditions of "labor
shortage" in different parts of eastern Africa likely gave able-bodied men some leverage, if they could stay healthy.[70] While labor migration created opportunities for
workers to earn cash, gain practical knowledge, and experience wider geographies
and economies, these individuals also changed gendered labor dynamics in the

communities they left behind. In these ways, wartime violence was transformative, laying the basis for new patterns of gender relations after the war.

Thus, when the war ended, masculine hierarchies realigned to accommodate new socioeconomic realities. Marriage practices changed as well, reflecting an intensification of state and missionary interventions in managing marriages between African men and women, as well as African efforts to use these mechanisms to their benefit.[71] In the precolonial and into the colonial period, older men controlled younger men's marriage prospects through their control of livestock herds that formed the basis of bridewealth, a fundamental aspect of arranging respectable marriages between men and women. But after the war, with access to livestock diminished, and young men earning cash as migrant laborers, they exercised more freedom in selecting marriage partners, without necessarily needing to seek the approval of older men. This interaction between gender and age thus shaped categories of authority and power in society.

For women, wartime violence often meant fleeing to escape the columns' depredations. Stories of family dispersal dominate the collective memory of communities most affected by German and Allied maneuvers between 1916 and 1918, as in the southern highlands or in Ugogo. Women bore most of the responsibility for caring for children, limiting their mobility and increasing their risk during periods of dispersal. Men in turn could use these vulnerabilities to argue for a heightened need to protect women and children, thus bolstering their own claims to masculine authority.[72] On the other hand, though, women mobilized Christian idioms and family networks for support in the face of absent men, in order to protect their interests and those of their children.[73] Birth-spacing practices may have increased, and birth rates may have decreased in some places owing to poor health conditions. Witchcraft accusations, disproportionately leveled against women in times of economic and environmental hardship, also may have increased during the influenza pandemic.[74]

Poverty resulting from the convergence of the columns' logic of military necessity in requisitioning goods and livestock, rampant disease, and crop failures in the latter stages of the campaign spilled into the postwar period. Women felt such poverty in distinct ways, since they were charged with caring for families and administering households, while men increasingly joined the migrant labor force. For example, because women's work typically included finding and carrying water for household consumption, any change in the conditions under which they collected water (e.g., distance to the nearest source, security of routes to the source) also affected women's work regimes. In all these ways, wartime violence shaped gender relations into the postwar period in British-ruled Tanganyika.

CONCLUSION

An analysis of gender and violence in a lesser-known theater of the war enhances our ability to discern patterns of violence and the effects of such violence in the global war beyond those normally associated with Europe's Western Front battlefields. Yet much more work remains to be done to better connect the gendered meanings of the war's violence across its many different contexts. This work depends on the availability of source materials that can help historians reconstruct the local and regional histories of the war and its aftermaths. In the case of German East Africa/Tanganyika, for instance, many written sources went missing or were damaged during the conflict. Those that survived are dispersed throughout archives in Tanzania, Britain, Germany, Belgium, and elsewhere. Considerable synthetic work remains to be done in reconstructing Tanganyikan experiences of the First World War and the transition to British rule generally. This appears to be the case in other areas that transitioned from colony to mandate in the early 1920s.

Further exploration of the relationship between gender and violence in the East African campaign could take several paths that might prove useful within African historiography, and which will enable historians to make more robust connections to the global history of the First World War. The violence of war often continues, in one form another, after the war's end because grief, suffering, and losses fundamentally alter how families and communities function.[75] The subject of how Tanganyikans, Malawians, Kenyans, and many others coped with the magnitude of death and suffering they encountered, including losses of family and community members, is an area in need of further study. Interesting evidence exists for understanding African expressions and practices of mourning and bereavement, and it connects with emerging research in other contexts.[76]

Expressive cultures are also useful places to look for evidence of changing patterns of performance reflective of the war's violence and related trauma. In eastern Africa, competitive dance associations known as *ngoma* expanded rapidly during and after the war, and they encompassed gendered understandings of authority, wealth, generosity, and violence.[77] Devastating occurrences from the period 1914–1918, including famine, disease, and military attacks, appear in labor songs collected among the Sukuma of northwestern Tanzania, and these too express gendered understandings of the war.[78] Are there equivalent new forms of expressive cultures in postwar Europe, or in the postwar Middle East? If so, what do they reveal about gender and violence in the First World War?

Mourning and commemoration are additional areas in need of further transnational research. European memoirs and diaries from the war in East Africa sometimes make note of African burial practices, as do some oral histories.[79] Did men and women mourn differently in these contexts? In what ways were expressions of grief gendered? How did the cause of death affect mourning practices, and how were these gendered? What kinds of memorial cultures evolved, and what role did gender play in their maintenance? How did the interaction of race and gender shape violence during and after the war? What commonalities and differences do we see if we compare African and Western experiences of gender and mourning? It is also worth considering how the colonial context may have shaped expressions of grief and memory cultures. How does war-related bereavement take place among subject populations that lack citizenship, or whose humanity is devalued by colonial legal codes, labor practices, and education systems? Pursuing answers to these sorts of questions may shed light on how wartime violence shaped gender relations after the war.

Another potential research area that emerges from the German East Africa/ Tanganyika context relates to the transition from German to British rule. Given that other theaters of the war also went through such transitions, do patterns in the relationships between gender and violence emerge? How did different occupying powers seek to manage the effects of violence on postwar societies in gendered ways? Did men and women experience these effects in different ways, or not? What place did disabled veterans—as visible, feminized reminders of the war's violent effects—occupy in these settings? What role did veterans' organizations or other kinds of mutual aid associations play in shaping gender norms in these fluid postwar landscapes? The violence of World War I and its complicated aftermath offer rich opportunities to discern continuity and change in gender relations globally. The stories that might emerge from such analysis will help us better grasp the ways that war, with the different kinds of violence it unleashes, can solidify, dissolve, or reconstitute gender norms.

ACKNOWLEDGMENTS

I gratefully acknowledge Andrea Rosengarten's careful reading of an earlier draft of this chapter, which helped refine the argument in key places. I would also like to thank Susan Grayzel and Tammy Proctor for their encouragement and critical feedback throughout the writing process.

NOTES

1. Robert Gerwarth and John Horne, *War in Peace: Paramilitary Violence in Europe after the Great War* (Oxford: Oxford University Press, 2012).

2. Stéphane Audoin-Rouzeau and Annette Becker, *14–18: Understanding the Great War* (New York: Hill and Wang, 2000), 61.

3. Compare to Nancy M. Wingfield and Maria Bucur, "Introduction: Gender and War in Twentieth-Century Eastern Europe," in *Gender and War in Twentieth-Century Eastern Europe*, ed. Nancy M. Wingfield and Maria Bucur (Bloomington: Indiana University Press, 2006), 1.

4. Christa Hämmerle, Oswald Überegger, and Birgitta Bader Zaar, "Introduction: Women's and Gender History of the First World War—Topics, Concepts, Perspectives," in, *Gender and the First World War*, ed. Christa Hämmerle, Oswald Überegger, and Birgitta Bader Zaar (New York: Palgrave Macmillan, 2014), 7–9.

5. My definition relies on that provided in Nancy Scheper-Hughes and Philippe Bourgois, "Making Sense of Violence," introduction to *Violence in War and Peace: An Anthology*, ed. Nancy Scheper-Hughes and Philippe Bourgois (Oxford: Blackwell, 2004), 1. See also Heike I. Schmidt, *Colonialism and Violence in Zimbabwe: A History of Suffering* (Woodbridge, UK: James Currey, 2013), 9.

6. Richard Bessel, *Violence: A Modern Obsession* (London: Simon and Schuster, 2015), 15.

7. Hew Strachan, *The First World War in Africa* (Oxford: Oxford University Press, 2004), 3.

8. Heather Jones, "As the Centenary Approaches: The Regeneration of First World War Historiography," *Historical Journal* 56, no. 3 (2013): 858, 870. These older questions are: "why did war break out; why did the Allies win; were the generals . . . to blame for the high casualty rates; how did men endure trench warfare; and to what extent did civilian society accept and endorse the war effort?"

9. Jonathan Gumz, *The Resurrection and Collapse of Empire in Habsburg Serbia, 1914–1918* (New York: Cambridge University Press, 2009), 9.

10. John Horne and Alan Kramer, *German Atrocities, 1914: A History of Denial* (New Haven, CT: Yale University Press, 2001), 1.

11. Horne and Kramer do not advance an explicitly gendered analysis of the francs-tireurs, but they describe the irregulars as antithetical to German soldierly masculine ideals because they did not conform to German expectations of how opposing armies should behave. See Horne and Kramer, *German Atrocities*, 152–153. See also Isabel Hull, *Absolute Destruction: Military Culture and the Practices of War in Imperial Germany* (Ithaca, NY: Cornell University Press, 2005), 117–122. For more on how different styles of soldiering become categorized as masculine or feminine in a different context, see Susan Jeffords, *The Remasculinization of America: Gender and the Vietnam War* (Bloomington: Indiana University Press, 1989), 144–167. See also George L. Mosse, *The Image of Man: The Creation of Modern Masculinity* (New York: Oxford University Press, 1996), 56–76, on the making of "modern masculinity" in opposition to "marginal" versions of masculinity exemplified by the figure of the "wandering Jew," among others. More recently, see Jason Crouthamel, *An Intimate History of the Front: Masculinity, Sexuality, and German Soldiers in the First World War* (New York: Palgrave Macmillan, 2014), 15–20, on the making of a German hegemonic masculinity that was based on martial qualities. William Ian Miller, *The Mystery of Courage* (Cambridge, MA: Harvard University Press, 2000), 234–239, offers a useful reflection on cowardice as a diminished form of masculinity. Finally, see Ute Frevert's overview of the links between hegemonic masculinity and honor in "Wartime Emotions: Honour, Shame, and the Ecstasy of Sacrifice," *1914–1918-Online—International Encyclopedia of the First World War*, ed. Ute Daniel et al. (Berlin: Freie Universität, 2014). DOI: 10.15463/ie1418.10409.

12. Horne and Kramer, *German Atrocities*, 129–138. On European manly ideals, see Mosse, *Image of Man*, 107–119. For a useful critique of Mosse's formulation as overly rigid, see David Glover and Cora Kaplan, *Genders* (London: Routledge, 2000), 56–69. For a comparative case on the Eastern Front, see Laura Engelstein, "'A Belgium of Our Own': The Sack of Russian Kalisz, August 1914," *Kritika: Explorations in Russian and Eurasian History* 10, no. 3 (2009): 441–473.

13. Horne and Kramer, *German Atrocities*, 199. See also Tammy Proctor, *Civilians in a World at War, 1914–1918* (New York: New York University Press, 2010), 124–129.

14. Susan Grayzel, *Women and the First World War* (Harlow: Longman, 2002), 52.

15. Grayzel, *Women and the First World War*, 57. See also Billie Melman, "Introduction," in *Borderlines: Genders and Identities in War and Peace, 1870–1930*, ed. Billie Melman (New York: Routledge, 1998), 11.

16. Anton Holzer, *Das Lächeln der Henker: Der unbekannte Krieg gegen die Zivilbevölkerung 1914–1918* (Darmstadt: Primus-Verlag, 2014), 96–98.

17. See, for example, Maureen Healy, "Civilizing the Soldier in Postwar Austria," in *Gender and War in Twentieth-Century Eastern Europe*, ed. Nancy M. Wingfield and Maria Bucur (Bloomington,: Indiana University Press, 2015), 47–69.

18. Andrew Tait Jarboe and Richard S. Fogarty, "Introduction: An Imperial Turn in First World War Studies," in *Empires in World War I: Frontiers and Imperial Dynamics in a Global Conflict*, ed. Andrew Tait Jarboe and Richard S. Fogarty (London: I. B. Tauris, 2014), 1–20.

19. But see Joshua Sanborn, *Imperial Apocalypse: The Great War and the Destruction of the Russian Empire* (Oxford: Oxford University Press, 2014).

20. German East Africa encompassed today's mainland Tanzania, Rwanda, and Burundi.

21. Columns were narrow, but long, military formations of foot soldiers. All colonial armies operating in Africa from the late nineteenth century on used these formations.

22. Charles Miller, *Battle for the Bundu: The First World War in East Africa* (London: Macdonald and Janes, 1974), 326. Also cited in Leonard Mosley, *Duel for Kilimanjaro: An Account of the East African Campaign, 1914–1918* (London: Weidenfeld and Nicolson, 1963), 223; and John Iliffe, *A Modern History of Tanganyika* (Cambridge: Cambridge University Press, 1979), 245.

23. Brian Gardner, *German East: The Story of the First World War in East Africa* (London: Cassell, 1963), 193–194. See also Miller, *Battle for the Bundu*, 325–326.

24. Paul von Lettow-Vorbeck, *My Reminiscences of East Africa* (Nashville, TN: Battery Classics, n.d.), 177, 225, 244; Richard Wenig, *Kriegs-Safari: Erlebnisse und Eindrücke uaf den Zügen Lettow-Vorbecks durch das östliche Afrika* (Berlin: August Scherl, 1920).

25. See, for example, Heinrich Schnee, *Deutsch-Ostafrika im Weltkriege: Wie wir lebten und kämpften* (Leipzig: Verlag Quelle & Meyer, 1919), 393; Wilhelm Arning, *Vier Jahre Weltkrieg in Deutsch-Ostafrika* (Hannover: Gebrüder Jäneke, 1919), 319.

26. Gardner, *German East*, 167.

27. Hugh Clifford, *The Gold Coast Regiment in the East African Campaign* (1920; repr., Nashville, TN: Battery Press, 1995), 76.

28. John Lynn, *Women, Armies, and Warfare in Early Modern Europe* (New York: Cambridge University Press, 2008), 18.

29. Ludwig Deppe, *Mit Lettow-Vorbeck durch Afrika* (Berlin: August Scherl, 1919), 446.

30. Deppe, *Mit Lettow-Vorbeck durch Afrika*, 447, 449.

31. August Hauer, *Kumbuke: Erlebnisse eines Arztes in Deutsch-Ostafrika* (Berlin: Reimar Hobbing, 1923), 192.

32. Hauer, *Kumbuke*, 222. See also Marcia Wright, *Strategies of Slaves and Women: Life Stories from East/Central Africa* (New York: Lilian Barber Press, 1993), for more context.

33. Michelle Moyd, *Violent Intermediaries: African Soldiers, Conquest, and Everyday Colonialism in German East Africa* (Athens: Ohio University Press, 2014), 126–129. For comparison, see Linda Grant De Pauw, *Battle Cries and Lullabies: Women in War from Prehistory to the Present* (Norman: University of Oklahoma Press, 1998), 16–25; Cynthia Enloe, *Does Khaki Become You? The Militarization of Women's Lives* (London: Pandora, 1988); Catherine Lutz, *Homefront: A Military City and the American Twentieth Century* (Boston: Beacon Press, 2001).

34. Hauer, *Kumbuke*, 222.

35. Hauer, *Kumbuke*, 192; Nachlass (NL) Schnee, "Manuskript 'Meine Abenteuer in Deutsch-Ostafrika,'" Nr. 17, pp. 36, 37–38, Geheimes Staatsarchiv (GStA), Preussisches Kulturbesitz, Berlin; Hoskins to Chief of the Imperial General Staff (CIGS), 22/1/17, The National Archives, (TNA) CO 691/9).

36. Holly A. Mayer, *Belonging to the Army: Camp Followers and Community during the American Revolution* (Columbia: University of South Carolina Press, 1996), 6. See also Holly A. Mayer, "From Forts to Families: Following the Army into Western Pennsylvania, 1758–1766," *Pennsylvania Magazine of History and Biography* 130, no. 1 (2006): 6.

37. For a general discussion of military masculinities, see David H. J. Morgan, "Theater of War: Combat, the Military, and Masculinities," in *Theorizing Masculinities*, ed. Harry Brod and Michael Kaufman (Thousand Oaks, CA: Sage, 1994), 165–182.

38. German colonizers called their African male servants "boy," apparently adopting the term from their British colonial neighbors. Askari, in turn, called their servants, who were also often soldiers' apprentices, "askariboys."

39. NL Schnee, "Manuskript," p. 86, GStA,

40. Joe Lunn, "Les Races Guerrières: Racial Preconceptions in the French Military about West African Soldiers during the First World War," *Journal of Contemporary History* 34, no. 4 (1999): 517–536.

41. See also Timothy Stapleton, *No Insignificant Part: The Rhodesia Native Regiment and the East Africa Campaign of the First World War* (Waterloo, ON: Wilfrid Laurier University Press, 2006), 44–45. Stapleton makes the point that white soldiers in the British Empire were not subject to the same kinds of brutal punishments that African troops routinely experienced.

42. Wenig, *Kriegs-Safari*, 32; Hauer, *Kumbuke*, 44–47, 173, 207; NL Schnee, pp. 53–54, GStA.

43. Hauer, *Kumbuke*, 196.

44. See especially Karen Hagemann and Stefanie Schüler-Springorum, *Home/Front: The Military, War and Gender in Twentieth-Century Germany* (Oxford: Berg, 2002); Hämmerle, Überegger, and Bader Zaar, *Gender and the First World War*; and Proctor, *Civilians in a World at War*.

45. See also Susan R. Grayzel, *At Home and under Fire: Air Raids and Culture in Britain from the Great War to the Blitz* (New York: Cambridge University Press, 2012).

46. Research on the Middle Eastern theaters reflects similarities to the German East Africa case. See, for example, Abigail Jacobson, *From Empire to Empire: Jerusalem between Ottoman and British Rule* (Syracuse, NY: Syracuse University Press, 2011); Proctor, *Civilians in a World at War*, 143–144; Melanie Tanalien, "Feeding the City: The Beirut Municipality and Civilian Provisioning during World War I," *International Journal of Middle East Studies* 46 (2014): 737–758; and Edward C. Woodfin, *Camp and Combat on the Sinai and Palestine Front: The Experience of the British Empire Soldier, 1916–18* (Houndmills: Palgrave Macmillan, 2012), 126–128.

47. Lynn, *Women, Armies, and Warfare in Early Modern Europe*, 18.

48. Hull, *Absolute Destruction*, 122–124.

49. NL Schnee, p. 40, GStA.

50. Francis Brett Young, *Marching on Tanga: With General Smuts in East Africa* (1917; repr., Gloucester, UK: Alan Sutton, 1984), 71.

51. For an overview of the theme of population displacement in recent European historiography, see Peter Gatrell, "Introduction: World Wars and Population Displacement in Europe in the Twentieth Century," *Contemporary European History* 16, no. 4 (2007): 415–426.

52. On "sexual violence" as a broad term for understanding a range of acts, including but going beyond "rape," see Elizabeth D. Heineman, "Introduction: The History of Sexual Violence in Conflict Zones," in *Sexual Violence in Conflict Zones: From the Ancient World to the Era of Human Rights*, ed. Elizabeth Heineman (Philadelphia: University of Pennsylvania Press, 2011), 2. "According to the United Nations, 'sexual violence' includes (but is not limited to) rape, sexual mutilation, sexual humiliation, forced prostitution, and forced pregnancy. Victims can be female or male, of any age."

53. Jones, "As the Centenary Approaches," 876.

54. For useful commentary on related questions for the Second World War, see Judith Surkis, "Introduction: What Gender Historians Do," *Journal of Women's History* 26, no. 3 (2014): 129–130.

55. Wenig, *Kriegs-Safari*, 99–100. See also Bror MacDonell, *Mzee Ali: The Biography of an African Slave Raider Turned Askari and Scout* (Pinetown, South Africa: 30 Degrees South Publishers, 2008), 185.

56. Wenig, *Kriegs-Safari*, 100.

57. Compare to James Giblin, "The Victimization of Women in Late Precolonial and Early Colonial Warfare in Tanzania," in *Sexual Violence in Conflict Zones*, ed. Elizabeth Heineman (Philadelphia: University of Pennsylvania Press, 2011), 101.

58. Wenig, *Kriegs-Safari*, 100.

59. Wenig, *Kriegs-Safari*, 105. *Ngali* or *ugali* is a stiff porridge made of boiled millet, sorghum, or maize. It is a widespread staple food in East Africa.

60. Wenig, *Kriegs-Safari*, 105. For a similar anecdote from an earlier period in *Schutztruppe* history, see Ernst Nigmann, *Schwarze Schwänke: Fröhliche Geschichten aus unserem schönen alten Deutsch-Ostafrika* (Berlin: Safari Verlag, 1922), 137–144. This text is analyzed in Wright, *Strategies of Slaves and Women*, 206–208.

61. For her insights on the possible effects and meanings of "rape" for African families, I am grateful to Professor Sandra Greene (personal communication, November 2007). See A. T. Culwick and G. M. Culwick, *Ubena of the Rivers* (London: George Allen and Unwin, 1935), 209, 372, 360–369, 414–416, for customs of marriage and handling "adultery" among the Wabena of southern Tanzania.

62. Wenig, *Kriegs-Safari*, 102–104.

63. Gregory Maddox, "*Mtunya*: Famine in Central Tanzania, 1917–20," *Journal of African History* 31, no. 2 (1990): 183, 184. For British observations regarding harsh German conscription practices in Njombe, see also E. A. Northey war diary, December 2, 1916, p. 213, TNA CO 691/1.

64. Maddox, "*Mtunya*," 181.

65. District Political Officer, Bukoba to Sec State Col, July 16, 1918, TNA CO 691/15, pp. 343–344. See also Iliffe, *Modern History of Tanganyika*, 251.

66. Ludwig Deppe, *Mit Lettow-Vorbeck durch Afrika* (Berlin: August Scherl, 1919), 393.

67. Byatt to Sec State Col, February 5, 1919, TNA CO 691/21, pp. 179–180.

68. Iliffe, *Modern History of Tanganyika*, 270; Edward Paice, *How the Great War Razed East Africa*, Africa Research Institute, July 2014, http://www.africaresearchinstitute.org/publications/counterpoints/how-the-great-war-razed-east-africa/.

69. James Giblin, *The Politics of Environmental Control in Northeastern Tanzania, 1840–1940* (Philadelphia: University of Pennsylvania Press, 1992), 154–155.

70. "Influenza," *Nyasaland Times* 21, no. 52, December 26, 1918.

71. Derek R. Peterson, "Morality Plays: Marriage, Church Courts, and Colonial Agency in Central Tanganyika, ca. 1876–1928," *American Historical Review* 111, no. 4 (2006): 983–1010.

72. James Giblin, *A History of the Excluded: Making Family a Refuge from State in Twentieth-Century Tanzania* (Athens: Ohio University Press, 2005), 39–40, 75–84, 100.

73. Giblin, *History of the Excluded*, 95–96; Gregory H. Maddox, "Gender and Famine in Central Tanzania: 1916–1961," *African Studies Review* 39, no. 1 (1996): 90.

74. "Influenza."

75. Tammy M. Proctor, "The Everyday as Involved in War," *1914-1918 Online—International Encyclopedia of the First World War*, ed. Ute Daniel, et al. (Berlin: Freie Universität, 2014), DOI: 10.15463/ie1418.10453.

76. See, for example, Margaret Higonnet, "The 2005 ACLA Presidential Address: Whose Can(n)on? World War I and Literary Empires," *Comparative Literature* 57, no. 3 (2005): xiii–xvii. See also Christa Hämmerle's work on nurses' experiences of violence in central Europe, and the traumas they experienced as a result, which suggests interesting new paths to assessing the effects of combat violence on "noncombatants." Christa Hämmerle, " 'Mentally Broken, Physically a Wreck . . .': Violence in War Accounts of Nurses in Austro-Hungarian Service," in *Gender and the First World War*, ed. Christa Hämmerle, Oswald Überegger, and Birgitta Bader Zaar (Houndmills: Palgrave Macmillan, 2014), 89–107.

77. Melvin Page, *The Chiwaya War: Malawians and the First World War* (Boulder, CO: Westview Press, 2000), 185–189.

78. Frank Gunderson, *Sukuma Labor Songs from Western Tanzania* (Leiden: Brill, 2010), 302–303.

79. Burkhard Vieweg, *Macho Porini: Die Augen im Busch* (Weikersheim: Margraf, 1996), 412; Page, *Chiwaya War*, 148–149.

11

Gender and Mourning

Joy Damousi

THE WORLD WAS plunged into mourning as the First World War continued relentlessly over four long years to create communities united in grief across the globe. From the East to the West and across all parts of the world, the war produced scales of collective and individual mourning unprecedented to that point in time. As the first truly global war, no nation was untouched. Wilfred Owen's poem "Song of Songs" captures the poignancy of loss of those left to mourn the dead: "Sing me at midnight with your murmurous heart/And let its moaning like a chord be heard/ Surging through you and sobbing unsubdued."[1] In an effort to understand these texts and others, this chapter examines the responses to mass death produced by the war and takes a transnational approach to explore the shifting patterns of mourning across cultures, nations, and societies. In so doing, it captures the genuinely global impact of the war across communities. It also considers how men and women mourned in ways that were similar and different.

A consideration of gender is central to this discussion, for mourning in war is shaped by cultural understandings of masculinity and femininity. How are these notions fashioned by wartime experience? Men and women mourned the dead in different ways. Mourning was perceived as a *feminine* response as it involved the open expression of emotion, pain, and anguish. In contrast to this, war defined masculinity as heroic, stoic and violent, which meant the suppression of emotion, including exercising restraint when mourning the dead. In wartime, propaganda portrayed women as mourners and men as warriors. But such public pronouncements did not always match daily experience. Men mourned, too, in ways unexpected and often unacknowledged publicly, and women were often stoic, showing great forbearance in the aftermath of unprecedented violence and devastation. The rhetoric surrounding war and battle enforced gender stereotypes, but the experience and reality of it, paradoxically, often challenged crude gender representations.

This transnational approach allows for an examination of the enduring impact of the war and its different responses to the same emotional experience of loss and grief. In some cultures, such as that in Britain, the spiritualist movement was supported by many widows and mothers in an effort to deal with their loss. In Eastern traditions, however, this was not the response to the enduring grief that engulfed their societies. In Orthodox Christianity, commemoration of the war and its losses did not result in a move toward alternative religions. In many countries of Orthodox belief, church and state remained inseparable, and for this reason war commemoration and mourning the dead became firmly embedded within religious ceremonies and the ecumenical calendar.[2] A transnational approach to mourning and the First World War further points to the universality of women as central to the cultural practices of mourning, yet it also reveals profound cultural differences in mourning rituals surrounding the war dead.

THE TRANSNATIONALISM OF WAR GRIEF AND LOSS

The unprecedented scale of the trauma of loss left an enduring legacy on those who remained to absorb the impact of individual and national tragedies. Rituals of mourning became embedded in cultural life during the interwar years in ways not seen before or since. The end of the war may have signaled an end to hostilities, but the community of mourners it created in its wake struggled to escape from the persistent shadow of bereavement. The wide circle of those affected—mothers, fathers, siblings, wives, uncles, aunts, cousins, friends—faced devastating loss after the war.[3]

It was during these years that mourning became much more than a private or familial matter. Those who died in the war were commemorated publicly: monuments and memorials honored the men who had made the ultimate sacrifice. The battlefields where combatants had fallen became places of pilgrimage for mourners, who were irresistibly drawn to where the carnage took place, and to the cemeteries where their loved ones were buried, seeking an intimacy with the dead as a way for their own emotional wounds to begin to heal. At the same time, the public process of commemoration, memorial, and reconciliation of grief also took on a nonphysical form in which artistic expression, spiritualism, and religion were utilized to imbue the war and the mourners' individual loss with meaning and a sense of higher purpose.[4] The different contexts of the war produced very different mourning practices, and these behaviors varied according to the circumstances encountered by global communities.

Women became the quintessential figures of mourning and bereavement during the Great War. In Canada, Britain, Australia, and the United States, women were prominent as the "public face" of wartime grief.[5] In Eastern Europe, too, women played a central role in performing mourning rituals and rites and in postwar commemorations.[6] Across all communities, the grieving process was complicated in many instances by the absence of the soldier's body as it was not common practice to return the body of the deceased. The bereaved on the home front, invariably women, were often left too with a sense of wanting to know what the dead had experienced: of wanting to relive their last moments and understand something of what they had gone through. No body, no service, no eulogy, no family and friends to provide comfort at the grave; all this left loved ones in a state of limbo, in search of solace, and in need of some kind of reassurance about the spiritual welfare of the departed. But these similarities mask the complexity and range of mourning across communities.

MOTHERS AND WIDOWS

After the war, a generation of grieving mothers searched for new ways to articulate their grief, to commemorate their losses, and to live with their bereavement. The cruel and enduring loss of those who continued to live with the shadow cast by war allowed the experience of women and mothers in particular to find a place in the history of the Great War. Around the globe, war widows who were not perceived to have upheld the memory of their husbands via their moral conduct were vilified.[7] In many cultures, mothers were expected to disavow their grief and channel it into forms of patriotism and heightened nationalistic pride.

The numbers are staggering and vast. The war left some 600,000 widows in France,[8] 200,000 in Great Britain,[9] and more than 500,000 in Germany,[10] while 200,000 were recorded in Italy.[11] Although widows' pensions were belatedly introduced in Germany and France, in the view of widows, there were strict controls on the private activities of aid recipients to ensure that they would be "dutiful widows."[12] In Germany, they remained the war's neglected victims.[13] During the interwar years, those British war widows who did not remarry were dependent on limited state pensions and low-paid employment that guaranteed that they remained on the lowest rungs of the socioeconomic ladder.[14] Italian war widows came similarly under examination for their moral behavior. In a predominantly Catholic culture, they occupied an ambivalent status after the war, viewed as either victims of war or a threat to social harmony.[15]

SEPARATION OF BATTLEFRONT AND HOME FRONT

In Australia, a mother's stature increased with the number of sons she had serving at the front. In 1916, Australian Mrs. Annie J. Williams was one of many mothers around the world who had multiple sons on active service; at that time she had four sons serving. They had all been at Gallipoli, two of them invalided and another two wounded. The reportage of a sacrificial mother such as Annie Williams was used by the press to boost morale, support the war effort, and allow mothers to share the honor of their sons. But mothers' association with patriotism and heroism hid the agony and pain felt by these grieving women when they lost their sons. Ellen Derham supported her son Alfred in his enlistment for the war. "I want no Victoria Cross—I want my son," she insisted, but claimed that she was "thankful that my son is not and never has been a coward and I know you will do whatever you consider your duty." Although she hoped for a happy ending, she wrote, "But it is still a nightmare to me & it will be until I hear that you are coming home again." When her second son, Frank, enlisted, she expressed her anguish: "My heart is . . . full of tears all the time; but I am only one of [a] million of other sad mothers. If I could only fire myself instead of my sons! I am weeping now for you both but oh my son I am proud that my sons are to be of use to their country."[16] For mothers like Williams and Derham, whose sons fought on the Western Front, there was an expectation and deep hope that their sons would return. When their sons did not come home, the grief of mothers and widows became an integral part of public mourning and commemoration.

In 1918, newspaper reports described how Australian widows were "clad in the deepest mourning . . . with eyes wet with tears, brave smiles forced upon grim set faces. Many wore photographs of their dead ones upon their breasts. In every face lurked the sadness wrought of the memory of one they had held dear . . . . Brave women!"[17] During 1919, widows and orphans of fallen soldiers took prominent roles in public commemorations.[18] By 1920, mothers had come to occupy a central place in the country's memory of the war, and public tributes were paid to them for their sacrifices. For instance, in the Armistice Day commemorations of 1920, the Centre for Soldiers' Wives and Mothers organized a public procession, which extended for more than a mile and was crowded with widows and bereaved mothers.[19] Soldiers' wives and mothers became the particular audience addressed by chaplains speaking at these events, as the *Daily Telegraph* reported:

> The mothers and widows of those men bowed their heads as the chaplain spoke. The tears rolled down unrestrained. All days were days of commemoration to them. They wouldn't forget. There were well nigh 60,000 of our men who have fallen on the fields of battle . . . . A day like this brings your sorrow back afresh again to you. While you mourn there is a spirit of gratitude and pride in your breasts that you are associated with such men . . . . It was a sad sight this glimpse into the mothers' hearts.[20]

The Sydney suburb of Woolloomooloo—where soldiers passed through to board their ships bound for battle—became an important site for the commemoration of women's loss. Laying down wreaths here was a ritual that had been initiated by the Centre for Soldiers' Wives and Mothers in 1918 and an event that celebrated the heroism of their men.[21] Each Anzac Day, the public event honoring the war dead, mothers and widows would gather to remember and commemorate the deaths of their sons and husbands. "Wives' and Mothers' Tribute" was the way in which the Anzac commemorations of 1924 announced the service to be held at the Woolloomooloo gates where "wreaths and beautiful blossoms . . . covered the gates."[22] In 1925, the identity and the memory of the mother were writ large in the commemorative celebrations in the daily press. The *Daily Telegraph* noted how "one could not study those sacred emblems and their messages without a lump rising in the throat. 'In memory of my only son,' and 'In remembrance of my two sons' were samples of many nestled beside those of many brave-hearted mothers."[23]

Two years later, the *Daily Telegraph* noted that the Anzac Day ritual "was an occasion of remembrance" undertaken by old ladies, "dressed in black, who needed no adventitious aid to memory," where a "profusion of wreaths, of white, purple, and red flowers, rioted on the gates; and the fountain opposite, erected by the Soldiers' Mothers and Wives' Association, was dressed with soft foliage and flowers. Time may have softened the sorrow, but it has not lessened the love for those who gave their all."[24]

Grief in this context, however, was not as straightforward as public declaration and acknowledgment of patriotic loss. It could emerge in more subtle ways. Uniquely in Australia, compulsory military service was not introduced by the government but put to a referendum by Prime Minister W. H. Hughes on two occasions—in October 1916 and December 1917. The referenda failed on both occasions, so unlike most countries, which introduced compulsory military service, Australia sent a volunteer army. During the fiercely debated conscription campaigns, pro-conscriptionists argued that a mother's sacrifice was synonymous with citizenship and patriotism. They believed that it was incomprehensible that women should stop men from assisting those who had already gone to the front. Those opposed argued it was a mother's maternal duty not to send her sons to kill another mother's son.[25]

Mothers' grief came to the surface on both sides when they publicly and violently clashed. At one meeting in 1917 in Brisbane, where a group of conservative women physically attacked women pacifists, among the women leading the violence were several members of the Women's Compulsory Service Petition League whose sons or relatives had been killed or badly wounded. Grief over war loss was transformed into aggression, fury, and violent force. In this context, emotional intensity coalesced around grief that drove violent behavior by women against women.[26]

RUSSIAN GRIEF AND THE BATTLEFIELD

On the Eastern Front, mothers and wives grieved in different ways from those in the West. In the Russian context, where an estimated 500,000 to 600,000 men perished in two years,[27] and in peasant communities, soldiers were not expected to return. In such circumstances, mourning took place before the battle.

In this context, death was not perceived as a "natural" death in the course of the life cycle but instead as one where there was no body, and so no peace. In the rituals of the Orthodox traditions, the body has to be intact to be resurrected, which of course was very difficult in wartime.[28] Traditional funeral rites could not be practiced on the battlefield, and often the most minimal of death rituals were performed, such as covering a face or placing an individual cross with a name on the grave. These makeshift funeral rites were also applied to civilians as many dead civilians and refugees were often buried in mass graves without ceremony.[29] The grind of everyday death drew responses that often necessitated a hardening by soldiers as a tactic of survival by resisting grief and distancing themselves from expressing it. For the civilian population, too, there was little room for grief and mourning in the context of mass death. Children played with corpses; in one instance, they made a snowman, using a stiff corpse as its core.[30]

However, in the Russian Orthodox Church, there was some continuity with prewar and wartime mourning. The rituals of prayers, requiem services, liturgies, the lighting of candles, and the serving of holy bread continued. But the rites could not be the same. Widows who had the means and connections found their husbands' bodies and got them returned, but this was not the norm. Even so, Russia was slow to modernize and secularize its mourning practices. The Orthodox Church, with its heavily ritualized practices, was politically embedded within the state, and it continued to play a central role in the lives of Russians; thus, when bodies were returned, the full burial rites were performed. The Russian Revolution of 1917, separating church from state, complicated how the war was remembered and the dead honored. Following the Revolution, there were no formal memorials erected in honor of fallen men nor mourning of them. The country moved into a civil war that produced more death. [31]

INNER TURMOIL

In Germany, the artist Käthe Kollwitz created a visual landscape of mourning that remains distinctive and haunting. She represents the generation of mothers who lived under the shadow of mourning—a loss that consumed her creative as well as personal life. In October 1914, Kollwitz's eighteen-year-old son, Peter, died in battle in Flanders. Her creative work, as well as her personal letters and diaries, reveal the intense grief and prolonged mourning she endured. As many commentators have noted, Kollwitz's maternal identity was intimately connected to the sacrifice of her son.[32] On January 17, 1916, she wrote:

> All has changed forever. Changed, and I am impoverished. My whole life as a mother is really behind me now. I often have a terrible longing to have it back again—to have children, my boys, one to the right and one to the left; to dance with them as formerly when spring arrived and Peter came with flowers and we danced a springtide dance.[33]

The anniversary of Peter's death, in October 1916, was cause for further reflection, communication, and intimacy with her son, as she recorded in her diary:

> You are united, all of you who swore you would die for Germany You are dead two years now, and turned wholly to earth. Your spiritual part—where is it? I can hope for this kind of reunion—that to one another, run together like two streams. Do not withhold yourself from me. Perfect your form in mine.... Sometimes I have felt you, my boy—Oh, many, many times. You sent signs. Wasn't it a sign when on October 13 I visited the place where your memorial is to stand, and there was the same flower that I gave you when you departed?[34]

She drew inspiration from her son to continue living. "Strength is what I need," she wrote. "It's the one thing which seems worthy of succeeding Peter."[35] Käthe Kollwitz's sculpture and artwork became an expression of her mourning. In her striking and stunning sculpture *The Parents*, she aimed to make the two figures "simplicity in feeling, but expressing the totality of grief." For many who had been affected by war, it was as if they themselves had died.[36]

Themes of grief and mourning similarly dominate the work of the German poet Frida Bettingen, who lost her son in October 1914 at Verdun. According to her biographer, this was a turning point in her life. In 1917, she was diagnosed with a depressive illness and subsequently spent prolonged periods in psychiatric clinics. Bettingen's poetry drew directly from her experience of maternal grief and the loss of her son. In her writing, her grief is all-consuming, and it is through writing that she confronts and manages this emotion. Bettingen's verse is an attempt to mediate her own personal experience of loss. She describes the tension between her desire to recreate the relationship with her son and the impossibility of doing so as a "funeral for which there are no words."[37] While a vast majority of mothers did not develop psychological illnesses, the increased number of cases of melancholic depression among women reported in countries such as Germany during the war point to the underrecognized occurrence of civilian trauma. The impact of war and its trauma was not confined to soldiers, as civilians also experienced trauma.[38] In contrast, the expectation that men who remained at home would be stoic and firm under such duress suggests that even if they endured such stress, they were more likely not to reveal or expose their emotional vulnerabilities.[39]

At a more public level, the practice of pilgrimages to war graves by mothers and widows of British, American, and Australian families was not replicated in the German context. The German War Graves Commission did not cover the cost of travel by the families to gravesites. Unlike the practice in victorious nations, where the families played a role in public commemoration, the bereaved did not assume a high profile here. Symbolically, too, the contribution of mothers was publicly recognized in Canada, Australia, the United States, and Italy with medals such as the Golden Star or Silver Cross, but this was not a practice that was adopted in vanquished nations such as Germany.[40]

ORTHODOX PRACTICES

The war casualties in the East were the highest as men in the Balkans—in Serbia, Turkey, Romania, and Bulgaria—perished in the largest numbers. In terms of civilian casualties, the figures are disproportionate, with more than 6 million deaths in the East and fewer than 50,000 in the West.[41] In this context, the gender divide was clear: the emotional and cultural work of mourning fell on women. They were the

Käthe Kollwitz's moving sculpture *The Parents* is a central feature in a large German cemetery in Belgium, where the sculptor's son, who was killed in 1914, is buried. The separate statues of a stiff upright father and a mother bent in agony show the artist's understanding of how grief is gendered, that women could collapse into their unbearable sorrow while men remained able to face the world, and of how her own loss may have been channeled into her art. *Photo by Tammy Proctor*

custodians of the ritual practices of the Orthodox religion and so were expected to ensure these traditions were followed as closely as possible under wartime and postwar conditions. Orthodox religions at the time tied feminine identity to the domestic realm. They thus understood women's devout religiosity as an emotional response to death and part of their feminine role in upholding the rituals of war and mourning according to the scriptures as far as was possible in times of turbulence and conflict.

Rural villages such as those in Romania had to address the mourning rituals for the dead well before state authorities could intervene. Communities began locating bones and bodies in nearby former battlefields. This involved priests, widows, teachers, police, and other members of the community, as well as soldiers. In this instance, the memory and commemoration of the dead remained close to home rather than in a distant cemetery. Even if the bodies of their own sons, brothers, or fathers could not be found, relatives could honor them by retrieving and respecting the bones of others who had died and then conducting Orthodox funeral rites. Heroes Day, the Romanian day of commemoration, was established in 1920, but local communities created their own rituals and observance of mourning typically arranged by women, which carried more significance for their small towns and villages. [42]

While there were unprecedented events in mourning and commemorating the dead after 1918, for Orthodox communities such as those in Romania, there was a continuity rather than a break in mourning rituals where the cult of the dead was a key aspect of cultural practice. Funerary rituals remained highly gendered as women continued to be largely responsible for undertaking them. War commemoration also became intertwined with Orthodox religious holidays and commemorations, and so mourning the losses in the war evolved into part of the religious calendar. [43]

MASCULINITY, RELIGION, AND MOURNING

The clergy played a key role in offering support for mourners in the British context. Contrary to expectations of masculinity and war at the time, these men often showed intense emotion and sympathy. For example, the Scottish Presbyterian chaplain James T. Hall wrote to the mother of the soldier W. B. Binning, who had died in combat, expressing his deepest condolences and providing details of the final stages of death, which was often what the families craved. Introducing himself as Presbyterian chaplain for the Number 2 Casualty Clearing Station, Hall wrote of the last meeting with the woman's son:

I saw him when he came in on Sunday night and engaged in prayer with him, and again on Monday morning when I also engaged in prayer with him. He was most grateful for my ministrations and expressed himself as such. On both occasions that I saw him, though he was suffering he was very brave and bright. He was hoping for recovery, but at the same time recognized the possibility of not getting better, for he asked me to write to you in case anything should happen to him.[44]

In an attempt to make the mourning more tolerable, Hall stated that it would surely "console you to know that doctors and nurses did all in their power for your son and his last hours were made as comfortable as possible." He tried to reassure Binning's mother the body and burial arrangements would be appropriately respectful and dignified: "The most reverent care is taken of our soldiers' graves by the Graves' Registration Commission," which included marking the grave with a cross, "to be inscribed 'with metal lettering, his name, rank, regiment, date and cause of death.'" Hall offered to provide a photograph of the grave and send it to her. His sentiments were genuine, offering his "deep sympathy" in her "great loss" and attempting to comfort her. He reassured her that she had "much to comfort and sustain you in your hours of trial the knowledge that your son died as a brave man should, that he gave his life for others, following in the footsteps of Him 'who loved us and gave Himself for us.'" Hall offered the Christian response of the afterlife, for "the life he is now living is infinitely better and happier than the best that this earth can offer, and the certainty that you will meet him again in that world where there is no death, no separation, no sorrow."[45] Hall was in the privileged position of having witnessed the final moments of death, and of seeing the body of a deceased soldier. Being unable to see the body of dead loved ones deeply frustrated and disturbed relatives. Hall's role was to communicate his experience of seeing the body in considerable detail, which he understood many relatives found comforting and reassuring.

Devout religious followers interpreted the war as God's war. Catholics mourned through highly ritualized processes of prayer sermons, evoking soldiers on a given saint's day. The French used such mourning rituals to create religious and political memory. Religious imagery mixed with military sacrifices; the sacrifice of the Christian soldier could echo the sacrifice of Christ. This can also be seen in the Baines family of Putney, who sought comfort, solace, and consolation through their Catholic faith. Ralph Baines lost three brothers—two on the Somme and the third in 1917. The family structured their mourning around Catholic ritual: the local priest delivered a requiem mass; nuns made a shrine to the Baines brothers; Ralph was ordained, and he insisted his sister's fiancé convert to Catholicism. The fact that the church could not take allegiance, as Catholics on both side of the battle were being killed, did not diminish the power of the spiritual message for mourners from across the military divide who sought comfort in it.[46] The role of the male clergy in administering religious rites as a form of managing grief was central in these families' efforts to make sense of their loss.

The challenge to the masculinity of fathers and soldiers is another central issue when considering how men mourned differently from women. Expressing open emotion was not expected of men from the Edwardian age, but emotional expressions of mourning and loss can be commonly found among men in the British armies. In this regard, conventional understandings of masculinity and war, which insisted on stoicism, were not always followed. Major Charrington wrote to Mrs. Carr in May 1918, offering details of the last phase of her son's life: "To me it was a tremendous blow when I heard . . . that he had died of wounds. I had so hoped he would pull through. For he had been through all that heavy fighting from Mar 21st with the battalion all the time and throughout he had done magnificent work." The performance of Mrs. Carr's son under battle was exceptional and defied his years: "His coolness under heavy fire was wonderful and saved several almost desparate [sic] situations. His company did splendidly. For one of his age he showed an amazing grasp of the situation—which added to his great gallantry made him invaluable as an officer. . . . Believe me his name will not be forgotten in this battalion, nor his personality by his few intimate friends that are still here."[47]

The mourning of soldiers who were less well known or even strangers also reveals how men coped with their emotions about the dead. In a May 1917 letter, the British soldier E. S. Campbell finds the body of a soldier, discovers his identity and that of a woman attached to him, and writes to her from "Firing Line, France" with great power and emotion, seeming to share her grief. He thinks the woman is a girlfriend, but instead he is writing to the soldier's mother. The tone is sad and melancholic:

I hardly know how to commence this letter to you, but I feel that I write and tell you of a sorrowful incident that happened yesterday. Whilst crossing a portion of our old trenches, I noticed the body of a soldier which had been almost buried by the explosions of a shell. In his pockets were several things—a testament, some letters and all the little trifles that a man carries with him, of no value, but which may be treasured by his relations at home. How sad and mournful those trifles seem—the links that bound them to life and are now forgotten in death. There were several photos also, but they were nearly all destroyed by the water and mud that had soaked them through.

This death was sad and tragic, but not in vain:

Your friend has died for the honour of his country. . . . So he lies at rest—until the great mystery called life and death is made known to us,—in that noblest of all tombs, a soldier's grave . . . . I send you my sincerest sympathy for the loss of your friend, do not grieve; his death is honourable.[48]

The recipient of this letter, the soldier's mother, lost three of her four sons in the war—Edward, Ernest, and Robert. The remaining son, Charles Taylor, treasured this letter, and his mother valued it forever.

The deaths of multiple sons could result in devastation for their fathers as well as mothers. The Smith family from Barnard Castle in County Durham lost five of its six sons in the trenches, two in 1916, two in 1917, and one in 1918. Their broken father himself died in 1918. The intervention in 1918 of the local vicar's wife in writing to Queen Mary may well have saved the life of Mrs. Smith's only surviving son, Wilfred. Buckingham Palace contacted the War Office, and he was spared serving on the front lines. Wilfred went on to have five children and lived to the age of seventy-two. Records at the time do not document how many sets of brothers were killed, or indeed how many groups of fathers and sons or other relations. Only now are we able to ascertain the full extent of these multiple disasters for families. In the Gallipoli campaign, for instance, no fewer than 196 pairs of brothers were killed.[49]

Fathers facing such losses were meant to be stoic and firm, upholding dominant versions of Edwardian masculinity. Yet this facade hid the pain and anguish of many fathers across all cultures. In Germany, for instance, the expression of bereavement and mourning was similar to that in other parts of Europe where the management of grief and emotion within the family was deemed to be the task of women. Outside the family, few depictions of fathers' mourning appeared in the public domain, and there was an expectation that fathers would transfer their own grief to mothers within the household.[50]

THE IMPACT OF MOURNING AND RISE OF SPIRITUALISM

One way to cope with loss for some mourners was to connect with the spirit of the dead. Spiritualism emerged in the nineteenth century and was a popular but not widespread practice. The resurgence of spiritualism after the war was an attempt by families, especially women, to make contact with their beloved dead and assist in their grieving process. The growth and appeal of spiritualism after the war are undeniable. In Britain by the mid-1930s, there were reportedly more than 200 local spiritualist societies, with a total membership that exceeded a quarter of a million.[51]

Spiritualism provided a specific avenue of hope for *direct* and physical rather than spiritual contact with the dead. In his *History of Spiritualism*, one of the leaders of the spiritualist movement, Arthur Conan Doyle, describes several instances of the spirits and ghosts of soldiers making contact with their families and of psychic photography identifying their presence. Doyle argued that the war heightened interest in the afterlife, and although the spiritualist movement "counted its believers in millions before the war," most Britons did not recognize it or its achievements. The war, he noted, "changed all that."[52] Doyle cites many cases of mothers and wives connecting with the dead. In one such case, a mother reported seeing her dead son returned to her. The Reverend G. Vale Owen describes how George Leaf, who attended one of his Bible classes, was killed. He then powerfully recounts:

> Some weeks later his mother was tidying up the hearth in the sitting-room. She was on her knees before the grate when she felt an impulse to turn round and look at the door that opened into the entrance hall. She did so, and saw her son clad in his working clothes, just as he used to come home every evening when he was alive. He took off his coat and hung it upon the door, an old familiar habit. Then he turned to her, nodded and smiled, and walked through to the back kitchen, where he had been in the habit of washing before sitting down to his evening meal. It was all quite natural and lifelike.[53]

The identity of the boy was unmistakable, and the mourner validated the testimony unconditionally:

> She knew that it was her dead boy who had come to show her that he was alive in the spirit land and living a natural life, well, happy and content. Also that smile of love told her that his heart was still with the old folks at home. She is a sensible woman and I did not doubt her story for a moment. As a matter of fact, since his death he had been seen in Orford Church, which he used to attend, and has been seen in various places since.[54]

In another instance cited by Doyle, a bereaved widow testified to feeling the death of her husband:

> Her husband, a sergeant in the Devons, went to France on July 25th, 1915. She had received letters regularly from him, all of which were very happy and cheerful, and so she began to be quite reassured in her mind about him, feeling certain that whatsoever danger he had to face he would come safely through. On the evening of September 25th, 1915, at about ten o'clock, she was sitting on

her bed in her room talking to another girl, who was sharing it with her. The light was full on, and neither of them had as yet thought of getting into bed, so deep were they in their chat about the events of the day and the war.[55]

There was an immediate disturbance, at which point the wife's behavior dramatically shifted:

And then suddenly there came a silence. The wife had broken off sharply in the middle of a sentence and sat there staring into space. For, standing there before her in uniform was her husband. For two or three minutes she remained there looking at him, and she was struck by the expression of sadness in his eyes.[56]

She then sought to make contact with what she saw and moved very swiftly. Getting up quickly, she advanced to the spot where he was standing, but by the time she had reached it, the vision had disappeared. Though only that morning the wife had had a letter saying her husband was safe and well, she felt sure that the vision foreboded evil. She was right. Soon afterward she received a letter from the War Office, saying that he had been killed in the Battle of Loos on September 25, 1915, the very date she had seemed to see him stand beside her bed.[57]

These testimonies collected by Doyle point to the nature of mourning across place, but there were also differences. While in Orthodox cultures mourners drew on prewar religious symbolism and rituals and situated their mourning within these rituals, in the English context, the growth of spiritualism points to an increasing disillusionment among some with existing religious rituals, and a willingness to seek less conventional practices to converse more directly with the dead in new forms. This, of course, was not the only means of postwar mourning of the dead, as memorials and monuments soon rose and pilgrimages to the sites of death quickly became sites of mourning for women in Britain, Australia, and the United States in particular.[58]

But trying to commune with the dead does mark a distinctive contrast to the ways in which mourning and bereavement were undertaken across nations. Mourning the war dead was more central to religious practice in Romania, for example. Here, women also retained a crucial role, as they had done throughout the war, in attempting to uphold traditional rituals. But, strikingly, this also meant that women remained central to public war commemoration. In 1919, Heroes Cult became an official holiday at the same time as the religious day of the Ascension. The National Orthodox Society of Romanian Women suggested that the commemoration be held on the second day of Easter and in so doing kept a ritual that was familiar to them and in which their role was central.[59] A similarity shared between traditional religious traditions and newer forms was the expectation that the mourners would be women, in large part because they were left behind to mourn the dead. But these expectations also spoke to assumptions that the feminine response would be an emotive one.

Vera Brittain, grieving her fiancé and brother, reflected in *A Chronicle of Youth* how "terrible tragedies of youth are too merciless, too complete, to be readily relieved by even the sincerest sympathy. Loss is loss, shattering, immeasurable."[60] The Great War created a generation of mourners across the globe in staggering numbers. While women became in many cultures symbols of mourning, and they played an essential but varying role in national, cultural, and religious commemorations. The war devastated family members and left an enduring loss in its wake.

The literature on the Great War is extensive, but one area of research where there is still much to learn is how the war defined mourning practices along gender lines. New directions in future research on mourning and gender should explore several aspects that have yet to attract the widespread attention of historians. These would include, first, focusing on how civilians were mourned, and moving attention away from exclusively examining the soldiers who perished. How was the narrative of civilian death embedded in war memory? The neglect of such losses involved a question of gender, as many of the civilians who died in war were women and children. Second, the enduring mourning of siblings in the context of war requires more analysis. Sisters and brothers lived with the shadow of death for many years after a sibling or siblings died in the war. How did siblings mourn within families? Was there an expectation that sisters would carry the emotional burden of grief, and in ways that were different than for their brothers? Finally, there has been much written about soldiers and commemorating and mourning their deaths, but what of nurses who died in the line of duty? How have they been mourned? In what way has the notion of the ultimate sacrifice on the battlefield by male soldiers overshadowed other deaths, of women and nurses in particular? These examples point not only to the extent of mourning throughout communities and societies but also to its complexity, its depth, and its cultural and social endurance. The mourning of war dead reverberated across many relationships, in both public and private arenas, throughout the twentieth century and into the twenty-first century. It is incumbent on historians in the future to extend our current understandings of the powerful legacy the war left on those men and women who remained to grieve and mourn. Their stories—of how they did so individually and collectively—are vital to adding further complexity to our historical understandings of gender, mourning, and war.

NOTES

1. Wilfred Owen, "Song Of Songs," in *The First World War Poetry Digital Archive*, http://www.oucs.ox.ac.uk/wwIlit/collections/item/3347.

2. Joy Damousi, "Mourning Practices," in *The Cambridge History of the First World War*, vol. 3, *Civil Society*, ed. Jay Winter (Cambridge: Cambridge University Press, 2014), 378.

3. Damousi, "Mourning Practices," 358.

4. Damousi, "Mourning Practices," 358.

5. Claudia Siebrecht, "Imagining the Absent Dead: Rituals of Bereavement and the Place of the War Dead in German Women's Art during the First World War," *German History* 29, no. 2 (2011): 202–223. See also Erika Kuhlmann, *Of Little Comfort: War Widows, Fallen Soldiers, and the Remembering of the Nation after the Great War* (New York: New York University Press, 2012); Susan Grayzel, *Women's Identities at War: Gender, Motherhood, and Politics in Britain and France during the First World War* (Chapel Hill: University of North Carolina Pres, 1999); Joy Damousi, *The Labour of Loss: Mourning, Memory, and Wartime Bereavement in Australia* (Cambridge: Cambridge University Press, 1999); Pat Jalland, *Death in War and Peace: A History of Loss and Grief in England, 1914–1970* (Oxford: Oxford University Press, 2010).

6. Maria Bucur, *Heroes and Victims: Remembering War in Twentieth-Century Romania* (Bloomington: Indiana University Press, 2009), 101.

7. Georges Duby and Michelle Perrot, eds., *A History of Women in the West: V. Towards a Cultural Identity in the Twentieth Century* (Cambridge, MA: Harvard University Press, 1994), 53.

8. Colin Dyer, *Population and Society in Twentieth Century France* (London: Hodder and Stoughton, 1978), 43.

9. J. M. Winter, *The Great War and the British People* (London: Macmillan, 1985), 274.

10. Richard Bessel, *Germany after the First World War* (Oxford: Clarendon Press, 1993), 275.

11. Francesa Lagorio, "Italian Widows of the First World War," in *Authority, Identity and the Social History of the Great War*, ed. Frans Coetzee and Marilyn Shevin-Coetzee (Oxford: Berghahn Books, 1995), 177.

12. Lagorio, "Italian Widows of the First World War," 53.

13. Lagorio, "Italian Widows of the First World War," 53; see Karin Hausen, "The German Nation's Obligations to the Heroes' Widows of World War I," in *Behind the Lines: Gender and the Two World Wars*, ed. Margaret Higonnet et al. (New Haven, CT: Yale University Press, 1987); Robert Weldon Whalen, *Bitter Wounds: German Victims of the Great War, 1914–1939* (Ithaca, NY: Cornell University Press, 1984), 69–81.

14. Bessel, *Germany after the First World War*, 226–228; E. Sylvia Pankhurst, *The Homefront: A Mirror to Life in England during the First World War* (London: Cressett Library, 1987), 18–30.

15. Lagorio, "Italian Widows of the First World War," 177.

16. Mother to Alfred, n.d., "Tues. Even.," letters from Mother Ellen Derham and Father Thos Derham, 1914–27, 7/2/1/1, Derham Papers, University of Melbourne Archives.

17. *Daily Telegraph*, April 26, 1918, 5.

18. *Daily Telegraph*, July 21, 1919, 14.

19. *Daily Telegraph*, November 12, 1920, 5.

20. *Daily Telegraph*, April 26, 1920, 6.

21. *Sydney Morning Herald*, April 26, 1921, 8.

22. *Daily Telegraph*, April 26, 1924, 8.

23. *Daily Telegraph*, April 27, 1925, 5.

24. *Daily Telegraph*, April 26, 1927, 8.

25. Joy Damousi, "Socialist Women and Gendered Space: Ant-conscription and Anti-war Campaigns 1914–1918," in *Gender and War: Australians at War in the Twentieth Century*, ed. Joy Damousi and Marilyn Lake (Cambridge: Cambridge University Press, 1995), 254–273.

26. Raymond Evans, " 'All the Passion of Our Womanhood': Margaret Thorp and the Battle of the Brisbane School of Arts," in *Gender and War: Australians at War in the Twentieth Century*, 239–253.

27. Nik Cornish, *The Russian Army and the First World War* (Stroud: Tempus, 2006).

28. Svetlana Malysheva, "Bereavement and Mourning (Russian Empire)," in *1914-1918-Online— International Encyclopedia of the First World War*, ed. Ute Daniel et al. (Berlin: Freie Universität, 2014), DOI: 10.15463/ie1418.10190.

29. Malysheva, "Bereavement and Mourning (Russian Empire)."

30. Malysheva, "Bereavement and Mourning (Russian Empire)."

31. Malysheva, "Bereavement and Mourning (Russian Empire)."

32. Regina Schulte, "Käthe Kollwitz's Sacrifice," trans. Pamela Selwyn, *History Workshop Journal* 41 (1996): 193–221.

33. Hans Kollwitz, ed., *The Diary and Letters of Käthe Kollwitz*, trans. Richard Winston and Clara Winston (Chicago: Henry Regnery, 1955), 67.

34. Kollwitz, *Diary and Letters of Käthe Kollwitz*, entry October 13, 1916, 76.

35. Kollwitz, *The Diary and Letters of Käthe Kollwitz*, February 1917, 78.

36. Kollwitz, *Diary and Letters of Käthe Kollwitz*, entries December 17, 1917, 86–87; March 19, 1918, 87.

37. Catherine Smale, "Aus Blut und Schmerz geboren": Maternal Grief and the Poetry of Frida Bettingen," *German Life and Letters* 61, no. 3 (2008): 328–329; Gill Plain, " 'Great Expectations': Rehabilitating the Reluctant War Poets," *Feminist Review* 51:1 (1995): 56.

38. For an example of the overwhelming grief of one French woman that provides evidence of grief-induced trauma for civilians, see the case of Madame O in Gregory M. Thomas, *Soldiers, Civilians and Psychiatry in France, 1914–1940* (Baton Rouge: Louisiana State University Press, 2009), 80.

39. See Damousi, "Mourning Practices," 367–371.

40. Silke Fehlemann, "Bereavement and Mourning (Germany)," in *1914-1918-Online— International Encyclopedia of the First World War*, ed. Ute Daniel et al. (Berlin: Freie Universität, 2014), DOI: 10.15463/ie1418.10177.

41. Bucur, *Heroes and Victims*, 51.

42. Bucur, *Heroes and Victims*, 49–51

43. Bucur, *Heroes and Victims*, 19, 60.

44. Letter to William Binning's parents from the Church of Scotland minister, First World War Poetry Archive, http://www.oucs.ox.ac.uk/ww1lit/gwa/document/9626/8660.

45. Letter to William Binning's parents from the Church of Scotland minister.

46. Adrian Gregory, *The Last Great War: British Society and the First World War* (Cambridge: Cambridge University Press, 2008), 33–34.

47. Letter from Major C. Charrington to Mrs. C. Carr re death of Leslie George Carr, First World War Poetry Digital Archive, http://www.oucs.ox.ac.uk/ww1lit/gwa/document/8867/3109.

48. "Letter to My Grandmother," the Great War Archive, University of Oxford/Primary Contributor via *First World War Poetry Digital Archive*, http://www.oucs.ox.ac.uk/ww1lit/gwa/document/8778. The letter was contributed by Donald Taylor, the recipient's grandson.

49. Anthony Seldon, "First World War: Losing one child in war is a terrible thing so just imagine losing five," Daily Telegraph, February 21, 2014. http://www.telegraph.co.uk/history/

50. Fehlemann, "Bereavement and Mourning (Germany)."

51. David Cannadine, "War and Death, Grief and Mourning in Modern Britain," in *Mirrors of Mortality: Studies in the Social History of Death*, ed. Joachim Whaley (London: Europa, 1981), 229.

52. Arthur Conan Doyle, *History of Spiritualism*, vol. 2 (1926), available from Project Guttenberg Australia, http://gutenberg.net.au/ebooks03/0301061.txt.

53. Doyle, *History of Spiritualism*.

54. Doyle, *History of Spiritualism*.

55. Doyle, *History of Spiritualism*.

56. Doyle, *History of Spiritualism*.

57. Doyle, *History of Spiritualism*.

58. See David Lloyd, *Battlefields Tourism: Pilgrimage and the Commemoration of the Great War in Britain, Australia and Canada 1919–1939* (Oxford: Berg, 1998).

59. Bucur, *Heroes and Victims*, 101.

60. Alan Bishop with Terry Smart, eds., *Vera Brittain: War Diary 1913–1917: Chronicle of Youth* (London, Victor Gollancz, 1981), 14.

12

Gender and Memory

Karen Petrone

WHAT MAKES WAR thinkable? That is a key question posed by historian Jay Winter in seeking to understand how states and societies throughout the ages argued for and justified the need for their soldiers to commit organized violence on behalf of the state or the nation.[1] One important answer to this question is war memory—how states and societies represented the nature of war, its sacrifices, and its outcomes in the aftermath of war. War memory is a complex and multifaceted public phenomenon, created by the interplay between official state-centered narratives about wars and popular opinions regarding these same events. It is fashioned through official histories and governmental reports, memoirs, letters, diaries, the press, art, architecture, literature, music, memorials, monuments, civic ceremonies, and rituals.

Gender plays a critical role in the construction of war memory. While the importance of gender to war memory can be traced all the way back to the beginnings of recorded history, gender is particularly crucial to the memory of the First World War. The Great War of 1914–1918 was the first total war, where the home front was no longer separated from the battlefront, and millions of women both contributed to the war effort and became victims of the fighting. The transformation of war from an overwhelmingly male phenomenon to one that encompassed the actions of millions of women fundamentally changed the nature of war and its memory. Because of this dramatic change, it is essential to consider the interaction of gender and war memory in the decades after the First World War.

"War memory" is not a singular phenomenon. From the day that the First World War began, there were competing narratives about the nature of that war, both within each warring country and across national lines. The study of war memory records this competition as various actors sought to shape first the interpretation of the war as it was occurring, and then how it would be remembered after it was over. The historian of memory explores the full range of differing interpretations and then demonstrates how and why some of them were "winners" in this competition as they gained prominence at a particular place and time, whereas others were "losers" who disappeared from sight.[2]

Nor is war memory static; it is, in the words of historian Jay Winter, "unstable, plastic, synthetic, and repeatedly reshaped."[3] For this reason, analysts of war memory must be attentive to change over time, as the commonplace narratives of war memory today were not necessarily always the most broadly accepted accounts. These memories may have emerged and gained prominence over other accounts under very particular historical circumstances. For example, in the Soviet Union under Stalin in the 1930s, much of the literature about the First World War that had been produced in the more open 1920s was systematically censored and repressed. As a result, the First World War nearly disappeared from historical memory until it was revived in post-Soviet Russia as part of the new Russian national project.[4]

The first of two debates that we can analyze through the gendered memory of the First World War revolves around the struggle for citizenship. During the war, ideas of citizenship were greatly in flux. In the course of the nineteenth century, both men and women had fought for suffrage and citizenship rights. In the wake of the French Revolution, many connected the willingness to bear arms and commit violence in the name of one's country with both ideal citizenship and ideal masculinity. Male soldiers, in return for their honorable service to their nation, received the privileges of inclusion in the national community as full citizens.[5] Because the First World War created a situation of extreme national emergency in the context of the first modern total war, states called upon all members of their societies to contribute to the war effort. As women, members of minority groups (such as African Americans in the United States), and colonial peoples (such as African troops fighting for France and Indian troops for England) sacrificed for their countries (or their empires), they developed and nurtured expectations that they too might be included in their national communities or gain political independence with rights equal to those of white male European and American soldiers.

The Russian Provisional Government that came to power in March 1917 after the abdication of Tsar Nicholas II provides an interesting prism through which to view the complex connections between gender, soldiering, and citizenship in a newly created state, one that survived for barely eight months. The upheaval of the

February Revolution had destroyed the army's will to fight, but the new democratic Provisional Government affirmed its commitment to continue the war effort along-side its democratic allies. During this dire emergency, the Provisional Government simultaneously gave women the vote and organized units of women to serve in combat roles in the army, thus demonstrating the intimate connection between citizenship and soldiering. One goal of the women's units was to raise morale by demonstrating devotion to the war effort, but another was to shame male soldiers into fighting for the new Russian nation. The heroic actions of women soldiers chal-lenged the masculinity of men who were unwilling to fight. Ultimately, however, the Provisional Government's attempts to rally the war-weary nation were unsuccessful after three years of brutal and devastating warfare.[6] Nevertheless, this failure should not obscure the fact that the exigencies of total war offered possibilities to reshape fundamentally both citizenship and gender roles.

At the end of the war, women gained full voting rights in the United States and limited suffrage in Europe and Canada, even as colonial peoples in Africa and Asia remained under imperial rule. In the United States, African American veterans struggled to access the rights to which they were formally entitled in the Jim Crow South, and the return of black veterans led to a wave of lynching and mob violence, as white supremacists denied African American soldiers recognition for their ser-vice to the nation and rejected their demands for rights. As societies adjusted to the extension of citizenship rights to some women, and the simultaneous denial of rights to certain veterans, the extent to which war memory celebrated or downplayed the participation of women, African Americans, and colonial peoples in the First World War contributed to ongoing debates about gender roles, rights for colonized and minority peoples, and the nature of citizenship in general.

The other central debate to which memory of the First World War contributed was the disagreement over the nature of war itself. From the very outbreak of war, there emerged debate about whether war was an appropriate and just way to solve the political problems of Europe. Some observers saw war as an abomination, sent by God to punish Europe for its sins, while others understood the war as a "holy" war and equated victory with God's favor bestowed on the nation. While many social-ists abandoned their avowed internationalism to support the national war efforts in their own countries, some socialists declared a "war on war" and identified capitalist competition for markets as the cause of all wars. For leaders such as Vladimir Lenin, willing participation in the "imperialist" war was an illegitimate act, a betrayal of the interests of the working classes who were forced by capitalists to serve as "cannon meat." While some viewed war as a national catastrophe, others, such as the Italian Futurist writers, celebrated war as an opportunity for men of honor to prove their worth through enacting violence in sublime sacrifice to the nation. In several of the combatant countries, the press was tightly controlled to prevent representations of war that were unfavorable to morale and the war effort. Nevertheless, a diversity of opinions about the war emerged as the fighting unfolded, and continued into the postwar period.

Moreover, each combatant country witnessed a distinct internal postwar debate about the nature of war based on its individual political and social context. These contexts were dramatically different in the United States, for example, which entered the war in April 1917 and whose soldiers saw fighting only in 1918, than in the countries whose combatants had experienced four years of grueling trench warfare. It was markedly distinct for those (surprisingly few) countries whose governments survived the war than for the many new states and regimes that emerged in the aftermath of the war. Nevertheless, in each country, gender was central to war memory in a variety of ways.

For the "victors," notably England, France, and the United States, which had emerged from the war politically intact, war memory celebrated the sacrifices of male citizens and recognized the achievements of veterans. Having understood the high cost of "winning," some veterans' organizations in these countries opposed future wars, while others emphasized the debt owed to veterans in ways that promoted military culture. Generally speaking, war memory in Britain and France emphasized mourning and gratitude to veterans over militarization, but this mourning and remembrance were heavily skewed toward the male victims of war.[7] The emphasis on the nation's military honor was much more pronounced in defeated or disappointed nations such as Germany and Italy, in which war memory served as one of the means of repairing the damage to masculine honor that the war had caused.

War memory was even more fraught in the new Eastern European nations created as a result of the First World War, many of whose current citizens had actually fought against each other as soldiers of the now defunct Russian Empire or Austro-Hungarian Empire. In Poland and Czechoslovakia, volunteers in the Czech and Polish legions, who had fought on the side of the Entente during the First World War in exchange for promises of national independence from the Austro-Hungarian Empire, gained prominence in postwar memory. These countries erased the memory of fratricidal civil war between 1914 and 1918 in celebration of the founding of their new nations.

The new nations articulated national identities based on culture, language, and religion. National leaders often saw women as the carriers of national culture and as mothers of the nation. Because these nations had been created out of armed conflict, however, the heroic figures of the soldier and the legionnaire gained particular prominence as the protectors of the (usually female-gendered) nation. In such places as the Cemetery of the Defenders of Lwów (now in Lviv, Ukraine), Polish leaders honored soldiers as well as teenage gymnasium and university students, the "eaglets," who fought and died defending Lwów from a Ukrainian bid for independence in 1918. Later, one body from this cemetery, chosen symbolically by the mother of a soldier who went missing in a nearby battle, was brought to Warsaw to be buried in the Tomb of the Unknown Soldier. In contrast, between 1922 and 1930, in Hoover Square in Warsaw (named after Herbert Hoover), there stood a monument by Xawery Dunikowski honoring American food relief by depicting an anguished woman holding her two hungry children. However, this monument, which showed the tragedy of war for noncombatants and the inability of Polish leaders to protect and sustain their own women and children, was taken down for repairs in 1930 and never restored.[8] All across Europe, political leaders employed war memory and "war forgetting" to foster prescribed national, patriotic, and gender identities.

In the interwar period, the anxieties about the potential for another war created a heightened awareness of demography; states increasingly put emphasis on raising the birth rate and on readying the male population for military service.[9] In this context, debates about the nature of war intersected with anxieties about the survival of the nation. How states and societies represented the First World War could have a tangible effect on military morale and on the creation of pacifistic or militaristic tendencies among the males of fighting age. Simultaneously, representations of women as helpless victims of war or as exalted mothers of the nation could shape their attitudes toward producing and educating the next generation of soldiers.[10] In short, there was a lot at stake for both gendered individuals and their states in how the First World War was remembered.

THE CENTRALITY OF THE MALE IN MEMORIALIZATION

First and foremost, those constructing the memory of the First World War focused on memorializing the unprecedented numbers of the dead and commemorating their sacrifices. During the war, propaganda often depicted horrifying atrocities against civilian women in their efforts to mobilize their populations,[11] but postwar memory concentrated much more fully on the actions and experiences of soldiers, especially on those who gave their lives. One notable remembrance of German brutality against a civilian woman did cross over into postwar memory, however; in 1920, a statue to nurse Edith Cavell was unveiled in London. The Germans had executed Cavell in Brussels in 1915, for aiding British soldiers to escape to neutral Holland. The monument praised Cavell's sacrifice "For King and Country" and for being "Faithful until Death." The statue was multivalent, as, in 1924, its base was inscribed with Cavell's remarkable words before the firing squad: "Patriotism is not enough. I must have no hatred or bitterness for anyone."

But monuments to individual heroes were rare, and many families did not even have an individual gravesite at which to mourn. For those families who were not able to retrieve the bodies of their loved ones for private burial and private mourning, sites such as the Cenotaph in London and the various tombs of unknown soldiers served as places of private as well as public mourning.[12] At the same time that nations developed memorials to soldiers at home, they also constructed powerful monuments at war cemeteries near the actual battlefields and arranged for pilgrimages of families to these sites. While some of the US dead, for example, were repatriated at the request of their families, the government also created the opportunity for "Gold Star Mothers" to travel to their sons' graves in Europe, privileging the mourning of mothers.[13] Thus, the dead and missing men were memorialized in multiple ways: in private graves, town and village memorials, national memorials, and war cemeteries on foreign soil.

The inscription on London's Cenotaph to "The Glorious Dead" does not specify gender or race, but the word "glorious" underscores the notion that the memorial was dedicated to those heroic individuals who actively served their countries. The tradition of honoring an unknown soldier is more specific; the Unknown Soldier is a male fallen in battle who symbolizes all the soldiers missing in action and the nation as a whole. In this latter type of commemoration especially, the figure of the national citizen-soldier who gave his life for his country takes precedence over civilian casualties and sacrifices. While no doubt memorial sites were also sites of mourning for civilian losses, they nonetheless prioritized the male soldier as the focal point of commemoration and the epitome of the nation. In doing so, they underscored the special status of male soldiers as citizens and affirmed their political and social status. In Germany such sites became the locus of a civic religion of nationalism that sacralized the fallen male soldiers.[14] Because military contributions to the war effort trumped civilian efforts and could even be understood to be in the realm of the sacred, the result of commemoration was to reinforce the dominant status of men in building the nation.

An exception to this tendency can be found in the commemoration of female nurses and medical personnel who sacrificed (and sometimes gave their lives) for the war effort. In 1926, for example, the Canadian Association of Trained Nurses sponsored a memorial to the nurses who lost their lives in the First World War in the Canadian Parliament Hall of Honour in Ottawa. The prime minister of Canada, William King, broadened the nurses' original idea for a World War I memorial by advocating for a historical tableau that included the experiences of Canadian women across four centuries of the nation's history.[15] This modification preserved

the terrain of war as a male-gendered space while recognizing a particularly feminine contribution to the nation. While the memorial recognized the nurses who
"gave their lives in the Great War," it also according to the official documentation
underscored woman's "tender ministrations to those in need," throughout Canadian
history.[16] Both the Canadian nurses' memorial and the Women's Services relief at
the Scottish National War Memorial showed nurses tending to wounded men; thus,
the sacrifices of male soldiers remained central to the memorials' iconography.[17]

While fallen nurses were sometimes commemorated, a few memorials honored
the women of the nation in general for their "labours, sympathy and prayers," and
memorial sites such as the Five Sisters Window memorial at York Minster Cathedral
listed all the women of the British Empire who died as a result of their service in
the war, most war memorials did not commemorate women's war experiences.[18]
However, there were numerous female figures on war memorials nonetheless. One
subset of female images was allegorical—representing peace, justice, and various
personifications of the nation. For example, the sculpture erected inside the Greek
Temple Monument, the First World War memorial in Atlantic City, New Jersey,
featured the provocative image titled *Liberty in Distress*. This 1929 statue by Frederic
MacMonnies depicted a physically attractive and young female Liberty, naked and
shouting in pain, with a bare-chested dead soldier lying across her thigh.[19] Here,
Liberty combined two typically female functions: the first to stand as a symbol of
the entire nation, and the second to mourn for the loss of the dead soldiers. In this
particular statue, both the mourning nation and the fallen soldier were eroticized,
providing an emotionally charged representation of the relationship of the male citizen to the nation, and of the devastating cost of war.

While there were also some depictions of male mourners in interwar memorials, the female mourner appeared much more frequently as an element of interwar
monumental art. There were many variations of mourning mothers, wives, angels,
and female representations of the nation, and some of them drew on the explicitly
religious image of the pietà. This particular rendering of mourning sanctified the
dead soldier by likening his sacrifice to Christ's martyrdom. Whether in a secular or
a religious context, the male soldier sacrificing his life stood in counterpoint to the
passive female mourner who could do nothing but grieve for the loss of her husband,
brother, or son or more abstractly for the soldiers of her nation.[20]

However, the gender order as represented in interwar memory did not necessarily
correspond to the lived experience of men and women at the time, or exert influence
over real men and women. It was one of the many strands of postwar culture that
both reflected and reinforced traditional social relations between men and women,
but it was always in competition with other cultural interpretations. The significance of using gender to analyze interwar memory is that it reveals war memory

to be a vital component of the strands of postwar culture that undercut female and nonwhite arguments about equality, and thus worked toward stabilizing white male dominance through valorizing male heroism and sacrifice alone.

In the vast majority of cases, First World War monuments celebrated males of European descent, though there are some notable exceptions. Near the bloodiest battle sites of the war, monuments such as the Menin Gate in Ypres, Belgium, which was dedicated to the missing soldiers of the British Commonwealth, recognized Indian troops by name alongside British, Canadian, and Australian troops. French war cemeteries at Verdun and elsewhere honored the colonial dead in special Muslim sections. On Indian soil, the India Gate (or All India War Memorial) in the very center of New Delhi was designed by Edward Lutyens, also the architect of the Cenotaph in London. Resembling the Arc de Triomphe in Paris, this majestic monument was dedicated to the 70,000 Indian soldiers who died in the First World War. More than 13,000 names were inscribed on the monument.

On the whole, however, commemorations of the war dead tended to privilege European men. There were few US monuments commemorating African Americans in the First World War, and figurative monuments of soldiers depicted ethnically European types by default. In interwar memory, the contributions of colonial and African American troops, as well as those of women, were very often obscured by the centrality of the white male soldier in memorialization. Despite the shifting gender and ethnic power relations in various societies after the First World War, the typical forms of war commemoration shored up notions of the superiority of white male citizenship in public culture.

Many local interwar memorials used abstract forms rather than representational ones, such as stone obelisks, tablets, or steles, often with the names of the dead inscribed upon them. In such cases (along with the Cenotaph and the India Gate), the viewer had to imagine the image of the fallen soldier. The possibility of listing all the individual names of the fallen, or the dedication of a monument "to the fallen" in general, at least allowed for the possibility of inclusivity. In the former case, the individual names of women and nonwhites could potentially be included. In the latter, individual mourners could define their losses personally and did not have to restrict this definition to soldiers in battle.

DEBATES ABOUT SOLDIERLY MASCULINITY IN MEMOIRS AND LITERATURE

Just because war memory focused on the canonical image of the male soldier did not mean that the creators of war memory agreed about the nature of war and the ideal attributes of this heroic male soldier. The various ways in which figurative monuments depicted soldiers reveal sharp differences in how individual communities viewed the nature of war and of soldierly masculinity. Some monuments supported and some challenged the notion that the First World War could be described as "glorious." Literature and memoirs, with their greater capacity to describe soldiers' experiences in detail, also expressed conflicting ideas about the war.

Interwar writing conveyed complex and contradictory messages about the relationship of soldiering to manliness and honor, as well as about the nature of women's roles in wartime. The powerful impact of the memory of the First World War as articulated in the antiwar novels, memoirs, and poetry of the late war years and the 1920s sometimes obscures the fact that, in both Europe and the United States, these works represented only one strand of opinion about the war. While their notion that the war was a futile bloodbath that failed to solve Europe's problems is dominant today, in the interwar period these ideas competed vigorously with a discourse about the war that celebrated the honor, heroism, and valor of those who sacrificed their lives in the First World War.[21] This debate was one that touched upon the masculinity of the soldier in a variety of ways—both in understanding the effects of the war on the manliness of the soldier and in evaluating the extent to which his actions could be understood as "honorable."

German memoirs and literature perhaps demonstrated the sharpest conflict in notions about the war and masculinity. On the one hand, memoirists such as Ernst Junger in *The Storm of Steel* celebrated the First World War as a testing ground on which men could prove their honor and masculinity. Junger called the four years of war "schooling" and explained that even if their aim had not been achieved, the soldiers "learned to stand for a cause and if necessary to fall as befitted men. Hardened as scarcely another generation ever was in fire and flame, we could go into life as though from the anvil; . . . It is not every generation that is so favored."[22] For Junger, and others who wrote literature about what Germans called the "Time of Greatness," the front was a desirable, exclusively masculine sphere in which men could be "hardened" like steel by their heroic actions.[23] Despite the suffering of the German nation in wartime, Junger and other writers who shared his views saw war as a means of maturing and strengthening German men and, through this tempering process, constructing a powerful German nation.

In contrast to Junger, the German novelist Erich Maria Remarque believed that the war destroyed a generation of young men. His *All Quiet on the Western Front* (1929) became an international phenomenon, selling millions of copies in twenty languages. By late 1930, a French journal named Remarque the "author today with the largest audience in the world."[24] Remarque's novel came to epitomize "the truth" about the war, and the tragedy of the "lost generation," forever changed by its brutal war experience. In 1930, the Hollywood director Lewis Milestone expanded the reach of the novel even further when he brought the story to the screen in a powerful Academy Award–winning film.

In *All Quiet on the Western Front*, Remarque celebrated the comradeship of male soldiers as the only way to cope with war, but he rejected the idea that war could build a nation or turn boys into ideal heroic men. Instead, as Remarque explained in the novel's epigraph, the book was about "a generation of men who, even though they may have escaped its shells, were destroyed by the war." The novel showed the systematic annihilation of the soldiers, as war crushed their innocence, maimed their bodies, dulled their minds, and ultimately took their lives. Remarque's pacifist and internationalist novel posited that the ordinary French and German soldiers had more in common with one another than with those who started the war and ordered them into battle. In one of the most famous scenes, the protagonist Paul Baumer kills a Frenchman and then is trapped in a shell hole with the dead body. He vows, "I will fight against this, that has struck us both down; from you—taken life and from me?—Life also."[25] The novel firmly denied the idea that manliness and honor could be gained through combat against men of other nations.

Needless to say, Remarque's war memory, which challenged the efficacy of war for gaining honor and manliness and for solving international conflicts, was not well received by the leaders of the German army, the Nazi Party, or, later, the militarizing Nazi state. Critics of the novel attacked Remarque's war record, suggesting that his version of events was inauthentic because he had not been a true front-line soldier.[26] In 1930, Joseph Goebbels and his Storm Troopers (SA) disrupted the Berlin premiere of the American film version of *All Quiet on the Western Front* by throwing smoke bombs and sneezing powder in the movie theater and then beating cinema patrons who objected. When the Nazis came to power, Remarque's book was one of the first to be destroyed in the notorious 1933 book-burning ceremonies. As the book was thrown into the fire, the participants took an oath to educate "the nation in the spirit of standing to battle."[27]

These dramatic episodes clearly demonstrate the sharp differences of opinion in interwar memory about the relationship of warfare to masculinity, and what was at stake for the adherents of one side or another. Remarque's powerful book argued against all wars because of their negative impact on men as soldiers and citizens. The Nazi project required men to embrace their roles as soldiers, and so the Nazi leaders did all they could to suppress and discredit pacifist war memory. Although Junger distanced himself from the Nazi Party, his works were promulgated by Nazi propagandists as promoting a particular kind of soldierly masculinity that was in sync with Nazi ideals.

The Soviet government in the 1930s also waged war on Soviet memoirs and literature from the 1920s that represented war as emasculating and dehumanizing men, though its efforts were less dramatic than the Germans'. Memoirs that lingered on the physical costs of war—injuries to the genitals that turned men into eunuchs, shell shock, body-destroying diseases, and death—were censored in the 1930s and no longer appeared in print. Likewise, the Soviet government began to censor accounts of war that recognized its moral ambiguities, showing soldiers behaving dishonorably against civilians, raping, looting, and enacting violence not only against the enemy but also against innocent civilians from their own country and the enemy's, and even their own family members. The censors sometimes went so far as to eliminate depictions of soldiers showing fear in battle, leaving readers with one-dimensional depictions of courageous and chivalric soldiers who fiercely fought the enemy in battle but protected innocent civilians and the enemy wounded, and who never had any doubts about whether their actions were just or moral.[28]

Like Nazi Germany, the militarizing Soviet Union required war memory that promoted the soldier as hero and celebrated war against the enemy as an unambiguously positive manly duty. Because these two dictatorships practiced censorship, it is relatively easy to document the ways in which they manipulated war memoirs and literature to support state projects. In democratic and pluralistic states, the situation was more fluid, and trends in war memory were less sharply defined.

Women's memoirs likewise registered broad differences of opinion about the efficacy of war and the desirability of participating in it. A unique memoir of the period was *Yashka, My Life as Peasant, Officer, and Exile*, recording the life of the Russian female soldier (and later officer) Maria Bochkareva.[29] Bochkareva had received the tsar's special permission to join the army in early 1915 as a soldier rather than as a nurse, and she fought in the regular tsarist army. After the February Revolution, she led the Women's Battalion of Death, the first all-female Russian military unit. She fled Russia after the Bolsheviks took power and wrote her memoirs in exile. She later returned to Russia to join the anti-Bolshevik forces, and the Bolsheviks captured and executed her in 1920.

In her descriptions of the First World War, Bochkareva recounted her dedication to her comrades and her poise under fire and demonstrated her strong commitment to fighting the war to a successful conclusion. She showed herself to be a model of patriotism and loyalty, first to Tsar Nicholas II and then to the Provisional Government. Her memoirs appeared in English in the United States and were not subject to censorship, but they nonetheless embodied the same patriotic (some might even say jingoistic) spirit that could be found in official tsarist government publications in 1914. As the work of an émigré writer, however, Bochkareva's contribution to war memory did not influence narratives within Russia; instead, it helped to shape a Russian diaspora narrative of an honorable war effort undermined by Bolshevik treachery.

The memoirs of Vera Brittain, *Testament of Youth: One Woman's Haunting Record of the First World War*, stand in sharp contrast to Bochkareva's enthusiasm about war. Brittain, a middle-class university student who became a V.A.D. nurse on the front lines in France, and who lost her fiancé, her only sibling, and several other dear friends to the war, cataloged the agony of her wartime experience. She recalled "ambulance trains jolting noisily into the siding, all day, all night—gassed men on stretchers, clawing the air—dying men, reeking with mud and foul green-stained bandages, shrieking and writhing in a grotesque travesty of manhood—dead men with fixed empty eyes and shiny, yellow faces." Like Remarque, she showed the psychological and physical destruction of the front-line men and women of her generation and registered her own difficulty in adjusting to the trivialities of civilian life, in which people discussed only "the price of butter" and "the incompetence of the latest 'temporary' [servant]."[30] Thus, the sharp European debates about the nature of the war and its effects on youth could found in the works of European women as well as those of European men.

VISUAL REPRESENTATIONS AND DIVERGING OPINIONS OF WAR

Although monumental art could not convey interwar memory in as much depth and complexity as could literature and memoirs, there was nonetheless still a wide variety of ways to represent the nature of war and its impact on men and women using figurative means. Each community commemorating the dead of the First World War made aesthetic choices based on tradition and finances, as well as local imagination and creativity. In the United States, a prominent figurative depiction was that of the American "doughboy." Approximately 400 such monuments were built across the United States. Although some of these monuments were original, one-of-a-kind images, several artists were mass-producing doughboy monuments, including sculptors John Paulding and E. M. Viquesney. Viquesney organized a system of mass production of *The Spirit of the American Doughboy* in pressed copper, so that communities all over the country could have their own monuments at the relatively inexpensive price of a thousand dollars. By comparison, the Atlantic City statue *Liberty in Distress* cost $19,000. Viquesney's statue also appeared in thousands upon thousands of mass-produced figurines and even as the base of a doughboy lamp.[31] It is worth, then, considering what images of masculinity and war memory this popular statue conveyed.

A magazine advertisement for E. M. Viquesney's mass-produced statuette, *The Spirit of the American Doughboy*, demonstrates the manly ideal for postwar monuments in the United States. Mass-produced doughboy statues appeared across the United States after the war and cemented an image of the active male American soldier for citizens. *The American Legion National Headquarters*

The figure represented in *American Doughboy* stands in full battle gear, striding forward with a rifle in his left hand. His right arm is held high above his head, in preparation for throwing the grenade he holds in his right hand. He appears to be crossing no man's land, as indicated by the tree stumps and barbed wire at his feet. The John Paulding version of the statue is titled *Over the Top*, making it even more explicit that the soldier is staging an attack. Thus, the quintessential American figurative image of remembrance of the First World War is a soldier poised to kill the enemy in battle, boldly striding forward with his weapons at the ready. This much-reproduced statue embraces an image of war as a noble and manly endeavor. Numerous other monuments in the United States and Europe celebrated the dead through depicting battle scenes and soldiers taking part in military action, for example, charging with their bayonets. These demonstrated the persistence of a heroic image of the soldier throughout the interwar period, upholding the ideal of perpetrating violence on behalf of the state as a central component of male citizenship.

The widespread image of the heroic soldier in battle belied the realities of everyday army life, in which large numbers of soldiers served as laborers rather than combatants. Soldier-laborers dug trenches, built roads, transported supplies, and provided housing, food, and other necessities for the front-line soldiers. But the work of supporting the front-line soldiers was virtually erased from visual war memory, and with it the war experience of most African American and colonial troops, who were more likely to be assigned to labor battalions. War memory's concentration on the combat soldier as the exemplar of national masculinity both whitened the image of the warrior by excluding nonwhite soldier-laborers from the ranks of the heroes and undercut women's claims to citizenship as they, too, carried out the kinds of work conducted by soldier-laborers.

There were, however, other memorial images that competed with the image of the heroic soldier in battle. Images of mourning also appeared on many memorials in the United States and Europe, often focusing on the mourner alone, with the male soldier's body conspicuous by its absence. One example of this kind of monument is the moving tribute of the German artist Käthe Kollwitz to her son Peter. Kollwitz, whose art was later labeled "degenerate" by the Nazis, produced a monument for the German military cemetery in which her son was buried in Vladslo, Belgium. The piece is composed of two statues depicting a grieving mother and father, both on their knees, with the mother's head bowed in sorrow and the father staring straight ahead at his son's gravestone. This work focuses on the sorrow and loss of war and does not valorize the soldier's actions.

Other statues show soldiers with their heads bowed, mourning the loss of their comrades in arms. Typical of these works is a soldier in full uniform, with his gun reversed; the soldier holds the barrel of the rifle and bows his head in remembrance of his lost peers. The memorial thus recognizes the actions of the mourning soldier who has done his duty, as well as commemorating the soldier who has fallen. This variant of mourning does not show the limp and suffering body of the dying or dead soldier as does the pietà-style memorial but instead displays the manly value of stoicism in the face of loss. This wide variation in memorials reflects the broad spectrum of opinion about the costs of war and about soldierly masculinity and also demonstrates the complexity of interwar dialogues about both gender and war.

Representations of war as a manly field of honor for European men served as a conservative force in postwar dialogues about the relationship of the war to citizenship. The privileging of white male combatants in memorials weakened the claims of women, nonwhites, and noncombatants to equal recognition, honor, and rights in the postwar period. Despite the achievements of various movements for peace and civil rights in the 1920s, war memory aided in shoring up elements of prewar militarism and the race and gender order in spite of such changes. War memory in the interwar period was multifaceted, and there were exceptions that reinforced pacifism and the claims of women and nonwhites for equality. Overall, however, the field of war memory tended toward reinforcing and stabilizing traditional prewar and military roles.

There is still much work to be done in the field of gender and the memory of the First World War. In recent years, the dominance of research on the Western Front has been challenged by scholars working on gender and memory in the founding of the new nations of Eastern Europe. However, the tendency of new nations in the interwar years to eclipse the First World War in favor of their own founding myths, followed by the cataclysm of the Second World War, has made it difficult to trace the shape of Eastern European war memory. There is still more work to be done on the impact of the war on Eastern European men and women. The transnational reception of war memory and the construction of war memory in diasporic communities separated from their native lands also deserve more attention. The transformation of gendered memory as it crosses borders can reveal a great deal about the construction of national and transnational identities.

It is also important for researchers to examine atypical war memory and the narratives about war that have been marginalized and erased. Studying the versions of gendered, racialized, and national identities that have lost their battles with prevailing narratives reveals much about social and political conflict in the process of forming dominant national identities. Retrieving lost narratives and bringing them to light allows an examination of alternative historical paths and identities that are not any less important because they failed to thrive at an earlier time.

Diverse ideas about whether the war was heroic or destructive emerged all over Europe and the United States. In England, France, and the United States, martial representations coexisted with depictions of mourning in a dialogue about the nature of war and its effects on the combatants. Images of heroic warfare, of adoring family members sending their soldiers off to war, and of noble and stoic soldiers all contributed to making war thinkable as they represented the soldier as the honored masculine ideal and perhaps even as sacred. While not all war memory conveyed this positive message about soldierly masculinity, the notion of honor on the battle-field survived the First World War, even though the actual fighting conditions did not allow for the knightly chivalry of old. However, the two intensely militarizing states of Eastern and Central Europe sought to silence debates about war and masculinity with censorship. In Nazi Germany and the Soviet Union, war memory that bemoaned the effects of war on the masculinity, bodily integrity, and moral bearing of the soldier disappeared from sight, leaving only heroic notions of war in public discourse. Because of the actions of these two countries, war became "thinkable" again in 1939.

NOTES

1. Jay Winter, *Remembering War: The Great War between Memory and History in the Twentieth Century* (New Haven, CT: Yale University Press, 2006), introduction.

2. Here I am relying on the work of Alon Confino, "Collective Memory and Cultural History: Problems of Method," *American Historical Review* 102, no. 5 (1997): 1391.

3. Winter, *Remembering War*, 3–4.

4. Karen Petrone, *The Great War in Russian Memory* (Bloomington: Indiana University Press, 2011); Karen Petrone "'Now Russia Returns Its History to Itself': Russia Celebrates the Centennial of World War I," in *Remembering the First World War*, ed. Bart Ziino (New York: Routledge, 2014), 129–145.

5. On masculinity and state violence, see Joshua Sanborn, *Drafting the Russian Nation: Military Conscription, Total War, and Mass Politics, 1905–1925* (DeKalb: Northern Illinois University Press, 2003).

6. Laurie S. Stoff, *They Fought for the Motherland: Russia's Women Soldiers in World War I and the Revolution* (Lawrence: University Press of Kansas, 2006); Melissa Stockdale, "'My Death for the Motherland Is Happiness': Women, Patriotism, and Soldiering in Russia's Great War, 1914–1917," *American Historical Review* 109, no. 1 (2004): 79, 91, 115.

7. Jay Winter, *Sites of Memory, Sites of Mourning: The Great War in European Cultural History* (Cambridge: Cambridge University Press, 1995).

8. Quoted in Maciej Maria Gorny, "All Quiet? The Memory and Historiography of the First World War in Poland," *Rubrica Contemporanea* 3, no. 6 (2014): 39.

9. David L. Hoffmann and Annette F. Timm, "Utopian Biopolitics: Reproductive Policies, Gender Roles, and Sexuality in Nazi Germany and the Soviet Union," in *Beyond Totalitarianism: Stalinism and Nazism Compared*, ed. Michael Geyer and Sheila Fitzpatrick (Cambridge: Cambridge University Press, 2009), 87–132.

246 ◦_ Gender and the Great War

10. For a discussion of the centrality of motherhood to wartime identities, see Susan R. Grayzel, *Women's Identities at War: Gender, Motherhood, and Politics in Britain and France during the First World War* (Chapel Hill: University of North Carolina Press, 1999).

11. See John N. Horne and Alan Kramer, *German Atrocities 1914: A History of Denial* (New Haven, CT: Yale University Press, 2001).

12. Winter, *Sites of Memory, Sites of Mourning*.

13. The "Gold Star Mother" program privileged mothers over widows and fathers. It also remained segregated, and the mothers of black soldiers had to travel separately to the graves of their sons. See Lisa Budreau, *Bodies of War: World War I and the Politics of Commemoration in America, 1919–1933* (New York: New York University Press, 2010). See also Suzanne Evans, *Mothers of Heroes, Mothers of Martyrs: World War I and the Politics of Grief* (Montreal: McGill-Queen's University Press, 2007).

14. George L. Mosse, *Fallen Soldiers: Reshaping the Memory of the World Wars* (New York: Oxford University Press, 1990).

15. See Daniel J. Sherman, *The Construction of Memory in Interwar France* (Chicago: University of Chicago Press, 1999).

16. Parliament of Canada website, http://www.parl.gc.ca/collections/collection_profiles/CP_nurses-e.htm.

17. Scottish National War Memorial website, http://www.snwm.org/content/tour/?view=station_5.

18. Scottish National War Memorial website; York Minster Cathedral website, http://www.yorkminster.org/first-world-war/events-activities-and-services/memorial-trail.html; Susan R. Grayzel, *Women and the First World War* (Harlow: Longman, 2002).

19. Online Exhibit, "Nucky's Empire: The Prohibition Years," The Atlantic City Experience, Atlantic City Free Public Library. http://atlanticcityexperience.org/10001-experience-the/prohibition-1920-1933/218-greek-temple-monument.html.

20. Sherman, *Construction of Memory in Interwar France*, 303.

21. For the deconstruction of this myth, see Samuel Hynes, *A War Imagined: The First World War and English Culture* (London: Bodley Head, 1990); Terri Blom Crocker, *The Christmas Truce: Myth, Memory and the First World War* (Lexington: University Press of Kentucky, 2015).

22. Ernst Junger, *The Storm of Steel: From the Diary of a German Storm-Troop Officer on the Western Front* (1929; repr., New York: Howard Fertig, 1975), 316–317.

23. See Wolfgang G. Natter, *Literature at War 1914–1940: Representing the "Time of Greatness" in Germany* (New Haven, CT: Yale University Press, 1999).

24. Quoted in Modris Eksteins, *Rites of Spring: The Great War and the Birth of the Modern Age* (New York: Mariner Books, 2000), 276.

25. Erich Maria Remarque, *All Quiet on the Western Front* (1929; repr., New York: Ballantine Books, 1982), epigraph, 226.

26. Eksteins, *Rites of Spring*, 278.

27. US Holocaust Memorial Museum website, http://www.ushmm.org/outreach/en/article.php?ModuleId=10007677; http://www.ushmm.org/wlc/en/article.php?ModuleId=10007520.

28. See Petrone, *Great War in Russian Memory*, for further discussion of the disappearance of pacifist war literature. The censored works include Kirill Levin, *Notes from Captivity* (Zapiski iz plena); Sof'ia Fedorchenko, *The People at War* (Narod na voine); and Mikhail Sholokhov, *Quiet Flows the Don* (Tikhii Don).

29. Maria Bochkareva, *Yashka: My Life as Peasant, Officer and Exile* (New York: F. A. Stokes, 1919). This is sometimes written as Botchkareva.

30. Vera Brittain, *Testament of Youth: One Woman's Haunting Record of the First World War* (1933; repr., New York: Penguin, 1989), 423, 429.

31. Jennifer Wingate, *Sculpting Doughboys: Memory, Gender and Taste in America's World War I Memorials* (Farnham, UK: Ashgate, 2013), 1, 24. See also the website produced by community researchers Les Kopel and Earl Goldsmith, "The E. M. Viquesney Spirit of the American Doughboy Database," http://doughboysearcher.weebly.com.

13

The Scholarship of the First World War

Susan R. Grayzel and Tammy M. Proctor

DURING THE CENTENARY of the First World War, scholars around the world are re-examining this important conflict and its global impact on the twentieth century. Historians are investigating virtually all aspects of the war and its short- and long-term impacts and employing multiple theoretical tools, analytical frameworks, and newly opened (or revisited) archives. One of the crucial and relatively new tools for analyzing the First World War is gender, a category that came to prominence in the 1980s and 1990s. Our book has brought together a multinational group of historians to catalog some of the major scholarship produced on gender and the First World War to explain "where we have been" while also laying out contemporary themes in gender history, demonstrating their significance for understanding the Great War, and suggesting future areas of inquiry, or "what needs to be done." This brief chapter provides a bit of historiographic background and introduces a select list of important works in the field.

Since the war itself, historians have been studying the war's origins and impact. National histories in the 1920s chronicled the course of the war and outlined major effects of the conflict on nations and regions of the world. Many of the historians had been participants in the war themselves, giving them a particular kind of perspective.[1] However, the scholarly trajectory of the war was in many ways interrupted and displaced by the cataclysm of World War II, which involved even greater numbers of people and places. Faced with the destruction and scope of this second global conflict, scholars allowed World War I to fade from view. Even today, a glance at the history shelves in a popular bookstore or university library will demonstrate the enduring interest in World War II, while a much smaller section is devoted to the earlier conflict.

Given this chronology, scholarship on World War I is easily grouped into four major periods, three of which are described in detail by Jay Winter and Antoine Prost in *The Great War in History: Debates and Controversies, 1914 to the Present*.[2] In this work, which was published in English in 2005, Winter and Prost identify three groups of historians and approaches. The first generation of scholars asked diplomatic, economic, and political questions about the war.[3] This first phase, Winter and Prost argue, continued into the post–World War II era with a major debate about the origins of the war sparked by the publication of Fritz Fischer's *Germany's Aims in the First World War*.[4] This earlier group of scholars established the field. The second and third phases reflect a sea change in the historical profession itself, with an emphasis on social history and history from below in the second iteration, and a turn to cultural and comparative history in the third phase.[5] The social history generation coincided with the study of underrepresented groups and created interest in the lives of women, and important works about the history of women and war emerged in the 1980s especially.[6] However, gender history only coalesced as a field in the period after the 1986 publication of Joan Wallach Scott's article "Gender: A Useful Category of Historical Analysis."[7] Soon after, historical publications on World War I appeared that used gender as a framework.[8]

The fourth period in World War I scholarship has emerged in the twenty-first century. These scholarly works aim to reach across national lines with a comparative or transnational approach.[9] The new transnational focus for World War I scholarship has exposed gaps in understanding and coverage of the war, making room for a new generation of scholars. Additionally, the methodological changes of the past few decades have led to more cross-pollination between historical schools. For example, diplomatic historians now frequently employ gender as a tool for understanding the intricacies of international politics. Subjects that had been considered peripheral to the war experience in the past now have become legitimate subjects for study— food, sexuality, and environment, to name just a few. While there are many ways of approaching missing elements in the history of the war, three important insights have emerged just in the period since the centennial of the war came into focus or roughly the last decade.

First, many historians now realize that the dominant narrative of the war, especially in English-language publications has been built heavily around the Western Front. Students of history often know little about the First World War beyond the trope that it was a stalemate in which millions died for no real aims. As part of this version of the story, alliances between states led almost inexorably toward an inevitable and futile conflict, erasing the agency of political decision-makers and obscuring the broader historical context. In short, while this trope of war might contain a kernel of truth, it does a disservice to the complexity of the war and its participants. Several historians have begun to pick apart this war narrative, with one of the best examples of new interpretations of old debates that aim to challenge orthodox views of the war being Christopher Clark's work *The Sleepwalkers*, which reopens the debate about the war's origins and the belligerents' war aims by giving Serbia a more prominent place in the narrative.[10]

A second area that has seen significant scholarly activity in recent years is the notion of a global war. The interest in the trench warfare of Belgium and France has obscured the larger realities of war on other fronts; it has skewed many of the debates about wartime origins and impacts toward a few countries. Additionally, revolution and political upheaval in the former Russian, Habsburg, and Ottoman Empires meant that histories of the First World War in those regions received less attention than in other nations. Scholars are now trying to redress the balance by exploring the archives of nations that had been part of the non–Western Front experience of war. In particular, valuable work has emerged in the past two decades explaining war in the Russian, Austro-Hungarian, and Italian contexts.[11] Increasingly younger scholars are also writing histories of the war's impact in the Balkans, Mesopotamia and other places in the former Ottoman empire, all of Asia, and various parts of the African continent. In so doing, some are extending the timespan of the war as well, beginning as early as 1911 and ending in 1923.[12]

The last area that has proved important in recent scholarship is the displacement and movement of peoples during war and the responses the international community created to deal with this massive problem. Several scholars have located the origins of modern humanitarianism in the period of the war, when populations faced famine, loss of their homes and livelihoods, and often loss of their statehood.[13] Other scholars have honed in on the experience of refugees and forced population exchange.[14] In all these studies, authors identify a fundamental shift in ethnic politics, global understanding, and citizenship as a result of the First World War.

The broadening of the scholarship of World War I to include multiple fronts and participants has provided depth and new interest in the period surrounding the war. Alan Kramer published an important two-part article surveying much of this recent historiography that is useful to any scholar or student of the war.[15] One of the things that is apparent in Kramer's overview is the way in which gender analysis has become a central feature of studying the First World War, particularly in work that explains war's impact on so-called home fronts and in occupied zones. However, there are still significant gaps in our understanding of the interaction of war and gendered expectations that this collection has explored.

The gender history of the First World War began as women's history. To a great extent, this history dates to the war itself. Accounts of the contributions of women to the war effort in various nations appeared throughout the war years. Most recounted the new labor being performed by women, whether in Britain in Helen Fraser's *Women and War Work* (1918); France in Léon Abensour's *Les vaillantes: Héroïnes, martyres ou remplaçantes* (1917); or Germany as shown in the testimonies recounted in *Deutsche Frauen—Deutsche Treue!* (1917). So, too, can we find from the start of the war the appearance of appeals to women to respond to the war either as call to support, such as suffragette Christabel Pankhurst pamphlet "The War" (1914), or in anguished protest throughout suffragist Helena Swanwick's *Women and War* (1915). In participant states, then, there is ample evidence to support a vision of the war as a marked turning point for women, and this has had an influence on the writing of such history.

However, an analysis of the meanings of women's wartime experiences and contributions would wait more than fifty years to appear. There are several explanations for why the attention paid to women during the war faded as the war ended. In part this occurred because of how wartime memory and commemorations highlighted the suffering and sacrifices of soldiers. A decade after the war's end, an interpretation of the war had emerged across the West, certainly, that suggested that the war was a catastrophe for a generation of young men who fell in valiant if futile combat, a bloodletting due to incompetent military and civilian leadership. There was little room in this version to acknowledge the contributions of all of society to total war except to blame civilians, epitomized perhaps as women, for failing to understand the horrors that had just occurred. A more fundamental reason for the disappearance of women from the wartime narrative is apparent in the work of political scientist Cynthia Enloe, whose investigations into the study of women and war demonstrate how efforts to place women in roles removed from the allegedly real work of war help justify the continuing emphasis on elevating what male soldiers do in a heroic story of conflict.[16]

It was arguably not until the combination of the fiftieth anniversary of the war and the rise of the women's movement that the study of the war in the new field of women's history emerged. From roughly the 1970s to the 1990s, the study of women and the war opened up in part due to an Imperial War Museum exhibit and its companion volume by Arthur Marwick, *Women at War 1914–1918*. In this book, filled with illustrations from the Imperial War Museum's substantial Women's Work Collection, Marwick postulated that the war had been of benefit to women, helping them to achieve access to new forms of employment and, as a result, to public life.[17]

The idea that the war was somehow liberating for women also captured the attention of literary scholars. Using textual and visual evidence, Sandra Gilbert's influential essay "Soldier's Heart: Literary Men, Literary Women and the Great War" (1983) argued that the war caused young men to become "increasingly alienated from their pre-war selves." As a result, women "become, as if by some uncanny swing of history's pendulum, ever more powerful."[18] Largely using male-authored texts, Gilbert shows how they painted a worldview where women thrived as men died. While this model of the war as emancipating women seized the imagination of those looking to cultural evidence, social historians of Britain and France, such as Gail Braybon, James McMillan, and Deborah Thom, by the late 1970s and early 1980s were investigating the lives of women workers and finding that the war offered temporary and limited opportunities for working-class women. There were a few attempts at a national synthesis such as Françoise Thébaud's *La femme au temps de la guerre de 14* (1986), but here too the emphasis remained on what women could do and did during the duration of the war.[19]

Another important way to conceptualize the contradictory experience of the war for women came in the mid-1980s in Margaret Higonnet and Patrice Higonnet's essay on "The Double Helix" in the pivotal volume *Behind the Lines* (published in 1987, but based on a 1984 conference). Here, the Higonnets argued that the metaphor of the double helix offers a useful way to understand the dynamics at work between men and women during the war: "relationships of domination and subordination" (with men always retaining power over women) get maintained "through discourses that systematically designate unequal gender relationships."[20] In the same volume, Joan Scott urged women's historians to rewrite the history of war.

While many of the theoretical models for thinking about women and the war came largely from an Anglo-American context, work on women and the war in other participant states also emerged in the 1970s and 1980s, especially in Germany. This included the insights offered in the overview of women in Germany by Ute Frevert, *Frauen-Geschichte: Zwischen Bürgerlicher Verbesserung und Neuer Weiblichkeit* (1986), and the specific study of working-class women found in Ute Daniel's *Arbeiterfrauen in der Kriegsgesellschaft: Beruf, Familie und Politik im Ersten Weltkrieg* (1989).[21] Like much of the scholarship to this point, these studies focused on the economic, political, and social impact of women's wartime mobilization, especially for working-class women.

By the early 1990s, another important model for how to see the impact of the war on conceptions of gender, especially of femininity, came in the work of Susan Kingsley Kent and Mary Louise Roberts.[22] Using the case studies of Britain and France, respectively, these two cultural historians cull from a range of textual and visual evidence to argue that whatever transformations occurred from 1914 to 1918, the postwar era represented a "backlash" against any of these gains. In the aftermath of the war, feminism failed as those in power curtailed the options available to women, emphasizing instead their essential domestic nature as wives and mothers. It is worth noting that they chose countries where the most visible sign of feminist triumph as an immediate result of the war—the winning of female enfranchisement—either failed to be realized (France) or came on unequal terms with men (Britain). Nonetheless, this narrative of liberation and then backlash seemed to make sense of the absence of women from the story of the First World War, as well as the ways in which the very visible changes evident in the Imperial War Museum's photographs seemed to have disappeared almost overnight.

Complicating the history of women and the war, which, like much of the literature on the war itself, focused on the Western Front and the clash of nations, there came histories that extended the geographical range of a scholarly field that continued to focus primarily on women. Essays by Barbara Engel helped illuminate the activism of women in Russia, while Belinda Davis offered an important contribution to understanding women and everyday life in wartime Berlin.[23] Nicole Dombrowski edited a 1999 collection that questioned what it meant for men and women to "enlist" in war across several national boundaries.[24] Other histories took up the investigation of new kinds of work for women, including espionage, police work, medicine, and even, in the case of revolutionary Russia, combat.[25]

Many of these studies enabled the broadening of a conversation about the impact of the war on gender roles. While emphasizing war's effect on women, they suggested that this opened up questions about gender—the intermingling and dynamic ways in which men as well as women saw themselves in relationship to prevailing norms. Another wave of historians in the 1990s sought to portray a nuanced view of women during the war, looking to analyze both culture and politics, including the politics of the workplace, to see the lasting impact of the war on gender policies as well as practices. These include Susan Pedersen tracing the origins of the welfare state in ideas about state support for soldier's dependents, Laura Lee Downs examining changes in women's and men's roles in wartime metalworking, Janet Watson illustrating how men and women fought "different" wars in concert, and Susan Grayzel showing how even a normative ideal like motherhood could be put by and for women to contradictory ends—both radical and conservative.[26]

Part of the challenge that historians have faced in analyzing gender and this war has been figuring out how to incorporate the parallel story of the fight for extending the franchise to include women. Many women's historians tried to use the war and women's contribution to help explain the advances of the movement for women's suffrage, especially in the war's direct aftermath. Yet as Nicoletta Gullace demonstrated in her book on the British suffrage debates, the story was often much more complicated than the vote serving as a reward or recognition solely for women's war-time service.[27] Suffragists were shrewd political actors who used the war to their advantage when possible, but the leaders of the women's suffrage movement never had a singular vision of women's role in wartime or a single response to this war. At the International Women's Peace Conference at The Hague in 1915, feminists from warring and neutral countries (including Germany, Britain, the Netherlands, the United States, and Hungary) met and attempted to forge a manifesto that tied peace in part to a world of enfranchised women.[28] This meeting was an outgrowth of the dynamic prewar women's movement, exemplified by the International Women's Suffrage Alliance, and gave rise to one key postwar global organization, the Women's International League for Peace and Freedom (WILPF). However, until WILPF's second congress took place after the war ended in 1919, no real progress toward an international feminist organization could be made, although a feminist periodical, *Jus Suffragi*, continued publication throughout the war. At the national level, splits within campaigns for women's suffrage occurred over questions of pacifism, political alignment, class, and race, and splinter organizations formed in many cases. The history of organized feminist activity around the vote remains a component of the years 1914–1918, but it is not necessarily the most important feature in the history of gender and this war.[29]

One of the more recent developments in gender history in the war is the shift from studies such as those listed here that might consider gender but are clearly focused on and derived from women's history. A new wave of scholarship on masculinity and this war has yielded some valuable insights that undermine ideas that there was one overarching male experience of the war, or that it was only about war making, or that it was entirely separate from the world of home and women. Joanna Bourke's *Dismembering the Male*, Santanu Das's *Touch and Intimacy in First World War Literature*, Michael Roper's *The Secret Battle*, Jessica Meyer's *Men at War*, and Jason Crouthamel's *An Intimate History of the Front* all employ the testimony of soldiers to offer nuanced interpretations of the war as being complicated for men trying to understand themselves as men. The experience of noncombatant men is also slowly coming to be written.[30]

Expanding the scope of such studies beyond the canonical war zones has produced a new and rich literature on gender and the global context of the war. Work by Africanists such as Joe Lunn in *Memoirs of the Maelstrom* has revealed how much the encounters between Senegalese troops and European civilians, especially women, transformed the lives and expectations of veterans.[31] Several of the essays in Santanu Das's *Race, Empire and First World War Writing* consider the intimate history of Indian troops, the complex experiences of Asian laborers from China and Vietnam in France, and the uneasy ways in which national regimes tried to incorporate the experience of racialized imperial subjects in Australia and New Zealand.[32] In addition, methodological work by Joanna Bourke in *Dismembering the Male* and *An Intimate History of Killing* as well as Laura Doan in *Disturbing Practices* has opened up the very category of the subject and added a transformed understanding of the embodied self to the list of insights offered by gender history.[33]

This short chapter has only been able to touch upon a few of the important debates and continuing conversations about gender and the Great War. The chapters in this volume have added to the conversation while also opening up fruitful new veins of scholarly inquiry in the future. The select bibliography again is meant only as a starting point for further reading, but it does provide some idea of the richness and scope of work on the First World War and gender history. As scholars of this subject, all of the contributors to this book look forward to seeing what what the next generation will uncover.

NOTES

1. Good examples of such national histories, often with a strong ideological purpose, include Henri Pirenne, *La Belgique et la guerre mondiale* (Paris: Les Presses Universitaires de France, 1929), and C. E. W. Bean, *The Official History of Australia in the War of 1914-1918*, which constituted twelve volumes published between 1920 and the early 1940s. Pirenne spent more than two years in German internment, and Bean served as a war correspondent, traveling with Australian forces.

2. Jay Winter and Antoine Prost, *The Great War in History: Debates and Controversies, 1914 to the Present* (Cambridge: Cambridge University Press, 2005).

3. This work encompasses the huge 132-volume economic history of the war series produced by the Carnegie Endowment for International Peace.

4. Fritz Fischer, *Germany's Aims in the First World War* (New York: Norton, 1967).

5. The 1960s marks the beginning of social history as a field, which expanded inquiry to include marginalized groups. The convergence of World War I and social history approaches hits a high-water mark in the 1970s and 1980s with work by scholars such as Jay Winter, Jean-Jacques Becker, and John Keegan. Cultural history emerged under the influence of literary theory and cultural anthropology, which broadened historians' use of sources especially. The cultural turn in the history of World War I is epitomized by the 1990s scholarship of Stéphane Audoin-Rouzeau and Annette Becker in France.

6. Examples here include Angela Woollacott, *On Her Their Lives Depend: Munitions Workers in the Great War* (Berkeley: University of California Press, 1994), and Margaret Darrow, *French Women and the First World War: War Stories of the Home Front* (Oxford: Berg, 2000).

7. Joan Wallach Scott, "Gender: A Useful Category of Historical Analysis," *American Historical Review* 91, no. 5 (1986): 1053–1075.

8. One of the first of such gender histories was the collection Margaret Higonnet et al., eds., *Behind the Lines: Gender and the Two World Wars* (New Haven, CT: Yale University Press, 1987). A good example of a comparative gender history is Susan R. Grayzel's *Women's Identities at*

War: Gender, Motherhood, and Politics in Britain and France during the First World War (Chapel Hill: University of North Carolina Press, 1999).

9. Examples of such scholarship include Peter Englund's book *The Beauty and the Sorrow: An Intimate History of the First World War* (New York: Vintage, 2012), and Tammy Proctor's *Civilians in a World at War, 1914–1918* (New York: New York University Press, 2010).

10. Christopher Clark, *The Sleepwalkers: How Europe Went to War in 1914* (New York: Harper, 2012).

11. See, for instance, Joshua Sanborn, *Drafting the Russian Nation: Military Conscription, Total War, and Mass Politics, 1905–1925* (DeKalb: Northern Illinois University Press, 2003); Maureen Healy, *Vienna and the Fall of the Habsburg Empire: Total War and Everyday Life in World War I* (Cambridge: Cambridge University Press, 2004); and Mark Thompson, *The White War: Life and Death on the Italian Front* (London: Faber, 2008).

12. See, for example, Eugene Rogan, *The Fall of the Ottomans: The Great War in the Middle East* (New York: Basic Books, 2015); Leila Tarazi Fawaz, *A Land of Aching Hearts: The Middle East in the Great War* (Cambridge, MA: Harvard University Press, 2014); Abigail Jacobson, *From Empire to Empire: Jerusalem between Ottoman and British Rule* (Syracuse, NY: Syracuse University Press, 2011); Frederick R. Dickinson, *War and National Reinvention: Japan in the Great War, 1914–1919* (Cambridge, MA: Harvard University Press, 2001); Xu Guoqi, *China and the Great War: China's Pursuit of a New National Identity and Internationalization* (Cambridge: Cambridge University Press, 2011); Bill Nasson, *Springboks on the Somme: South Africa in the Great War 1914–1918* (Johannesburg: Penguin, 1998); Michelle R. Moyd, *Violent Intermediaries: African Soldiers, Conquest and Everyday Colonialism in German East Africa* (Athens: Ohio University Press, 2014). Chronology is particularly addressed in essays in Robert Gerwarth and Erez Manela, eds., *Empires at War: 1911–1923* (Oxford: Oxford University Press, 2014).

13. Recent examples include Bruno Cabanes, *The Great War and the Origins of Humanitarianism 1918–1924* (Cambridge: Cambridge University Press, 2014); Julia Irwin, *Making the World Safe: The American Red Cross and a Nation's Humanitarian Awakening* (New York: Oxford University Press, 2013); and Keith Watenpaugh, *Bread from Stones: The Middle East and the Making of Modern Humanitarianism* (Berkeley: University of California Press, 2015).

14. Michaël Amara, *Des Belges à l'épreuve de l'Exil: Les réfugiés de la première guerre mondiale* (Brussels: ULB, 2008); Peter Gatrell, *A Whole Empire Walking: Refugees in Russia during World War I* (Bloomington: Indiana University Press, 1999); and Evangelia Balta, *The Exchange of Populations: Historiography and Refugee Memory* (Istanbul: ISTOS, 2014).

15. Alan Kramer, "Recent Historiography of the First World War," *Journal of Modern European History* 12, nos. 1/2 (2014): 5–27, 155–174.

16. See Cynthia Enloe, *Does Khaki Become You? The Militarization of Women's Lives* (London: Pandora, 1988); Cynthia Enloe, *Maneuvers: The International Politics of Militarizing Women's Lives* (Berkeley: University of California Press, 2000). Similarly, writer and cultural critic Nancy Huston has asserted that the roles of men and women in wartime break down into who narrates the war story and who weeps to hear it. See Nancy Huston, *A l'amour comme à la guerre* (Paris: Seuil, 1984); Nancy Huston, "Tales of War and Tears of Women," *Women's Studies International Forum* 1 (1982), 271–282.

17. Arthur Marwick, *Women at War 1914–1918* (London: Fontana, 1977). That Marwick used propaganda photos as evidence has been remarked upon by Gail Braybon and Deborah Thom. See Gail Braybon, "Winners or Losers: Women's Role in the War Story," in *Evidence, History and*

the Great War: Historians and the Impact of 1914–1918, ed. Gail Braybon (New York: Berghahn, 2003), 86–113; Deborah Thom, "Making Spectaculars: Museums and How We Remember Gender in Wartime," in *Evidence, History and the Great War: Historians and the Impact of 1914– 1918*, ed. Gail Braybon (Oxford: Berghahn, 2003), 48–66.

18. Sandra Gilbert, "Soldier's Heart: Literary Men, Literary Women and the Great War," *Signs* 8, no. 3 (1983): 425.

19. Gail Braybon, *Women Workers in the First World War* (London: Croom Helm, 1981); James McMillan, *Housewife or Harlot?* (New York: St. Martin's Press, 1981); Deborah Thom, *Nice Girls and Rude Girls: Women Workers and the First World War* (London: I. B. Tauris, 1999); and Françoise Thébaud, *La femme au temps de la guerre de 14* (Paris: Stock, 1986).

20. Margaret Higonnet and Patrice Higonnet, "The Double Helix," in *Behind the Lines: Gender and the Two World Wars*, ed. Margaret Higonnet et al. (New Haven, CT: Yale University Press, 1987), 31–47.

21. Ute Frevert, *Frauen-Geschicte: Zwischen Bürgerlicher Verbesserung und Neuer Weiblichkeit* (Frankfurt: Suhrkamp, 1986); Ute Daniel, *Arbeiterfrauen in der Kriegsgesellschaft. Beruf, Familie und Politik im Ersten Weltkrieg* (Göttingen: Vandenhoeck & Ruprecht, 1989), published as a modified translation in *The War from Within: German Working-Class Women in the First World War* (Oxford: Berg, 1997).

22. Susan Kingsley Kent, *Sex and Suffrage in Britain, 1860-1914* (Princeton: Princeton University Press, 1987), and Mary Louise Roberts, *Civilization without Sexes: Reconstructing Gender in Postwar France, 1917–1927* (Chicago: University of Chicago Press, 1994).

23. Barbara Engel, "Not by Bread Alone: Subsistence Riots in Russia during World War." *Journal of Modern History* 69, no. 4 (1997): 696–721, and.Belinda Davis, *Home Fires Burning: Food, Politics and Everyday Life in World War I Berlin* (Chapel Hill: University of North Carolina Press, 2000).

24. Nicole Ann Dombrowski, ed., *Women and War in the Twentieth Century: Enlisted with or without Consent* (New York: Routledge, 1999).

25. Tammy Proctor, *Female Intelligence: Women and Espionage in the First World War* (New York: New York University Press, 2003); Philippa Levine, "Walking the Streets in a Way No Decent Woman Should: Women Police in WWI," *Journal of Modern History* 66, no. 1 (1994): 34–78; Leah Leneman, *In the Service of Life: Story of Elsie Inglis and Scottish Women's Hospitals* (Edinburgh: Mercat Press, 1994); Kimberly Jensen, "Feminist Transnational Activism and International Health: The Medical Women's International Association and the American Women's Hospitals, 1919-1948," in *Women and Transnational Activism in International Perspective*, ed. Kimberly Jensen and Erika Kuhlman (Dordrecht: Republic of Letters, 2010), 143– 172; and Laurie S. Stoff, *They Fought for the Motherland: Russia's Women Soldiers in World War I and the Revolution* (Lawrence: University Press of Kansas, 2006).

26. Susan Pedersen, *Family, Dependence and the Origins of the Welfare State, Britain and France, 1914-1945* (Cambridge: Cambridge University Press, 1993); Laura Lee Downs, *Manufacturing Inequality: Gender Division in the French and British Metalworking Industries, 1914–1939* (Ithaca, NY: Cornell University Press, 1995); Janet S. K. Watson, *Fighting Different Wars: Experience, Memory and the First World War in Britain* (Cambridge: Cambridge University Press, 2004); Grayzel, *Women's Identities at War.*

27. Nicoletta F. Gullace, *The Blood of Our Sons: Men, Women and the Renegotiation of British Citizenship during the Great War* (New York: Palgrave Macmillan, 2002).

28. For a good transnational overview of some of these issues, see Alison S. Fell and Ingrid Sharp, eds., *The Women's Movement in Wartime: International Perspectives, 1914–1919* (Houndmills: Palgrave Macmillan, 2007).

29. Johanna Alberti, *Beyond Suffrage: Feminists in War and Peace, 1914–1928* (Houndmills: Macmillan, 1989); Birgitta Bader Zaar, "Women's Suffrage and War: World War I and Political Reform in Comparative Perspective," in *Suffrage, Gender and Citizenship: International Perspectives on Parliamentary Reforms*, ed. Irma Sulkunen, Seija-Leena Nevala-Nurmi, and Pirjo Markkola (Cambridge: Cambridge Scholars Press, 2009); Nancy F. Cott, *The Grounding of Modern Feminism* (New Haven, CT: Yale University Press, 1987); Richard J. Evans, *The Feminists: Women's Emancipation Movements in Europe, America and Australasia 1840–1920* (London: Croom Helm, 1987); Gullace, *The Blood of Our Sons*; Steven C. Hause with Anne R. Kenney, *Women's Suffrage and Social Politics in the French Third Republic* (Princeton, NJ: Princeton University Press, 1984); Karen Offen, *European Feminisms 1700–1950: A Political History* (Stanford, CA: Stanford University Press, 2000); Ingrid Sharp and Matthew Stibbe, eds., *Aftermaths of War: Women's Movements and Female Activists, 1918–1923* (Leiden: Brill, 2010); Paul Smith, *Feminism and the Third Republic: Women's Political and Civil Rights in France, 1918–1945* (Oxford: Clarendon, 1996).

30. Joanna Bourke, *Dismembering the Male: Men's Bodies, Britain and the Great War* (London: Reaktion, 1996); Santanu Das, *Touch and Intimacy in First World War Literature* (Cambridge: Cambridge University Press, 2005); Michael Roper, *The Secret Battle: Emotional Survival in the Great War* (Manchester: Manchester University Press, 2009); Jessica Meyer, *Men at War: Masculinity and the First World War in Britain* (New York: Palgrave Macmillan, 2009); and Jason Crouthamel, *An Intimate History of the Front: Masculinity, Sexuality, and German Soldiers in the First World War* (New York: Palgrave Macmillan, 2014).

31. Joe Lunn, *Memoirs of the Maelstrom: A Senegalese Oral History of the First World War* (Portsmouth, NH: Heinemann, 1999).

32. Santanu Das, ed., *Race, Empire and First World War Writing* (Cambridge: Cambridge University Press, 2011).

33. Bourke, *Dismembering the Male*; Joanna Bourke, *An Intimate History of Killing: Face-to-Face Killing in Twentieth-Century Warfare* (New York: Basic Books, 1999); Laura Doan, *Disturbing Practices: History, Sexuality, and Women's Experience of Modern War* (Chicago: University of Chicago Press, 2013).

SELECTED BIBLIOGRAPHY

Adams, Katherine H., and Michael L. Keene. *Alice Paul and the American Suffrage Campaign.* Urbana: University of Illinois Press, 2008.

Alberti, Johanna. *Beyond Suffrage: Feminists in War and Peace, 1914–1928.* Houndmills: Macmillan, 1989.

Allen, Keith. "Sharing Scarcity: Bread Rationing and the First World War in Berlin, 1914–1923." *Journal of Social History* 32, no. 2 (1998): 371–393.

Amad, Paula. *Counter-archive: Film, the Everyday, and Albert Kahn's Archives de la Planète.* New York: Columbia University Press, 2010.

Amara, Michaël. *Des Belges à l'épreuve de l'Exil: Les réfugiés de la première guerre mondiale.* Brussels: ULB, 2008.

Anderson, Benedict. *Imagined Communities: Reflections on the Origin and Spread of Nationalism.* Rev. ed. New York: Verso, 1991.

Anderson, Julie. *War, Disability and Rehabilitation in Britain: Soul of a Nation.* Manchester: Manchester University Press, 2011.

Audoin-Rouzeau, Stéphane. "Children and the Primary Schools of France, 1914–1918." In *State, Society and Mobilization in Europe during the First World War*, edited by John Horne, 39–52. Cambridge: Cambridge University Press, 1997.

———. *La guerre des enfants, 1914–1918.* Paris: Armand Colin, 1993.

———. *14–18 Les combattants des tranchées.* Paris: Armand Colin, 1986.

Audoin-Rouzeau, Stéphane, and Annette Becker. *14–18: Understanding the Great War.* New York: Hill and Wang, 2000.

Bader Zaar, Birgitta. "Women's Suffrage and War: World War I and Political Reform in Comparative Perspective." In *Suffrage, Gender and Citizenship: International Perspectives on Parliamentary Reforms*, edited by Irma Sulkunen, Seija-Leena Nevala-Nurmi, and Pirjo Markkola, 193–218. Cambridge: Cambridge Scholars Press, 2009.

Baldwin, M. Page. "Subject to Empire: Married Women and the British Nationality and Status of Aliens Act." *Journal of British Studies* 40, no. 4 (2001): 522–556.

Ballhatchet, Kenneth. *Race, Sex and Class under the Raj: Imperial Attitudes and Policies and Their Critics, 1793–1905*. London: Weidenfeld and Nicolson, 1980.

Balta, Evangelia. *The Exchange of Populations: Historiography and Refugee Memory*. Istanbul: ISTOS, 2014.

Bean, C. E. W. *The Official History of Australia in the War of 1914–1918*. 12 vols. Sydney: Angus and Robertson, 1921–1942.

Becker, Annette. *Les cicatrices rouges, 14–18, France et Belgique occupées*. Paris: Fayard, 2010.

———. *Oubliés de la Grande Guerre: Humanitaire et culture de guerre, 1914–1918: Populations occupées, déportés civils, prisonniers de guerre*. Paris: Noêsis, 1998.

Beckett, Ian F. W. *The Great War, 1914–1918*. Harlow, UK: Longman, 2001.

———. *Home Front 1914–1918: How Britain Survived the Great War*. Kew: National Archives, 2006.

Bekraoui, Mohammed. *Les Marocains dans la Grande Guerre 1914–1919*. Rabat: Publications de la Commission Marocaine d'Histoire Militaire, 2009.

Berg, Justin Allen. "Subjective Age Identity during the Transition to Adulthood: Psychological and Sociological Perspectives." *Social Thought and Research* 28 (2007): 145–163.

Bessel, Richard. *Germany after the First World War*. Oxford: Clarendon Press, 1993.

———. *Violence: A Modern Obsession*. London: Simon and Schuster, 2015.

Bette, Peggy. "Women's Mobilization for War (France)." Translated by Susan Emanuel. In *1914-1918-Online—International Encyclopedia of the First World War*, edited by Ute Daniel, Peter Gatrell, Oliver Janz, Heather Jones, Jennifer Keene, Alan Kramer, and Bill Nasson. Berlin: Freie Universität, 2014. doi:http://dx.doi.org/10.15463/ie1418.10027.

Birchard, Robert S. *Cecil B. DeMille's Hollywood*. Lexington: University Press of Kentucky, 2004.

Bishop, Alan, with Terry Smart, eds. *Vera Brittain: War Diary 1913–1917: Chronicle of Youth*. London: Victor Gollancz, 1981.

Bland, Lucy. "White Women and Men of Colour: Miscegenation Fears in Britain after the Great War." *Gender and History* 17, no. 1 (2005): 29–61.

Blobaum, Robert. "Warsaw's Forgotten War." *Remembrance and Solidarity Studies* 2 (2014): 185–207.

Blobaum, Robert, and Donata Blobaum. "A Different Kind of Home Front: War, Gender and Propaganda in Warsaw, 1914–1918." In *World War I and Propaganda*, edited by Troy R. E. Paddock, 247–272. Leiden: Brill, 2014.

Blom, Philipp. *The Vertigo Years: Europe, 1900–1914*. New York: Basic Books, 2010.

Boittin, Jennifer Anne. *Colonial Metropolis: The Urban Grounds of Anti-imperialism and Feminism in Interwar Paris*. Lincoln: University of Nebraska Press, 2010.

Bourke, Joanna. *Dismembering the Male: Men's Bodies, Britain and the Great War*. London: Reaktion, 1996.

———. *Fear: A Cultural History*. Emeryville, CA: Avalon, 2006.

———. "Gender Roles in Killing Zones." In *The Cambridge History of the First World War*, 3 vols., edited by Jay Winter, 3:153–177. Cambridge: Cambridge University Press, 2014.

——. *An Intimate History of Killing: Face-to-Face Killing in twentieth-century Warfare.* New York: Basic Books, 1999.

Boxwell, David A. "The Follies of War: Cross-Dressing and Popular Theater on the British Front." *Modernism/Modernity* 9, no. 1 (2002): 1–20.

Brantlinger, Patrick. *Rule of Darkness: British Literature and Imperialism, 1830–1914.* Ithaca, NY: Cornell University Press, 1990.

Braybon, Gail. "Winners or Losers: Women's Symbolic Role in the War Story." In *Evidence, History and the Great War: Historians and the Impact of 1914–18,* edited by Gail Braybon, 86–112. New York: Berghahn, 2003.

——. "Women, War, and Work." In *The Oxford Illustrated History of the First World War,* edited by Hew Strachan, 149–162. Oxford: Oxford University Press, 1998.

——. *Women Workers in the First World War.* London: Croom Helm, 1981.

Bredbenner, Candice. "A Duty to Defend? The Evolution of Aliens' Military Obligations to the United States, 1792–1946." *Journal of Policy History* 24, no. 2 (2012): 224–262.

——. *A Nationality of Her Own: Women, Marriage and the Law of Citizenship.* Berkeley: University of California Press, 1998.

Brown, Frederic. *Chemical Warfare: A Study in Restraints.* 1968. Reprint, New Brunswick, NJ: Transaction, 2006.

Brown, Nikki. *Private Politics and Public Voices: Black Women's Activism from World War I to the New Deal.* Bloomington: Indiana University Press, 2006.

Brookfield, Tarah. "Divided by the Ballot Box: The Montreal Council of Women and the Election of 1917." *Canadian Historical Review* 89, no. 4 (2008): 473–501.

Brownell, Penelope. "The Women's Committees of the First World War: Women in Government, 1917–1919." PhD diss., Brown University, 2002.

Browning, Christopher R. *Ordinary Men: Reserve Police Battalion and the Final Solution in Poland.* New York: HarperCollins, 1992.

Bucur, Maria. *Heroes and Victims: Remembering War in Twentieth-Century Romania.* Bloomington: Indiana University Press, 2009.

Budreau, Lisa. *Bodies of War: World War I and the Politics of Commemoration in America, 1919–1933.* New York: New York University Press, 2010.

Byrnes, Joseph F. *Catholic and French Forever: Religious and National Identity in Modern France.* University Park: Pennsylvania State University Press, 2005.

Cabanes, Bruno. *The Great War and the Origins of Humanitarianism 1918–1924.* Cambridge: Cambridge University Press, 2014.

Cannadine, David. "War and Death, Grief and Mourning in Modern Britain." In *Mirrors of Mortality: Studies in the Social History of Death,* edited by Joachim Whaley, 187–242. London: Europa, 1981.

Cannady, Margot. *The Straight State: Sexuality and Citizenship in Twentieth-Century America.* Princeton, NJ: Princeton University Press, 2009.

Capozzola, Christopher. *Uncle Sam Wants You: World War I and the Making of the Modern American Citizen.* New York: Oxford University Press, 2008.

Carden-Coyne, Ana. *The Politics of Wounds: Military Patients and Medical Power in the First World War.* Oxford: Oxford University Press, 2014.

——. *Reconstructing the Body: Classicism, Modernism and the First World War.* Oxford: Oxford University Press, 2009.

Chaudhuri, Nupur, and Margaret Strobel, eds. *Western Women and Imperialism: Complicity and Resistance*. Bloomington: Indiana University Press, 1992.

Chickering, Roger. *The Great War and Urban Life in Germany*. Cambridge: Cambridge University Press, 2007.

Clancy-Smith, Julia, and Frances Gouda, eds. *Domesticating the Empire: Race, Gender, and Family Life in French and Dutch Colonialism*. Charlottesville: University Press of Virginia, 1998.

Clark, Christopher. *The Sleepwalkers: How Europe Went to War in 1914*. New York: Harper, 2012.

Clifford, Hugh. *The Gold Coast Regiment in the East African Campaign*. 1920. Reprint, Nashville, TN: Battery Press, 1995.

Clothier, Norman. *Black Valour: The South African Native Labour Contingent, 1916–1918, and the Sinking of the Mendi*. Pietermaritzburg, South Africa: University of Natal Press, 1987.

Cole, Sarah. *Modernism, Male Friendship and the First World War*. Cambridge: Cambridge University Press, 2003.

Compagnon, Olivier, and Pierre Purseigle. "Géographies de la mobilisation et territoires de la belligérance durant la Première Guerre mondiale." *Annales* 71, no. 1 (2016): 39–63.

Condell, Diana, and Jean Liddiard. *Working for Victory: Images of Women in the First World War*. London: Routledge, 1987.

Confino, Alon. "Collective Memory and Cultural History: Problems of Method." *American Historical Review* 102, no. 5 (1997): 1386–1403.

Conklin, Alice L. *A Mission to Civilize: The Republican Idea of Empire in France and West Africa, 1895–1930*. Stanford, CA: Stanford University Press, 1997.

Connolly, James E. "*Mauvaise conduite*: Complicity and Respectability in the Occupied Nord, 1914–1918." *First World War Studies* 4, no. 1 (2013): 7–21.

Cook, Tim. "Against God-Inspired Conscience: The Perception of Gas Warfare as a Weapon of Mass Destruction, 1915–1939." *War and Society* 18, no. 1 (2000): 47–69.

Cornish, Nik. *The Russian Army and the First World War*. Stroud: Spellmount, 2006.

Corrigan, Gordon. *Sepoys in the Trenches: The Indian Corps on the Western Front, 1914–15*. Kent, UK: Spellmount, 1999.

Cott, Nancy F. *The Grounding of Modern Feminism*. New Haven, CT: Yale University Press, 1987.

Cousturier, Lucie. *Des inconnus chez moi*. Paris: Sirène, 1920.

Cox, Mary Elisabeth. "Hunger Games: Or How the Allied Blockade in the First World War Deprived German Children of Nutrition, and Allied Food Aid Subsequently Saved Them." *Economic History Review* 68, no. 2 (2015): 600–631.

Crenshaw, Kimberle. "Mapping the Margins: Intersectionality, Identity Politics, and Violence against Women of Color." *Stanford Law Review* 43, no. 6 (1991): 1241–1299.

Crocker, Terri Blom. *The Christmas Truce: Myth, Memory and the First World War*. Lexington: University Press of Kentucky, 2015.

Crouthamel, Jason. *The Great War and German Memory: Society, Politics and Psychological Trauma, 1914–1945*. Exeter: University of Exeter Press, 2009.

———. *An Intimate History of the Front: Masculinity, Sexuality, and German Soldiers in the First World War*. New York: Palgrave, 2014.

———. "Male Sexuality and Psychological Trauma: Soldiers and Sexual 'Disorder' in World War I and Weimar Germany." *Journal of the History of Sexuality* 17, no. 1 (2008): 60–84.

Culwick, A. T., and G. M. Culwick. *Ubena of the Rivers*. London: George Allen and Unwin, 1935.

Damousi, Joy. *The Labour of Loss: Mourning, Memory, and Wartime Bereavement in Australia*. New York: Cambridge University Press, 1999.

———. "Mourning Practices." In *The Cambridge History of the First World War*. Vol. 3, *Civil Society*, edited by Jay Winter, 358–386. Cambridge: Cambridge University Press, 2014.

———. "Socialist Women and Gendered Space: Anti-conscription and Anti-war Campaigns 1914–1918." In *Gender and War: Australians at War in the Twentieth Century*, edited by Joy Damousi and Marilyn Lake, 254–273. Cambridge: Cambridge University Press, 1995.

Daniel, Ute. *The War from Within: German Working-Class Women in the First World War*. Oxford: Berg, 1997.

Daniels, Gordon. "Humanitarianism or Politics? Japanese Red Cross Nurses in Britain 1915–1916." In *Japanese Women: Emerging from Subservience, 1868–1945*, edited by Hiroko Tomida and Gordon Daniels, 222–231. Kent, UK: Global Oriental, 2005.

Darrow, Margaret. *French Women and the First World War: War Stories of the Home Front*. Oxford: Berg, 2000.

Das, Santanu, ed. *Race, Empire and First World War Writing*. Cambridge: Cambridge University Press, 2011.

———. *Touch and Intimacy in First World War Literature*. Cambridge: Cambridge University Press, 2005.

Daughton, James P. "Sketches of the Poilu's World: Trench Cartoons from the Great War." In *World War I and the Cultures of Modernity*, edited by Douglas Peter Mackaman and Michael Mays, 35–67. Jackson: University Press of Mississippi, 2000.

Davis, Belinda J. "Food, Politics and Women's Everyday Life during the First World War." In *Home/Front: The Military, War and Gender in Twentieth-Century Germany*, edited by Karen Hagemann and Stefanie Schüler-Springorum. Oxford: Berg, 2002.

———. "Food Scarcity and the Empowerment of the Female Consumer in World War I Berlin." In *The Sex of Things: Gender and Consumption in Historical Perspective*, edited by Victoria de Grazia and Ellen Furlough, 287–310. Berkeley: University of California Press, 1996.

———. *Home Fires Burning: Food, Politics, and Everyday Life in World War I Berlin*. Chapel Hill: University of North Carolina Press, 2000.

Dayan, Jacques, and Betrand Olliac. "From Hysteria and Shell Shock to Posttraumatic Stress Disorder: Comments on Psychoanalytic and Neuropsychological Approaches." *Journal of Physiology-Paris* 104, no. 6 (2010): 296–302.

Dayton, Cornelia H., and Lisa Levenstein. "The Big Tent of U.S. Women's and Gender History: A State of the Field." *Journal of American History* 99, no. 3 (2012): 793–817.

DeBauche, Leslie Midkiff. *Reel Patriotism: The Movies and World War I*. Madison: University of Wisconsin Press, 1997.

DeGroot, Gerard. *Blighty: British Society in the Era of the Great War*. Harlow: Longman, 1996.

De Pauw, Linda Grant. *Battle Cries and Lullabies: Women in War from Prehistory to the Present*. Norman: University of Oklahoma Press, 1998.

Depkat, Volker. "Remembering War the Transnational Way: The U.S.-American Memory of World War I." In *Transnational American Memories*, edited by Udo J. Hebel, 185–214. New York: Walter de Gruyter, 2009.

De Schaepdrijver, Sophie. "Military Occupation, Political Imaginations, and the First World War." *First World War Studies* 4, no. 1 (2013): 1–5.

———. "Occupation, Propaganda, and the Idea of Belgium." In *European Culture in the Great War: The Arts, Entertainment, and Propaganda, 1914–1918*, edited by Aviel Roshwald and Richard Stites, 267–294. Cambridge: Cambridge University Press, 1999.

Dibbets, Karel, and Bert Hogenkamp. *Film and the First World War*. Amsterdam: Amsterdam University Press, 1995.

Dickinson, Frederick R. *War and National Reinvention: Japan in the Great War, 1914–1919*. Cambridge, MA: Harvard University Press, 2001.

Doan, Laura. *Disturbing Practices: History, Sexuality, and Women's Experience of Modern War*. Chicago: University of Chicago Press, 2013.

———. "Sex Education and the Great War Soldier: A Queer Analysis of the Practice of 'Hetero' Sex." *Journal of British Studies* 51, no. 3 (2012): 641–663.

Doan, Laura, and Jane Garrity, eds. *Sapphic Modernities: Sexuality, Women and National Culture*. New York: Palgrave Macmillan, 2006.

Dombrowski, Nicole Ann, ed. *Women and War in the Twentieth Century: Enlisted with or without Consent*. New York: Routledge, 1998.

Donner, Henriette. "Under the Cross: Why V.A.D.s Performed the Filthiest Task in the Dirtiest War: Red Cross Women Volunteers, 1914–1918." *Journal of Social History* 30, no. 3 (1997): 687–704.

Donson, Andrew. *Youth in the Fatherless Land: War Pedagogy, Nationalism, and Authority in Germany, 1914–1918*. Cambridge, MA: Harvard University Press, 2010.

Downing, Lisa. *The Cambridge Introduction to Michel Foucault*. Cambridge: Cambridge University Press, 2008.

Downs, Laura Lee. *Manufacturing Inequality: Gender Division in the French and British Metalworking Industries, 1914–1939*. Ithaca, NY: Cornell University Press, 1995.

Duby, Georges, and Michelle Perrot, eds. *A History of Women in the West: V. Towards a Cultural Identity in the Twentieth Century*. Cambridge, MA: Harvard University Press, 1994.

Dumenil, Lynn. "Women's Reform Organizations and Wartime Mobilization in World War I–Era Los Angeles." *Journal of the Gilded Age and Progressive Era* 10, no. 2 (2011): 213–245.

Dyer, Colin. *Population and Society in Twentieth Century France*. London: Hodder and Stoughton, 1978.

Early, Frances H. *A World without War: How U.S. Feminists and Pacifists Resisted World War I*. Syracuse, NY: Syracuse University Press, 2007.

Eckert, Henri. "Les militaires indochinois au service de la France (1859–1939)." 2 vols. Thèse de doctorat, L'Université de Paris IV, 1998.

Eichenberg, Julia, and John Paul Newman, eds. *The Great War and International Veterans' Organizations*. Basingstoke: Palgrave Macmillan, 2013.

Eksteins, Modris. *Rites of Spring: The Great War and the Birth of the Modern Age*. New York: Mariner Books, 2000.

Engel, Barbara. "Not by Bread Alone: Subsistence Riots in Russia during World War." *Journal of Modern History* 69, no. 4 (1997): 696–721.

Engelstein, Laura. "'A Belgium of Our Own': The Sack of Russian Kalisz, August 1914." *Kritika: Explorations in Russian and Eurasian History* 10, no. 3 (2009): 441–473.

Englund, Peter. *The Beauty and the Sorrow: An Intimate History of the First World War.* New York: Vintage, 2012.

Enloe, Cynthia. *Does Khaki Become You? The Militarization of Women's Lives.* London: Pandora, 1988.

———. *Maneuvers: The International Politics of Militarizing Women's Lives.* Berkeley: University of California Press, 2000.

Ermacora, Matteo. "Rural Society." In *1914-1918-Online—International Encyclopedia of the First World War,* edited by Ute Daniel, Peter Gatrell, Oliver Janz, Heather Jones, Jennifer Keene, Alan Kramer, and Bill Nasson. Berlin: Freie Universität, 2014. DOI: 10.15463/ie1418.10530.

Evans, Raymond. "'All the Passion of Our Womanhood': Margaret Thorp and the Battle of the Brisbane School of Arts." In *Gender and War: Australians at War in the Twentieth Century,* edited by Joy Damousi and Marilyn Lake, 239–253. Cambridge: Cambridge University Press, 1995.

Evans, Richard J. *The Feminists: Women's Emancipation Movements in Europe, America and Australasia 1840–1920.* London: Croom Helm, 1987.

Evans, Suzanne. *Mothers of Heroes, Mothers of Martyrs: World War I and the Politics of Grief.* Montreal: McGill-Queen's University Press, 2007.

Favre-Le Van Ho, Mireille. "Un milieu porteur de modernisation: Travailleurs et tirailleurs vietnamiens en France pendant la première guerre mondiale." 2 vols. Thèse de doctorat, École nationale des chartes, 1986.

Fawaz, Leila Tarazi. *A Land of Aching Hearts: The Middle East in the Great War.* Cambridge, MA: Harvard University Press, 2014.

Fedorchenko, Sof'ia. *The People at War.* New York: Oxford University Press, 2008.

Fehlemann, Silke. "Bereavement and Mourning (Germany)." In *1914-1918-Online—International Encyclopedia of the First World War,* edited by Ute Daniel, Peter Gatrell, Oliver Janz, Heather Jones, Jennifer Keene, Alan Kramer, and Bill Nasson. Berlin: Freie Universität Berlin, 2014. DOI: 10.15463/ie1418.10177.

Feimster, Crystal N. "The Impact of Racial and Sexual Politics on Women's History." *Journal of American History* 99, no. 3 (2012): 822–826.

Fell, Alison S., and Ingrid Sharp, eds. *The Women's Movement in Wartime: International Perspectives, 1914–1919.* Houndmills: Palgrave Macmillan, 2007.

Fischer, Fritz. *Germany's Aims in the First World War.* New York: Norton, 1967.

Fisher, Susan. *Boys and Girls in No Man's Land: English-Canadian Children and the First World War.* Toronto: University of Toronto Press, 2011.

Fogarty, Richard S. "Eugenics in Europe." In *International Encyclopedia of Social and Behavioral Sciences,* 2nd ed., 237–245. Oxford: Elsevier, 2015.

———. *Race and War in France: Colonial Subjects in the French Army, 1914–1918.* Baltimore: Johns Hopkins University Press, 2008.

Foster, Catherine. *Women for All Seasons: The Story of the Women's International League for Peace and Freedom.* Athens: University of Georgia Press, 1989.

Foucault, Michel. *The History of Sexuality.* London: Penguin, 1976.

Frank, Dana. "Housewives, Socialists, and the Politics of Food: The 1917 New York Cost-of-Living Protests." *Feminist Studies* 11, no. 2 (1985): 255–285.

Frémaux, Jacques. *Les colonies dans la Grande Guerre: Combats et épreuves des peuples d'outre-mer.* Saint-Cloud: Éditions 14–18, 2006.

Frevert, Ute. *Frauen-Geschicte: Zwischen Bürgerlicher Verbesserung und Neuer Weiblichkeit.* Frankfurt: Suhrkamp, 1986.

———. "Wartime Emotions: Honour, Shame, and the Ecstasy of Sacrifice." In *1914-1918-Online—International Encyclopedia of the First World War*, edited by Ute Daniel et al. Berlin: Freie Universität, 2014. DOI: 10.15463/ie1418.10409.

Frey, Marc. "Bullying the Neutrals: The Case of the Netherlands." In *Great War, Total War: Combat and Mobilization on the Western Front, 1914–1918*, edited by R. Chickering and S. Förster, 227–244. Cambridge: Cambridge University Press, 2000.

Gardner, Brian. *German East: The Story of the First World War in East Africa.* London: Cassell, 1963.

Gardner, Martha. *The Qualities of a Citizen: Women, Immigration, and Citizenship, 1870–1965.* Princeton, NJ: Princeton University Press, 2005.

Garton, Stephen. "The Dominions, Ireland and India." In *Empires at War: 1911–1923*, edited by Robert Gerwarth and Erez Manela, 152–178. Oxford: Oxford University Press, 2014.

Gatrell, Peter. "Introduction: World Wars and Population Displacement in Europe in the Twentieth Century." *Contemporary European History* 16, no. 4 (2007): 415–426.

———. *A Whole Empire Walking: Refugees in Russia during World War I.* Bloomington: Indiana University Press, 1999.

Gervereau, Laurent, and Christophe Prochasson, eds. *Images de 17.* Paris: BDIC, 1987.

Gerwarth, Robert, and John Horne. *War in Peace: Paramilitary Violence in Europe after the Great War.* Oxford: Oxford University Press, 2012.

Gerwarth, Robert, and Erez Manela, eds. *Empires at War: 1911–1923.* Oxford: Oxford University Press, 2014.

Giblin, James. *A History of the Excluded: Making Family a Refuge from State in Twentieth-Century Tanzania.* Athens: Ohio University Press, 2005.

———. *The Politics of Environmental Control in Northeastern Tanzania, 1840–1940.* Philadelphia: University of Pennsylvania Press, 1992.

———. "The Victimization of Women in Late Precolonial and Early Colonial Warfare in Tanzania." In *Sexual Violence in Conflict Zones*, edited by Elizabeth Heineman, 89–102. Philadelphia: University of Pennsylvania Press, 2011.

Gibson, Craig. *Behind the Front: British Soldiers and French Civilians, 1914–1918.* Cambridge: Cambridge University Press, 2014.

Gilbert, Sandra. "Soldier's Heart: Literary Men, Literary Women and the Great War." *Signs* 8, no. 3 (1983): 422–450.

Giles, Kevin S. *Flight of the Dove: The Experience of Jeannette Rankin.* Beaverton, OR: Touchstone Press, 1980.

Gilje, Paul A. *Rioting in America.* Bloomington: Indiana University Press, 1996.

Girard, Marion. *A Stange and Formidable Weapon: British Responses to World War I Poison Gas.* Lincoln, NE: University of Nebraska Press, 2008.

Glover, David, and Cora Kaplan. *Genders.* London: Routledge, 2000.

Goebel, Stefan. "Exhibitions." In *Capital Cities at War: Paris, London, Berlin 1914–1919.* Vol. 2, *A Cultural History*, edited by Jay Winter and Jean-Louis Robert, 143–187. Cambridge: Cambridge University Press, 2007.

Goldman, Wendy Z. *Women at the Gates: Gender and Industry in Stalin's Russia.* Cambridge: Cambridge University Press, 2002.

Gorny, Maciej Maria. "All Quiet? The Memory and Historiography of the First World War in Poland." *Rubrica Contemporanea* 3, no. 6 (2014): 37–46.

Gould, Jenny. "Women's Military Services in First World War Britain." In *Behind the Lines: Gender and the Two World Wars*, edited by Margaret Higonnet, Jane Jenson, Sonya Michel, and Margaret Collins Weitz, 114–125. New Haven, CT: Yale University Press, 1987.

Graham, Sarah Hunter. *Woman Suffrage and the New Democracy*. New Haven, CT: Yale University Press, 1996.

Grayzel, Susan R. *At Home and Under Fire: Air Raids and Culture in Britain from the Great War to the Blitz*. Cambridge: Cambridge University Press, 2012.

———. "Defence against the Indefensible: The Gas Mask, the State and British Culture during and after the First World War." *Twentieth Century British History* 25, no. 3 (2014): 418–434.

———. "Liberating Women? Examining Gender, Morality, and Sexuality in First World War Britain and France." In *Evidence, History and the Great War: Historians and the Impact of 1914–18*, edited by Gail Braybon, 113–134. New York: Berghahn, 2003.

———. "Men and Women at Home." In *The Cambridge History of the First World War*, 3 vols., edited by Jay Winter, 3:96–120. Cambridge: Cambridge University Press, 2014.

———. "Mothers, Marraines, and Prostitutes: Morale and Morality in First World War France." *International History Review* 19, no. 1 (1997): 66–82.

———. " 'The Outward and Visible Sign of Her Patriotism': Women, Uniforms, and National Service during the First World War." *Twentieth Century British History* 8, no. 2 (1997): 145–164.

———. *Women and the First World War*. Harlow: Longman, 2002.

———. *Women's Identities at War: Gender, Motherhood, and Politics in Britain and France during the First World War*. Chapel Hill: University of North Carolina Press, 1999.

Greenhut, Jeffrey. "The Imperial Reserve: The Indian Corps on the Western Front, 1914–15." *Journal of Imperial and Commonwealth History* 12, no. 1 (1983): 54–73.

———. "Race, Sex, and War: The Impact of Race and Sex on Morale and Health Services for the Indian Corps on the Western Front, 1914." *Military Affairs* 45, no. 2 (1981): 71–74.

Greenwald, Maurine Weiner. *Women, War, and Work: The Impact of World War I on Women Workers in the United States*. Ithaca, NY: Cornell University Press, 1980.

Gregory, Adrian. *The Last Great War: British Society and the First World War*. Cambridge: Cambridge University Press, 2008.

Grundling, Albert. *Fighting Their Own War: South African Blacks and the First World War*. Johannesburg: Ravan Press, 1987.

Gullace, Nicoletta F. "Allied Propaganda and World War I: Interwar Legacies, Media Studies and the Politics of War Guilt." *History Compass* 9, no. 9 (2011): 686–700.

———. *The Blood of Our Sons: Men, Women, and the Renegotiation of British Citizenship during the Great War*. New York: Palgrave Macmillan, 2002.

———. "Sexual Violence and Family Honor: British Propaganda and International Law during the First World War." *American Historical Review* 102, no. 3 (1997): 714–747.

Gumz, Jonathan. *The Resurrection and Collapse of Empire in Habsburg Serbia, 1914–1918*. Cambridge: Cambridge University Press, 2009.

Gunderson, Frank. *Sukuma Labor Songs from Western Tanzania*. Leiden: Brill, 2010.

Guoqi, Xu. *China and the Great War: China's Pursuit of a New National Identity and Internationalization*. Cambridge: Cambridge University Press, 2011.

Haber, L. F. *The Poisonous Cloud: Chemical Warfare in the First World War*. Oxford: Clarendon, 1986.

Hagemann, Karen, and Stefanie Schüler-Springorum. *Home/Front: The Military, War and Gender in Twentieth-Century Germany.* Oxford: Berg, 2002.

Hall, Lesley. *Hidden Anxieties: Male Sexuality, 1900–1950.* Cambridge: Polity Press, 1991.

———. "Impotent Ghosts from No Man's Land, Flappers' Boyfriends or Cryptopatriarchs? Men, Sex and Social Change in 1920s Britain." *Social History* 21, no. 1 (1996): 54–70.

Hallett, Christine E. "'This Fiendish Mode of Warfare': Nursing the Victims of Gas Poisoning in the First World War." In *One Hundred Years of Wartime Nursing Practices*, edited by Jane Brooks and Christine E. Hallett, 81–100. Manchester: Manchester University Press, 2015.

Hallett, Christine E., and Alison S. Fell. "Introduction." In *First World War Nursing: New Perspectives*, edited by Allison S. Fell and Christine E. Hallett, 1–16. New York: Routledge, 2013.

Hämmerle, Christa, Oswald Überegger, and Birgitta Bader Zaar, eds. *Gender and the First World War.* Houndmills, Basingstoke, Hampshire: Palgrave Macmillan, 2014.

———. "Introduction: Women's and Gender History of the First World War—Topics, Concepts, Perspectives." In *Gender and the First World War*, edited by Hämmerle et al., 1–15. Houndmills, Basingstoke, Hampshire: Palgrave Macmillan, 2014.

Hampf, Michaela. *Release a Man for Combat: The Women's Army Corps during World War II.* Cologne: Böhlau, 2010.

Hanna, Martha. *The Mobilization of Intellect: French Scholars and Writers during the Great War.* Cambridge, MA: Harvard University Press, 1996.

———. *Your Death Would Be Mine: Paul and Marie Pireaud in the Great War.* Cambridge, MA: Harvard University Press, 2006.

Harris, Jose. "Bureaucrats and Businessmen in British Food Control, 1916–19." In *War and the State: The Transformation of British Government, 1914–1919*, edited by Kathleen Burk, 135–156. London: Routledge, 1982.

Harris, Ruth. "The 'Child of the Barbarian': Rape, Race and Nationalism in France during the First World War." *Past and Present*, no. 141 (1993): 170–206.

Harrison, Mark. "The British Army and the Problem of Venereal Disease in France and Egypt during the First World War." *Medical History* 39, no. 2 (1995): 133–158.

Hau, Michael. *The Cult of Health and Beauty in Germany: A Social History, 1890–1930.* Chicago: University of Chicago Press, 2003.

Hause, Steven C., with Anne R. Kenney. *Women's Suffrage and Social Politics in the French Third Republic.* Princeton, NJ: Princeton University Press, 1984.

Hausen, Karin. "The German Nation's Obligations to the Heroes' Widows of World War I." In *Behind the Lines: Gender and the Two World Wars*, edited by Margaret Higonnet, Jane Jenson, Sonya Michel, and Margaret Wietz, 126–140. New Haven, CT: Yale University Press, 1987.

Healy, Maureen. "Civilizing the Soldier in Postwar Austria." In *Gender and War in Twentieth-Century Eastern Europe*, edited by Nancy M. Wingfield and Maria Bucur, 47–69. Bloomington: Indiana University Press, 2015.

———. *Vienna and the Fall of the Habsburg Empire: Total War and Everyday Life in World War I.* Cambridge: Cambridge University Press, 2004.

Heineman, Elizabeth D. "Introduction: The History of Sexual Violence in Conflict Zones." In *Sexual Violence in Conflict Zones: From the Ancient World to the Era of Human Rights*, edited by Elizabeth Heineman, 1–24. Philadelphia: University of Pennsylvania Press, 2011.

Hendley, Matthew. *Organized Patriotism and the Crucible of War: Popular Imperialism in Britain, 1914–1932*. Montreal: McGill-Queen's University Press, 2012.

Henry, Louis. "Perturbations de la nuptialité resultant de la guerre 1914–1918." *Population* 21, no. 2 (1966): 273–332.

Herwig, Holger. *The First World War: Germany and Austria Hungary, 1914–1918 Modern Wars*. London: Bloomsbury Academic, 1996.

Herzog, Dagmar. *Sexuality in Europe: A Twentieth-Century History*. Cambridge: Cambridge University Press, 2011.

Higonnet, Margaret R. "The 2005 ACLA Presidential Address: Whose Can(n)on? World War I and Literary Empires." *Comparative Literature* 57, no. 3 (2005): xiii–xvii.

———, ed. *Lines of Fire: Women Writers of World War I*. (New York: Plume, 1991)

Higonnet, Margaret, Jane Jenson, Sonya Michel, Margaret Collins Weitz, eds. *Behind the Lines: Gender and the Two World Wars*. New Haven, CT: Yale University Press, 1987.

Higonnet, Margaret R., and Patrice Higonnet. "The Double Helix." In *Behind the Lines: Gender and the Two World Wars*, edited by Margaret Higonnet, Jane Jenson, Sonya Michel, and Margaret Collins Weitz, 31–47. New Haven, CT: Yale University Press, 1987.

Hill, Kimloan. "A Westward Journey, an Enlightened Path: Vietnamese Linh Tho, 1915–30." PhD diss., University of Oregon, 2001.

Hirschfeld, Magnus. *The Sexual History of the World War*. 1934. Reprint, Honolulu: University Press of the Pacific, 2006.

Hochschild, Adam. *To End All Wars: A Story of Loyalty and Rebellion, 1914–1918*. Boston: Mariner Books, 2011.

Hoffmann, David L., and Annette F. Timm. "Utopian Biopolitics: Reproductive Policies, Gender Roles, and Sexuality in Nazi Germany and the Soviet Union." In *Beyond Totalitarianism: Stalinism and Nazism Compared*, edited by Michael Geyer and Sheila Fitzpatrick, 87–132. Cambridge: Cambridge University Press, 2009.

Holmes, Katie. "Day Mothers and Night Sisters: World War I Nurses and Sexuality." In *Gender and War: Australians at War in the Twentieth Century*, edited by Joy Damousi and Marilyn Lake, 43–59. Cambridge: Cambridge University Press, 1995.

Holzer, Anton. *Das Lächeln der Henker: Der unbekannte Krieg gegen die Zivilbevölkerung 1914–1918*. Darmstadt: Primus-Verlag, 2014.

Horne, John. "Immigrant Workers in France during World War I." *French Historical Studies* 14, no. 1 (1985): 57–88.

———, ed. *State, Society and Mobilization in Europe during the First World War*. Cambridge: Cambridge University Press, 1997.

Horne, John, and Alan Kramer. *German Atrocities 1914: A History of Denial*. New Haven, CT: Yale University Press, 2001.

Howe, Glenford. *Race, War, and Nationalism: A Social History of West Indians in the First World War*. Kingston, Jamaica: Ian Randle, 2002.

Hull, Isabel. *Absolute Destruction: Military Culture and the Practices of War in Imperial Germany*. Ithaca, NY: Cornell University Press, 2005.

———. *A Scrap of Paper: Breaking and Making International Law during the Great War*. Ithaca, NY: Cornell University Press, 2014.

Hunt, Karen. "Gendering the Politics of the Working Woman's Home." In *Women and the Making of Built Space in England, 1870–1950*, edited by E. Darling and L. Whitworth, 107–122. Padstow, Cornwall: Aldershot, 2007.

———. "A Heroine at Home: The Housewife on the WWI Home Front." In *The Home Front in Britain: Images, Myths and Forgotten Experiences since 1914*, edited by Maggie Andrews and Janis Lomas, 73–91. London: Palgrave Macmillan, 2014.

———. "Negotiating the Boundaries of the Domestic: British Socialist Women and the Politics of Consumption." *Women's History Review* 9, no. 2 (2000): 389–410.

———. "The Politics of Food and Women's Neighborhood Activism in First World War Britain." *International Labor and Working-Class History* 77, no. 1 (2010): 8–26.

Huston, Nancy. *A l'amour comme à la guerre*. Paris: Seuil, 1984.

Hyam, Ronald. *Empire and Sexuality: The British Experience*. Manchester: Manchester University Press, 1990.

Hylton, Stuart. *Leisure in Post-war Britain*. Stroud: Amberley, 2013.

Hynes, Samuel. *A War Imagined: The First World War and English Culture*. London: Bodley Head, 1990.

Iliffe, John. *A Modern History of Tanganyika*. New York: Cambridge University Press, 1979.

Ineson, Antonia, and Deborah Thom. "TNT Poisoning and the Employment of Women Workers in the First World War." In *The Social History of Occupational Health*, edited by Paul Weindling, 89–102. London: Croom Helm, 1985.

Irwin, Julia. *Making the World Safe: The American Red Cross and a Nation's Humanitarian Awakening*. New York: Oxford University Press, 2013.

Jack, George Morton. "The Indian Army on the Western Front, 1914–1915: A Portrait of Collaboration." *War in History* 13, no. 3 (2006): 329–362.

Jacobson, Abigail. *From Empire to Empire: Jerusalem between Ottoman and British Rule*. Syracuse, NY: Syracuse University Press, 2011.

Jahn, Hubertus F. *Patriotic Culture in Russia during World War I*. Ithaca, NY: Cornell University Press 1995.

Jalland, Pat. *Death in War and Peace: A History of Loss and Grief in England, 1914–1970*. Oxford: Oxford University Press, 2010.

Jarboe, Andrew Tait. "Soldiers of Empire: Indian Sepoys in and beyond the Imperial Metropole during the First World War, 1914–1919." PhD diss., Northeastern University, 2013.

Jarboe, Andrew Tait, and Richard S. Fogarty. "Introduction: An Imperial Turn in First World War Studies." In *Empires in World War I: Frontiers and Imperial Dynamics in a Global Conflict*, edited by Andrew Tait Jarboe and Richard S. Fogarty, 1–20. London: I. B. Tauris, 2014.

———, eds. *Empires in World War I: Shifting Frontiers and Imperial Dynamics in a Global Conflict*. London: I. B. Tauris, 2014.

Jeffords, Susan. *The Remasculinization of America: Gender and the Vietnam War*. Bloomington: Indiana University Press, 1989.

Jennings, Rebecca. *A Lesbian History of Britain: Love and Sex between Women since 1500*. Westport, CT: Greenwood Press, 2007.

Jensen, Kimberly. "Feminist Transnational Activism and International Health: The Medical Women's International Association and the American Women's Hospitals, 1919–1948." In *Women and Transnational Activism in International Perspective*, edited by Kimberly Jensen and Erika Kuhlman, 143–172. Dordrecht: Republic of Letters, 2010.

———. "From Citizens to Enemy Aliens: Oregon Women, Marriage, and the Surveillance State during the First World War." *Oregon Historical Quarterly* 114, no. 4 (2014): 427–442.

———. *Mobilizing Minerva: American Women in the First World War.* Urbana: University of Illinois Press, 2008.

———. *Oregon's Doctor to the World: Esther Pohl Lovejoy and a Life in Activism.* Seattle: University of Washington Press, 2012.

———. "Volunteers, Auxiliaries, and Women's Mobilization: The First World War and Beyond." In *The Brill Companion to Women's Military History*, edited by Barton C. Hacker and Margaret Vining, 189–232. Leiden: Brill, 2012.

Jones, Edgar. "Terror Weapons: The British Experience of Gas and Its Treatment in the First World War." *War in History* 21, no. 3 (2014): 355–375.

Jones, Heather. "As the Centenary Approaches: The Regeneration of First World War Historiography." *Historical Journal* 56, no. 3 (2013): 857–878.

———. "International or Transnational? Humanitarian Action during the First World War." *European Review of History* 16, no. 5 (2009): 697–713.

Junger, Ernst. *The Storm of Steel: From the Diary of a German Storm-Troop Officer on the Western Front.* 1929. Reprint, New York: Howard Fertig, 1975.

Kaplan, Temma. "Women and Communal Strikes in the Crisis of 1917–22." In *Becoming Visible: Women in European History*, edited by Renate Bridenthal, Claudia Koonz, and Susan Stuard, 429–449. 2nd ed. Boston: Houghton Mifflin, 1987.

Kauffmann, Jesse. *Elusive Alliance: The German Occupation of Poland in World War I.* Cambridge, MA: Harvard University Press, 2015.

Keith, Jeanette. *Rich Man's War, Poor Man's Fight: Race, Class and Power in the Rural South during the First World War.* Chapel Hill: University of North Carolina Press, 2004.

Kennedy, Kathleen. *Disloyal Mothers and Scurrilous Citizens: Women and Subversion during World War I.* Bloomington: Indiana University Press, 1999.

Kennedy, Rosie. *The Children's War, Britain 1914–1918.* Houndmills: Palgrave Macmillan, 2014.

Kennett, Lee. *The First Air War 1914–1918.* New York: Free Press, 1991.

Kent, Susan Kingsley. *Making Peace: The Reconstruction of Gender in Interwar Britain.* Princeton: Princeton University Press, 1994.

———. *Sex and Suffrage in Britain, 1860–1914.* Princeton: Princeton University Press, 1987.

Kerber, Linda K. *No Constitutional Right to Be Ladies: Women and the Obligations of Citizenship.* New York: Hill and Wang, 1998.

Kestien, Kate. "A Night in a German Munitions Factory." In *Women's Writing on the First World War*, edited by Agnès Cardinal, Dorothy Goldman, Judith Hattaway, 114–115. Oxford: Oxford University Press, 1999.

Knežević, Jovana. "Prostitutes as a Threat to National Honor in Habsburg-Occupied Serbia during the Great War." *Journal of the History of Sexuality* 20, no. 1 (2011): 312–335.

Kollwitz, Hans, ed. *The Diary and Letters of Käthe Kollwitz.* Translated by Richard Winston and Clara Winston. Chicago: Henry Regnery, 1955.

Kramer, Alan. *Dynamic of Destruction: Culture and Mass Killing in the First World War.* Oxford: Oxford University Press, 2007.

———. "Recent Historiography of the First World War," *Journal of Modern European History* 12, nos. 1/2 (2014): 5–27, 155–174.

Kramer, Ann. *Conscientious Objectors of the First World War: A Determined Resistance.* Barnsley, South Yorkshire: Pen and Sword Books, 2013.

Kuhlman, Erika. *Of Little Comfort: War Widows, Fallen Soldiers, and the Remaking of the Nation after the Great War*. New York: New York University Press, 2012.

———. *Petticoats and White Feathers: Gender Conformity, Race, the Progressive Peace Movement, and the Debate over War, 1895–1919*. Westport, CT: Greenwood Press, 1997.

———. *Reconstructing Patriarchy after the Great War: Women, Gender, and Postwar Reconciliation between Nations*. New York: Palgrave, 2008.

Lagorio, Francesca. "Italian Widows of the First World War." In *Authority, Identity and the Social History of the Great War*, edited by Frans Coetzee and Marilyn Shevin-Coetzee, 175–198. Oxford: Berghan Books, 1995.

Laite, Julia. *Common Citizens and Ordinary Prostitutes: Commercial Sex in London, 1885–1960*. Basingstoke: Palgrave Macmillan, 2012.

Leed, Eric J. *No Man's Land: Combat and Identity in World War I*. Cambridge: Cambridge University Press, 1979.

le Naour, Jean-Yves. *La Honte Noire: L'Allemagne et les troupes coloniales françaises, 1914–1945*. Paris: Hachette, 2003.

Leneman, Leah. *In the Service of Life: Story of Elsie Inglis and Scottish Women's Hospitals*. Edinburgh: Mercat Press, 1994.

———. "Medical Women at War, 1914–1918." *Medical History* 38, no. 2 (1994): 160–177.

Lentz-Smith, Adriane Danette. *Freedom Struggles: African Americans and World War I*. Cambridge, MA: Harvard University Press, 2009.

Le Pick, Olivier. "Des gaz et des hommes." In *Gaz! Gaz! Gaz! La guerre chimique 1914–1918*, 25–53. Péronne: Historial de la Grande Guerre, 2010.

Levine, Philippa. "Battle Colors: Race, Sex, and Colonial Soldiery in World War I." *Journal of Women's History* 9, no. 4 (1998): 104–130.

———. "'Walking the Streets in a Way No Decent Woman Should': Women Police in World War I." *Journal of Modern History* 66, no. 1 (1994): 34–78.

Liulevicius, Vejas Gabriel. *War Land on the Eastern Front: Culture, National Identity, and German Occupation in World War I*. New York: Cambridge University Press, 2000.

Livingstone, Thomas. *Tommy's War: A First World War Diary*. Hammersmith: Harmper Press, 2008.

Lloyd, David. *Battlefield Tourism: Pilgrimage and the Commemoration of the Great War in Britain, Australia and Canada 1919–1939*. Oxford: Berg, 1998.

Loughran, Tracey. "Shell Shock, Trauma, and the First World War: The Making of a Diagnosis and Its Histories." *Journal of the History of Medicine and Allied Sciences* 67, no. 1 (2012): 94–119.

Lunardini, Christine A. *From Equal Suffrage to Equal Rights: Alice Paul and the National Woman's Party, 1910–1928*. New York: New York University Press, 1986.

Lunn, Joe. *Memoirs of the Maelstrom: A Senegalese Oral History of the First World War*. Portsmouth, NH: Heinemann, 1999.

———. "Les races guerrières: Racial Preconceptions in the French Military about West African Soldiers during the First World War." *Journal of Contemporary History* 34, no. 4 (1999): 517–536.

Lutz, Catherine. *Homefront: A Military City and the American Twentieth Century*. Boston: Beacon Press, 2001.

Lynn, John. *Women, Armies, and Warfare in Early Modern Europe*. New York: Cambridge University Press, 2008.

Ma, Li, ed. *Les travailleurs chinois en France pendant la Grande Guerre*. Paris: CNRS Editions, 2012.

MacDonell, Bror. *Mzee Ali: The Biography of an African Slave Raider Turned Askari and Scout.* Pinetown, South Africa: 30 Degrees South Publishers, 2008.

Maddox, Gregory H. "Gender and Famine in Central Tanzania: 1916–1961." *African Studies Review* 39, no. 1 (1996): 83–101.

———. "*Mtunya:* Famine in Central Tanzania, 1917–20." *Journal of African History* 31, no. 2 (1990): 181–197.

Maghraoui, Driss. "Moroccan Colonial Troops: History, Memory and the Culture of French Colonialism." PhD diss., University of California, Santa Cruz, 2000.

Majerus, Benoit. "La prostitution à Bruxelles pendant la Grande Guerre: Contrôle et pratique." *Crime, Histoire Sociétés* 7, no. 1 (2003): 5–42.

Malysheva, Svetlana. "Bereavement and Mourning (Russian Empire)." Translated by Trevor Goronwy. In *1914-1918-Online—International Encyclopedia of the First World War*, edited by Ute Daniel, Peter Gatrell, Oliver Janz, Heather Jones, Jennifer Keene, Alan Kramer, and Bill Nasson. Berlin: Freie Universität, 2014. DOI: 10.15463/ie1418.10190.

Mann, Gregory. *Native Sons: West African Veterans and France in the Twentieth Century.* Durham, NC: Duke University Press, 2006.

Martin, Ian. " 'When Needs Must'—The Acceptance of Volunteer Aids in British and Australian Military Hospitals in WWI." *Health and Society* 4, no. 1 (2002): 88–98.

Marwick, Arthur. *Women at War 1914–1918.* London: Fontana, 1977.

Mayer, Holly A. *Belonging to the Army: Camp Followers and Community during the American Revolution.* Columbia: University of South Carolina Press, 1996.

———. "From Forts to Families: Following the Army into Western Pennsylvania, 1758–1766." *Pennsylvania Magazine of History and Biography* 130, no. 1 (2006): 5–43.

Mayerhofer, Lisa. *Zwischen Freund und Feind—Deutsche Besatzung in Rumänien 1916–1918.* Frankfurt am Main: Peter Lang, 2010.

Mayhall, Laura E. Nym. *The Militant Suffrage Movement: Citizenship and Resistance in Britain, 1860–1930.* Oxford: Oxford University Press, 2003.

McDaniel, Susan A. "Born at the Right Time? Gendered Generations and Webs of Entitlement and Responsibility." *Canadian Journal of Sociology* 26, no. 2 (2001): 193–214.

McMillan, James R. "The Great War and Gender Relations: the Case of French Women and the First World War Revisited." In *Evidence, History and the Great War*, edited by Gail Braybon, 135–153. New York: Berghahn Books, 2005.

———. *Housewife or Harlot?* New York: St. Martin's Press, 1981.

Melman, Billie. "Introduction." In *Borderlines: Genders and Identities in War and Peace, 1870–1930*, edited by Billie Melman, 1–26. New York: Routledge, 1998.

Meyer, Jessica. *Men at War: Masculinity and the First World War in Britain.* New York: Palgrave Macmillan, 2009.

Meyerowitz, Joanne J. "Transnational Sex and U.S. History." *American Historical Review* 114, no. 5 (2009): 1273–1286.

Meynier, Gilbert. *L'Algérie révélée: La guerre de 1914–1918 et le premier quart du XXᵉ siècle.* Geneva: Droz, 1981.

Michel, Marc. *L'Appel à L'Afrique: Contributions et réactions à l'effort de guerre en AOF, 1914–1919.* Paris: Publications de la Sorbonne, 1982.

Miller, Charles. *Battle for the Bundu: The First World War in East Africa.* London: Macdonald and Janes, 1974.

Miller, William Ian. *The Mystery of Courage.* Cambridge, MA: Harvard University Press, 2000.

Mjolsness, Lora. "Animated Propaganda: Visualizing the Great War in Russia." Paper presented at the conference "Europe and the World: World War I as Crisis of Universalism," University of California at Irvine, December 2014.

Morgan, David H. J. "Theater of War: Combat, the Military, and Masculinities." In *Theorizing Masculinities*, edited by Harry Brod and Michael Kaufman, 165–182. Thousand Oaks, CA: Sage, 1994.

Morrow, John H., Jr. *The Great War: An Imperial History*. New York: Routledge, 2004.

Morton, Desmond. "Supporting Soldiers' Wives and Families in the Great War: What Was Transformed?" In *A Sisterhood of Suffering and Service: Women and Girls of Canada and Newfoundland during the First World War*, edited by Sarah Glassford and Amy Shaw, 195–218. Vancouver: University of British Columbia Press, 2012.

Mosley, Leonard. *Duel for Kilimanjaro: An Account of the East African Campaign, 1914–1918*. London: Weidenfeld and Nicolson, 1963.

Mosse, George L. *Fallen Soldiers: Reshaping the Memory of the World Wars*. New York: Oxford University Press, 1990.

———. *The Image of Man: The Creation of Modern Masculinity*. New York: Oxford University Press, 1996.

Moyd, Michelle R. *Violent Intermediaries: African Soldiers, Conquest, and Everyday Colonialism in German East Africa*. Athens: Ohio University Press, 2014.

Murphy, Libby. "Trespassing on the 'Trench-Fighter's Story': (Re)-Imagining the Female Combatant of the First World War." In *Gender and Conflict since 1914: Historical and Interdisciplinary Perspectives*, edited by Ana Carden-Coyne, 55–68. New York: Palgrave Macmillan, 2012.

Nagler, Jorg. "Enemy Aliens in the USA, 1914–1918." In *Minorities in Wartime: National and Racial Groupings in Europe, North America and Australia during the Two World Wars*, edited by Panikos Panayi, 191–215. Oxford: Berg, 1993.

Nash, Jennifer C. "Re-thinking Intersectionality." *Feminist Review* 89, no. 1 (2008): 1–15.

Nasson, Bill. *Springboks on the Somme: South Africa in the Great War 1914–1918*. Johannesburg: Penguin, 2007.

Natter, Wolfgang G. *Literature at War 1914–1940: Representing the "Time of Greatness" in Germany*. New Haven, CT: Yale University Press, 1999.

Neiberg, Michael S. *Fighting the Great War: A Global History*. Cambridge, MA: Harvard University Press, 2006.

Nogaro, Bertrand, and Lucien Weil. *La main d'oeuvre étrangère et coloniale pendant la guerre*. Paris: Presses Universitaires de France, 1926.

Norman, Allison. "'In Defense of the Empire': The Six Nations of the Grand River and the Great War." In *A Sisterhood of Suffering and Service: Women and Girls of Canada and Newfoundland during the First World War*, edited by Sarah Glassford and Amy Shaw, 29–50. Vancouver: University of British Columbia Press, 2012.

Oddy, Derek J. *From Plain Fare to Fusion Food: British Diet from the 1890s to the 1990s*. Woodbridge: Boydell Press, 2003.

Offen, Karen. *European Feminisms 1700–1950: A Political History*. Stanford, CA: Stanford University Press, 2000.

Omissi, David, ed. *Indian Voices of the Great War: Soldiers' Letters, 1914–18*. New York: St. Martin's Press, 1999.

Oram, Alison. *Her Husband Was a Woman! Women's Gender-Crossing in Modern British Popular Culture.* London: Routledge, 2007.

Ortega, Simonetta. "Italian Women during the Great War." In *Evidence, History and the Great War: Historians and the Impact of 1914–18*, edited by Gail Braybon, 216–237. New York: Berghahn Books, 2005.

Özaydin, Zuhal. "Upper Social Strata Women in Nursing in Turkey." *Nursing History Review* 14 (2006): 161–174.

Page, Melvin. *The Chiwaya War: Malawians and the First World War.* Boulder, CO: Westview Press, 2000.

Pedersen, Susan. *Family, Dependence and the Origins of the Welfare State: Britain and France, 1914–1945.* Cambridge: Cambridge University Press, 1993.

Pejović, Marko. "Beogradska štampa o sudjenjima za saradnju sa okupatorima u Srbiji 1918–1920 godine." *Godišnjak za društvenu istoriju* 12: 1–3 (2005), 85–109.

Peterson, Derek R. "Morality Plays: Marriage, Church Courts, and Colonial Agency in Central Tanganyika, ca. 1876–1928." *American Historical Review* 111, no. 4 (2006): 983–1010.

Petrone, Karen. "Family, Masculinity, and Heroism in Russian War Posters of the First World War." In *Borderlines: Genders and Identities in War and Peace 1870–1930*, edited by Billie Melman, 95–120. New York: Routledge, 1998.

——. *The Great War in Russian Memory.* Bloomington: Indiana University Press, 2011.

——. " 'Now Russia Returns Its History to Itself': Russia Celebrates the Centennial of World War I." In *Remembering the First World War*, edited by Bart Ziino, 129–145. New York: Routledge, 2014.

Pick, Daniel. *Faces of Degeneration: A European Disorder, c. 1848–1918.* Cambridge: Cambridge University Press, 1993.

Pignot, Manon. "French Boys and Girls in the Great War: Gender and the History of Children's Experiences, 1914–1918." In *Gender and the First World War*, edited by Christa Hämmerle, Oswald Überegger, and Birgitta Bader Zaar, 163–175. Basingstoke: Palgrave Macmillan, 2014.

Pirenne, Henri. *La Belgique et la guerre mondiale.* Paris: Les Presses Universitaires de France, 1929.

Plain, Gill. " 'Great Expectations': Rehabilitating the Recalcitrant War Poets." *Feminist Review* 51, no. 1 (1995): 41–65.

Plascka, Richard Georg, Horst Haselsteinger, and Arnold Suppan. *Innere Front: Militärassistenz, Widerstand un Umsturz in der Donaumonarchie 1918.* Munich: R. Oldenbourg Verlag, 1974.

Plastas, Melinda. *A Band of Noble Women: Racial Politics in the Peace Movement.* Syracuse, NY: Syracuse University Press, 2011.

Polman, Linda. *The Crisis Caravan: What's Wrong with Humanitarian Aid?* Translated by Liz Waters. New York: Metropolitan Books, 2010.

Price, Richard M. *The Chemical Weapons Taboo.* Ithaca, NY: Cornell University Press, 1997.

Proctor, Tammy M. *Civilians in a World at War, 1914–1918.* New York: New York University Press, 2010.

——. "*La Dame Blanche*: Gender and Espionage in Occupied Belgium." In *Uncovered Fields: Perspectives in First World War Studies*, edited by Jenny Macleod and Pierre Purseigle, 227–242. Leiden: Brill, 2004.

——. "The Everyday as Involved in War." *1914-1918-Online—International Encyclopedia of the First World War*, edited by Ute Daniel, Peter Gatrell, Oliver Janz, Heather Jones, Jennifer Keene, Alan Kramer, and Bill Nasson. Berlin: Freie Universität, 2014. DOI: 10.15463/ie1418.10453.

———. *Female Intelligence: Women and Espionage in the First World War*. New York: New York University Press, 2003.

———. *On My Honour: Guides and Scouts in Interwar Britain*. Philadelphia: American Philosophical Society, 2002.

———. *Scouting for Girls: A Century of Girl Guides and Girl Scouts*. Santa Barbara, CA: Praeger, 2009.

Rachamimov, Alon. "The Disruptive Comforts of Drag: (Trans)Gender Performances among Prisoners of War in Russia, 1914–1920." *American Historical Review* 111, no. 2 (2006): 362–382.

———. "'Female Generals' and 'Siberian Angels': Aristocratic Nurses and the Austro-Hungarian POW Relief." In *Gender and War in Twentieth-Century Eastern Europe*, edited by Nancy M. Wingfield and Maria Bucur, 23–46. Bloomington: Indiana University Press, 2006.

Razafindranaly, Jacques. *Les soldats de la grande île: D'une guerre à l'autre, 1895–1918*. Paris: L'Harmattan, 2000.

Regele, Oskar. *Gericht über Habsburgs Wehrmacht: Letzte Siege und Untergang unter dem Armee-Oberkommando Kaiser Karls I. Generaloberst Arz von Straussenburg*. Vienna: Herold, 1968.

Reilly, Catherine, ed. *Scars upon My Heart: Women's Poetry and Verse of the First World War*. London: Virago, 1981.

Rich, Norman. *The Age of Nationalism and Reform: 1850–1890*. New York: Norton, 1976.

Robert, Jean-Louis. "The Image of the Profiteer." In *Capital Cities at War: Paris, London, Berlin, 1914–1919*, volume 1, ed. Jay Winter and Jean-Louis Robert, 104–132. Cambridge: Cambridge University Press, 1999.

Roberts, Mary Louise. *Civilization without Sexes: Reconstructing Gender in Postwar France, 1917–1927*. Chicago: University of Chicago Press, 1994.

Rogan, Eugene. *The Fall of the Ottomans: The Great War in the Middle East*. New York: Basic Books, 2015.

Roos, Julia. "Nationalism, Racism, and Propaganda in Early Weimar Germany: Contradictions in the Campaign against the 'Black Horror on the Rhine.'" *German History* 30, no. 1 (2012): 45–74.

———. "Racist Hysteria to Pragmatic Rapprochement? The German Debate about Rhenish 'Occupation Children,' 1920–1930." *Contemporary European History* 22, no. 2 (2013): 155–180.

Roper, Michael. *The Secret Battle: Emotional Survival in the Great War*. Manchester: Manchester University Press, 2009.

Rose, Sonya O. "The Politics of Service and Sacrifice in WWI Ireland and India." *Twentieth Century British History* 25, no. 3 (2014): 368–390.

Rupp, Leila. *Worlds of Women: The Making of an International Women's Movement*. Princeton, NJ: Princeton University Press, 1997.

Sabol, Steven. "'It Was a Pretty Good War, but They Stopped It Too Soon': The American Empire, Native Americans and World War I." In *Empires in World War I: Shifting Frontiers and Imperial Dynamics in a Global Conflict*, edited by Andrew Tair Jarvoe and Richard S. Fogarty, 193–216. New York: Palgrave Macmillan, 2014.

Salter, Heather Streets. *Martial Races: The Military, Race, and Masculinity in British Imperial Culture, 1857–1914*. Manchester: Manchester University Press, 2004.

Sanborn, Joshua. *Drafting the Russian Nation: Military Conscription, Total War, and Mass Politics, 1905–1925*. DeKalb: Northern Illinois University Press, 2003.

──────. *Imperial Apocalypse: The Great War and the Destruction of the Russian Empire*. Oxford: Oxford University Press, 2014.

Sauerteig, Lutz. "Sex, Medicine and Morality during the First World War." In *War, Medicine and Modernity*, edited by Roger Cooter, Mark Harrison, and Steve Sturdy, 167–188. Stroud: Sutton, 1998.

Scardino Belzer, Allison. *Women and the Great War: Femininity under Fire in Italy*. Basingstoke: Palgrave Macmillan, 2010.

Scheer, Tamara. *Zwischen Front und Heimat: Österreich-Ungarns Militärverwaltungen im Ersten Weltkrieg*. Frankfurt am Main: Peter Lang, Internationaler Verlag der Wissenschaften, 2009.

Scheper-Hughes, Nancy, and Philippe Bourgois. "Making Sense of Violence." In *Violence in War and Peace: An Anthology*, edited by Nancy Scheper-Hughes and Philippe Bourgois, 1–32. Oxford: Blackwell, 2004.

Schmidt, Heike I. *Colonialism and Violence in Zimbabwe: A History of Suffering*. Woodbridge, UK: James Currey, 2013.

Schönberger, Bianca. "'Motherly Heroines and Adventurous Girls': Red Cross Nurses and Women Army Auxiliaries in the First World War." In *Home/Front: The Military, War and Gender in Twentieth-Century Germany*, edited by Karen Hagemann and Stefanie Schüler-Springorum, 87–114. New York: Berg, 2002.

Scott, Joan Wallach. "Feminism's History." *Journal of Women's History* 16, no. 2 (2004): 10–29.

──────. "Gender: A Useful Category of Historical Analysis." *American Historical Review* 91, no. 5 (1986): 1053–1075.

Schulte, Regina. "Käthe Kollwitz's Sacrifice." Translated by Pamela Selwyn. *History Workshop Journal* 41 (1996): 193–221.

Sharp, Ingrid. "Feminist Peace Activism: 1915 and 2010: Are We Nearly There Yet?" *Peace and Change: A Journal of Peace Research* 38, no. 2 (2013): 155–180.

Sharp, Ingrid, and Matthew Stibbe, eds. *Aftermaths of War: Women's Movements and Female Activists, 1918–1923*. Leiden: Brill, 2010.

Sheffy, Yigal. "Chemical Warfare and the Palestine Campaign, 1916–1918." *Journal of Military History* 73, no. 3 (2009): 803–843.

Shephard, Ben. *War of Nerves: Soldiers and Psychiatrists in the Twentieth Century*. Cambridge, MA: Harvard University Press, 2003.

Sherman, Daniel J. *The Construction of Memory in Interwar France*. Chicago: University of Chicago Press, 1999.

Shover, Michael J. "Roles and Images of Women in World War I Propaganda." *Politics and Society* 5, no. 4 (1975): 469–486.

Showalter, Elaine. *The Female Malady: Women, Madness and English Culture 1830–1980*. London: Virago, 1987.

Siebrecht, Claudia. "Imagining the Absent Dead: Rituals of Bereavement and the Place of the War Dead in German Women's Art during the First World War." *German History* 29, no. 2 (2011): 202–223.

Singh, Gajendra. "India and the Great War: Colonial Fantasies, Anxieties, and Discontent." *Studies in Ethnicity and Nationalism* 14, no. 2 (2014): 343–361.

Sinha, Mrinalini. *Colonial Masculinity: The "Manly Englishman" and the "Effeminate Bengali" in the Late Nineteenth Century*. Manchester: Manchester University Press, 1995.

Sluga, Glenda. "What Is National Self-Determination? Nationality and Psychology during 'The Apogee of Nationalism.'" *Nations and Nationalism* 11, no. 1 (2005): 1–20.

Smale, Catherine. "'Aus Blut und Schmerz geboren': Maternal Grief and the Poetry of Frida Bettingen." *German Life and Letters* 61, no. 3 (2008): 328–343.

Smart, Judith. "Feminists, Food and the Fair Price: The Cost of Living Demonstrations in Melbourne, August–September 1917." *Labour History* 50 (1986): 113–131.

———. "Sex, the State, and the 'Scarlet Scourge': Gender, Citizenship and Venereal Diseases Regulation in Australia during the Great War." *Women's History Review* 7, no. 1 (1998): 5–36.

Smith, Leonard V. *Between Mutiny and Obedience: The Case of the French Fifth Infantry Division during World War I*. Princeton, NJ: Princeton University Press, 1994.

Smith, Leonard V., Stéphane Audoin-Rouzeau, and Annette Becker. *France and the Great War, 1914–1918*. Cambridge: Cambridge University Press, 2003.

Smith, Paul. *Feminism and the Third Republic: Women's Political and Civil Rights in France, 1918–1945*. Oxford: Clarendon, 1996.

Smith, Richard. *Jamaican Volunteers in the First World War: Race, Masculinity and the Development of a National Consciousness*. Manchester: Manchester University Press, 2004.

———. "World War I and the Permanent West Indian Soldier." In *Empires in World War I: Shifting Frontiers and Imperial Dynamics in a Global Conflict*, edited by Andrew Tait Jarboe and Richard S. Fogarty, 304–327. London: I. B. Tauris, 2014.

Snyder, R. Claire *Citizen-Soldiers and Manly Warriors: Military Service and Gender in the Civic Republican Tradition*. Lanham, MD: Rowman and Littlefield, 1999.

Sondhaus, Lawrence. *World War One: The Global Revolution*. Cambridge: Cambridge University Press, 2011.

Stapleton, Timothy. *No Insignificant Part: The Rhodesia Native Regiment and the East Africa Campaign of the First World War*. Waterloo, ON: Wilfrid Laurier University Press, 2006.

Stibbe, Matthew. "Elisabeth Rotten and the 'Auskunfts und Hilfsstelle für Deutsche im Ausland und Ausländer in Deutschland' 1914–1919." In *The Women's Movement in Wartime: International Perspectives 1914–19*, edited by Alison Fell and Ingrid Sharp, 194–210. London: Palgrave Macmillan, 2007.

Stiehm, Judith Hicks. "The Protected, the Protector, the Defender." *Women's Studies International Forum* 5 (1982): 367–376.

Stockdale, Melissa K. "'My Death for the Motherland Is Happiness': Women, Patriotism, and Soldiering in Russia's Great War, 1914–1917." *American Historical Review* 109, no. 1 (2004): 78–116.

Stoff, Laurie. *They Fought for the Motherland: Russia's Women Soldiers in World War I and the Revolution*. Lawrence: University Press of Kansas, 2006.

Stoler, Ann Laura. *Carnal Knowledge and Imperial Power: Race and the Intimate in Colonial Rule*. Berkeley: University of California Press, 2002.

———. *Race and the Education of Desire: Foucault's History of Sexuality and the Colonial Order of Things*. Durham, NC: Duke University Press, 1995.

Storey, William Kelleher. *The First World War: A Concise Global History*. New York: Rowman and Littlefield, 2010.

Stovall, Tyler. "Colour-Blind France? Colonial Workers during the First World War." *Race and Class* 35, no. 2 (1993): 35–55.

———. "The Color Line behind the Lines: Racial Violence in France during the Great War." *American Historical Review* 103, no. 3 (1998): 737–769.

———. "Love, Labor, and Race: Colonial Men and White Women in France during the Great War." In *French Civilization and Its Discontents: Nationalism, Colonialism, Race*, edited by Tyler Stovall and Georges Van Den Abbeele, 297–321. Lanham, MD: Lexington, 2003.

———. *Paris and the Spirit of 1919: Consumer Struggles, Transnationalism, and Revolution*. Cambridge: Cambridge University Press, 2012.

———. *Paris Noir: African Americans in the City of Light*. New York: Houghton Mifflin, 1996.

Strachan, Hew. *The First World War*. Vol. 1, *To Arms*. Oxford: Oxford University Press, 2001.

———. "The First World War as a Global War." *First World War Studies* 1, no. 1 (2010): 3–14.

———. *The First World War in Africa*. Oxford: Oxford University Press, 2004.

Strauss, Edward M., trans. *Poilu: The World War I Notebooks of Corporal Louis Barthas, Barrelmaker 1914–1918*. New Haven, CT: Yale University Press, 2014.

Strobel, Margaret. "Gender, Sex, and Empire." In *Islamic and European Expansion: The Forging of a Global Order*, edited by Michael Adas, 345–375. Philadelphia: Temple University Press, 1993.

Stryker, Laurinda. "Mental Cases: British Shellshock and the Politics of Interpretation." In *Evidence, History and the Great War: Historians and the Impact of 1914–18*, edited by Gail Braybon, 154–171. New York: Berghahn, 2003.

Stynen, Ludo, and Sylvia Van Peteghem, eds. *In Oorlogsnood: Virginie Lovelings Dagboek, 1914–1918*. Gent: Koninklijke Academie voor Nederlandse Taal-en Letterkunde, 1999.

Surkis, Judith. "Introduction: What Gender Historians Do." *Journal of Women's History* 26, no. 3 (2014): 129–130.

Sweeney, Regina. "Harmony and Disharmony: French Singing and Musical Entertainment during the Great War." PhD diss., University of California at Berkeley, 1992.

———. *Singing Our Way to Victory: French Cultural Politics and Music during the Great War*. Middletown, CT: Wesleyan University Press, 2001.

Tanalien, Melanie. "Feeding the City: The Beirut Municipality and Civilian Provisioning during World War I." *International Journal of Middle East Studies* 46 (2014): 737–758.

———. "Politics of Wartime Relief in Ottoman Beirut (1914–1918)." *Journal of First World War Studies* 5, no. 1 (2014): 69–82.

Taylor, Lynne. "Food Riots Revisited." *Journal of Social History* 30, no. 2 (1996): 483–496.

Thébaud, Françoise. *La femme au temps de la guerre de 14*. Paris: Stock, 1986.

Theweleit, Klaus. *Male Fantasies*. Translated by Stephen Conway. Minneapolis: University of Minnesota Press, 1989.

Thom, Deborah. "The Bundle of Sticks." In *Unequal Opportunities Women's Employment in England, 1800–1918*, edited by Angela John, 261–289. Oxford: Blackwell, 1986.

———. "Making Spectaculars: Museums and How We Remember Gender in Wartime." In *Evidence, History and the Great War: Historians and the Impact of 1914–1918*, edited by Gail Braybon, 48–66. New York: Berghahn, 2003.

———. *Nice Girls and Rude Girls: Women Workers and the First World War*. London: I. B. Tauris, 1998.

Thomas, Gregory M. *Soldiers, Civilians and Psychiatry in France, 1914–1940*. Baton Rouge: Louisiana State University Press, 2009.

Thompson, J. Lee. *Politicians, the Press and Propaganda: Lord Northcliffe and the Great War, 1914–1919*. Kent, OH: Kent State University Press, 1999.

Thompson, Mark. *The White War: Life and Death on the Italian Front*. London: Faber, 2008.

Üngör, Uğor Ümit. "Orphans, Converts, and Prostitutes: Social Consequences of War and Persecution in the Ottoman Empire, 1914–1923." *War in History* 19, no. 2 (2012): 175–176.

Valensky, Chantal. *Le soldat occulté: Les Malgaches de l'Armée française, 1884–1920*. Paris: L'Harmattan, 1995.

Van Bergen, Leo. *Before My Helpless Sight: Suffering, Dying, and Military Medicine on the Western Front, 1914–1918*. Farnham, UK: Ashgate, 2009.

Van Galen Last, Dick. *Black Shame: African Soldiers in Europe, 1914–1922*. London: Bloomsbury, 2015.

Van Ypersele, Laurence. "En guise de conclusion, Les résistances belges et françaises en 14–18." In *La résistance en France et en Belgique occupées 1914–1918: Actes de la journée d'études, bondues, 30 Janvier 2010*, edited by Robert Vandenbussche, 207–216. Villeneuve-d'Ascq: Institut de recherches historiques du Septentrion, 2012.

Vieweg, Burkhard. *Macho Porini: Die augen im Busch*. Weikersheim: Margraf, 1996.

Ward, Margaret. *In Their Own Voice: Women and Irish Nationalism*. Dublin: Attic, 2001.

Watenpaugh, Keith. *Bread from Stones: The Middle East and the Making of Modern Humanitarianism*. Berkeley: University of California Press, 2015.

Waters, Chris. "Sexology." In *Palgrave Advances in the Modern History of Sexuality*, edited by H. G. Cocks and Matt Houlbrook, 41–63. Basingstoke: Palgrave Macmillan, 2006.

Watson, Alexander. *Enduring the Great War: Combat, Morale, and Collapse in the German and British Armies, 1914–1918*. Cambridge: Cambridge University Press, 2008.

———. *Ring of Steel. Germany and Austria-Hungary at War, 1914–1918*. London: Basic Books, 2014.

Watson, Janet S. K. *Fighting Different Wars: Experience, Memory, and the First World War in Britain*. Cambridge: Cambridge University Press, 2004.

———. "Khaki Girls, VADs, and Tommy's Sisters: Gender and Class in First World War Britain." *International History Review* 19, no. 1 (1997): 32–51.

———. "Wars in the Wards: The Social Construction of Medical Work in First World War Britain." *Journal of British Studies* 41, no. 4 (2002): 484–510.

Weingard, Timothy C. *For King and Kanata: Canadian Indians and the First World War*. Winnipeg: University of Manitoba Press, 2012.

———. *Indigenous Peoples of the British Dominions and the First World War*. Cambridge: Cambridge University Press, 2012.

Whalen, Robert Weldon. *Bitter Wounds: German Victims of the Great War, 1914–1939*. Ithaca, NY: Cornell University Press, 1984.

Whelan, Mark. *American Culture in the 1910s*. Edinburgh: Edinburgh University Press, 2010.

Willan, Brian P. "The South African Native Labour Contingent, 1916–1918." *Journal of African History* 19, no. 1 (1978): 61–86.

Williams, Chad L. *Torchbearers of Democracy: African American Soldiers in the World War I Era*. Chapel Hill: University of North Carolina Press, 2010.

Wilmers, Annika. "Zwischen den fronten: Friedensdiskurse in der Internationalen Frauenfriedensbewegung, 1914–1919." In *Frieden—Gewalt—Geschlecht: Friedens und Konfliktforschung als Geschlechterforschung*, edited by Jennifer A. Davy, Karen Hagemann, and Ute Kaetzel, 123–143. Essen: Klartext Verlag, 2005.

Wingate, Jennifer. *Sculpting Doughboys: Memory, Gender and Taste in America's World War I Memorials*. Farnham, UK: Ashgate, 2013.

Wingfield, Nancy M., and Maria Bucur, eds. *Gender and War in Twentieth-Century Eastern Europe*. Bloomington: Indiana University Press, 2006.

———. "Introduction: Gender and War in Twentieth-Century Eastern Europe." In *Gender and War in Twentieth-Century Eastern Europe*, edited by Nancy M. Wingfield and Maria Bucur, 1–22. Bloomington: Indiana University Press, 2006.

Winter, J. M. *The Great War and the British People*. London: Macmillan, 1985.

———. *Remembering War: The Great War between Memory and History in the Twentieth Century*. New Haven, CT: Yale University Press, 2006.

———. *Sites of Memory, Sites of Mourning: The Great War in European Cultural History*. Cambridge: Cambridge University Press, 1995.

———. "Some Aspects of the Demographic Consequences of the First World War in Britain." *Population Studies* 30, no. 3 (1976): 539–552.

Winter, Jay, and Antoine Prost. *The Great War in History: Debates and Controversies, 1914 to the Present*. Cambridge: Cambridge University Press, 2005.

Woodfin, Edward C. *Camp and Combat on the Sinai and Palestine Front: The Experience of the British Empire Soldier, 1916–18*. Houndmills: Palgrave Macmillan, 2012.

Woollacott, Angela. "'Khaki Fever' and Its Control: Gender, Class, Age and Sexual Morality on the British Home Front in the First World War." *Journal of Contemporary History* 29 (1994): 325–347.

———. *On Her Their Lives Depend: Munitions Workers in the Great War*. Berkeley: University of California Press, 1994.

Wright, Marcia. *Strategies of Slaves and Women: Life Stories from East/Central Africa*. New York: Lilian Barber Press, 1993.

Zeiger, Susan. *In Uncle Sam's Service: Women Workers with the American Expeditionary Force, 1917–1919*. Ithaca, NY: Cornell University Press, 1999.

Ziemann, Benjamin. *War Experiences in Rural Germany, 1914–23*. Oxford: Berg, 2007.

INDEX

adulthood, 116, 127

Africa, 4, 8, 82, 85, 155, 169, 188–9, 197
  East Africa, 188–9, 191–2, 196–9, 202, 204–5
  South Africa, 4, 68, 72, 188–9, 197
  West Africa, 72, 75, 76, 195

air power, 169, 173–4, 180
  ace (pilot), 169, 173
  aerial bombing and warfare, 124, 169, 173–4,
    180–1, 183, 194
  airplane, 4, 52, 55, 61, 169, 173, 180

Albania, 133

Allies, 15, 35, 51, 56, 82, 156, 165, 197, 232

atrocities, 123, 136–8, 139, 172, 190, 234
  Bryce Report, 135–6
  Reiss Report, 135–6

Australia, 4, 12, 13, 52, 63, 72, 101, 117, 128, 182,
  213, 214–16, 218, 225

Austria-Hungary. *See* Habsburg Empire

Balkans, 218, 250
  Balkan wars, 3, 143, 218

Baltic States, 13

Belgium, 143–4, 146, 155, 169, 177–8

body, 49, 62, 95, 190, 213, 216
  deceased, 213, 216, 221, 222, 234, 239,
    240, 243–4

female, 98, 136
  male, 94, 240, 243

Britain. *See* United Kingdom

Brusilov offensive, 4

Canada, 4, 12, 13, 16, 17, 33, 52, 60–1, 63, 68, 72,
  137, 182, 213, 218, 232, 235

cavalry, 72, 170

censorship, 12, 79, 110, 139, 142, 174, 177, 240, 245

Central Powers, 4, 165, 190

children, 7, 41, 47, 49, 52, 59, 61, 74, 75, 79, 80,
  115–16, 117, 118, 120, 121, 123, 124–7, 128–9,
  136, 143, 158, 160–2, 164, 169, 174, 177, 179,
  180, 181, 183, 187, 189, 191, 192, 193, 194,
  197, 198, 199, 200, 202, 203, 216, 217, 223,
  226, 234

China, 3, 55, 68, 72, 77, 78, 254

chivalry, 174, 245

cinema, 63, 178–9, 239

citizenship, 5, 6, 10–13, 15, 16, 17–23

civilians, 28, 40, 68, 75, 95, 110, 120, 134, 135, 137,
  139, 141, 143, 145, 150, 151, 153–8, 163, 170,
  172, 174, 179–83, 189–90, 198, 216, 218, 226,
  234–5, 240–1, 251, 254

class. *See* social class

collaboration, 51, 57, 94, 119, 123, 133, 134, 144

colonialism, 70, 74, 81, 85, 197
color line, 71, 75, 77, 81–4
columns (military), 188, 191–201, 202, 203
combatants, 1, 4, 6, 7, 71, 110, 170, 174, 189–90,
    194, 212, 233, 244, 245
    combatant nations, 10, 19, 21, 51, 53–4, 57, 59,
        93, 154, 233

democracy, 17, 19, 50, 63
deportation, 137, 139, 145
dilution, 54, 57
discourse, 16, 21, 85, 93, 95, 136, 145, 238, 245, 252
dogfight, 173

education, 2, 13, 63, 97, 99, 116, 119, 120, 121, 125,
    127, 205
elderly, 115, 122, 127, 160, 189, 202
empire, 2–6, 11, 12, 15, 68, 70, 71–2, 74, 76,
    79, 80, 85, 95, 117, 134, 177, 187, 195, 231,
    250, 254–5
espionage, 12, 32, 19, 123, 141, 253
eugenics, 73

famine, 60, 154, 179, 189, 202, 204, 250
fatherhood, 12, 33, 75–7, 101, 116, 125, 126, 177–8,
    180, 200, 201, 212, 220, 222–3, 243
femininity, 27–8, 31–2, 43, 70, 97–8, 110, 121, 143,
    177, 182, 187, 191, 211, 252
feminism, 18, 28, 98, 182, 253
food
    bread, 5, 46, 49, 57, 156, 160, 216
    prices, 56, 149, 150–1, 155, 156, 165
    queues, 152, 157, 160–3
    riots, 2, 12, 57, 149, 152, 153, 155, 159, 161–2
    shortages, 56, 149, 153–8, 161, 164–5
forgetting, 234
France, 2–4, 6, 13–19, 22, 28, 38, 42, 47, 50–8,
    62–3, 67–8, 70–2, 74–5, 77–85, 98, 120,
    122–3, 125, 127–8, 133–4, 136–8, 140–1,
    143–4, 146, 154–5, 169, 171, 173, 178,
    188–9, 195, 213, 222, 224, 231, 233, 241,
    244, 250–4
Franz-Ferdinand, Habsburg heir, 2, 3

Galicia, 2
Gallipoli, 214, 223
gender and gender theory, 1, 4–6, 8, 10, 11, 13,
    14, 18–20, 23, 28–30, 31–3, 35, 36, 41–3,

46–8, 49, 52, 56, 59, 67–8, 70–5, 77, 84–5,
    91, 93–5, 96, 98–101, 105, 109–10, 115–16,
    118, 121, 123–4, 126–7, 135–6, 140, 145–6,
    149–50, 152, 154, 158–9, 162–3, 165, 169–70,
    174, 176–7, 179, 182, 187–95, 197, 199,
    201–5, 211–12, 218, 220, 226, 230, 231–7,
    244, 248, 249, 250–5
generation, 5, 53, 73, 115–18, 121, 123–4, 127, 129,
    213, 217, 226, 234, 238–9, 249, 251, 255
Germany, 2–4, 6, 14, 16, 20–1, 26n43, 28, 30–3,
    35–7, 39, 41, 48, 49, 49–58, 61, 63, 68, 71, 84,
    94–5, 98, 117–20, 122–3, 125–8, 133–5,
    137–43, 149–57, 159–60, 162, 164, 171–2,
    174, 177–9, 188–99, 201–5, 213, 217–18, 223,
    233–5, 238–40, 243, 245, 249, 251–2, 254
Great Britain. See United Kingdom
grief, 39, 121, 127, 170, 204–5, 211–18, 222–3, 226

Habsburg Empire, 4, 12, 125, 135, 140, 142–4, 250
health, 5, 22, 41, 47, 49, 58, 61, 74, 95, 110, 142,
    152, 202, 203
heroism, 5, 144, 169, 190, 214, 237, 238
Hohenzollern Empire. See Germany
home front, 12, 94, 118, 122, 128, 134, 138, 143, 150,
    153–4, 157–61, 163–5, 169, 180, 189, 194, 197,
    214, 230
homosocial, 75, 100–101
hospitals, 13–15, 22, 29, 54, 56, 75–6, 79-80-1,
    99–101, 104–9, 114n42, 125, 161, 174
household, 53, 56, 122–3, 150, 155–6, 158, 181, 189,
    194, 196, 197, 199–201, 203, 223

imperialism, 1, 2, 11, 15, 51, 63, 71–2, 74, 80, 101,
    106, 142, 154, 191, 232, 255
intimacy, 68, 70, 79, 94, 99–100, 105, 106, 109,
    212, 217, 254
invasion, 4, 39, 40, 51, 57, 124, 134–7, 139, 145–6,
    164, 169, 176, 178–80, 189–90
Italy, 3–4, 6, 8, 47, 50, 53–4, 57, 71, 110, 133,
    213–14, 218, 232–3, 250

Japan, 3, 15, 72
July Crisis, 3

logistics, 188, 195, 197–8
looting, 240

male body. See body, male

marriage, 20–1, 33, 39, 53, 54, 75, 76, 79, 97, 99, 105–6, 110, 117–18, 121–2, 128, 194, 200–201, 203
martyrdom, 135, 137, 139, 172, 236
Marxism. *See* socialism
masculinity, 5, 10, 13, 19, 22, 27, 32–3, 35, 38, 41–2, 48, 70, 73, 74, 78, 94, 95, 97–8, 99–100, 101, 106, 109, 110, 117, 118–20, 129, 140, 159, 170, 173, 174, 179, 182, 187, 189, 190, 192, 193, 197, 200, 201, 203, 211, 220–3, 237–8, 239, 241, 243, 244, 245
media, 5, 57, 96, 116, 123, 126, 173, 178, 180–1
memory, 58–9, 129, 146, 182, 189, 197, 203, 205, 213, 214–15, 220, 226, 230–4, 236–8, 239, 240–1, 243, 244–5, 251
militarism, 2, 17, 23, 34, 98, 182, 244
Montenegro, 47, 133
monuments, 225, 230, 234–8, 241, 243
morale, 56, 78, 142, 150–1, 153, 173, 214, 232–4
morality, 50, 94–5, 97, 109–10, 140–3, 200
mourning, 211–14, 216–18, 220–6, 233, 235–6, 243–4, 245

nationalism, 2, 5, 7, 21, 34, 38–9, 125, 145, 235
negotiation, 30, 43, 200–201
ngoma, 204
norms, 18, 28, 32–3, 71, 93, 96, 99, 100, 110, 127, 152, 200, 205, 253
nostalgia, 2
nurses, 1, 2, 7, 14–15, 29, 40, 49, 56, 57, 62, 76, 81, 96, 100, 101, 105–6, 109, 121, 123, 134, 137, 172, 190–1, 197, 221, 226, 234, 235–6, 240, 241

occupation, military, 5, 115, 127, 133–46, 169, 180, 189–90, 200
Ottoman Empire, 3–4, 6, 8, 12, 14, 71–2, 127, 172, 179, 182, 250

pacifism, 21, 28–9, 34, 38, 244, 254
paternalism, 58, 200
Poland, 2, 16, 101, 128, 133, 142, 190, 233
poverty, 18, 121, 158, 203
Princip, Gavrilo, 2, 3
propaganda, 12, 50, 57, 98, 116, 117, 121, 124–7, 134–6, 138–9, 145, 173, 176–7, 179, 190, 211, 234

queer, 18, 93

race and racism, 7, 11, 17–18, 23, 39, 67–72, 73–5, 77–5, 94–5, 172, 190, 195, 205, 235, 244, 254
riots, 12–13, 78
rape, 40, 70, 77, 84–5, 94, 123, 127, 136, 138–9, 145, 190, 196, 200–201
rationing, 2, 7, 10, 126, 152, 154–7, 161, 164, 179, 194
Red Cross, 12–13, 15, 29, 39–40, 174
refugees, 2, 7, 40, 47, 51, 59, 68, 122, 128, 143, 250
religion, 10, 67, 99, 212, 213, 220, 233, 235
    Orthodox Christian, 212, 216, 220, 225
    Roman Catholic, 13, 134, 214, 221
Romania, 13, 47, 133, 139, 218, 220, 225
Romanov Empire. *See* Russia
Russia, 2–4, 6, 12–15, 28, 47–9, 51–2, 54, 57, 63–4, 68, 71–2, 98, 101, 133–4, 157, 161–2, 164, 177–8, 216–17, 231–3, 240–1, 250, 253

sacrifice, 6, 7, 15, 16, 52, 57–8, 116–17, 125, 134, 138, 144, 149, 212, 214, 216–17, 221, 226, 230–8, 251
Second World War, 97, 117, 127, 244
Serbia, 3, 6, 13, 22, 47, 101, 127, 133, 135–6, 140–4, 190, 218, 250
sexology, 94–7, 110
sex-talk, 99
sexuality, 11, 19, 23, 67, 70–1, 73–4, 78, 84, 85, 93–9, 105, 109–10
skill, 13, 29, 48, 51, 54–6, 59, 62, 73, 99, 110, 121, 165, 181, 195
social class, 1, 3, 11, 15, 18, 23, 29, 46, 47, 53, 57, 59, 63, 70, 77, 91, 95–101, 106, 109–10, 115, 117–19, 122, 125–6, 153, 155, 157–8, 163, 178, 224, 232, 241, 252, 254
socialism, 3, 28, 49
Somme, battle of, 4, 221
Soviet Union, 16, 22, 134, 231, 240, 245
substitution, 31, 54, 115
suffrage, 2, 7, 10, 11, 13–17, 21, 22, 23, 31–2, 34–6, 39, 42, 51, 63–4, 163, 231–2, 251, 253–4

teenagers, 2, 5, 20, 53, 116–18, 120, 125–7, 217, 234
TNT, 52, 61
total war, 1, 7, 10, 99, 150, 152, 154, 165, 181, 230–2, 251
Turkey. *See* Ottoman Empire

uniforms, 5, 51, 101, 119, 190

United Kingdom, 3–6, 12, 13, 15, 20–1, 29, 31, 32, 37, 42–3, 52–3, 57, 61–3, 68, 72, 74–5, 78–81, 83, 91, 95–6, 98, 100, 101, 106, 117–18, 123, 125, 126, 129, 135, 137, 149, 152, 154–5, 157, 160, 162, 164, 171–3, 177, 179–81, 191–2, 195, 197, 202–5, 213, 218, 220, 222, 234, 236–7, 253

United States, 1–4, 12–21, 28–31, 34, 40–3, 48, 52–4, 67–8, 70, 72, 82–5, 120–2, 126, 136, 155, 162, 178–9, 182, 218, 225, 231–4, 237–41, 243, 252, 254

Verdun, battle of, 218, 237

veterans, 37–8, 191, 205, 232, 233

victimhood, 38–9, 41, 45, 67, 123, 127–8, 135, 136, 138–9, 144–5, 180, 188, 194, 213–14, 230, 233–4

Vienna, 2, 126, 150, 153, 160–1, 163–4, 180

violence, 1, 3, 6, 10–11, 19–20, 22, 29, 34, 36, 39, 70, 73, 78, 84–5, 94, 105, 124, 128–9, 134–9, 145, 153, 155, 162, 170, 176–8, 181–2, 187–97, 199–201, 203–5, 211, 212, 216, 230–2, 240, 243

volunteers, 7, 12–15, 28–9, 32–3, 47, 53, 57, 59, 62, 115, 117, 125, 155, 177, 179–80, 233

wages, 47–8, 56, 63

war, global, 1, 4, 14, 68, 71, 72, 85, 154, 187–8, 190–1, 204, 211, 248, 250, 254

war, total, 1, 7, 10, 28, 99, 150–2, 154, 165, 169, 181, 230–2, 251

war service, 5, 52, 57, 59, 61, 117–18, 121–2, 125

weapons, 4, 42, 149, 152, 169–73, 243
    artillery, 2, 4, 52, 76, 170, 176, 179, 182
    bayonets, 170, 174, 243
    poison gas, 4, 39, 52, 169–73, 176, 181–3, 241

widows, 16, 41, 53, 77, 116, 121, 128, 212–15, 216, 218, 224–5

women's work, 11, 13, 46–64, 122, 137, 140, 197, 203, 251, 252

YMCA, 17, 41, 82, 118, 121

youth, 1, 5, 28, 58, 61, 75–7, 80, 106, 115–19, 120–7, 129, 134, 137, 155, 158, 177, 180–1, 189, 193–4, 202–3, 226, 238, 241, 251–2

Zeppelin, 4, 61, 173–4, 180